CAPITALISM BEYOND MUTUALITY?

CAPITALISM BEYOND MUTUALITY?

Perspectives Integrating Philosophy and Social Science

Edited by

SUBRAMANIAN RANGAN

OXFORD

UNIVERSITY PRESS

OXFORD
UNIVERSITY PRESS

Great Clarendon Street, Oxford OX2 6DP,
United Kingdom

Oxford University Press is a department of the University of Oxford.
It furthers the University's objective of excellence in research, scholarship,
and education by publishing worldwide. Oxford is a registered trade mark of
Oxford University Press in the UK and in certain other countries

British Library Cataloguing in Publication Data

Data available

Library of Congress Control Number: 2017960661

ISBN 978-0-19-882506-7

Printed and bound by
CPI Group (UK) Ltd, Croydon, CR0 4YY

To Ken Arrow

PREFACE

THE essays in this volume outline and explore concrete approaches to concerns originating in the contemporary practice and theory of our liberal decentralized market-based economic system (aka "capitalism"). In this system, mutuality has been established and accepted as a prime principle in addressing our interdependence. Now, however, mounting regulations notwithstanding, doubts about the sufficiency of this principle are not only increasingly widespread, they are also increasingly confirmed. Accordingly, the essays here explore whether and how we might help the economic system evolve further into one where mutuality is more systematically complemented by morality. Some such evolution seems necessary and even unavoidable if the economy is to abet desirable outcomes and not only output. When it comes to economic power, its regulation was clearly meant to complement not substitute its education.

Philosophy has a natural role in informing such reflection, and the essays here integrate its moral perspectives with the analysis of social science. Indeed, one core feature of this volume is that, by design, the majority of the essays are co-authored by philosophers and social scientists. (It is not every day that reputed scholars of finance co-author with distinguished moral philosophers.) The aim has been to explore which assumptions of standard social science imported into the world of business merit scrutiny and evolution—how even in a liberal economy moral ideals and reasoning might inform and influence economic action. What processes of reasoning (including those suggested in constructivist philosophy) offer promise? What organizational and systemic evolution may be necessary to enact a more philosophical (as opposed to a more political) economy? What future research and role for education is required to shape and "correct" actors' interests, preferences, and conduct?

Moral reasoning more than material (economic and technical) reasoning is needed to help ground theory on why, how, and which economic actors might better integrate performance and progress. Moral logics are going to be indispensable because we need to reason about ends and not only means; and because we need to discuss multiple values, not all of which can be compared or exchanged. Material reasoning depends largely on prices, exchange rates, and marginal and dynamic effects. To this logic based on self-regarding "consequences," moral reasoning can usefully integrate a logic based on other-regarding "appropriateness."

The essays, developed expressly for this volume, are aimed primarily at scholars in the fields of management, strategy, economics and finance, decision science, marketing science, and organization theory. If business scholars are to help advance the economic system, then they must better address units of analysis typical in philosophy, viz. the individual, society, and humanity including other sentient creatures. Ideas such as fairness, well-being, humaneness, esteem, inclusion, justice, and progress all attach to these units of analysis. Scholars in moral and social philosophy with an interest in the dilemmas of the decentralized economic system will likewise find the essays useful. Last but not least, executives drawn to reflection and graduate students in business schools should also find the perspectives discussed in this volume enlightening.

The essays cover an array of topics including climate change, intergenerational obligations, life satisfaction, value endogeneity, education as a complement to regulation, the role of "purpose" in organizations, organizing for hybrid goals, representation and deliberation within business firms, wealth inequality, trust, future discounting, new technology-enabled "platform capitalism," and government's catalytic (as opposed to controlling) role.

The essays contained here were first presented and discussed at the Society for Progress' second assembly, which was held at the Royal Society in London during November 2015. (Brief summaries of the discussions appear at the end of each essay.) This work and the assemblies of the Society for Progress were all made possible thanks to a substantial grant from the Abu Dhabi Department of Education and Knowledge (ADEK) to my home school INSEAD. My chair at the school, which has afforded me time to work on this project, is endowed by the Abu Dhabi Crown Prince Court (CPC). I am profoundly and genuinely grateful to ADEK, the CPC, and their respective leaders Dr. Ali Al Nuaimi and Mohamed Mubarak Al Mazrouei.

I am fortunate and grateful for the tremendous support of the INSEAD community, including faculty and staff colleagues, students, alumni, board members, the development team, and of course the Deans.

I thank Oxford University Press, and in particular Clare Kennedy and Adam Swallow, for taking interest in this work and showing care and attention during its review. I appreciate the four scholars that diligently reviewed and helped evolve the framing and structure of this volume. It is much improved thanks to their rigorous input.

Over the course of this long project I have been blessed by the support of several other people. I wish to express my gratitude to the following for their encouragement, input, and assistance: Ron Adner, Jose Luis Alvarez, Antonio Batista, Henri Claude de Bettignies, Mike Brimm, Laurence Capron, Karel Cool, Jean Dermine, Aldemir Drummond, Anne Fournier, Charlotte Fraizy, Catherine Galitzine, Frederic Godart, Henrich Greve, Denis Gromb, Pierre Hillion, Jeremy Jurgens, Kevin Kaiser, Manfred Kets de Vries, Ilze Kivleniece, Robert Lawrence, Miguel Lobo, Sheila Loxham, Massimo Massa, Tomasz Obloj, Urs Peyer, Michele Plu, Eric Ponsonnet, Mark Roberts, Mel Rogers, Metin Sengul, Ithai Stern, Heinz Thanheiser, Tim Van Zandt, Theo Vermaelen, and Alexis Von Busekist.

For a variety of reasons, in such projects, one ends up drawing more on some people. In this category I wish to mention and express deep personal appreciation to Emerson Almeida, Phil Anderson, Oleg Bagrin, Jacques Bel, Pascal Berend, Hervé Beuret,

Frank Brown, Antonio Fatas, Umesh Ganjam, Fadi Ghandour, Andre Hoffmann, Sophie Hook, Alison James, Claude and Tuulikki Janssen, Ravi Kailas, Dr. Mugheer al Khaili, Guilherme Leal, Ilian Mihov, David Musson, Jean Claude Noel, Nitin Nohria, Indra Nooyi, Babu and Satish Padmanabhan, Pedro Passos, Shantanu Prakash, Gisela Sánchez, Luiz Seabra, Hilde and Klaus Schwab, Kumari Shibulal, Birgitte Hagemann Snabe, Vikas Tibrewala, Ruben and Veronika Vardanyan, and Peter Zemsky.

I would be remiss not to acknowledge explicitly the engagement and efforts of the distinguished contributors, especially the elders Jim March, John Meyer, and Amartya Sen. With the enthusiastic agreement of all, we dedicate this volume to Ken Arrow who passed away during its preparation and for which he was preparing an essay. Though everyone associated with the project knows this, I would like to state for everyone else that Ken's mentoring and support made all the difference: for me, for the project, and for all of us associated with him. His amazing intellect was matched by his warmth and wit.

In closing, I would like especially to highlight and thank five individuals: Gareth Dyas, Mike Fuerstein, Javier Gimeno, Ebba Hansmeyer, and Anthony Appiah. I have called liberally (and at times excessively) on their guidance, assistance, and abiding friendship. In the same profound vein, I thank my family, including my loving parents, my caring brother and sister, and most of all, my exceptionally supportive wife, and our two children.

S.R.

Fontainebleau, France

Contents

PART I THE PARADIGM PROBLEM

PART II THE AGENCY PROBLEM

List of Figures

LIST OF TABLES

LIST OF CONTRIBUTORS

Rabih Abouchakra is the founder and Managing Director of the Office of Strategic Affairs at the Abu Dhabi Crown Prince Court. He was previously a Vice President and Partner at Booz & Company, heading the firm's Organization and Strategy practice in the Middle East and focusing on public administration modernization, policy formulation, and large-scale transformation. Prior to that Mr. Abouchakra was a Senior Associate Consultant at Bain & Company in Canada and the United Kingdom. Mr. Abouchakra sits on the boards of Al-Qattara Investments Company, Al Bayt-Mitwahid Association, and the 2019 Special Olympics Local Organizing Committee. He is also a member of the advisory boards of INSEAD Abu Dhabi and University of Zurich Department of Economics. Mr. Abouchakra has co-authored three books: *Looking Ahead: The 50 Global Trends that Matter* (Thinkers50, 2016); *Government for a New Age: The Transformation Agenda* (Thinkers50, 2015); and *Leading Smart Transformation: A Roadmap for World Class Government* (Palgrave, 2011). Mr. Abouchakra holds an MBA from INSEAD, and a Master of Telecommunication Engineering and a Bachelor of Electrical Engineering with Top of Class honors from McGill University in Canada.

Elizabeth Anderson is Arthur F. Thurnau Professor and John Dewey Distinguished University Professor of Philosophy and Women's Studies at the University of Michigan, Ann Arbor. She earned her PhD from Harvard University in 1987 and previously taught at Swarthmore College. She is a Guggenheim Fellow, an ACLS Fellow, a member of the American Academy of Arts and Sciences, and former President of the Central Division of the American Philosophical Association. She is the author of *Value in Ethics and Economics* (Harvard University Press, 1993), *The Imperative of Integration* (Princeton University Press, 2010), *Private Government* (Princeton University Press, 2017), and over sixty articles in journals of philosophy, law, and economics. She specializes in moral and political philosophy, social and feminist epistemology, and the philosophy of the social sciences. Her current project is a history of egalitarianism from the Levellers to the present, with a special focus on the organization of the workplace and labor relations, markets, and contracts.

Kwame Anthony Appiah is Professor of Philosophy and Law at New York University. He was born in London, grew up in Ghana, and took both BA and PhD degrees in philosophy at Cambridge University. He has taught in Ghana, France, Britain, and the United States. From 2002 to 2013, he was a member of the Princeton University faculty. He has published widely in philosophy as well as in African and African American literary and cultural studies. His books include *The Ethics of Identity* (Princeton University Press, 2005), *Cosmopolitanism: Ethics in a World of Strangers* (Princeton University Press, 2005), which won the Arthur Ross Award of the Council on Foreign Relations, *The Honor Code: How Moral Revolutions Happen* (W.W. Norton, 2010), and *Lines of Descent: W. E. B. Du Bois and the Emergence of Identity* (Harvard University Press, 2014).

David Autor is Ford Professor of Economics and Associate Head of the MIT Department of Economics. His scholarship explores the labor market impacts of technological change and globalization, earnings inequality, and disability insurance and labor supply. Autor has received several awards for his scholarship—the National Science Foundation Career Award, an Alfred P. Sloan Foundation Fellowship, the Sherwin Rosen Prize for outstanding contributions in the field of labor economics—and for his teaching: MIT's James A. and Ruth Levitan Award for excellence in teaching, the Undergraduate Economic Association Teaching Award, and the Faculty Appreciation Award from the MIT TPP program. He is an elected Fellow of the Econometrics Society, the Society of Labor Economists, and the American Academy of Arts and Sciences, and a Faculty Research Associate of the National Bureau of Economic Research and the Abdul Latif Jameel Poverty Action Lab. He is also Director of the NBER Disability Research Consortium, and Co-Director of the MIT School Effectiveness and Inequality Initiative. Autor earned a BA in Psychology from Tufts University and a PhD in Public Policy from Harvard's Kennedy School of Government in 1999. Prior to graduate study, he spent three years directing computer skills education for economically disadvantaged children and adults in San Francisco and South Africa.

Jay B. Barney is Presidential Professor of Strategic Management and holds the Pierre Lassonde Chair in Social Entrepreneurship at the David Eccles School of Business at the University of Utah. He has held honorary visiting appointments at Peking University (Beijing), Sun Yat Sen University (Guangzhou), Waikato University (New Zealand), and Brunel University (UK), and has received three honorary doctorate degrees (Lund University, Copenhagen Business School, and the Universidad Pontificia Comillas, Madrid). He served as an officer of both the Strategic Management Division of the Academy of Management and the Strategic Management Society, and was elected a Fellow of the Academy of Management and a Fellow of the Strategic Management Society. He received the Irwin Outstanding Educator Award for the Business Policy and Strategy Division of AOM and the Outstanding Contributions to Scholarship Award at AOM. Professor Barney is currently the Editor-in-Chief at the *Academy of Management Review*. He has published over one hundred articles and book chapters, and six books. His research focuses on identifying the attributes of firm resources and capabilities that enable firms to gain and sustain a competitive advantage. In addition, he has begun doing research on entrepreneurship and corporate social responsibility, with special emphasis on entrepreneurship among the abject poor.

Julie Battilana is the Joseph C. Wilson Professor of Business Administration in the Organizational Behavior unit at Harvard Business School and the Alan L. Gleitsman Professor of Social Innovation at Harvard Kennedy School, where she is also the founder and academic co-director of the Social Innovation and Change Initiative. Her research examines the processes by which organizations and individuals initiate and implement changes that diverge from the taken-for-granted norms in a field of activity. Professor Battilana's research aims to elucidate what it takes to initiate divergent change, and how to succeed in its implementation. To do so, she has developed two streams of research that address divergent change at different levels of analysis. The first focuses on understanding the conditions that enable individuals to initiate and implement divergent change within their organizations. The second examines how organizations themselves can diverge from deeply seated organizational forms. She has focused on hybrid organizations that diverge from typical businesses and typical charities by combining aspects of both. Her aim is to understand whether, and if so how, these hybrid organizations can achieve high levels of social and financial performance. She has articles published in the *Academy of Management Annals, Academy of Management Journal, Harvard Business Review, Journal of Business Ethics, Leadership Quarterly, Management Science, Organization, Organization Science, Organization Studies, Research in Organizational Behavior, Stanford Social Innovation Review,* and *Strategic Organization.* Professor Battilana earned a BA in sociology and economics, an MA in political sociology, and an MSc in organizational sociology and public policy from École Normale Supérieure de Cachan in France. She also holds a degree from HEC Business School, and a joint PhD in organizational behavior from INSEAD and in management and economics from École Normale Supérieure de Cachan.

Ing-Haw Cheng is Assistant Professor of Business Administration at the Tuck School of Business, Dartmouth College. Professor Cheng received his PhD in Economics from Princeton University in 2009. He has published in leading academic journals such as the *American Economic Review, Journal of Finance,* and *Review of Financial Studies.*

Bertrand Collomb is Honorary Chairman of Lafarge, a worldwide leader in building materials that merged with Holcim to form LafargeHolcim, of which he is a director. He is a member of the Institut de France and was chairman of the Académie des sciences morales et politiques in 2013. A graduate of the École Polytechnique and the École des Mines in Paris, he also holds a French law degree and a PhD in Management (University of Texas). He founded the Center for Management Research at the École Polytechnique. From 1966 to 1975, he worked with the French government in various positions. He joined Lafarge in 1975. After several responsibilities in various areas of the group, including CEO of Lafarge Corporation, the North American arm of the group (1985–8), he was appointed chairman and CEO of Lafarge in August 1989. He was Chairman of Lafarge from 2003 to 2007. He led Lafarge to become a global leader, while maintaining a people-oriented culture. He is a proponent of sustainable development, a founding member of WBCSD (World Business Council for Sustainable Development), of which he was the chairman in 2004–5. He was also a member of the European Round Table of Industrialists (ERT) and chairman of Institut de l'Entreprise and AFEP (the association of French large international companies). He has been a director of several international companies including Allianz, Unilever, DuPont, and Total.

Gerald F. Davis received his PhD from the Graduate School of Business at Stanford University and taught at Northwestern and Columbia before moving to the University of Michigan, where he is Associate Dean for Business+Impact and the Gilbert and Ruth Whitaker Professor of Business Administration and Professor of Sociology. He has published widely in management, sociology, and finance on topics ranging from corporate governance and new forms of enterprise to inequality and social movements. Recent books include *Social Movements and Organization Theory* (Cambridge University Press, 2005), *Organizations and Organizing* (Pearson Prentice Hall, 2007), *Managed by the Markets: How Finance Reshaped America* (Oxford University Press, 2009), *Grassroots Social Innovation* (Harvard Business Press, 2015), and *The Vanishing American Corporation: Navigating the Hazards of a New Economy* (Berrett-Koehler, 2016).

Robert Frank is the H. J. Louis Professor of Management and Professor of Economics at Cornell's Johnson School of Management. His "Economic View" column appears monthly in the *New York Times*. He is a Distinguished Senior Fellow at Demos. He received his BSc in mathematics from Georgia Tech, then taught math and science for two years as a Peace Corps Volunteer in rural Nepal. He holds an MA in statistics and a PhD in economics, both from the University of California at Berkeley. His papers have appeared in the *American Economic Review*, *Econometrica*, *Journal of Political Economy*, and other leading journals. His books, which include *Choosing the Right Pond* (Oxford University Press, 1985), *Passions Within Reason* (W.W. Norton, 1988), *Microeconomics and Behavior* (McGraw-Hill, 2014), *Principles of Economics* (with Ben Bernanke, McGraw-Hill, 2016), *Luxury Fever* (Princeton University Press, 1999), *What Price the Moral High Ground?* (Princeton University Press, 2004), *Falling Behind* (University of California Press, 2007), *The Economic Naturalist* (Basic Books, 2009), *The Darwin Economy* (Princeton University Press, 2012), and *Success and Luck* (Princeton University Press, 2016), have been translated into twenty-four languages. *The Winner-Take-All Society* (Free Press, 1995), co-authored with Philip Cook, received a Critic's Choice Award. He is a co-recipient of the 2004 Leontief Prize for Advancing the Frontiers of Economic Thought. He was awarded the Johnson School's Stephen Russell Distinguished teaching award in 2004, 2010, and 2012, and its Apple Distinguished Teaching Award in 2005.

Michael Fuerstein is Associate Professor of Philosophy at St. Olaf College in Northfield, Minnesota. His research focuses on the norms and practices that contribute to knowledge in social and political contexts. He completed his PhD at Columbia

University in 2009 and, following that, held a post-doc at the Center for Cultural Analysis at Rutgers University. For the 2016–17 year he held a visiting professorship at INSEAD. He has been a recipient of grants/fellowships from the National Endowment for the Humanities, the Mellon Foundation, the Whiting Foundation, the DeKarman Foundation, the Institute for Social and Economic Research and Policy, and the Institute for Humane Studies. His work has appeared in a variety of scholarly venues, including *The Journal of Political Philosophy*, *Social Theory and Practice*, *Episteme*, and others. He currently serves on the Editorial Board of the *Journal of Political Philosophy* and *Academy of Management Review*. A current book project—tentatively titled *Experiments of Social Living*—seeks to model the role of democracy in episodes of moral progress. As an undergraduate, he completed a dual-degree program at Tufts University and the New England Conservatory of Music, where he studied jazz saxophone. He continues to perform actively as a musician.

Mona Hammami is a Director at the Office of Strategic Affairs, Abu Dhabi Crown Prince Court. Her role includes providing advisory support to leadership on local and global social and economic developments, as well as heading the think-tank arm of the office, which works on drafting publications and white papers for policymakers. Prior to joining the Crown Prince Court she worked at Booz & Company as part of the public sector practice team focusing on a range of issues, including social and labor policy, and macroeconomic policy. She worked as an economist with the International Monetary Fund (IMF) and the UN Economic and Social Commission for Western Asia. She has authored several papers including an IMF paper on the determinants of public–private partnerships. Her most recent work includes two books: *Looking Ahead: The 50 Trends that Matter* (Thinkers50, 2015), and *The Giving World: How Maximizing Three Financial Forces Could Revolutionize Global Development* (Infinite Ideas, 2016). Mona holds a PhD in Development Studies from the university of Oxford and a Masters in Public Administration International Development from Harvard Kennedy School. She is the founding Curator of the World Economic Forum Abu Dhabi Global Shapers Hub and a World Economic Forum Young Global Leader.

Ebba Abdon Hansmeyer is Executive Director of the Society for Progress. She was based previously at INSEAD's Abu Dhabi campus where she managed a portfolio of research and development projects. She has had research and project management roles in the private and public sector (including NGOs and the United Nations). She studied economic history at the London School of Economics, and Arabic at the American University of Beirut, and holds degrees in Philosophy from the Institut Catholique de Paris, and Human Rights Law from the University of Hong Kong. She is married with two young daughters.

Harrison Hong is Professor of Economics at Columbia University. He was previously the John Scully '66 Professor of Economics and Finance at Princeton University until July 2016. He received his BA in economics and statistics with highest distinction from the University of California at Berkeley in 1992 and his PhD in economics from MIT in 1997. His work has covered diverse topics, including behavioral finance and market efficiency, agency and biased decisions, organizational diseconomies and performance, social interaction and investor behavior, and social responsibility and the stock market. In 2009, he was awarded the Fischer Black Prize, given once every two years to the best American finance economist under the age of 40. He is a research associate at the National Bureau of Economic Research and currently an editor of the *International Journal of Central Banking*. He has been an associate editor at the *Journal of Finance* and the *Journal of Financial Intermediation* and a Director of the American Finance Association.

Philip Kitcher was born in 1947 in London. He received his BA from Cambridge University and his PhD from Princeton. He has taught at several American universities, and is currently John Dewey Professor of Philosophy at Columbia. He is the author of books on topics ranging from the philosophy of mathematics, the philosophy of biology, the growth of science, the role of science in society, naturalistic ethics, pragmatism, Wagner's *Ring*, Joyce's *Finnegans Wake*, and Mann's *Death in Venice*. He has been President of the American Philosophical Association (Pacific Division) and Editor-in-Chief of *Philosophy of Science*. A Fellow of the American Academy of Arts and Sciences, he was also the first recipient of the Prometheus Prize, awarded by the American Philosophical Association for work in expanding the frontiers of Science and Philosophy. He has been named a "Friend of Darwin" by the National Committee on Science Education, and received a Lannan Foundation Notable Book Award for *Living With Darwin* (Oxford University Press, 2007). He has been a Fellow at the Wissenschaftskolleg zu Berlin, where he was partially supported by a prize from the Humboldt Foundation, and in the autumn of 2015 he was the Daimler Fellow at the American Academy in Berlin. His most recent books are *Life After Faith: The Case for Secular Humanism* (Yale University Press, 2014), and *The Seasons Alter: How to Save our Planet in Six Acts*, co-authored with Evelyn Fox Keller (W.W. Norton, 2017). He is currently at work on a systematic version of Deweyan pragmatism, tentatively entitled *Progress, Truth, and Values*.

Mike Lee is a Doctoral Candidate in Management at Harvard Business School and studies novel organizational designs and how formal structure can be leveraged to foster greater organizational effectiveness. His dissertation research explores the dynamics and consequences of radical approaches to less hierarchical organizing, focusing on a novel organizational system called Holacracy. His other research explores how formal structure can be used to foster positive change in teams and organizations. He uses ethnographic observation and interviews, field experiments, survey methods, and computer modeling to study these phenomena. Michael has worked in a variety of organizational contexts and sectors. Most recently, he served as an engagement leader for a global management consulting firm. Michael earned his AB magna cum laude in Social Studies from Harvard University and an MBA from University of California, Berkeley's Haas School of Business.

James G. March is Professor Emeritus at Stanford University, where he has been on the faculty since 1970. He holds appointments in the Graduate Schools of Business and Education and in the Departments of Political Science and Sociology. He received his BA degree from the University of Wisconsin and his MA and PhD from Yale University. He has received honorary doctorates and honorary professorships from several European and North American universities and has been elected to membership in the National Academy of Science, the American Academy of Arts and Sciences, the American Philosophical Society, the National Academy of Public Administration, and the National Academy of Education, as well as several overseas academies. He received the Wilbur Cross Medal from Yale University in 1968, the Academy of Management Award for Scholarly Contributions to Management in 1984, the Walter J. Gores Award for Excellence in Teaching from Stanford University in 1995, the John Gaus Award from the American Political Science Association in 1997, the Distinguished Scholar Award from the Academy of Management in 1999, the Viipuri Award from the Viipuri Society in 2004, the Aaron Wildavsky Award from the Public Policy Society in 2004, the Herbert Simon Award from Laslo Raik College (Budapest) in 2005, and a Progress Medal from the Society for Progress in 2016. In 1995 he was made a Knight First Class in the Royal Norwegian (Olav V) Order of Merit, and in 1999 he was made a Commander of the Order of the Lion of Finland. He has been a member of the National Science Board (1969–74) and the National Council on Educational Research (1975–8). From 1984 to 1994 he was a member, and from 1991 to 1993 Chair, of the Board of Trustees of the Russell Sage Foundation. He is best known professionally for his writings on decision making and organizations, including *Organizations* (Wiley, 1958), *A Behavioral Theory of the Firm* (Prentice-Hall, 1963), *Leadership and Ambiguity* (Harvard Business School Press, 1974), *Ambiguity and Choice in Organizations* (Universitetsforlaget, 1976), *Decisions and Organizations* (Basil Blackwell, 1988), *Rediscovering Institutions* (Free Press/Macmillan, 1989), *The Pursuit of Organizational Intelligence* (Blackwell, 1999), *Democratic Governance* (Free Press, 1995), *A Primer on Decision Making* (Free Press, 1994), *The Dynamics of Rules* (Stanford University Press, 2000), *Explorations in Organizations* (Stanford University Press, 2008), *On Leadership* (Blackwell, 2005), and *The Ambiguities of Experience* (Cornell University Press, 2010). He has also written thirteen books of poetry and two films.

Ramón Mendiola is CEO of Florida Ice & Farm Company (FIFCO), a leading company with three main businesses: beverages and food, retail, and real estate and hotels, with operations in Central America and the United States. Five years ago, he led the company through a breakthrough transformation merging the company business strategy with its sustainability strategy to make FIFCO a triple-bottom-line company where its executives' compensation is linked to economic, social, and environmental goals. FIFCO was chosen as one of the Sustainability Champions of the World Economic Forum. A few years ago, FIFCO discovered its purpose and since then, the company has been creating positive value across its value chain. Mendiola has a business administration and marketing degree from Babson College and he has an

MBA, with an emphasis on international business marketing and strategy, from the Kellogg Graduate School of Management at Northwestern University.

John W. Meyer is Professor of Sociology, emeritus, at Stanford. He has contributed to organizational theory, comparative education, and the sociology of education, developing sociological institutional theory. He has studied the national impacts of global society (some papers are collected in *Weltkultur*, Suhrkamp, 2005; a more extensive set is in *World Society: The Writings of John W. Meyer*, Oxford University Press, 2009). One collaborative study examines worldwide science and its national effects (Drori et al., *Science in the Modern World Polity*, Stanford University Press, 2003). More recent collaborative projects are on the organizational impact of globalization (Drori et al., *Globalization and Organization*, Oxford University Press, 2006; Bromley and Meyer, *Hyper-Organization: Global Organizational Expansion*, Oxford University Press, 2015). He now studies the global human rights regime, world curricula in mass and higher education, and the worldwide expansion of managerialism. He is a member of the US National Academy of Education, and has honorary doctorates from the Stockholm School of Economics and the Universities of Bielefeld and Lucerne. He received the Academy of Management's award for lifetime contributions to organization theory; the American Sociological Association's section awards for lifetime contributions to the sociology of education and the study of globalization; and the Association's du Bois award for lifetime contributions to sociology.

Susan Neiman is Director of the Einstein Forum, an independent public think tank in Potsdam, Germany. Before coming to the Einstein Forum in 2000 Neiman was Professor of Philosophy at Yale and Tel Aviv University. Born in Atlanta, Georgia, she studied philosophy at Harvard, where she took her PhD with John Rawls, and the Freie Universität Berlin. Her books, translated into many languages, include *Slow Fire: Jewish Notes from Berlin* (Schocken Books, 1992), *The Unity of Reason: Rereading Kant* (Oxford University Press, 1994), *Evil in Modern Thought: An Alternative History of Philosophy* (Princeton University Press, 2002), *Fremde Sehen Anders* (Suhrkamp, 2005), *Moral Clarity: A Guide for Grownup Idealists* (Harcourt, 2008), *Why Grow Up?* (Penguin, 2014), *Widerstand der Vernunft* (Ecowin, 2017). She has also published more than eighty essays and articles.

Philip Pettit is a dual citizen of Ireland and Australia and divides his time between Princeton University, where he is L. S. Rockefeller University Professor of Politics and Human Values, and the Australian National University, where he is Distinguished Professor of Philosophy. His books include *Republicanism* (Oxford University Press, 1997), *The Economy of Esteem* (Oxford University Press, 2004) with G. Brennan, *Group Agency* (Oxford University Press, 2011) with C. List, *On the People's Terms* (Cambridge University Press, 2012), *Just Freedom* (W.W. Norton, 2014), *The Robust Demands of the Good* (Oxford University Press, 2015), and *The Birth of Ethics* (Oxford University Press, 2018). He is a Fellow of the American Academy of Arts and Sciences, the British Academy and the Royal Irish Academy, as well as the Australian Academies of

Humanities and Social Sciences. In 2017 he was named a Companion of the Order of Australia. *Common Minds: Themes from the Philosophy of Philip Pettit*, edited by G. Brennan et al., was published by Oxford University Press in 2007.

Subramanian Rangan   is Professor of Strategy and Management at INSEAD. He holds the Abu Dhabi Crown Prince Court Endowed Chair in Societal Progress. He received an MBA from the MIT Sloan School of Management and a PhD in Political Economy from Harvard University. His current work explores the future of capitalism and in particular how enterprises may better integrate performance and progress. In 2013 he initiated the Society for Progress, a fellowship of eminent philosophers, social scientists, and business leaders.[1] Their first work was published in a volume entitled *Performance and Progress: Essays on Capitalism, Business, and Society* (Oxford University Press, 2015). His other research explores the political sociology of discrimination in foreign transnational firms and these firms' non-market strategies. In 1998 he won the Academy of International Business' Eldridge Haynes Prize for the best original work in international business. In 1995 that academy awarded their Best Dissertation Award to his doctoral thesis. In 2010 his research won the Emerald award for top fifty papers in management. His articles appear in the *Administrative Science Quarterly*, *Academy of Management Review*, *Brookings Papers on Economic Activity*, *Journal of International Business Studies*, *Strategic Management Journal*, *Sloan Management Review*, and *Harvard Business Review*. Rangan is co-author of two books, *Manager in the International Economy* (Pearson, 1995), and *A Prism on Globalization* (Brookings Institution Press, 1999). He is associate editor of the *Academy of Management Review*; former chair of the World Economic Forum's Global Agenda Council on Emerging Multinationals; a member of the board of trustees of Fundacao Dom Cabral, a leading business school in Brazil; and a member of the Board of Directors of the Schwab Foundation for Social Entrepreneurship. He directs INSEAD's top executive seminar AVIRA: Awareness, Vision, Imagination, Role, and Action. He is married and has a daughter and son.

Mathias Risse   is a German-born political philosopher. He is Professor of Philosophy and Public Policy at the John F. Kennedy School of Government at Harvard University. Previously he taught in the Department of Philosophy at Yale University, having received his PhD from Princeton University in 2000. His work addresses global justice, ethics, decision theory, and nineteenth-century German philosophy, especially Nietzsche. In addition to the Kennedy School he teaches in Harvard College and the Harvard Extension School, and has also been involved with executive education. Risse is the author of *On Global Justice* (Princeton University Press, 2012) and *Global Political Philosophy* (Palgrave Macmillan, 2012). *On Global Justice* is known for introducing the "ground-of-justice" approach to global political thought. *Global Political Philosophy* is an unconventional introduction to political philosophy that begins at the

---

[1]   <http://www.societyforprogress.org>.

global level. At Harvard, Risse is affiliated with the Safra Center for Ethics, the Carr Center for Human Rights Policy, and the Weatherhead Center for International Affairs. He is also the director of the McCloy Scholarship program, a prestigious fellowship program for German students. Risse has been the organizer of several major inter-disciplinary conferences at Harvard over the years. Moreover, he believes political philosophers reflecting on global questions should do their share in building global connections. In recent times, accordingly, his interests have expanded to East and South East Asia. Having traveled extensively in the region, he was a Visiting Professor at the National University of Singapore in 2013. He has also organized or co-organized several international conferences at Fudan University in Shanghai as well as at the National University of Singapore. He has been a visiting professor at New York University Abu Dhabi and Leuphana University in Germany, as well as a visiting fellow at the Center for Human Values at Princeton University.

David Schmidtz is Kendrick Professor of Philosophy (College of Social and Behavior Sciences), Eller Chair of Service-Dominant Logic (College of Management), founding Director of the Center for Philosophy of Freedom, founding Head of the Department of Political Economy and Moral Sciences, and editor in chief of *Social Philosophy & Policy*, at the University of Arizona.

Amartya Sen is Thomas W. Lamont University Professor, and Professor of Economics and Philosophy, at Harvard University, and was until 2004 the Master of Trinity College, Cambridge. He is also Senior Fellow at the Harvard Society of Fellows. Earlier he was Professor of Economics at Jadavpur University Calcutta, the Delhi School of Economics, and the London School of Economics, and Drummond Professor of Political Economy at Oxford University. Sen has served as President of the Econometric Society, the American Economic Association, the Indian Economic Association, and the International Economic Association. He was formerly Honorary President of OXFAM and is now its Honorary Advisor. His research has ranged over social choice theory, economic theory, ethics and political philosophy, welfare economics, theory of measurement, decision theory, development economics, public health, and gender studies. Sen's books have been translated into more than thirty languages, and include *Choice of Techniques* (Oxford University Press, 1960), *Growth Economics* (Penguin, 1970), *Collective Choice and Social Welfare* (Holden Day, 1970), *On Economic Inequality* (Clarendon Press, 1973, 1997), *Poverty and Famines* (Clarendon Press, 1981), *Utilitarianism and Beyond* (jointly with Bernard Williams, Cambridge University Press, 1982), *Choice, Welfare and Measurement* (Basil Blackwell, 1982), *Commodities and Capabilities* (North-Holland, 1985), *The Standard of Living* (Cambridge University Press, 1987), *On Ethics and Economics* (Basil Blackwell, 1987), *Hunger and Public Action* (jointly with Jean Drèze, Clarendon Press, 1989), *Inequality Re-examined* (Clarendon Press, 1992), *The Quality of Life* (jointly with Martha Nussbaum, Clarendon Press, 1993), *Development as Freedom* (Alfred Knopf, 1999), *Rationality and Freedom* (Harvard University Press, 2002), *The Argumentative Indian* (Penguin,

2005), *Identity and Violence: The Illusion of Destiny* (W. W. Norton, 2006), *The Idea of Justice* (Harvard University Press, 2009), *An Uncertain Glory: India and Its Contradictions* (jointly with Jean Drèze, Penguin, 2013), and *The Country of First Boys* (Oxford University Press, 2015). Sen's awards include Bhar Ratna (India); Commandeur de la Legion d'Honneur (France); the National Humanities Medal (USA); Ordem do Merito Cientifico (Brazil); Honorary Companion of Honour (UK); the Aztec Eagle (Mexico); the Edinburgh Medal (UK); the George Marshall Award (USA); the Eisenhower Medal (USA); the Johan Skytte Prize in Political Science; and the Nobel Prize in Economics.

S. D. Shibulal co-founded Infosys in 1981 and has led the company in different capacities since its inception. He was a member of the Board of Infosys and was its CEO and MD between 2011 and 2014. He is especially proud of being instrumental in creating the Global Delivery Model, which established a new standard for delivery of outsourced IT services. He serves on several global leadership forums and advisory boards. In 2014, Shibulal co-founded Axilor Ventures—a new-generation platform to improve the odds of success of entrepreneurs. With three distinct programs—accelerator, scale-up, and early stage funding—Axilor provides infrastructure, mentoring, and capital for high-impact, India-centered start-ups (in the areas of e-commerce, healthcare, and clean-tech). Shibulal serves on the board of several organizations promoting education. He is Trustee of the Infosys Science Foundation, a not-for-profit trust; a Member of the Board of Trustees, Boston University; a Member of the Board of Governors of Indraprastha Institute of Information Technology, Delhi, and a Member of the Board of Managers of Haverford College, Philadelphia. He is also the Chairman of the Information and Communication Technology Academy of Kerala.

Jim Hagemann Snabe is Chairman of A. P. Moller Maersk, incoming Chairman of Siemens, and Vice Chairman of Allianz. He serves on the Board of Trustees at World Economic Forum. His twenty-five years of experience in the IT industry culminated in his role as co-CEO of SAP, the leading enterprise software company. Snabe is currently focused on leadership around innovation, digitization, and societal progress. As co-CEO of SAP he was, together with Bill McDermott, instrumental in driving the strategic development of SAP to double the value of the company and play a more responsible role in society. In 2013 he and co-CEO Bill McDermott were ranked number two on Glassdoor.com's listing of the fifty best-rated CEOs, based on their 99 percent approval rating from employees. Snabe is involved in a number of activities focused on societal progress and the role of business in society. His views on leadership are shaped by his commitment to solving societal issues and his trust in human potential. Snabe received a master's degree in operational research from the Aarhus School of Business in Denmark. In 2016 he was appointed Adjunct Professor at Copenhagen Business School based on his work around digital transformation and its impact on business and society. He lives with his family in Copenhagen, Denmark.

Kotaro Suzumura is Professor Emeritus of Hitotsubashi University, Professor Emeritus and Honorary Fellow of Waseda University, and Member of the Japan Academy. Born in 1944, Professor Suzumura graduated from the Department of Economics, Hitotsubashi University, and received a PhD in Economics from the same institution. His main field of research is welfare economics and social choice theory. His major publications are *Rational Choice, Collective Decisions and Social Welfare* (Cambridge University Press, 1983), *Consistency, Choice, and Rationality* (Harvard University Press, 2010) (a joint work with Walter Bossert), *Consequences, Opportunities, and Procedures: Selected Papers on Social Choice and Welfare* (Harvard University Press, forthcoming). He was a joint editor of the *Handbook of Social Choice and Welfare* (North-Holland/Elsevier, 2002 and 2011), jointly with Kenneth Arrow and Amartya Sen. He was Lecturer at the London School of Economics and Political Science, Visiting Associate Professor at Stanford University, Visiting Fellow at All Souls College, Oxford University, Fulbright Senior Fellow at Harvard University, and Visiting Fellow Commoner at Trinity College, Cambridge University. He was also President of the Japanese Economic Association as well as of the international Society for Social Choice and Welfare, Inaugural Director of the Competition Policy Research Centre, Fair Trade Commission of Japan, and Vice-President of the Science Council of Japan. He was elected a Fellow of the Econometric Society in 1990.

Valerie Tiberius is the Paul W. Frenzel Chair in Liberal Arts and the chair of the Philosophy Department at the University of Minnesota, where she has taught since 1998. She earned her BA from the University of Toronto and her MA and PhD from the University of North Carolina at Chapel Hill. Her work explores the ways in which philosophy and psychology can both contribute to the study of well-being and virtue. She is the author of *The Reflective Life: Living Wisely With Our Limits* (Oxford University Press, 2008), which examines how we ought to think about practical wisdom and living a good life given what we now know about our psychological limitations from research in psychology. Her last book, *Moral Psychology: A Contemporary Introduction* (Routledge, 2015), brings together traditional philosophical approaches and new empirical approaches in order to investigate topics such as moral motivation, moral responsibility, and reasons to be moral. Her newest book, *Well-Being as Value Fulfillment: How We Can Help Each Other to Live Well* (Oxford University Press, forthcoming) develops the value fulfillment theory of well-being. She has also published numerous articles on the topics of practical reasoning, prudential virtues, well-being, and the relationship between positive psychology and ethics, and has received grants from the Templeton Foundation and the National Endowment for the Humanities. She is currently the Past President of the Central Division of the American Philosophical Association.

James P. Walsh (PhD, Northwestern University) is an Arthur F. Thurnau Professor and the Gerald and Esther Carey Professor of Business Administration at the University of Michigan's Ross School of Business. His research explores the purpose, accountability, control, and success of the firm, and even more generally, business itself. Contemplating these issues with his students, he does his best to prepare them to lead in and for society. A recipient of the Academy of Management's Career Distinguished Service Award, he has served both as the Dean of its Fellows Group and as its 65th president. The Academy of Management is comprised of nearly 20,000 management scholars from well over one hundred countries.

CHAPTER 1

....

INTRODUCTION

Capitalism Beyond Mutuality?

....

SUBRAMANIAN RANGAN

Abstract

Our quest for prosperity has produced great output (i.e. performance) but not always great outcomes (i.e. progress). Despite mounting regulation, when it comes to fairness, well-being, and the scope of our humanity, the modern economic system still leaves much to be desired. If practice is to evolve substantively and systematically, then we must help evolve an economic paradigm where mutuality is more systematically complemented by morality. The bases of this morality must rest, beyond the sympathetic sentiments envisaged by Adam Smith, on an expanded and intentional moral reasoning. Moral philosophy has a natural role in informing and influencing such a turn in our thinking, especially when education is the preferred vehicle of transformation. Indeed, rather than just regulate market power we must also better educate market power.

In the year 1870 John D. Rockefeller established the Standard Oil Company, whose subsequent break-up in the early twentieth century led to the establishment of Exxon. Today, though, Exxon is waging an "all-out campaign against" the Rockefeller family for "funding a conspiracy" alleged to impugn the firm's reputation on climate science.[1] The *New York Times* reports that at a January 2017 conference hosted at the Rockefeller family offices, "One potential subject of discussion suggested by a participant was 'to establish in [the] public's mind that Exxon is a corrupt institution that has pushed humanity (and all creation) toward climate chaos and grave harm.'"

In April 2014, in an ostensible bid to align pay with performance and incentivize the reverse, the board of the Coca-Cola Co. authorized a stock compensation plan that

---

[1] See John Schwartz, November 21, 2016. "Exxon Mobil Accuses the Rockefellers of a Climate Conspiracy." *New York Times.* <https://www.nytimes.com/2016/11/21/science/exxon-mobil-rockefellers-climate-change.html?_r=0> (accessed May 1, 2017).

would, by one major investor's estimate, "transfer $29.8 *billion* to managers."[2] Supporters of the plan disputed the estimate, but after news and disbelief spread, the plan was censured as "outrageously excessive" and eventually severely curtailed. Brows on the face of corporate governance were further raised when the largest stockholder in Coca-Cola, Warren Buffett via Berkshire Hathaway, disclosed that he had abstained from voting on the plan because he was torn between loyalty to Coke and distaste for super-sized executive compensation.[3]

In France meanwhile, in March 2017, poachers broke into a zoo in the west of Paris, killed a four-year-old caged rhino, chain-sawed off its bigger horn, and made off with the cruel booty.[4] A US Fish and Wildlife Service officer told reporters, "It's more valuable, pound for pound, than cocaine or heroin. By the time it gets to Vietnam or China or somewhere in Southeast Asia, a full horn will go for anywhere from $500,000 to $1 million." Depressing statistics from the World Wide Fund for Nature report that in 2016, in South Africa alone, more than 1,050 rhinos were poached (a staggering rise from the thirty-six recorded in the year 2006). One cannot be blamed for wondering who the beasts here are.

As the preceding and many similar stories suggest, our quest for prosperity has produced great output but not always great outcomes. The concerns and dissatisfactions that we experience today include, to list just a few, those pertaining to climate and natural capital, concentration of wealth and market power, employment and economic insecurity, conflicted corporate governance, lobbying and corruption, questionable industrialization of food and health, and immoderate and unhealthy consumerism. Fundamentally, when it comes to fairness, well-being, and the scope of our humanity, the modern economic system still leaves much to be desired.

To be clear, by historical standards, humanity is better off today on several fronts—including life expectancy, median income, and technology-enabled comforts. It is nonetheless difficult to deny that demand for profits has produced performance but not always progress. Demand for justice has produced regulation, but not always justice. Demand for economic security has produced a welfare state but not economic security. Demand for conservation has produced conversation, leaving scientists to fret about "collapse." Life expectancy appears to have outpaced life expectations.

These disquieting outcomes and worrying patterns cannot be explained away as only the product of the actions of a minority of delinquent actors (the "bad apples"). Rather, there appears to be something systemically unsatisfactory. The latter hypothesis must

---

[2] See Craig Giammona, October 1, 2014. "Coca-Cola Trims Stock Compensation Plan After Criticism." *Bloomberg News.* <https://www.bloomberg.com/news/articles/2014-10-01/coca-cola-reins-in-stock-compensation-plan-in-wake-of-criticism> (accessed May 1, 2017).

[3] Buffett's disapproval was eventually registered. See Linette Lopez, May 1, 2014. "Warren Buffett is Killing Coca-Cola's Wild Executive Compensation Plan." *Business Insider.*

[4] See Karin Brulliard, March 9, 2017. "A Rhino at a French Zoo was Killed for His Horn. Could that happen here?" *Washington Post.* <https://www.washingtonpost.com/news/animalia/wp/2017/03/09/a-rhino-at-a-french-zoo-was-killed-for-his-horn-could-that-happen-here/?utm_term=.c8a521189a08> (accessed May 1, 2017).

explain in good part why trust in the liberal market *system* (aka "capitalism") seems to have faded markedly, mounting regulations notwithstanding. Thus we witness in Europe and the United States a palpable pushback on global and even regional economic integration, the risks to growth, efficiency, and confidence notwithstanding. In Brazil, we witness a government and an economy being brought down in an exasperated bid to reform what is regarded as a corrupt system. Even the traditionally business-friendly Swiss brought to referendum a "say on pay" that sought to restrict CEO compensation to no more than twelve times junior workers' pay.[5]

In these and similar cases, often, the hesitation to embrace more radical action is sometimes explained by the clichéd acronym TINA, which is meant to remind us that "there is no alternative." Thankfully, a variety of forces—civic, political, cultural, economic, and intellectual—have been moving to constitute and retort with TIBA, "there is a better alternative." The contributions in this volume, authored by eminent philosophers, social scientists, and a handful of thoughtful business leaders, are submitted in this spirit. The thrust of the work is conveyed in the volume's titular question: *Capitalism Beyond Mutuality?*

Mutuality, or the exchange of benefits, has been established as the prime principle of action and interaction in addressing the chronic dilemma of human interdependence. Mutuality is a fundament in the social contract approach that has been adopted widely in liberal polities, and it continues to serve us well in guiding our design of social exchange arrangements. Yet, if we wish to address more robustly the concerns already outlined, then we need to conceive a *philosophical economy* that is anchored on a much richer spectrum of moral and normative requirements than mutuality alone. Specifically, we must help evolve an economic paradigm where mutuality is more systematically complemented by morality.[6] The bases of this morality must rest, beyond the sympathetic sentiments envisaged by Adam Smith, on expanded and intentional moral reasoning that deliberatively attends to fairness, well-being, and an expanded scope of humanity.

This implies, I will submit and elaborate below, that rather than just *regulate market power* we must also *educate market power*. Perhaps then our economy may evolve to be modern and moral, and we may obtain desirable output and outcomes. Otherwise the design of the state as protector and buffer between the market and society will remain the central and sole remedy. This will tend to overshoot into unproductive regulation and even authoritarianism, and is likely to just reproduce predictable disappointment. Moral philosophy has a natural role in informing and influencing such important turns

---

[5] See Catherine Bosley, November 25, 2013. "Swiss Voters Reject Strict CEO Pay Limits in Referendum." *Bloomberg News.* <https://www.bloomberg.com/news/articles/2013-11-24/swiss-voters-reject-strictest-executive-pay-limits> (accessed May 1, 2017).

[6] For a discussion on the definition of "morality," see Bernard Gert and Joshua Gert, "The Definition of Morality," *The Stanford Encyclopedia of Philosophy* (spring 2016 edition), Edward N. Zalta (ed.). <https://plato.stanford.edu/archives/spr2016/entries/morality-definition/>. In this Introduction, I have in mind what Gert and Gert refer to as a more universal or normative morality.

in our thinking, especially when education is the preferred vehicle of transformation. It is useful here to heed John Dewey's caution:

> For in spite of itself any movement that thinks and acts in terms of an 'ism becomes so involved in reaction against other 'isms that it is unwittingly controlled by them. For it then forms its principles by reaction against them instead of by a comprehensive, constructive survey of actual needs, problems, and possibilities.[7]

In the remainder of this introduction, I elaborate on the arguments that frame and motivate this exploratory work; outline the structure of the book; and clarify why philosophy & philosophers might play a useful role in the experiment. Before proceeding, I should note that the contributors to this volume also wrote essays for a prior volume entitled *Performance & Progress: Essays on Capitalism, Business, and Society* (Rangan, 2015, Oxford University Press). That volume focused on the problems of capitalism, including the erosion of trust related to the abuse of money power and insider status. Though clearly related, the two volumes may be appraised independently.

EDUCATING POWER

In comprehending socio-economic outcomes, a useful starting point may be conveyed by the equation $O \cong f(P \times I) + \varepsilon$. That is, outcomes tend to be principally a product of power and interests. If we can comprehend who has the power and what their interests are, then we may comprehend actions and outcomes.

An alluring corollary of the preceding is that if we wish to shape outcomes, then we must vigilantly check, assign, and/or seek power. Indeed, from Plato's *Republic*, to the English "magna carta," to Hobbes' *Leviathan*, to the French revolution, to US antitrust legislation, the role of power has been central in the human quest to shape and redress socio-economic outcomes. US Senator John Sherman, in proposing his eponymous and seminal 1890 antitrust legislation, argued: "If we will not endure a king as a political power we should not endure a king over the production, transportation, and sale of any of the necessaries of life."[8]

The importance of power in explaining outcomes has led scholars to identify its numerous correlates, which include size, resources, information, technology (including especially weapons), money, concentration, status, authority, convention, intelligence, charisma, allies and networks, reputation, and so on. The length and sophistication of the preceding list reflects the extent to which power has preoccupied all manner of thinkers (including philosophers, historians, political theorists, legalists, sociologists, psychologists, and economists).

---

[7] John Dewey, 1938. *Experience and Education.* New York, NY: Kappa Delta Pi.
[8] <https://en.wikipedia.org/wiki/History_of_United_States_antitrust_law> (accessed May 3, 2017).

The evolution of formal and informal institutions is in large part a response to the risk and reality of misuse and abuse of power. In the economic realm, at least since Adam Smith (who begrudged collusion and cartels), a central approach and action has been to check economic power with political power via regulation and occasionally even nationalization. Thus the market economy evolved to a regulated *political economy*. (Lobbying and capture have, perversely, often only redoubled efforts at regulation.) Labor too sought power by unionizing. The decline of unions and their bargaining power have been accompanied by a decline of labor's share in gross domestic product (GDP). All these would seem to validate the primacy of power in influencing socio-economic outcomes. Even in business theory, the "structural forces" model associated with Michael Porter explains and predicts outcomes at the level of industry via appeal to the relative power of the various actors and entities in the sector's economic web.

What about interests though? It is typically (and not wrongly) taken as self-evident that the term interests may be regarded as a truncation of self-interests. Interests relate to attention and to goals. Rational actors are thought to be goal-oriented; and their goals generally pertain to their own interests. Thus national leaders pursue their power and the national interest; business leaders may pursue their entrenchment, compensation, and the business interest; employees may pursue higher wages, benefits, and shorter working hours; investors may pursue higher and growing after-tax returns; consumers may pursue quantity and quality at low prices; and so on.

In grappling with the dilemma of human interdependence, we have of course considered interests. Thus retributive and deterrent punishment (that menace negative pay-offs), and eventually the social contract approach, have built on the premise of interest as self-interest. In its primitive form, the intersection of power and interests entails base egoism in which the powerful pursue their own wants even at the expense of others. If power is distributed, however, this yields to mutuality, i.e. an exchange of benefits. In liberal polities, a social arrangement that promises to protect or advance the self-interest of the actors involved has a good likelihood of adoption if and when it emerges. Hirschman develops the idea in his *Passions and the Interests*,[9] that the enterprise economy was permitted to blossom since for the rulers who were doing the permitting, profitable trade promised to stabilize society in an affordable and durable manner via an appeal to energetic citizens' self-interest. The principle of mutuality is found too in Adam Smith's "invisible hand," and as well in Elinor Ostrom's *"conditional cooperation"* that she found could sustain local collective commons.

Even in more recent arguments about stakeholder interests and "shared value," the reason for deviating from short-term egoism is meant to reside in actors' own, albeit long-term, interests. This is sometimes termed as the "business case" for corporate responsibility. Among the returns expected: perhaps talented millennials will be more attracted to join the organization (i.e. social capital redounds in human capital); or

[9] Albert O. Hirschman, 2013. *The Passions and the Interests: Political Arguments for Capitalism Before Its Triumph*. Princeton: Princeton University Press.

customers will be willing to pay more; or regulators may be more lenient in the event of violations, and so on. In these and similar instances, over a suitably broad time horizon and set of actors, mutuality remains a bedrock.

Fundamental though it is, does mutuality—i.e. the anticipation and exchange of self-interest—need to be the defining extent of economic actors' interests? After all, if power is coupled with what is essentially self-interest, then we should not be surprised to see in practice the limited extent of mutuality (as frequently found in "ultimatum game" experiments), and spectacular market failures (as with youth unemployment or environmental damage). That is, the efficiency of mutuality granted, it is the sufficiency of mutuality that trembles on the table.

Why, for instance, should enterprises ponder a living wage when minimum wage plus a dollar might do the job? Why might enterprises abstain from pursuing tax inversions so long as they're not illegal? Why not market and distribute dubious but profitable financial products after first lobbying for the right to do so? Why not raise the price of pharmaceuticals when one has the market power to do so? Why not file for instrumentally protective patents to ensure the preceding? What appreciable mutuality might one plausibly enact with distant future generations whose climate and resources we may forbear from despoiling? Or from animals whose humane treatment costs more?

Consumers and employees likewise may be engaged in micro-rational if macro-irrational pursuits, especially when interests are "positional" (i.e. influenced by social comparison). In the case of employees, why not as a rule take the job that pays more? We speak and ask after all of *gainful* rather than meaningful employment? Well-being may meanwhile be compromised at the altar of income or power itself. Likewise, why not buy the biggest house one can afford? For investors, why not invest in newfangled enterprises that may generate above-average returns though they may despoil the environment, displace livelihoods, or habituate needless consumerism via click-of-a-mouse and now voice-activated technologies?

Going beyond mutuality means becoming deliberatively other-regarding, and intentionally embracing and enacting a conception of interests more expansive than one's own (current) wants, even when this process leads to a certain (affordable) sacrifice. Though in the minority, there are enterprises and entrepreneurs that exercise their power in ways that would appear to go beyond mutuality in this sense. For instance, a major US coffee chain (Starbucks) has been training and recruiting thousands of veterans, and has since pledged that it would recruit and train 10,000 international refugees over the course of the next few years. It has urged similarly placed firms to do the same. A large Brazilian cosmetics firm (Natura) was among the earliest (if not the first) to cease animal testing. Happily this is now the industry practice. Likewise, so-called "social impact investing" has grown in leaps and bounds from nothing to something. A new category of organization referred to as "social enterprise" or "hybrid enterprise" has emerged too in the last decades. These enterprises attempt to employ business principles and creativity to do "good" while operating without the traditional but not always sustainable financial dependence on the philanthropy of benevolent individuals and organizations.

One can conjure a number of skeptical interpretations of the actions and developments just cited. Indeed, intentions aside, the actions may redound positively to the enterprises in question. This however is not the place or occasion to take up that debate on the integrity of intentions and instrumentalism.[10] Rather, the purpose here is more to pursue the idea implicit in what is referred to as Ostrom's Law, that "an arrangement that works in practice can work in theory."

Specifically, the aim here is vigorously and rigorously to explore and theorize why and how in a liberal economy moral ideals and reasoning might inform and influence interests in a systemic manner. What processes of reasoning, including those suggested in constructivist philosophy, may elicit and empower those ideals? Constructivism supports idealized processes of moral reasoning to arrive at proper courses of action.[11] Rather than take a substantivist perspective of discovering the "right" answer, constructivism recommends moral reasoning to develop it. Rather than relying primarily, let alone solely, on external governance, this approach recommends the self-governance of an "impartial agent" who is able to reason with integrity from a reflective distance. This approach is much closer in focusing on interests (or the exercise of power) rather than on power itself. So, to what extent can such moral reasoning and character-abiding reflection cause desirable actions and outcomes? How and to what extent can education (including and especially on the job) shape and influence economic actors' goals, interests, and conduct in a manner that is more morally oriented?

It is reported that undergraduate students *after* completing a basic course in microeconomics cooperate less (and defect more) in the standard prisoner's dilemma game. Education apparently can help reinforce self-regarding tendencies. Leading business schools attract students with the promise of a speedy passage into the corridors of corporate power. Via courses on power and politics, tyros are acquainted with such classics as Machiavelli's *The Prince* (to learn how strategically to exercise power to obtain and retain fortune). But can business schools also educate and shape the *aspirations* of high-flyers who often have the ambition and intelligence to ascend the ladder of power?

That is, beyond regulating economic power could we do more and better in terms of educating economic power?[12] Whatever the eventual empirical answer may be to this question, the realities we confront would appear coercive, and it is imperative that we take up the question and ponder further the role and our conception of interests in

---

[10] For a discussion on the integrity of intentions and moral actions, see Robert Shaver, "Egoism," *The Stanford Encyclopedia of Philosophy* (spring 2015 edition), Edward N. Zalta (ed.). <https://plato.stanford.edu/archives/spr2015/entries/egoism/>.

[11] See Carla Bagnoli, "Constructivism in Metaethics," *The Stanford Encyclopedia of Philosophy* (summer 2017 edition), Edward N. Zalta (ed.). <https://plato.stanford.edu/archives/sum2017/entries/constructivism-metaethics/>.

[12] Rakesh Khurana's *From Higher Aims to Hired Hands: The Social Transformation of American Business Schools and the Unfulfilled Promise of Management as a Profession* (Princeton: Princeton University Press, 2010) laments the history of business education and advances a salutary sociological perspective on the institution of "professions."

causing socio-economic outcomes. In so doing, we would be heeding a central message in Jared Diamond's book *Collapse*, that when potentially grave trouble is clearly perceptible but not yet invincible, it is critical for society to reconsider its core values.[13]

Though philosophical ideals and principles have influenced law and politics, their influence on business theory remains limited at best. Given the prominent and even pre-eminent role of enterprise in modern society, and given the nature of the dilemmas at hand, it is apropos and even essential that philosophy also contributes to shaping the evolution of our economic system. If philosophers can't be kings, perhaps kings can be (educated to think and act like) philosophers. This is not a novel proposition: the ageless *Bhagavad Gita*, which relates Krishna's moral dialogue with prince Arjuna on duty and sacrifice in the proper exercise of competence and power, famously adopts such an approach.

I must make one last point about the importance of reflecting more on our conception of interests. Well-being, it seems clear, is made up of a plurality of "goods," including especially social relations and leisure. The question of relative weights need not be settled for us to comprehend that there is more to well-being than income and consumption. There is thus a certain morality that we owe our future selves that recommends that we establish optimally in the present our goals, and especially how and to what we devote our time, energy, and attention. As several of the essays in this volume submit, the current (Western) neoliberal economic system feeds a propensity to reflexively displace life goals, degrade interests, and diminish well-being.

STRUCTURE OF THE VOLUME

If one allows that it is at the level of the economic paradigm and not just policy and practice that we must now explore and experiment, then it would follow that we must also attend to the constraints of the central actors that operate within the paradigm. Enterprises are among the central actors in the economic realm, and their managers are understandably contested on and constrained by the so-called agency duty, which pertains to the proper exercise of discretion vested in professional executives (who, in this design, are the agents of the owner principals). Why and when might such discretion encompass reasons to act even at the expense of the principal? And if we entertain the prospect of system evolution and reasoned enterprise engagement in intentionally causing desirable outcomes, then we must also reflect on the effectiveness and efficiency of ways to bring this about.

Accordingly, the essays in the first part of this volume—"The Paradigm Problem"— explore why the economic system is under pressure to evolve and why we may need to reflect on and reform the economic *paradigm* and not just policy and practice. Why is

---

[13] Jared Diamond, 2005. *Collapse: How Societies Choose to Fail or Succeed*. New York: Penguin.

mutuality supplemented by regulation no longer sufficient (if it ever was), and why is it appropriate to integrate moral reasoning into the microeconomic system? The essays in the second part of the volume—"The Agency Problem"—shed light on why, despite agency dilemmas, enterprises need to be prime actors in enacting greater fairness and well-being. The essays in the third part of the volume—"The Effectiveness Problem"—are oriented toward efficacy and explore and assess some specific approaches to system evolution and enterprise engagement.

Before proceeding to review the three themes—paradigm, agency, and effectiveness—along which are organized the essays in this volume, I must note that I encouraged the authors to interpret and develop variations that reflected their expertise and concerns. In practice then, the contributions reflect both broader and narrower interpretations. Complementing the ideas that propose improvements within the current paradigm (e.g. stakeholder theory and mutuality), these essays explore the fundaments of our economic system, including revisiting the economy–society relationship, the development and scope of our interests (across actors and time), and the integration of moral deliberation in our reasoning and action. The breadth of the subject matter is not an accident however. The fundamental premise of this volume is that if business scholars and actors are to improve on the current paradigm, they will need to embrace in a deep way the kinds of fundamental concerns—about our societies, our natural environment, our moral psychology, the nature of moral reasoning, and our education—that have traditionally occupied philosophers. All of the essays were drafted specifically for this volume, and some of the work reflects a novel direction in the authors' thinking.

THE PARADIGM PROBLEM

In the context of business, social science scholars (especially in economics and sociology) have been concerned with capabilities and contracts. Philosophers have reflected on the morality of markets. Yet, philosophers have not co-developed with social scientists economic perspectives at the nexus of mutuality and morality. As I have already submitted, there would seem a need for such collaboration. Writing about the natural sciences, Thomas Kuhn observed, "It is . . . particularly in periods of acknowledged crisis that scientists have turned to philosophical analysis as a device for unlocking the riddles of their field. Scientists have not generally needed or wanted to be philosophers."

Society's aspirations evolve. During the twentieth century, for a variety of reasons (technological but also social, geopolitical, and epistemological), societies were drawn to and embraced the idea of economic development, productivity growth, and competitiveness. During the latter half of that century, across a spectrum of political systems including in the East and the South, countries ushered in and liberalized markets and enterprises.

To justify and guide this liberalization, more societies adopted the paradigm (or exemplar "operating system") of a capitalism anchored on enlightened self-interest or mutuality. Supported by institutions to enforce contracts the "invisible hand" of mutuality encouraged an unprecedented division of labor, specialization, and impersonal voluntary exchange. Mutuality thrust economics and economic theory to the fore, and it now anchors the paradigm of capitalism on which enterprises have erected a marvel of productivity and performance. Rising output and incomes were joined by innovations in marketing, distribution, and finance. Mass investment and production were joined, and in some regions in the wake of globalization even surpassed, by mass consumption. Media reported on high-performing enterprises and wrote about the unprecedented wealth and life comforts of its owners and leaders. In turn, processes of social comparisons at the country, city, firm, household, and individual level then intensified the embrace of material modernity emanating from the West. The rest is, so to speak, recent history.

Now, in the twenty-first century, as already noted, the consequences of this consciously attempted convergence are chronicled with alarm and concern. Reminiscent of the "double movement" that Polanyi conjured in *The Great Transformation*, society seems anxious to foment a counter-move toward greater fairness, well-being, and an expanded scope for humanity. The call is out to all economic actors (especially enterprises) to better integrate economic performance and societal progress.

A paradigm of capitalism anchored primarily (let alone solely) on mutuality would seem inadequate to help enterprises deliver on these emerging aspirations. If the platform of capitalism is to stay upright and support enterprises and other economic actors as they figure out how to deliver on this new self-supported aspiration, then the anchor of mutuality will likely have to be supplemented by an anchor of morality. That is, the "operating system" of our modern economy will likely need a significant and brisk update.

The essays in the first section of this volume speak to this paradigm evolution. Several accounts exist for why paradigms evolve. Kuhn observed that paradigms tend to evolve when anomalies mount and confound the existing paradigm. Appiah has suggested that in the moral realm, paradigms may evolve when standards of honor, propriety, and legitimacy evolve.[14] It is also clear that elites (of the worlds of theory and practice) play a catalytic role.

The essay by Meyer and Risse outlines the sharply expanding public and collective awareness of global integration and interdependence. Their central observation relates to the development of a "world society" where, through social diffusion, there is a rising cognitive conception of injustice claims and expectations of rights. Moral philosophy, in parallel, has been developing universalistic frameworks of justice. Both approaches feature an expanding array of injustice claims related to liberal globalism. This essay traces how, more than just a sectoral or regional development, the very legitimacy and morality of the modern economic system are being contested.

Employing a dialogue format from the distinct vantage points of business leader and moral philosopher, Collomb and Neiman in their essay debate the anomalies of the current market paradigm. Does the pursuit of output have to lead to the sacrifice of

[14] Kwame Anthony Appiah, 2010. *The Honor Code: How Moral Revolutions Happen.* New York: W.W. Norton.

outcomes? Is the current paradigm in trouble because its practice has reversed the means–end relations? They conclude by agreeing that "if something is necessary to act morally, it is rational for us to believe in it." They agree too on an expanded role for education, especially in schools of business.

James G. March's essay is concerned too that the modern economic system has scrambled means and ends. Enacting scripts encoded in (and educated via) a rational decision-theoretic logic of consequences has tended to displace proper goals. If to be rational is to be calculating, then what is bigger may crowd out what is better. Output after all is not the same as outcomes. He submits that the economic paradigm can no longer ignore philosophy and overlook the endogeneity of values inherent in modern business decision theory. March acknowledges this is a "hard problem" to the extent that it requires us to reassess both the proper "puzzle" and the proper "solution" that the paradigm of the economic system must come to terms with.

In a subsequent essay, Appiah rejoins and reinforces March's call for moral philosophical reasoning to inform economic action more actively. Though Appiah and March write separate essays, they collaborated on developing their contributions for this volume. In consonance with March's call for a better integration of moral philosophical perspectives in the economic realm, Appiah submits that the economic paradigm has concentrated overly on reasons for doing and having (materialistic reasons) while neglecting reasons for being (existential reasons) and reasons for feeling (sentimental reasons). "Treating everything as tradable with everything else may be bad for the soul and society," he avers.

In the fifth and final essay in this section, Kotaro Suzumura takes up one of the most vexing anomalies in the modern economic paradigm, viz. that of better integrating the future into our reasons for acting and forbearing. The current economic paradigm is a poor guide on matters of distribution, both inter-actor and especially inter-temporal. Suzumura grounds his discussion on the specific dilemma of climate change, and argues why mutuality is an insufficient guide to our actions on this existential dilemma, and why unilateral moral reasoning must guide us going forward.

Beyond societal expectations and anomalies, pressure to evolve the current economic paradigm comes too from elites. The 2009 Sarkozy Commission study authored by Stiglitz, Sen, and Fitoussi soundly placed well-being on the intellectual and policy map. Piketty and his colleagues' research on inequality has entered the mainstream. Michael Porter and his colleagues have submitted the idea of "shared value" and have begun benchmarking social progress across nations (though, as noted earlier, Porter's approach sits within the mutualistic paradigm). In a variety of ways, elites in the real world too have signaled their leanings, including with the "giving pledge" embraced by some of the world's wealthiest, or the famous BlackRock "CEO letter" (now sent annually by the world's largest asset manager) that exhorts business leaders to heed seriously environ-mental, social, and governance issues. Even the widely revered Pope Francis has been voicing moral appeals on reforming capitalism.

In a crisis, a certain degree of chaos and experimentation are to be expected and even beneficial. Still, without intellectual confidence and plausible bases for public justification, experimental if proper action tends to be weak and uncoordinated. The coordinative power of a more appropriately evolved paradigm is, for this important reason too, crucial. As the quote attributed to Kurt Lewin avers: "There is nothing as practical as a good theory."

THE AGENCY PROBLEM

When it comes to the exercise of discretion in the economic realm there is an important distinction between enterprises and the individuals they employ and the households they serve. Whereas households and employees represent themselves, large enterprises (including family firms) are typically represented by hired managers, who stand in an agency relationship to the enterprises' owner principals.

At least since Berle and Means' 1932 classic entitled *The Modern Corporation and Private Property*,[15] the proper exercise of managerial discretion in this agent–principal architecture has posed a dilemma. For Berle and Means, the modern corporation "split the atom" in separating control from ownership. The business judgment rule notwithstanding, there is room and incentive for a conflict of interest between owners and their manager agents.

With Milton Friedman and later more dogmatic others at the forefront, this dilemma was eventually reframed as the extent to which enterprises were to operate only to maximize profits (accruing to the share owners) versus the extent to which they could also address societal goals, especially when pursuit of the latter brought uncertain returns to the former and sometimes even came at its expense.

Friedman famously propounded the view that the social responsibility of business was to generate profits.[16] In certain jurisdictions this view is written into statutes of incorporation. Today though, even among finance and economics professionals, few any longer support that orthodoxy. There has been a flurry of reflection and writing on a broader conception of the responsibility of firms, on stakeholder perspectives, sustainability, social entrepreneurship, impact investing, and triple bottom line measurement, accounting, and reporting. Indeed, in 2015 one of the largest pension funds, CALPERS (the California Public Employees Retirement System), revised its principles of investment and governance to demand "propriety" in the firms it invests in, "even at the expense of profitability."[17]

Paradigms in general seem to evolve gradually. Further, from the work of Adam Smith to Douglas North to Oliver Williamson and Elinor Ostrom, we observe that in

---

[15] Adolf A. Berle and Gardiner C. Means, 1932. *The Modern Corporation and Private Property*. New York: Harcourt, Brace & World, 2nd edition, 1968.

[16] Milton Friedman, September 13, 1970. "The Social Responsibility of Business is to Increase its Profits." *New York Times Magazine*.

[17] See Steven Davidoff Solomon, March 24, 2015. "The Thorny Task of Advocating Good Corporate Behavior." *New York Times*.

social science practice often leads theory. Thus in one recent case that attracted considerable media attention, the co-founder of a one hundred-person private enterprise in California (Gravity Payments) decided to set at $70,000 the *minimum* salary in his organization (an amount he felt could enable one to support a family with dignity). The owner's partner, who happened to be his older brother, filed a lawsuit alleging miscarriage of agency (which eventually failed to prevail).[18] In a much larger public enterprise in the retail sector (CVS Health), in 2014 the management decided to stop selling tobacco products. The firm estimated it would forego about $2 billion in annual revenue as a result of the action.[19] In even larger global and public firms (including PepsiCo and Unilever), CEOs have been working (but not without detractors) to make their firms more proactive on concerns related to sustainability, health, and inclusion.

While we cannot know the counterfactuals, some rightly suspect that these actions stand to impose a certain cost on the current owners of these enterprises. On what bases might business theory encourage and empower the exercise of such managerial discretion? If mutuality has to be systematically complemented by morality, theory will have to address the agency dilemma.[20]

Five essays in the second part of this volume pertain to these questions of authority and obligation of economic actors, especially enterprises, in ushering greater fairness, well-being, and an expanded scope of humanity.

In his essay Amartya Sen goes beyond compassion to address the concept of obligation. He submits that a reasoned sense of obligation emanates also from any "effective power" a person or organization may possess to prevent or alleviate suffering. In his reckoning, the "obligation of power" finds its justification in morality rather than mutuality. He underlines the point by acknowledging and discussing the likely asymmetry in consequences for the actor and object of the action. This perspective on obligation conveys a spirit of "I should because I can" (and contrasts with the more typical "I can because I should" dilemma). Sen focuses on climate concerns in his essay, but the pertinence of his message to the agency question is broader. Enterprises wield enormous effective power and the social responsibility for their "footprints" is founded partly on compensation for harm and partly on a demonstration of solidarity. Sen's obligation argument goes much further.

Another way to perceive the "effective power" of enterprises is to recognize that, at least in economically developed countries, people spend the bulk of their waking hours at work. Clearly beyond the mutuality of pay for work, enterprises have some effective power to influence the well-being of their employees, since work (if one is to avoid the

---

[18] Wikipedia entry on Gravity Payments. <https://en.wikipedia.org/wiki/Gravity_Payments> (accessed May 14, 2017).

[19] Rachel Abrams, September 3, 2014. "CVS Stores Stop Selling All Tobacco Products." *New York Times.* <https://www.nytimes.com/2014/09/03/business/cvs-stores-stop-selling-all-tobacco-products.html?_r=0> (accessed May 14, 2017).

[20] For a useful review of the issue, see Joshua D. Margolis and James P. Walsh, 2003. "Misery Loves Companies: Rethinking Social Initiatives by Business." *Administrative Science Quarterly* 48: 268–305.

"alienation" of Marx) should also feed into life satisfaction. In their essay, Autor and Kitcher recall this often neglected connection in the modern economy. They develop the philosophical idea of "life themes" and discuss (using US survey data) the extent to which "work" is a potent context in which people may (but today seldom) find meaning and expression. Autor and Kitcher discuss ways of better measuring the work–life link and point to an expanded role for education for individuals in reflecting on and articulating life themes. Of course, when business leaders include and attend more to the dignity and well-being of employees they may well impose a trade-off on profits. Autor and Kitcher's essay questions the morality of business leaders still operating within the conventional bounds of narrow fiduciary agency.

The essay by Hansmeyer, Mendiola, and Snabe (the latter two of whom are business leaders) suggests that the agency dilemma tends to be overstated. This essay and a couple of others in this volume imply that mutuality and morality need not be in opposition (even if they frequently are). In the view of these authors—and they share concrete experiences from their organizations—orienting business to society via "purpose" tends to redound in superior performance (especially via positive selection, engagement, and retention of employees). They sketch a "tesseract model" with purpose at its core and four vertices corresponding to economic, human, social, and environmental values. One question that this essay raises is that if performance and progress can both be better achieved via purpose, then what prevents more (if not all) managers from adopting this integrated approach? Perhaps the heart of the agency dilemma is most exposed by this question, which points to the importance of rethinking corporate governance and the standards against which we nominate, develop, evaluate, and reappoint organizational leaders.

In the subsequent essay, Barney and Schmidtz explore the question: "when are firm profits a crime?" They submit that in modern times great individual fortunes are generally generated via the instrument of the business firm. If we see rising inequality and are unsatisfied with that outcome, we must then ask how and for whom firms operate? Often enough the size and sustainability of firm profits reflect (more than sustained productivity) collusion between big business and big government to keep profits flowing to the former and contributions flowing to the latter. There can be little fairness or well-being when this state of affairs exists. The convenient mutuality between managers, owners, and regulators seems to come at the expense of society. The play of power and interests is never clearer. In showing the right way of doing the wrong things, agency theories have perhaps exceeded their scope if not usefulness.

In the final essay in this section, Davis and Shibulal touch upon the specter of the "gig economy" which they refer to as platform capitalism. They portray Internet-enabled "labor on demand" business models as a technology that can be "weaponized" to exploit workers and benefit highly compensated managers and owners. Their essay touches the issue of agency in the face of technologies that threaten massive substitution of labor by machines. In this view, the agency constraint reflects a mutuality design turned cancerous. The alternative vision that Davis and Shibulal articulate is that technology may enable community-based locally controlled alternatives to corporations and states. The specific solution they propose is not reform but wholesale architectural change that takes us toward cooperatives and more democratic platforms for integrating and rewarding the contributions of the many.

THE EFFECTIVENESS PROBLEM

Even if one were to accept that the economic system is ripe for a moral evolution, there is the challenge of discovering and designing effective ways to catalyze the adoption and support the enactment of moral reasoning. Some experiments have been under-way, and it is useful to assess the extent to which these are workable. As in any system, some of the enactment may need to be at the level of the system, and some at the level of the actors within the system.

In this section's opening essay, Frank and Pettit outline ideas for an "economy of esteem" where moral conduct would be at least partly observable and elicit social approval or disapproval. In their approach, an "intangible hand" of civil society would complement the "invisible hand" of the market and the "iron hand" of the law. To operate effectively in an economy of esteem, enterprises would professionalize (or, as they put it, "moralize") managers, enact explicit processes of deliberation that would include the voice of affected and potentially affected parties, make public commitments to societal priorities, and track and disclose progress on these commitments. The contribution here is not so much in the novelty of these ideas, as in the constructivist approach it implies. Recall, constructivism supports idealized processes of moral reasoning to arrive at proper courses of action.[21]

Along similar lines, but more from a managerial perspective, Battilana, Fuerstein, and Lee assess prospects for "organizational democracy." A central contention of these authors is that traditional hierarchical organization will be insufficient for attending to the dual goals of performance and progress. They propose distributed decision rights, deliberative decision making, and employee ownership. Bargaining power and negoti-ations are not the motor factors here in establishing ends and means. Rather—drawing on contemporary democratic theory—they suggest that trade-offs are to be addressed via collective deliberation with representation. The latter brings in voice and informa-tion that is often neglected; the former implies moral (as opposed to purely transac-tional) reasoning. Together these may influence interests in a manner that goes beyond self-interest to the interests of the collective, and informs the moral exercise of discretion. The authors illustrate their idea with field-based research and discuss limitations of their proposed approach.

In the subsequent essay, assessing approaches to reducing income inequality, Anderson, Cheng, and Hong explore philanthropy by the super-rich. (The appeal of the "giving pledge" and similar initiatives is growing.) In line with prior sociological

---

[21] Bagnoli, "Constructivism in Metaethics."

analysis, they show and submit that status plays a large role in what they term "conspicuous giving." Further, drawing on a quasi-natural experiment related to unanticipated tax policy changes in the US, the authors report that lowering taxes on the super-rich does not bolster giving, it reduces it. They conclude by discussing more promising private alternatives to philanthropy. The essay clearly suggests that status-for-charity mutuality is very much alive in conspicuous giving. The essay also suggests that policy remedies to income inequality are not straightforward. Relating this essay to the one by Barney and Schmidtz suggests that perhaps how entrepreneurs make money should be more important than how they spend this money. Clearly redistribution via government tax and transfer and private charitable transfers both carry drawbacks. If we could moralize the interests and inform the spending of the super-rich, outcomes could be better. More promising alternatives as outlined in this essay include impact investing and impact philanthropy (as illustrated by, say, the Gates Foundation) both of which start with moral interests and then track societal outcomes to guide spending.

As several essays in this volume imply, if we are to enact morality and not only mutuality then it is important to educate and develop our interests in a deliberative and reflective manner. Addressing the specific role of the educational system on this front, Tiberius and Walsh submit that it is time for universities to stop treating their students as "customers." This essay has a certain resonance with the one by Autor and Kitcher, in that it focuses on individuals and their well-being. The authors propose that students be exposed to a structured protocol and be encouraged to reflect on their values and develop a "philosophy of life." Tiberius and Walsh submit that when individual reflection is followed up by sharing and discussion with heterogeneous peers, then it will lead to a discovery and appreciation of our "shared humanity." They sketch a pedagogic tool to support their proposal. The confrontation of our views, beliefs, values, and goals with those of others would appear to be crucial in shaping and empowering morally appropriate choices. This in some sense would be like playing the prisoner's dilemma with communication and promising. Experiments show that under these conditions the rates of cooperation are uniformly higher.

In the final essay of the section and the volume, Abouchakra, Hammami, and Snabe (the first two of whom work in government), discuss how the state too is experimenting with novel approaches to address fairness and well-being. The authors submit that all governments are powerful and many have proper intentions, but the traditional machinery of government is not only often inadequate and underfunded, it is still overly focused on output rather than outcomes. They discuss how in recent times governments have begun incorporating behavioral and data-founded insights into their actions and practices. These include conditional taxes (such as a sugar tax aimed at obesity), innovative financing (such as issuance of social impact bonds), and use of big data (to measure interventions against outcomes in education, health, public services, and safety). These are all part of the new public practice (as opposed to policy) toolkit aimed at enabling well-being. Three things stand out here: greater attention to outcomes rather than output; a reliance not on blunt and difficult-to-enforce regulation but on feedback mechanisms to influence interests and endogenize individual and enterprise actions; and importantly, a good use of mutuality to better align interests. This essay too makes it amply clear that mutuality and morality need not be in opposition.

MERITS OF PHILOSOPHY AND THIS VOLUME FOR BUSINESS RESEARCH

Fairness, well-being, and the scope of our humanity were the concerns I highlighted at the top of this chapter. Fairness refers to distributional issues; well-being is constituted by a plurality of ends; and the concern about the scope of our humanity refers to the pain and interference we may inflict on other creatures in the pursuit of our own ends. These issues are not the forte of engineering and economics, the bedrock fields on which much business research is founded. Sociology and psychology come closer, but understandably in applications in business research their core concerns have for the most part remained positive rather than normative.

As I wrote in the introduction to *Performance & Progress* (p. 8), "The dilemmas we are grappling with are not only techno-economic in nature, but also moral-philosophical. They are not only about decisions but also about choices. They are not only about peace and prosperity but also propriety. Without proper foundations in propriety, peace and prosperity are fated to remain tentative."

It is customary in business schools that firms are the primary units of analysis, and that the secrets to their sustained performance are what motivate most of the research conducted in business schools. Starting in time and work studies, moving to optimization of operations and accounts, business schools eventually turned to the social sciences—especially psychology, economics, and sociology—to "ground" their research.

Business practice and business scholarship has, understandably, been concerned primarily with the idea of performance. Witness the focus on competitiveness, innovation, marketing, technology, and leadership. Lately however, beyond the conventional economic action–performance linkage, scholars, students, and practitioners are increasingly also interested in the linkage between economic action and societal progress. The spotlight has turned on the proper accountability and aspiration of business firms and economic actors more broadly.

Against that background, the essays in this volume have three distinctive merits.

(1) Whereas previous work has described the problems with capitalism and explored under what circumstances, how, and to what extent "doing good may lead to doing well" (i.e. the case for mutuality), the essays in this volume develop the titular idea that an evolved paradigm of capitalism within which economic actors may better integrate performance and progress will have to be anchored not only on mutuality but also on morality. This takes us beyond a standard social contract approach to human interdependence. Especially in the realm of climate change, and also in addressing

issues such as concentrated wealth and capsizing trust, this dual anchor design—based on mutuality *and* morality—seems desirable and perhaps even inescapable. This approach relaxes the constraint of the "Pareto-optimal" standard economic approach. It diminishes the overpopularized "no real trade-offs" claim implicit in the "doing well while doing good approach." Last but not least, unlike in the case of the standard model, diffuse adoption of the dual anchor would harken hope rather than concern. *If most actors adopt and adhere to the dual approach, our collective will be better off even as we avoid centralized design and direction.*

To be sure, this dual anchor model confronts considerable challenges in implementation. As already reviewed, several of the essays in this volume explore the implementation challenges.

(2) Another distinctive merit of the essays in this volume is that they are for the most part co-authored across philosophy and social science. While the workings of the decentralized economic system have conventionally been explored and developed within the confines of social science (especially economics, psychology, sociology, and political science), an economic system adapted to the expectations of the twenty-first century will likely have to draw from philosophy. Yet mainstream business management scholars (say in finance or organization theory) have typically not had to draw on philosophy, let alone collaborate with philosophers. Most of the essays in this volume attempt this novel pairing with promising results in the form of original and useful perspectives and proposals.

The pertinence of moral and social philosophy to more relevant and rigorous research by scholars in business schools may be appreciated in terms of reasoning (rigor), substance (relevance), and unit of analysis. First, moral reasoning more than material (economic and technical) reasoning is needed to help ground the work of business scholars who wish to theorize about why, how, and which economic actors might better integrate performance and progress. Moral philosophical logics are going to be indispensable because we will need to reason about ends and not only means; and because we will need to discuss multiple values, not all of which can be compared or exchanged, or sometimes even ordered according to preference. Material reasoning depends largely on prices, exchange rates, and marginal and dynamic effects. To this logic based on self-regarding "consequences," moral reasoning usefully integrates logics based on other-regarding "appropriateness."

Second, if business scholars are to advance research that is going to be relevant to business students and practitioners in the twenty-first century, they will have to draw on and integrate philosophical perspectives on what is "good" and what "should" be and not only what is "true" and what "can" be.[22] Economics, finance, psychology, sociology, and engineering may inform optimal decisions on means given ends (typically economic performance), but they are hardly well placed to reason adequately about optimal choices of ends. Further, while fields such as sociology and psychology

---

[22] Unlike in some moral theory, here "should" does not imply "can."

explore important concepts such as legitimacy and empathy, it is moral philosophy that is likely to give us substantively better purchase on notions such as propriety and progress. What is proper not in form but in substance is a complex and moral question. Empathy may be a psychological reflex, but obligations are a moral question.

Finally, the typical units of analyses in business research tend to be economic, viz. firms, workers, consumers, products, and markets. If business scholars are to contribute useful research on the future of the decentralized market-based economic system, then the units of analysis typical in moral philosophy, viz. individual, society, and humanity including other living creatures, must be better integrated. Important ideas such as dignity, satisfaction, esteem, inclusion, humaneness, fairness, well-being, and progress all attach to these other units of analyses.

(3) Last but not least, the essays in this volume cover in a somewhat concrete manner an impressive array of important topics. These include climate change, intergenerational obligations, life satisfaction, value endogeneity, education as a complement to regulation, organizing for hybrid goals, representation and deliberation within business firms, wealth inequality, trust, future discounting, new technology-enabled "platform capitalism," and government's catalytic (as opposed to controlling) role.

Markets in the long run may be self-correcting, but to travel from a less to a more optimal region of operation, its actors need good theories to justify and coordinate their shifts in that desirable direction. This volume contains essays that represent the "green shoots" of such theorizing on a capitalism beyond mutuality. Given the intellectually challenging nature of the dilemmas under consideration, it is vital that the best minds be called upon to reflect and contribute. The group of academics brought together here constitutes eminent scholars in the two respective domains. Further, bringing an insider's view on the practice, problems, and possibilities, a handful of thoughtful business leaders with experience in diverse sectors and countries also contribute. Accordingly, the work can claim some uniqueness in its orientation toward issues of fundamental, systematic importance, in the influence and stature of its contributors, and in its explicit orientation toward interdisciplinary engagement.

CONCLUSION

The starting premise of this project is that the paradigm of the decentralized market system is incomplete but not fundamentally incorrect. The contribution here is hence oriented to paradigm evolution rather than revolution. The incumbent mainstream paradigm has helped reduce absolute poverty in the world and unleashed unprecedented (though severely unequal) prosperity. The institutions of property rights and the informational content of market prices, albeit imperfect and incomplete, are powerful, and privately and socially useful. This part of the mainstream merits maintaining, at least insofar as it can be coupled to reforms across other dimensions of the market system.

It is clear that we must bring greater attention to fairness, well-being, and the scope of our humanity. Accordingly, the assumptions regarding the goals and sufficiency (of information, contracting, markets) of the current economic system must be re-examined and redressed.

The "mainstream" is therefore not to be discarded or dismissed but to be rectified and further developed. Adam Smith and successors are not wrong, but they focused overly on means and insufficiently on ends. Their regulators were more omniscient and omnipotent than the ones of reality. The externalities they considered were not pervasive or large. Nature's services and the ecosystem did not feature prominently. Distributional consequences were not primary in their analysis. Their humanity extended to those with whom one had relations; it mentions but does not really develop "non-relationist" reasoning on moral obligations. We should address these and other shortcomings while guarding the incentive and information properties of the decentralized economic system.

Having said all of this, I would hardly deny that there are viable criticisms of the mainstream approach. This volume, in effect, adopts the following approach: "Suppose we admit the basic paradigm of a decentralized market system; suppose we then gather some of the sharpest minds in philosophy, social science, and business; and suppose we then ask them: in what respects and how can that paradigm be improved to bring about greater fairness and well-being?" I submit that the answer to this question is important, even to those who might reject the paradigm.

At business schools worldwide there is a burning and growing need for rigorous treatment of concerns regarding the paradigm and practice of capitalism. The proposed volume is hence aimed at three audiences: business scholars, business students, and business practitioners. There is a growing interest among scholars (including especially doctoral students) in business schools to study, develop, and deepen the corpus of intellectual work on the issue. Yet, as argued in this chapter, there seems to be too little theoretical and philosophical grounding in this research, and the published work tends to be applied and empirical. The essays in this volume provide useful and meaningful grounding for future research. The fact that the essays here are authored by mainstream disciplinary scholars (as opposed to corporate social responsibility experts) is intended to attract future contributions from other mainstream scholars. The target business scholars work in such areas as management and leadership, organization theory, strategy, economics, finance, and decision science.

The essays make clear the role for education. Such education, especially in business schools and in business proper, needs content for reflection. Ideally, the content will be integrative; i.e. it will not be one-dimensional exhortations to do good. It has to be analytical and developmental (rather than polemical). Business school students both at the graduate and undergraduate level should benefit from (at least parts of) this volume. For them it is often unclear whether challenges related to social, natural, and human capital are even the proper realm of business and markets. If need be, they admit, some regulation and a handful of non-governmental organizations (NGOs) might be useful. In the typical MBA program, finance and economics tend to be interpreted by students as the final word. The students see too few (non-dogmatic) big names associated with concerns on capitalism. This hampers curiosity and receptivity, and leads to pre-judgment. The essays in this volume hope to open minds and make students more receptive to the debate on capitalism, business, and society, and, in turn, to their future role as enterprise managers and entrepreneurs in reconciling performance with progress. In the parlance of today, the time is nigh for business models to be complemented by business morals.[23]

[23] I am especially grateful to Mike Fuerstein, Javier Gimeno, and John Meyer for the time and comments they volunteered during the preparation of this chapter. Conversations with a number of other colleagues, including Karel Cool and Ithai Stern, were helpful too.

PART I

THE PARADIGM PROBLEM

CHAPTER 2

THINKING ABOUT
THE WORLD
Philosophy and Sociology

JOHN W. MEYER AND MATHIAS RISSE

Abstract

In recent decades the world has grown together in some unprecedented ways. This integration is linked to a greatly expanded public and collective awareness of global integration and interdependence. Academics across the social sciences and humanities have been trying to make sense of this expanded world within the confines of their disciplines. In sociology, since the 1970s, notions of the world as a society have become more and more prominent. John Meyer, among others, has put forward, theoretically and empirically, a general world society approach. In philosophy, much more recently, Mathias Risse has proposed the grounds-of-justice approach. Even though one is a social scientific approach and the other a philosophical one, the approaches of Meyer and Risse have much in common. Both call attention to the expanded array of injustice claims arising from unregulated globalization. This chapter brings these two approaches into a conversation.

INTRODUCTION

In recent decades the world has grown together in ways in which it had never been before. This integration is linked to a greatly expanded public and collective awareness of global integration. Academics across the social sciences and humanities have reacted to the expanded realities and perceptions, trying to make sense of the world within the confines of their disciplines. The matter is especially urgent—and normatively very colored—with respect to the very unequal world economy, built around capitalist logics but without the national infrastructures that have protected, legitimated, and tried to regulate national capitalist institutions. Thus a global society forcefully raises questions of global (especially economic) justice, without providing good answers. The issues are central to many chapters in this book (e.g. Chapters 3, 4, 5, 10, 13, and 14).

In sociology, since the 1970s, notions of the world as a society have become prominent. John Meyer, among others, has put forward, theoretically and empirically, a general world society approach. One defining feature is the rise of a world cultural frame that provides models, norms, and roles on a global scale. People, organizations, and national states are seen to act on normative and cognitive models that are global in character and aspiration (also see Frank and Pettit in this volume). It is less and less plausible to see world society in terms of explanations focusing only on power and interests. World society theory is concerned with (often competing) scripts whose institutionalization creates a world culture where general cognitive principles, values, and roles are broadly shared across countries and organizational contexts. This culture, faced with the little-legitimated inequalities generated by the world capitalist economy, has rapidly evolved legitimating regulatory models (of whatever actual effectiveness).

In philosophy, more recently, Mathias Risse has proposed the grounds-of-justice approach. Grounds are properties of individuals that make it the case that certain demands of justice apply among a group of people. The grounds he distinguishes are shared membership in states, common humanity, shared subjection to the trading system, membership in the global order, and humanity's collective ownership of the earth. A theory of global justice emerges from reflection on the various grounds.

The origins of this collaboration lie in our realization that, even though one approach is social scientific and the other philosophical, Meyer's world society approach and Risse's grounds-of-justice approach have much in common. This essay brings these two approaches into a conversation. The next section, written by Mathias Risse, traces philosophical reflection on the world across history. Section three, written by John W. Meyer, does the same for social scientific reflection on the world. The fourth section contains Mathias Risse's comments on John W. Meyer, and section five contains John W. Meyer's comments on Mathias Risse. The sixth section concludes.

THINKING ABOUT THE WORLD: PHILOSOPHY

Introduction: Political Philosophy and the World

Inevitably, most questions about living arrangements arise among people who interact regularly. Accordingly, most political philosophy has addressed local or regional matters. But rarely have humans simply stayed put. Thus they needed ways of thinking about how to treat those whom they encountered. Sometimes, though not always, a next step was taken to think about the world. The goal here is to look at a few ways in which philosophers have thought about the world, roughly in chronological order. There are perspectives that lie outside the Western canon, but coverage tends to be spotty.

From Polis to Kosmos

The Ancient Greeks lived in *poleis*, city states with hinterlands, averaging about the size of Liechtenstein.[1] In the fourth century BC Isocrates famously argued for Greek unity, insisting only an umbrella government capable of keeping all cities in line would cure incessant warfare. This thought of creating overarching structures for peacekeeping has echoed through the ages.

Soon, Philip of Macedon overran the *poleis*. His son vanquished much of the known world. Alexander has sometimes been hailed as a noble dreamer seeking to unify humanity.[2] Either way, it was Alexander's empire that rendered world unity a phantasy one could entertain. Later the Romans founded an empire that lasted for much longer and whose memory long after its demise fed the dream of unity.

Before all that came to pass, Greek political philosophy focused on the polis, and little else. In the *Republic*, Plato's Socrates theorized city states. He thought that to live the good life meant to flourish in a city. Aristotle's political philosophy, too, had little to say on what lay beyond the city state. In the *Nicomachean Ethics*, he reported that "some say there is one justice, as fire burns here and in Persia" (Book V, 7), and concurred. But nothing was said about how such justice might jointly apply to Greece and Persia.

The first European philosopher to articulate a cosmopolitan view was the Cynic Diogenes.[3] He called himself "a citizen of the world [*kosmopolitês*]." Apparently Diogenes merely meant to convey a negative message: it did not affect how he saw himself that he hailed from Sinope. Unsurprisingly, political thought that began with the *polis* would talk about the world by first ascertaining ways in which the world (*kosmos*) was a city (*polis*).

The Stoics provided a positive doctrine.[4] Much as *poleis* are governed by law, so is the *kosmos*. However, law governing cities is conventional whereas law governing the world is natural: right reason can discover it. Access to right reason sets humans apart from the rest of nature. Eventually each person capable of partaking of right reason would come to be appreciated in his (later also her) own right. The human rights movement still draws on these ideas. In the first century BC, Cicero took it for granted that the world is a city. But cosmopolitanism became thin at Cicero's hands. While *On Duties* has strong words for the importance of humanity, this recognition sounds hollow in light of the long list of special relations whose moral significance Cicero stresses in his theory of justice.[5]

---

[1] For a good overview of Greek political thought, see Ryan (2012: chapters 1–5).
[2] On Alexander as a dreamer of world unity, see Badian (1958). See also Baldry (1965: chapter 4).
[3] On the Cynics, see Moles (2000) and relevant sections in Parry (2014) and Kleingeld and Brown (2013).
[4] On the Stoics, see Baltzly (2013), Brown (2009), and Schofield (1991). See also Konstan (2009).
[5] On the connection between the Stoics and Cicero, see Baldry (1965: chapter 6).

All Under Heaven

In Chinese political thought the subject all along was empire. When in the eleventh century BC the Zhou replaced the Zhang, the justification for the overthrow spelled out the "mandate from heaven" that specified who got to rule. The implied contrast between "heaven" and "earth" made it natural to regard those over whom rule was exercised as "all under heaven" (*tianxia*). Confucius (around 500 BC), and later Mencius, advocated unity before the background of centuries of warfare, but they appealed to a unity that had existed before. However, while Chinese thought focused on something much bigger than the city, it also championed something much smaller: the family. All under heaven fall into concentric circles with the extended family at its core. For Confucius and Mencius the core notion was "ren," "meeting of people," which captures appropriate benevolence, humaneness.[6]

Since the 1990s, the doctrine of *tianxia* has seen a revival. In his 2005 book *The Tianxia System: A Philosophy for the World*, Zhao Tingyang aims to merge the idea of all under heaven with the Greek rational dialogue on the agora. What underlies the United Nations (UN), he says, are ideals of transnational democracy and rational communication, in continuation of the agora. However, the UN is an agora without a *polis*, which would have to be a global *polis*. Zhao believes the Chinese idea of all under heaven provides what is missing, harmonizing Greek and Chinese thought.

The Christian Middle Ages

Kosmopolis and natural law morphed into Christian thought. What especially fell on fertile soil was the Stoic tale of two cities. Both *polis* and *kosmopolis* made demands. Christians recast this tale: "Render therefore unto Caesar the things which are Caesar's; and unto God the things that are God's" (Matthew 22:21). In Augustine's appropriation, the polis became the worldly political domain. Worldly power was a playing field for deluded, violent characters. They could not ever know if they had achieved justice even if they tried. Justice means to give each his due. But if only God knows what that is, then the just world as a human creation is out of reach. The *kosmopolis* Augustine transforms into a spiritual sphere where people of all origins are eligible to become "fellow-citizens with the saints" (Ephesians 2:20). For Christianity, thinking about the world means to think about this whole world, but also always about the transcendent world that really matters.

Christianity kept alive a spiritualized vision of Roman rule as a driving ideal of empire. Central to cosmopolitan thought of antiquity was world *citizenship* rather than *government*. But it was the thought of the world being ruled by one government that became central in Dante's *De Monarchia* around 1300. To achieve human perfection

---

[6] For the themes in this section, see Angle (2012) and Bai (2012).

the whole species must pursue this task. The diversity of striving must be protected by a universal structure. But Dante's *humana civilitas* was not thought to inhabit all of the earth. Since the archaic Greeks, Western thought marked off a finite stretch of earth from the formless expanse surrounding it. The *orbis terrarum*, the realm where people lived, included Europe, Africa, and Asia, with the impassable ocean all around.[7]

European Expansionism

For the first time, European seafaring explorations raised questions about the division of the globe as such. There were sophisticated trade economies that included large parts of the known world before this period. But the world only now became the planet: "Columbus brought the two halves of the planet together."[8] Questions arose about how the conquerors should divide their spoils. Ancient ideas about the world resurfaced. Some argued that Native Americans were natural slaves (revitalizing an Aristotelian doctrine) who could not own property. Much later, with the advancement of science, this approach hardened into "scientific" racism. Others, notably Vitoria, insisted that natives had to be respected as humans who owned territory. But he too justified conquest.[9]

Considerations about proper land use became increasingly important. One guiding idea was the Stoic law-of-nature doctrine to let strangers use things one does not need. A case could be made that, if "savages" resisted occupation of land that, in the eyes of these beholders they could not meaningfully use, violence was appropriate. Then there was the view that humanity collectively owned the earth. This thought too goes back to the Stoa. More importantly, it is in the Old Testament. God's gift of the earth to humanity became the pivotal thought of seventeenth-century political philosophy.[10]

The great political development of the seventeenth century was the cementation of an order consisting of sovereign states. Wars made states, states made wars, but states also made nations and nations states.[11] The 1648 Treaty of Westphalia came to symbolize the initial stages of this process,[12] but the slogan of the 1555 Augsburg Religious Peace captures the era best: *cuius regio eius religio*, he who controls a region gets to choose its religion. To this day ours is a world of states. It was through centuries-long decolonization that the European system of order ultimately triumphed.

Several of the natural lawyers of the seventeenth century were social contract theorists. Grotius, Pufendorf, and others applied that model internationally and laid

---

[7] On Dante and the Christian Middle Ages, see Heater (1996: chapter 2). On Dante and medieval cosmology, see Bartelson (2009: chapter 3). On the boundaries of the world, see Romm (1992).

[8] Crosby (2003: 31).

[9] On Vitoria, see Pagden (2015: chapter 1); see also Nussbaum (1954: 79–84).

[10] See Tuck (2001).

[11] The formulation that states made wars and wars made states goes back to Tilly (1975).

[12] See Beaulac (2004) for the extent to which the importance of Westphalia has been overstated.

the foundation for international law.[13] However, what nowadays we recognize as international law largely emerged only in the nineteenth century. Initially, international law was designed to regulate interaction among colonial powers. Gradually more and more countries were created. The result was a world of artificially equal states operating in what eventually became a global system.

In a world that increasingly limits the policy space of nation states, questions arise about whether global order is still best described as a state system, and what the feasible alternatives could be. Let me just mention two approaches. In the middle of the last century Carl Schmitt argued that the world of states had expired in the nineteenth century when colonialism reached its limits. He saw the future in a world of great spaces, *Grossräume*, but rejected global oversight, insisting that whoever said humanity (a caring unimpeded by boundaries) sought to deceive.[14] Arguably, the current posturing of China expresses agreement with such an approach. A very different approach was recently adopted by David Held, whose work explores the shift from nation states to a world of "overlapping communities of fate" and how democratic standards and cosmopolitan values can be entrenched globally. Held supports the subordination of sovereignties to an overarching legal framework.[15]

Enlightenment and Individualism

During the Enlightenment initial steps were taken to ensure the political and legal map would also include individuals. For much of history, recognizing individuals as having any kind of status across borders could not have amounted to much. In the eighteenth century the American Declaration of Independence spoke of "a decent respect to the opinions of mankind." This wording was symptomatic of an emerging transnational public. The 1789 French Declaration of the Rights of Man and the Citizen was intended to make sure power was exercised also on behalf of individuals who often needed protection from states more than from anything else.

Organizations started to emerge to pursue concerns of individuals across state lines that would often not align with the interests of states. In the nineteenth century the paradigmatic movement was that of the working class. Eventually, the multifarious ways of protecting individuals fed into the Universal Declaration of Human Rights, and much subsequent international law. Individuals as such came to matter in the twentieth century as they never had before.[16]

One philosophical work from the end of the eighteenth century conceptualized the world in a novel, multifaceted way. Kant's *On Perpetual Peace* was guided by the idea that

---

[13] For the history of international law, see Nussbaum (1954) and Koskenniemi (2002).

[14] Schmitt develops his thoughts on international order most extensively in his 1950 *Nomos of the Earth*. The quote about humanity Schmitt attributes to Proudhon, but agrees with it; see Schmitt (1963: 55).

[15] See for instance Held (2004).

[16] On the history of the human rights movement, especially the predecessors, see Lauren (2011).

"the peoples of the earth have thus entered in varying degrees into a universal community, and it has developed to a point where a violation of rights in one part of the world is felt everywhere."[17] A federation to keep the peace was needed. Kant's world also gave status to individuals by acknowledging a cosmopolitan right of hospitality to protect individuals in dealings with foreign governments. The idea that humanity jointly inhabits a planet also arose: it is because we share a sphere rather than an infinite plane that we must regulate our affairs in ways respectful of all members of the moral community.

Into the Twentieth Century

The desire to build trade routes has instigated exploration throughout history. Artisans would copy foreign merchandises, ship's doctors study local herbs, and vessels add useful features spotted in foreign harbors. Animals and crops would be transplanted, and tried elsewhere.[18] But only the Industrial Revolution allowed for the mass production of goods, as well as for fast transportation.

In the nineteenth century, globalization incited fierce reactions. Marx and Engels regarded capitalism as inherently expansive, insisting that bourgeois ideology legitimatized "free" trade while impoverishing millions. They also held that across countries the proletariat had common interests. The *Communist Manifesto* ends with the rallying cry: "Working men of all countries, unite!" Communists juxtaposed the thought that trade makes the world with the thought that trade worsens oppression but thereby also hastens the revolution.

Politics became global in the first half of the twentieth century like never before. Communism, liberalism, and fascism were vying for supremacy. Fascism emphasizes authoritarian rule and subjection of individuals under collective control. But both liberalism and communism offer moral visions that make the individual central. Both also have found ways of losing sight of that commitment. For much of the remainder of the twentieth century a great deal of the world was divided between liberal-capitalist and communist countries.

Recent Thought

A stage-setting work in Anglo-American philosophy in the last third of the twentieth century was Rawls' *Theory of Justice*. The intensity and breadth of the work animated by Rawls mark these last decades as one of the most intense periods in the history of political philosophy. This should be of little surprise: better understanding of the

---

[17] See Kant (1991: 107–8).
[18] For how trade has shaped the world, see Bernstein (2008), Pomeranz and Topik (2006), and Findley and O'Rourke (2007).

functionings of society and of technology provides more policy tools than ever before; populations have grown enormously in the last 200 years, and many are well-educated and wish to participate actively in society; and both domestic societies and the world as such have become intensely intertwined, politically and economically.

Rawls' early work mostly concerned one state at a time. By the time he developed his thoughts on international affairs, in *Law of Peoples* in the late 1990s, the field had changed. "Global justice," thus the world, had become increasingly central. Even in *Law of Peoples*, however, Rawls saw the world through the lens of the foreign policy of the kind of state he favored. By then others had applied his approach globally. Rawls argued that it is the existence of a basic structure of political and economic institutions—those determining the fundamental parameters of interaction—that renders penetrating principles of justice applicable among those who share them. But as in the first instance, Beitz and Pogge insisted, such a basic structure exists globally.[19]

Pogge later argued that the basic global structure is arranged enduringly to inflict grievous injustices on the most vulnerable.[20] Dependency theory made a similar case, maintaining that the "periphery" of the global economy would continue to lose out given that its major contribution (resources) would increasingly decline in relative value. Nowadays most (not all) philosophers take a kind of moral cosmopolitanism for granted, recognizing some sort of human equality. Disagreement looms in assessing what such equality entails given that the world is a complex web of relationships (as Cicero knew). The views on the relationship between *polis* and *kosmopolis* that were open to the Stoics are now open to us.

Where Things Stand

The multifarious ways in which people have thought about the world are still with us. Our common humanity matters. Nothing serves better to illustrate this than the human rights movement, with its focus on the idea that something about us being human generates entitlements and corresponding obligations held by distant people. We no longer consider the earth a divine gift. But intellectuals, enlightened politicians, and foresighted citizens understand that we must see ourselves as having a relationship with our planet across generations. "Nature" is no longer independently given, but something we ourselves can shape.

Political and economic interconnectedness is mirrored in organizations and inter-governmental arrangements and the elaborate body of international laws that regulate transnational interactions. The diversity of ethnicities has too often fallen prey to rank ordering, with calamitous and even cataclysmic consequences. For many religious people the power of theology that compels them to think about the world as such rather than parts of it also forces them to see this world as merely an ephemeral one in a

---

[19] See Beitz (1979) and Pogge (1989).   [20] See Pogge (2006).

much larger scheme of things. This prevents them from seeking reasonable terms with others on an increasingly crowded planet.

States have withered but they have not withered away, as Engels predicted. Still, much that matters is no longer decided within states. International often trumps domestic rule-setting. International culture fuels domestic culture. The rising worship of the individual reflects the decline in worship of states, as well as the rising worship of the "world." However, the period during which individuality and equality have been praised has also been one of massive economic inequality. We are currently on the brink of a technological revolution. One result could be that we increasingly modify ourselves, perhaps creating untold numbers of blond, super-intelligent children who excel at sports. Another result could be an exacerbation of inequality. Those who know how to make or use technology will prosper. Others may become increasingly economically useless.

The thought that humans matter as such has also led to the thought that whatever makes us matter might also apply to other creatures. Some talk about "expanding circles" of moral concern, insisting our treatment of animals is abysmal.[21] Soon, our world may include machines equipped with artificial intelligence, which might pose a grave threat to humanity. Perhaps eventually we must confront aliens that may make demands on the resources of our planet.

The social world has become almost incomprehensibly complex. It is populated by states and individuals, and of course companies, many transnational, and some of those huge conglomerations. The last century has witnessed extraordinary growth of civil society. The relative importance of all these entities for bringing about change is debated, as is their importance for the kinds of questions that exercise philosophers, such as how to think about justice at the global level. These matters are urgent since they might help us navigate uncharted terrain to meet the challenge of our time: how to keep our flourishing species from ruining the very world of which we are part. If we fail, the planet will still be there. But the other senses in which we have come to think about the world may end up lacking a reference. Perhaps only a few humans will eventually remain to remember that there was once more to "the world."

THINKING ABOUT THE WORLD: SOCIOLOGY

Introduction

The social science disciplines arose after the Enlightenment, evolving out of philosophy. They developed over the nineteenth century, expanded in the twentieth century, and grew explosively since World War II. Their recent growth parallels a decline in the humanities (Frank and Gabler 2006; Drori and Moon 2006). Before the nineteenth

---

[21] See Singer (2011).

century, topics now considered social scientific were discussed by philosophers and theologians, not by specialists. The social sciences tended to take for granted as central the core ontological elements of the post-Enlightenment social world: the nation state and the individual (and a capitalist society built on individuals). Even now, the social sciences are relatively stronger in the West—especially the Protestant West (Frank et al. 1995). But the nation state system has spread to the whole world, and the social sciences have spread along with it: the end of the Cold War created an explosion of social science in the former communist countries. The tie of the social sciences to the nation state system has delayed their comprehension of a supranational society, falling behind popular awareness. The critics of "methodological nationalism" have a strong case (e.g. Beck 2000).

The Enlightenment, it has been said, "discovered society." Before, universalistic thought in Christendom tended to locate an ideal social order above a corrupted physical and social reality. After the Enlightenment, conceptions of society as a coherent system of interdependent parts and locus of purposive action arose. Society was seen in the plural, and the world was understood to be filled with them. Increasingly, with social Darwinism (as in Spencer 1896) they were seen to lie on an evolutionary or developmental scale. By the late nineteenth century all the major sociologists had a typology of societies along these lines (e.g. Durkheim (mechanical-organic), Toennies (*gemeinschaft-gesellschaft*), Marx (feudal-capitalist), Weber, or Comte). Primitive or pre-modern societies were seen as natural systems, embedded in nature and culture. Developed ones were rationalized and differentiated, often capitalist, and the consequence of purposive action: variously by individuals in liberal versions, and the state in illiberal ones (Toulmin 1990).

Society was depicted as an autonomous functional system, disembedded from history and culture: this, it was understood, was the source of the great success of the West. Society was thus seen as something of an organization, produced and maintained by the interaction among its purposive differentiated parts (individuals and organizations, or the state): "Man makes himself" is the idea. History may enter in through the interests built into the parts of the system, but not as a collective property. Culture, seen as a fabric of collective meaning, in pre-modern and primitive societies, was mainly left to the anthropologists. These images remain alive in social scientific understanding and in a dominant world ideology (Thornton et al. 2015).

Increasingly, notions of society became linked to the nation state (though sometimes a "civilization," as with the European colonial powers). The older ideas of a common universal transcendent moral order became secularized, developed into social scientific laws thought applicable everywhere—but found in their highest form in dominant countries. So by the twentieth century, the special Western religious status of the person was in part reformulated as citizenship in a national (often capitalist) economy, and thought to be functional for complex societies. Rationalization and differentiation create distinctive combinations of roles for individuals, producing the modern conscious individuated person (Simmel 1976 [1903] is the *locus classicus* here). Thus religious salvation was increasingly translated into compulsory education, seen as functional for economic, political, and social institutions (e.g. Parsons and Platt 1973; the parallel with earlier notions of salvation is made by Shils (1971)).

Social Scientific Models of Global Interdependence before World War II

The lines of thought noted here depict single societies. In practice, however, all these separate societies were interdependent—with exchanges of people, goods, and ideas; conflicts; and perceived collective problems. This produced specialized discussions of rules: interstate relations, trade, scientific matters, or piracy. They were matters for the interstate system to resolve. The nation state had sovereignty, however fictitious (Krasner 1999), attributed to Westphalia. So weak notions of a supranational order arose rather frequently, but nothing like a complete world society. This was the main social science situation until 1945. We can review the dimensions of the imagined partial world orders before World War II.

Political interdependencies within the system. Nation states needed to deal with each other, and a special field of international and diplomatic relations defined governing norms and their rationales. The society of states had rules, sometimes seen (in theory deriving from Hobbes and Machiavelli) as created by rational states in a global anarchy (e.g. Waltz 1979; Gilpin 2001). But sometimes this interstate system was seen more broadly as a society (following Grotius), reflecting older universalistic cultures (Bull 1977, and the English School—Buzan 2014).

Imperial linkages beyond the system. Western expansion created links to the wider world. Asymmetries of power turned most of these relations into imperial ones, culminating in the famous "Scramble for Africa" in the later nineteenth century. Justifications centered on evolutionary ideas: metropoles were extending civilization to their colonies, speeding their development: religious themes were prominent, with Protestant missionaries carrying nation state models of moral development, and Catholics (especially Jesuits) carrying distinct models (Casanova 2016; Woodberry 2012). In practice, over the whole post-Enlightenment period, colonies shifted into the canonical nation state status at increasing rates (Strang 1991): after World War II the rate increased even more, and the nation state became a completely dominant form.

World economic regulation. Beyond political and military relations, new international rules arose through the nineteenth and early twentieth centuries, attempting to manage economic transactions in a broadly capitalist regime. Intellectual developments were intensified by the Great Depression, partially analyzed as a creature of a world economy. The new rules tended to define economic interaction mainly as a network of capitalistic exchange relations, not a society: the contrast with the highly organized system (e.g. the World Trade Organization and the World Bank) that arose after World

War II is striking. Of course, the whole structure could be seen and analyzed (e.g. by Lenin) as rooted in capitalistic imperialism.

Individuals and civil or human rights. Similar patterns arose in domains we now call human rights: the Western system came down early on the theoretical point that savages had souls and thus polities, and deserved forms of respect. These were maintained even under the ugliest conditions of exploitation, as with the many treaties with the Native Americans, and the many efforts to recognize indigenous societies in Latin America (Casanova 2016). The main vision was of relationships among different societies, not an integrated society. But in good part deriving from the religious and cultural constitution of the nation state system, notions of the rights of individual humans expanded through the whole period (Lauren 2011).

The knowledge system. A shared international knowledge system continued: the old medieval universities recognized each other's degrees and sciences, and new nation states created many such universities (Riddle 1990). Notions were articulated that the knowledge system was global, and lay above the authority of states. The ambiguity of nation state legitimacy is illustrated by the dependence of these entities on a more universal knowledge system.

All of these arrangements—political, economic, and scientific or educational— expanded around the world, beyond any roots in Christendom. They were validated by the emerging social sciences, which legitimized the expansion. The spread was in part through a global process of colonization, but copying standard institutions continued at high rates. Universities are now found everywhere. So are the formal institutions of citizenship, with education, welfare, and human rights policies (and sometimes practices). But through the post-Enlightenment period, they make up an international system, not an articulated world society. Notions of a global society retain the status of visions. Perhaps the human race should collectively manage its reproduction: population control ideas changed into eugenics ones by the interwar period and then into a global population control movement (Barrett and Frank 1999). Similarly, there were global movements opposing war, to promote the health of children, to create common measures, or to improve education. And there were sentimental movements for global conservation, gradually developing into scientized environmentalism (Frank 1999). Mainly though, the social sciences focused on separate societies, not the world as a society.

Social Scientific Conceptions of World Society after World War II

The first half of the twentieth century saw interdependencies that undercut the picture of the world as made up of independent societies. Political, military, economic, moral, and social crises and disasters followed on from each other. All were understood to derive from the system of unregulated nationalist states, and all called for the creation of a global society that was more than the sum of national interests. The Great Depression was understood as an international failure. The League of Nations had failed, and a disastrous first war was followed by a disastrous second one. Genocidal forces, built on nationalist and racist claims, had been unleashed. Waves of social movements, clearly supranational, carried fascist or communist models around the world. A nuclear age made global interdependence obvious.

But social scientific conceptions in the early post-war period still saw the world as made up of independent national societies, with limited relations to each other: the new idea was that some of these relations could bring widespread progress. So aid for education, or national planning, or economic investments, or freed-up trade opportunities, or efficient states might be keys to national development universally. Strategies for improvement through religious change—the stock in trade of an older regime—were de-emphasized in preference for more scientific methods. The overall picture of the world was one of a classic bar chart: each nation had its own bar, and some were much taller than others. With the right social scientific strategies, all the bars could get higher. As one indicator, national plans were in vogue, and many countries formulated them (Hwang 2006).

With increasing interdependence, and with the many failures of the post-war faith in "development," expanded conceptions of the world as a global society arose. It became painfully clear that the recipes of social scientific development theories did not produce much progress in the Third World. Expanded education, rationalized state structures, and heavy economic investments did not add up to the promised growth. International economic equality showed little increase. There seemed to be no magic bullets for economic growth, and by some measures, the communist world was doing better.

Further, after World War II a whole set of explicitly supranational, and often global, conceptions developed, with a "world economy" or economic "world system," an "international political system," a recognition of international "human rights," and dramatically a world "ecosystem." A self-conscious global artistic and literary system arose, with celebrations of a common cultural heritage. Leading intellectual movements—usually with strong social scientific support—played central roles. The resulting structures took organizational forms, often linked to the emergent UN system, reflecting the dominance of liberal societies. But quite beyond these, all sorts of supranational organizations were formed (Boli and Thomas 1999).

These arrangements exploded, intensified by Cold War competition, and in recent decades, in each social scientific field, one can now find specialists on supranational dimensions. In sociology, proponents employed terms such as "world society," "world polity," "world system," or "global culture."

Heintz (1982), observing multidimensional supranational interdependence, called it world society (Heintz and Greve 2005). Luhmann (1982, and elsewhere) used the same term, locating the phenomenon in a global communication system. Tilly (1975) saw the core process as located in conflict. Robertson (1992) saw it as a cultural matter, a view also emphasized in Meyer (1980).

These ideas, though they received respectful attention, were given more deference than influence. Often, since social science has its own special conservatism, even the new global scholars saw the bigger world simply as a network of nations. But there has been a slow sea change, and assumptions about the global character of social change that would have been exotic a few decades ago now enter the most staid research ventures.

Research Foci on a World Society since the 1970s

There have been increasing tendencies to see the world as a society. Social scientists are heavily involved. Core grounding structures lie in several areas.

Human rights. Much research focuses on the rise of empowered conceptions of individuals as having common human rights around the world, to be supported by supranational rules (Elliott 2007). An older system in which rights were linked to citizenship is normatively superseded by universal human rights. More kinds of people are defined as having rights (women, children, the handicapped, the elderly, indigenous people, various minorities). More rights are defined beyond the classical civil, political, and social rights: culture and religion are now to be chosen by the individual, not the state. Further, there is theorized empowerment: people are thought able to further their own rights and those of others. In important ways, the sovereignty of the individual has tended to replace that of the national state, whose charisma (though not organizational power) declines.

Nature and the ecosystem. The extraordinary global expansion of science means that scientized conceptions of nature take on authority (Drori et al. 2003). These are linked to visions of a common global ecosystem, with common obligations around the world (Frank 1999). The world, formerly a unity in an abstract sense, comes to be defined concretely: air and water and earth are measured on a global scale, creating a mass of actual and perceived interdependencies.

Social organization. Filling in a void created by increasing interdependence in a world without its own state, there has been an enormous expansion in rules of reason and rationality. Conceptions have expanded of properly transparent and fair relations among commonly entitled humans. Matters formerly considered cultural are analyzed on unidimensional scales of corruption or irrationality. Social scientists are heavily involved, often in a global network of business schools prescribing universalized social structures (Moon and Wotipka 2006). In the same way, prescriptions for national states and state agencies are copied everywhere (Simmons et al. 2008; Meyer et al. 1997).

These transformations in the ontological cartography of humans have produced many globalized models. For example, integration brought to the fore earlier ideas that economic life is global: developments in one country affect progress elsewhere—perhaps negatively. Discussions, thus, focus on ideas of a world economy: statistical measures of the state of this economy became common. Radical conceptions—dependency theories, and "world systems" theories, often employing Marxian reasoning—see this economy as an unequalizing one (Wallerstein 1974, and the dependency theorists): capitalist systems of production and exchange produce and maintain the inequalities that are so striking in the world, suppressing the power of labor by shifting it to weak peripheries. Or dramatically unequal exchanges in the world economy monopolize the production of high-value goods, exchanging them for overproduced goods of the peripheries. All the new ideas stress that there is one big economy—a pie—and the winners, no longer autonomous bars on a chart, are excessive wedges in a pie. Rather than being success-ful, they are pigs. Less radical visions stress the need for protective and redistributive mechanisms to produce more equality: ideas of this sort are central to the policies of institutions like the World Bank. One illustrative symbol has been the high prices of medical drugs—out of reach for people in the peripheries. Health is increasingly seen as a basic human right, so the perception of injustice has been tangible (Inoue and Drori 2006).

Beyond economic foci, sociologists come to see more dimensions of social life as interdependent. Researchers increasingly focus on global diffusion, giving a global account of what were formerly seen as national institutions (Simmons et al. 2008). So contemporary sociologists attend to educational expansion as a global process (Ramirez and Boli 1987). Further, it becomes clear that despite all the cultural differences around the world, conceptions and institutions of schooling show remark-able homogeneity (Meyer et al. 1992; Frank and Gabler 2006): schooling systems (and universities) can thus now be ranked on unidimensional scales.

Other sociologists see global influences behind the rapid worldwide changes in norms of family life: the spread of formerly Western laws and practices in gender relations is analyzed as a global rather than local process (Bongaarts and Watkins 1996; Frank et al. 2010; Thornton et al. 2015). Even analyses of religious and cultural developments around the world now tend to stress global processes producing com-mon forms (Beyer 1994; Robertson 1992).

Similarly, analyses of organizational forms around the world stress diffusion, fol-lowing the prescriptions of the social sciences taught in the expanding business and professional schools (Bromley and Meyer 2015). Recognizably similar formal organ-izations appear in every country and social sector: private firms become formalized organizations; as (under the doctrines of the New Public Management) do government agencies. And a host of formerly distinct entities—churches, universities, hospitals, charities, and recreational associations—become "non-profit" formal organizations. Religious congregations have strategic plans, CEOs, information systems, and formal-ized structures to deal with all "stakeholders."

All these processes are analyzed as generating global integration, but this in no way indicates the rise of a more peaceful world. As societies coalesce on many dimensions into more global forms, conflict and competition is intensified. Simple differences come to be conflictful. Gender and age-group relations provide examples. If men and women and children have common rights, then variations among societies come to be grounds for conflict: customs of female circumcision become violations of women's rights, disciplinary arrangements become child abuse, gender choice becomes immorality. Global movements for women's and children's rights become aggressive, supported by social scientific thought: they generate much resistance too (Boyle 2002). Religious issues come to the fore: conflicts arise over headscarves, the consumption of tabooed foods, or the protection of animals; religious architecture offends, as with minarets.

The conceptions of a global society are very much in the making. Most social scientists prefer more conservative visions. They emphasize distinctive local patterns in social life, and de-emphasize the global processes that become apparent.

WORLD SOCIETY AND PLURALIST INTERNATIONALISM: MATHIAS RISSE COMMENTS ON JOHN W. MEYER

Introduction

My work has aimed to make the global central. Central to my theory is an account of different grounds of justice. Grounds are properties of individuals that make it the case that certain demands of justice apply among a group of people. The grounds I distinguish are shared membership in states, common humanity, shared subjection to the trading system, membership in the global order, and humanity's collective ownership of the earth. Each is associated with principles of justice. The grounds-of-justice approach incorporates several ways of thinking about the world we encountered in the overview.

An expansive deployment of considerations of distributive justice follows from making the global central. Justice captures the most stringent moral demands. Such demands arise in multifarious ways, including several that are global in nature. I see individuals as members of states, members of the global order, co-owners of the earth, participants in trade, and human beings. In all roles they are subject to demands of distributive justice.

Matching Ontologies, and Why it Matters

Meyer's account of the origins of the social sciences helps explain aloofness in some circles toward reflection on global justice. State-centered views naturally display that attitude. The explanations international relations realists tend to field turn on the kind of power states muster to pursue interests. International relations liberals make more room for values and focus on interstate cooperation. But they see cooperation as driven by the values states project upon the world. The global mostly enters by way of interstate affairs.

Explanations fielded by these approaches fail to make notions of the global central. But if normative and descriptive theory diverge in terms of how they see the world (in terms of ontology), ideal theory does not match with what is driving things. Such a mismatch nourishes the suspicion that either the empirical or the normative side got things wrong. In contradistinction to state-focused approaches, Wallerstein's world systems theory and like-minded views stress the historical significance of economic interconnectedness. This approach concurs with inquiries into global justice by way of seeing the world as an interconnected system where explanations cannot be largely reduced to activities of states. But it too matches uneasily with accounts of global justice to the extent that those theorize anything other than economic structures.

Social science matches uneasily with philosophical global justice inquiry if categories of the global or normative ideas are not granted explanatory power. As opposed to all these approaches, Meyer's world polity (or society) analysis matches well with global justice inquiries because it grants explanatory power to both. This approach views the world as one social system with a unified cultural framework that nonetheless is implemented in myriad conflicting variations. A polity or society is a system within which values and norms are defined and implemented through collective mechanisms that confer authority. A world polity is such a system with global dimensions. In a pluralist spirit this approach theorizes various kinds of actors, including states, companies, intergovernmental organizations, NGOs, and individuals. All play causal roles.

The defining feature of world polity—and this is how world polity analysis offers a unifying approach to global affairs—is that it provides norms and roles that jostle up against each other. World polity theory helps itself to normative ideas because it finds that people act on them. Praiseworthiness in norms, values, and roles helps explain why some, but not others, get accepted. Ideas about legitimacy, justice, and rights enter prominently.

World polity analysis adopts a rich ontology. The connection to my own similarly encompassing ontology is obvious. If both theories can be supported on their own terms, they would not stand awkwardly next to each other, as would realism and the grounds-of-justice approach. My work talks about a global order, the system of states, and the network of international organizations that aspires to international and even global problem solving. I have proposed a conception of human rights as membership rights in the global order. Meyer talks about world society. For my purposes I now think this is the better term. Talk about a global order underdescribes the extent to which ours is also, for instance, a world of human persons. So human rights are better described as membership rights *in world society*.

Basic Legitimacy of a World of States

I now identify three areas where world polity analysis supports views I have submitted. To begin with, the explanatory centrality of the adoption of successful scripts in world polity analysis indirectly supports my moderate justification of states. Second, world polity analysis allows for the extension to the global stage of a justificatory strategy in Rawls' *Political Liberalism* that I have adapted to that stage in another way. Third, world polity analysis offers an account of change that sits well with my approach.

Note that the explanation of change through the adoption of successful scripts connects to some of the themes in the philosophical survey. World polity analysis sees that polity largely as a product of Western intellectual tendencies, especially Christian notions of personhood and legitimacy. It was through the Church that Roman notions of law-governed community transpired to medieval Europe. Connecting to Stoic ideas of *kosmos* and equality, Christianity saw each human as created in God's image. This model of order that provided for a certain kind of rule and an ideal of personhood within a governed space (citizenship) spread globally. A world culture has emerged that triggers the formation of enactable cultures and organizations that elaborate world society further.

While the violence that colonialism projected plays a role in the emergence of this culture, world polity analysis also sees other factors at work in the spread of dominant scripts. To a large extent that spread can be explained through the voluntary adoption of successful models (e.g. states and citizenship). As an illustration, consider Michelangelo's *Creation of Adam*. It displays the moment when the spark of life is transmitted from a white, bearded male God to a young, white Adam. Adam is (almost) literally created in the divine image. That depiction of creation must offend many visitors, from women to non-Europeans. But all of them have adopted a way of thinking about themselves they saw as successful in white men. What once was alien became appropriated.

One implication is that the global system does not lose overall legitimacy because its origins are tarnished beyond repair. Part 4 of *On Global Justice* offers a moderate justification of states, pointing out their moral and prudential advantages and that we cannot theorize competing models of order sufficiently well for them to be action-guiding. Room needs to be made for potentially extensive reparations for past injustice. But it is reassuring that we can explain the emergence of world society in ways that emphasize processes of enacting successful scripts.

This might seem like an odd point. Readers may have wondered why the survey of ways of conceptualizing the global failed to mention Gilgamesh, the Bhagavad Gita, Popol Vuh, any Buddhist approach, or anything from Africa. The answer is that in our intellectual universe ideas of European origin play an outsized role. Does it add insult to injury to say that these ideas have spread by becoming accepted among those who were conquered? No. If that *is* what happened, it would be a peculiar form of orientalism to characterize the outcome in terms of insult added to injury. It has been difficult to form counter-Western approaches that provide an account of global order.

European conquerors themselves took scripts from earlier actors. Models of empire and citizenship were alien to Germanic invaders of Rome. But nowadays Danish writers can claim Cicero's legacy as much as Italian intellectuals can. But then Greek intellectuals have no more claims to counting Aristotle among their predecessors than Nigerian academics. All of them are what Husserl called "Funktionäre der Menschheit," civil servants of humanity, where how we think about humanity and other aspects of the global is the result of a centuries-long process that created a world culture, to the detriment of competing scripts that expired or got relegated.

World Polity, Human Rights, and Rawls' *Political Liberalism*

World polity analysis also connects to a justificatory strategy in Rawls' *Political Liberalism* that I have already developed in another context. *Political Liberalism* offers an account of justice designed to be applicable only in constitutional democracies. Rawls justifies his view by reference to ideas implicit in the culture of constitutional democracy. This includes conceptualizing humans as free and equal citizens.

Moral theories, we can say, drawing on Bernard Williams, must adopt a view of persons that is either factual or normative. A liberal theory may empirically see persons as autonomous choosers. But religious fundamentalists see them differently, say, as creatures of divine grace whose fates are ill-understood as resulting from autonomous choice. It seems practically impossible to settle this dispute. A theory may also treat individuals *as* persons with certain capacities for purposes of the theory, but defend that view without appeal to facts. Then we "need to identify a place in the world, a practice, which will give the set of concepts a grounding in reality" (Williams 2005: 21).

This grounding is the starting point from which to argue for the theory at hand. In this spirit, Rawls' view of personhood is supposed to be plausible only to those accustomed to democratic practices, citizens who *see* each other as free and equal (1993: 19f.). Individuals are not *empirically* free and equal. Instead, there are practices accompanied by moral ideas about citizenship. It is within those ideas—which refer to persons in idealizing ways—that individuals are *seen as* persons with certain powers. But there is also a connection between these ideas and the practices individuals engage in so that, again, it makes sense to say that being persons with such powers idealizes the roles individuals actually occupy. From there one can assess Rawls' arguments for why relations among free and equal citizens should be regulated by the principles of justice that he proposes.

On Global Justice applies this approach to humanity's collective ownership of the earth. Just as it is implicit in constitutional democracies that individuals are considered free and equal citizens, so it is implicit in the global order that they are seen as co-owners. The idea that individuals are co-owners is an idealization: empirically it might be false that they are respected as co-owners in any plausible way. But it is an idealization that not only emerges from our practices, but that we ought to care about in virtue of the considerations supporting collective ownership of the earth. Just as principles of domestic justice make states acceptable to citizens, so human rights make the global order acceptable to co-owners.

Now that the ontological connections between world society analysis and grounds-of-justice approach are visible, another parallel is available for world society as a whole. The point is to identify idealizations of personhood implicit in the practices of world society. From there one could argue that membership rights in world society should be acceptable to persons parallel to how principles of domestic justice should be acceptable to citizens and principles regulating resources and spaces of the earth to co-owners of the earth. One may only be the citizen of one or perhaps several countries, but citizenship is a global idea. World society analysis helps us see that we cannot only develop a justificatory strategy at the global level parallel to what Rawls does domestically, but that his own strategy *calls for* such a development.

Thinking about Political Change

On Global Justice says little about change. I take the global order as given to explore what principle of justice holds. Possibly other grounds will become actual in the future, much like membership in world society has in the last 200 years or so. At this stage we cannot theorize about a global order that would not essentially include the kind of power centers constitutive of states. So for the time being we should just consider world society to be possible rather than aim to create a different order.

In *Global Justice and Avant-Garde Political Agency*, Lea Ypi (2012) proposes a more ambitious understanding of change. Ypi is interested in activist political theory, theory that seeks to change the world. Activist theory gradually shifts public culture to advance progressive projects. Its main audience is the political avant-garde, politically conscious and engaged people who suffer from the injustices of an era and have taken it upon themselves to bring about change. Without the spearheads of political change there would be no activist theory to affect reality. Without activist theory we could not identify the avant-garde. Ypi proposes a general theory about the exchange between political theory and practice in history, thus also a theory of the role of intellectuals in political change.

World polity analysis conceptualizes change as a messy, multifaceted process: different scripts are in circulation and one or the other will eventually get adopted at a larger scale before there is renewed contestation. Different scripts might prevail in different regions, or be present in the same society and generate conflict. Our world is filled with activism, rule-setting, "othering," and so on. A diffuse understanding of change strikes me as more plausible than Ypi's model, which overemphasizes interaction between two kinds of actors without exploring how these actors blend into a background culture.

On the Philosophical Richness of "Decoupling"

A notion that becomes central in world society analysis is "decoupling." This notion is useful for philosophical analysis generally. Decoupling occurs if practices deviate from avowedly adopted scripts. Given the pressure toward isomorphism, decoupling is common, especially where scripts were adopted recently or conflict with other scripts.

For instance, decolonization generated an abundance of decoupling since new states were structured in ways unrelated to needs and conditions.

World polity analysis makes room for ideas even where they are not, or not yet, uniformly implemented. Agents might struggle to adjust to roles but fail. They might not be supported by their environment, not know how to proceed, or lack the means to do so. None of this shows that ideas cannot drive change. Decoupling is a natural aspect of change driven by ideas. Philosophical reflection on the global is a reservoir of examples of decoupling. Cicero's insistence on moral equality stood in stark contrast to the belligerent practices of Rome that Cicero supported as an official. Colonization in the name of natural law harbors enormous potential for decoupling. Vattel pointed out that natural law justification of conquest was a game too many can play. Liberalism and communism are political ideals driven by individualistic moral visions, but once institutionalized both were interpreted in ways that gave little relevance to those who did poorly in the system.

In *Nomos of the Earth*, Carl Schmitt explores the idea of humanity (1950: 71ff.). Conquest in the Americas led to the question of how to treat indigenous people. One stance was the Aristotelian view that "Barbaric people" were natural slaves, invoked by Sepúlveda. Stressing that Sepúlveda was a *humanist*, Schmitt thinks the idea of humanity generates a dialectic he seeks to capture in terms of his master notion of the political as driven by friend/enemy distinctions. Within a movement that makes *humanity* central, reflection on types of humanity eventually delivers the idea of a lowest type: *Unmensch* (inhuman). Once the *Unmensch* is seen as non-human, the dialectic delivers the distinction between *Übermensch* and *Untermensch* (superhuman, subhuman). For Schmitt this highlights the normative uselessness of the notion of humanity. But this is too limited an analysis. The differentiation among types of humanity shows that the idea of humanity spread and triggered responses. Such a spread of ideas will generate much decoupling because not all relevant actors can fit new ideas smoothly into their motivational framework. What Schmitt draws our attention to may be the symptoms of the successful adoption of a script.

A great danger that can be captured in terms of decoupling is the following. Two things happen currently that make for an alarming combination. The first is that climate change requires urgent action, but vested elites have little interest in engaging. The situation is much like in the many episodes of collapse Diamond (2005) recounts. At the same time, joining the elite is increasingly a matter of accomplishment. Wage income matters, coming from the ability to make technological change work for oneself. Talented people increasingly marry each other and found stable families. Much research shows that schooled professionals normally support change, but the danger is that such people, by joining the elite, adopt enlightened views decoupled from their membership in the elite that refuses to take our main challenge seriously.

Decoupling can sometimes also convey some optimism. There has been debate about how to think about the success of the human rights movement seventy years after the Universal Declaration of Human Rights. Some argue that not enough change occurs, that human rights talk is window dressing. But one may also say that there is a lot of decoupling going on as part of a long-winded process of making norms stick. Human rights are part of a world culture that worships individuality. So there is reason to be optimistic that human rights will catch on more.

REFLECTIONS ON GLOBALIZATION IN PHILOSOPHY: JOHN W. MEYER COMMENTS ON MATHIAS RISSE

Introduction

Ideas about justice, rights, and obligations depend on conceptions of the entities in which the rights inhere. They also depend on the frame within which they are seen. Globalization is changing both the conceptions of the entities seen as basic and the frames defining their relations. Mathias Risse considers the meaning of justice in frames that are globalized, in light of correspondingly changed conceptions of the humans involved. Universalized theoretical ideas about the standing of individuals, and thus about justice in their interrelations, have long histories in philosophical and religious thought. But they have functioned along with local social experience of inequality. With globalization there is an awareness of inconsistencies between the practices of inequality and the theories of equality.

The mix of fundamental entities in the world has changed with globalized frames. It follows that grounds of justice change too. It was one thing when societies were understood to differ in their development; it is another when globalized understandings see one society's development as undercutting another's (Chase-Dunn 1989).

I reflect here on the ontologies underlying the contemporary social world. I am concerned with three changes. First, there is the enlarged and globalized picture of the human individual, and the expansion of the properties of this individual relevant to considerations of justice (Frank and Meyer 2002; Meyer and Jepperson 2000). With now-equal individuals entitled and empowered on more dimensions, more differences and inequalities can be seen and organized as injustices: Risse spells out examples.

Second, there are conceptions of a global society, with economic, political, cultural, and especially ecosystemic models of interdependence (Frank et al. 2000). An inequality between A and B becomes more of a perceived injustice if A is seen as helping cause B's poverty. This makes possible more injustice claims.

Third, there is the relative weakening of the fundamental ontological status of the nation state and institutions, within which justice claims were organized, and the rise of claims about the world transcending any stabilizing polity (Meyer et al. 1997).

I reflect here on the consequences of these changes for an expansion of plausible injustice claims, and for social mobilization.

Globalized "Man": The Universalized and Expanded Public Individual

Universalistic notions about the individual—man—run very far back, as Risse emphasizes. Perhaps they have gotten more emphasis in the West than in other civilizations. They are ideas drawn from reflection, rather than practical experience, as they are put forward by people involved in much social stratification (e.g. slavery) and differentiation (e.g. between city states). In Greece, Rome, and Palo Alto, abstract ideas about justice among ultimately equal individuals prosper along with inequality. The sociological term for this is "decoupling," and it is fashionable (Bromley and Powell 2012), since contemporary society is filled with expanded normative ideas at variance with differentiating practice. Ideas about universal human rights coexist with a very unequal world society.

Risse makes it clear that tension between universalistic ideals and practical realities is of very long standing. It leads to classificatory boundaries, distinguishing between entitled "man" and other categories of human existence: barbarians and primitives, foreigners, women, children, subordinated social classes, ethnic groups and races, disabled people, and so on. In Western Christendom, the world of individual justice was sometimes restricted to "saved" Christian people. In parallel, in recent centuries, the entire natural human race, as produced by families and communities, has been deemed inadequate for the elevated category "man": almost universal programs of compulsory education repair people injured by family and community, in an institution under the national state. With the Education for All movement, this compulsion is now redefined as a global human right (Chabbott 2003). Schooling status is a central legitimizing ingredient of social stratification everywhere, making it difficult to legitimize inequalities on racial, ethnic, religious, historical, or even national status.

The social sciences are creatures of Western Christendom, and of an Enlightenment that evolved out of and reacted to earlier religious formulations. They are usually about individuals with citizenship in nation states. Seen against the long philosophic traditions, the social sciences look modern and scientific, but also parochial. With individual citizenship as a main identity, forms of traditional community are marginalized. A main dimension is scale: who "man" is. The ultimate units of social life are often culturally defined as families, communities, ethnic groups, or races—supra-individual corporate bodies. Modern thinking in both social science and philosophy tends to eliminate these structures as fundamental, reducing them to their individual components.

Thus, the social scientists and contemporary philosophers tend to converge on the individual human person as the focus of justice. In this, they reflect long-term institutional changes in advanced countries. The abstract ideas of earlier philosophers about "man" come to be concretized, and the philosophers join forces in the contemporary world that undercuts the ultimate authority of familial and ethnic (and now even national) communities in the name of individual rights.

The focus on the individual as the primordial unit of society has been enhanced by globalization in the period since World War II. Human rights ideologies and institutions have exploded on a global scale (Elliott 2007). They define more types of people as "men." They define more rights as inhering in "men." And they directly support justice claims by empowering "men" of all sorts to act on behalf of their expanded rights (Elliott 2007).

Overall, thus, abstract concepts of "man" become concretized around the expanded modern conception of the individual. And they become globalized, so that political, social, economic, and cultural matters become rights in a global frame.

Globalizing the Polity Within Which Justice is Defined

Social scientific and philosophical thinking focus on universalized notions of individual "man," but are also historically rooted in notions of a polity as a core collective structure with a similarly primordial status. (The underlying post-Enlightenment structure reflects the earlier Christian sacralization of both the Church as the Body of Christ, and the soul of the believer.) Correspondingly, there are ambivalent notions of justice: the provision of justice by the state—organized around its putative needs— can be different from the just entitlements of the nominally equal "men." Liberal models elide the distinction, imagining markets that merge individual and collective needs. Corporatist and statist models emphasize the distinction, often giving prefer-ence to collective needs and distributional principles rather than individual choice (Jepperson 2002).

In practice, societies embedded in the nation state system since the Enlightenment come to terms with the tension between the principle of the individual "man" as basic unit and the actual realities of great stratification. The term "structuration," from Giddens (1984), is employed, capturing the idea of boundaries between institutions and rules of justice. Risse uses the term "pluralism" to emphasize the institutional differentiation at the global level, in parallel with common analyses of modern national society. Thus some rights and obligations inhere in familial relationships, others in business organization, and still others in nation state polities.

Liberal societies, with their special stress on the rights and powers of the individual, tend to generate more institutional differentiation (Risse's pluralism) than others, since they have more distinct structures to bound, and empower more individual action. Corporatist or statist societies, giving more ontological status to the collective, may have simpler systems of stratification.

These systems have focused on the rules of and justice within an imagined national society, with a state as a frame. The rules for relationships cutting across the national boundaries are changing rapidly. Sociologists, for instance, have much research bearing on inequalities between Mexican American children in El Paso and Swedish American children in Minnesota: this research takes its interest from the normative baseline of equality. Little research compares the Mexican American children in El Paso with their cousins a mile away in Ciudad Juárez: and it is unclear what the frame is. This changes rapidly with globalization, which frames issues of justice on a supranational scale.

The naturalized pluralism of post-Enlightenment modernity goes global, with changed pictures of the rights of individuals and changed institutional frames differentiating different arenas. Education becomes an individual right on a global scale. Principles defining unfair treatment in the workplace expand: the son of the boss should really get an MBA before entering the firm. The rights of women in the family expand: marital rape is criminalized (see also Frank et al. 2010). The rights of the individual expand; the powers of the family decline. New entities come into place: rules of incorporation, for example, permit an explosion in organizational structures with internal boundaries and principles of justice.

These expansive changes are global. Organizational expansion, or educational expansion, or enhanced rights of women and children, occur in all sorts of countries as well as in an expanding international discourse (Meyer et al. 1997).

Risse's account emphasizes the rise of multiple dimensions of global interdependence, and hence multiple forms of justice. This permits (a) a clear discussion of the rapid changes in the recognized ontologies with (b) an internationalization that creates recognized interdependencies far transcending any state-like structure. The force of Risse's account is in its stress on a pluralism that transcends the state.

I can here simply summarize some dramatic changes in the ontological shape of social life, and call attention to consequences for forms of justice claims that drift toward institutionalization.

First, there is multidimensional internationalization of recognized social life: many more and stronger interdependencies—political, economic, military, and cultural. The social world is a much-expanded place. Each expanded interdependence creates grounds for claims, as Risse emphasizes. Dramatic instances of this involve the cultural construction and recognition of global ecosystemic interdependencies.

Second, the moral status of the individual is expanded and globalized. People have more recognized rights and powers, and these are explicitly extended to humans in supranational social locations. A massive human rights regime celebrates the ontological primacy of the equal individual. There are many more dimensions on which injustice claims can be defined. Risse's pluralism becomes more plural—across kinds of people and social functions. All this globalization occurs in a system with weak regulatory powers, so the pluralism can become inflationary. It is easy to define new areas of interdependence—squadrons of scientists are paid to do so—and thus new possible conceptions of injustice.

The Weakened Ontological Primacy of National State and Society

The rise of actualities and perceptions of a global society, and the reorganization of individuals as direct members of global society (with human rather than only citizen rights), weakens the primordial status of the nation state.

This means that claims for justice and order can more readily transcend national boundaries, as domestic rules and practices can be seen as violations of more universal rights and responsibilities. But it also means that many internal structures of pluralist society—structures that commonly depend on state-based legal frames—are weakened. The claims of the family on the individual weaken against human rights rules. Similarly weakened are all the institutions of communal authority—religious, ethnic, economic, and diffuse political communities. Local destructions of forests may be attacked as violations of global beliefs and agreement on the need to protect habitats and ecosystems. Or local economic practices may be seen as violations of global rules about trade. Global concepts of justice come into conflict with local ones.

Conclusion: Changes in the Plural Justice Frames

I outline here consequences of the changed ontology and frame already discussed. First, the expansion of legitimated individualism creates many possibilities for analyzed injustice (and consequent social mobilization). More people, of more sorts, are included. More qualities of these people (e.g. educational, medical, or cultural properties) are organized in an expanded pluralism, and are covered by expanding rules of justice. It is possible to see every transaction in the modern global economy as unjust.

Second, the weakening of the boundaries around the formerly charismatic national states expands comparative frames, and the capacity of people to mobilize. It is easy to create organizations pursuing global justice, and these grow exponentially (Boli and Thomas 1999).

Third, weakening nation state boundaries, and expanding global institutions, subject the states themselves—formerly the adjudicators of justice—to the wider claims of the supra-state system. Local people can now take issue with inconsistencies between their standing in the nation state and their human rights. But states can also make more claims in this arena: they increasingly depict themselves as assemblies of individuals, and claim legitimacy derived from the "people."

Fourth, the absence of a legitimately controlling center of the global system creates opportunities supporting organization and mobilization. The normative system involved has inflationary qualities, with many opportunities for expansion and few for restrictive control. Any good social scientist now has chances to "discover" and construct a new injustice. Risse's pluralism expands. The capacity to expand arenas of the pluralist system is a great resource for social movements.

Fifth, the global world becomes a frame within which claims can be made. It tends to be depicted as a closed system, intensified by analyses of a global ecosystem: a polity created by Nature. Imagery of climate change, species destruction, resource limitations, or disease developments and flows on a world scale, help construct a primordial conception of the world.

CONCLUSION

As a social scientist, Meyer offers descriptions of, and explanations for, phenomena in the world. As a philosopher, Risse makes normative proposals for what the world should be like. So in that sense they are engaged in very different activities. But there is also much convergence between them. Some of that is along dimensions that set them apart from other approaches in their respective disciplines.

One dimension of convergence is that both Meyer and Risse give a central role to cultural phenomena—norms, values, and cognitive models—in their approaches (see also Chapters 4, 5, 7, and 12). This is unsurprising as far as Risse is concerned since norms and values are the bread and butter of moral and political philosophers. Nonetheless, this is remarkable because it means Meyer ascribes a causal efficacy to the sort of cultural forms—now often structured at a global level—that philosophers explore in their normative approaches and whose efficacy is often de-emphasized by social scientists. If ontologies in different fields of inquiry fall apart one is left with the suspicion that at least one of them gets its approach to the world wrong. On the other hand, a field of academic inquiry gets some reassurance from the fact that another field of inquiry uses a similar ontology.

What is more, both Meyer and Risse make world society central to their inquiries, and do so in ways that pay close attention to the plurality of different kinds of entities that populate the world as conceived by their respective lines of inquiry. Meyer emphasized the term "world society" (or "world polity"), and much of this work in recent decades has sought to draw attention to the fact that phenomena we observe across countries are interconnected and are most plausibly explained as genuinely global phenomena. "World society" and "world polity" then become apt terms to describe human interaction at the macro scale. Individuals, states, companies, inter-governmental organizations, and organizations of various sorts in global civil society all populate world society, generating, propagating, and accepting global ideas and scripts.

Risse offers a theory of different grounds of justice of which several are global by nature. In particular, he conceives of human rights as membership rights in the world society or order, including the capitalist world economy. He also gives pride of place to humanity's relationship with the planet, as well as to common humanity. States continue to matter in Risse's approach because he also thinks that membership in states is a ground of justice in its own right. So unlike state-focused philosophers, Risse does indeed make the world central; but unlike other philosophers who do so as well, he thinks that structures that do not include the whole world matter from a standpoint of justice. (In addition to states there is also the international trading regime, with many capitalist properties, which is not aptly described as a unitary global system.)

Both Risse and Meyer, in other words, attend to the rapid globalization of recent decades, and to the new cultural models and ontologies this creates. Both call attention to the pluralistic character of the expansion. In Risse's case the focus is on the new, expanded, and multiple grounds of justice created. In Meyer's case the focus is on statelessness and the lack of integrating structure for the multiple dimensions of globalization, and thus the multiple kinds of injustice that can provide grounds for social mobilization.

Both analyses lead to the conclusion that globalization, integration, and conscious-ness lead to rapid increases in the kinds of injustices that are perceived and that can be the bases of conflictful claims—in a world society without strong mechanisms for stabilizing and legitimizing social and ideological controls. The world is a very diverse and very unequal place: rapid integration turns the diversity and inequalities into actual and potential injustice claims—which can readily be defended philosophically—and does so on an expanding set of pluralistic dimensions. As with many integrating but stateless situations, the present world provides many opportunities for contending lawyers and clerics—and frequently also for intranational and international episodes of violence.

Future research agendas, following our work, could focus on the rapid growth in claims about injustice in the contemporary world, and the new or changed ontological elements involved. An open world society, weakly regulated, can support a wide variety of mobilizations around normative issues. Against capitalism, or the West, or the dominant states and organizations, groups can mobilize around a wide range of claimed identities. Most of these are not the classic "class conflict" issues involving the mobilization of people as "labor." The roots of their claims are likely to be social, cultural, national, and religious in character—but global in aspiration and assertion. The pluralist character of an open world society provides incentives for the invention or discovery of normative claims based on changed or expanded ontologies.

· ·

COMMENTS AND DISCUSSION

Meyer and Risse's essay puts their respective takes on globalization into conversation, offering a comparative perspective on the normative (Risse) and descriptive (Meyer) dimensions of this notion. The world, on their view, has come increasingly to be defined by expanding notions of global interdependence, across social, institutional, and moral dimensions. This has important consequences, they suggest, for how we think about our moral obligations, and for how we conceive of our identity as moral and institutional actors.

> *In a world of growing interdependence, what is the normative significance of groups versus individuals in the global order? How should it bear on our models of decision making and our notions of responsibility?*

At the Society for Progress' second assembly, Pettit argued for the importance of treating individuals as primary bearers of moral significance while acknowledging, nonetheless, the crucial significance of groups as units of decision making. Nation states, for example, make decisions; but the moral goodness of those decisions is ultimately reducible in some way to how well individual people fare as a consequence of them. Organizations—political democracies, for example—can also play a crucial role in leading individuals to pursue good choices on a collective scale. On the moral primacy of the individual, Kitcher likewise observed that subordinating individual concerns to that of the group can too easily lead to a dangerous disregard for fundamental aspects of human welfare. Pointing to cases such as the EU, Fuerstein observed the striking contrast between the enlargement of the group perspective at the level of international political and economic institutions, and the sometimes violent rejection of those institutions at the street level. Here, the significance of the group is not situated against the individual; rather the significance of the local group—the nation state or the race—is situated against the cosmopolitan collective.

In the business context, these kinds of issues often play out in questions of corporate organization and responsibility. There has been a shift, Meyer noted, from the model of a corporate group, generically speaking, to that of a rational *organization*, where the latter implies a primary role for individuals as role-players in a formal decision-making structure. But to what extent are individuals primary in thinking about corporations? Barney noted that, in the case of the recent Volkswagen scandal, we could approach it either as a case of the malfeasance of particular individuals, who should then be subjected to appropriate punishments, or as a case of moral failure at the group level. In the latter case, the firm can be understood in terms of the aggregation of incentives, culture, and institutional and economic pressures that produced a particular choice. On this point, Anderson noted that seeing corporations in terms of a collection of role-playing individuals is part of an important "legitimation story" within the individualist framework. That way of looking at things, however, tends to obscure the distinctive kinds of structures that define internal corporate governance, which diverge significantly from the individualistic model that theorists might apply to democratic governments.

REFERENCES

Angle, S. 2012. *Contemporary Confucian Political Philosophy*. Malden: Polity.
Badian, E. 1958. "Alexander the Great and the Unity of Mankind." *Historia: Zeitschrift für Alte Geschichte* 7: 425–44.
Bai, T. 2012. *China: The Political Philosophy of the Middle Kingdom*. London: Zed Books.
Baldry, H. C. 1965. *The Unity of Mankind in Greek Thought*. Cambridge: Cambridge University Press.
Baltzly, D. 2013. "Stoicism." *Stanford Encyclopedia of Philosophy*.

Barrett, D. and Frank, D. 1999. "Population Control for National Development." In J. Boli and G. Thomas (eds.), *Constructing World Culture*. Stanford: Stanford University Press, 198–221.

Bartelson, J. 2009. *Visions of World Community*. Cambridge: Cambridge University Press.

Beaulac, S. 2004. *The Power of Language in the Making of International Law*. Leiden: Martinus Nijhoff Publishers.

Beck, U. 2000. "The Cosmopolitan Perspective." *British Journal of Sociology* 51(1): 79–105.

Beitz, C. 1979. *Political Theory and International Relations*. Princeton: Princeton University Press.

Bernstein, W. 2008. *A Splendid Exchange: How Trade Shaped the World*. New York: Atlantic Monthly.

Beyer, P. 1994. *Religion and Globalization*. Thousand Oaks: Sage.

Boli, J. and Thomas, G. M. 1999. *Constructing World Culture: International Nongovernmental Organizations Since 1875*. Stanford: Stanford University Press.

Bongaarts, J. and Watkins, S. C. 1996. "Social Interactions and Contemporary Fertility Transitions." *Population and Development Review* 22(4): 639–82.

Boyle, E. H. 2002. *Female Genital Cutting: Cultural Conflict in the Global Community*. Baltimore: Johns Hopkins University Press.

Bromley, P. and Meyer, J. 2015. *Hyper-Organization: The Global Expansion of Organization*. Oxford: Oxford University Press.

Bromley, P. and Powell, W. 2012. "From Smoke and Mirrors to Walking the Talk: Decoupling in the Contemporary World." *Academy of Management Annals* 6(1): 483–530.

Brown, E. 2009. "The Emergence of Natural Law and the Cosmopolis." In Stephen Salkever (ed.), *The Cambridge Companion to Greek Political Thought*. Cambridge: Cambridge University Press, 331–63.

Bull, H. 1977. *The Anarchical Society*. New York: Columbia University Press.

Buzan, B. 2014. *An Introduction to the English School of International Relations*. Cambridge: Polity Press.

Casanova, J. 2016. "Jesuits, Connectivity, and the Uneven Development of Global Consciousness since the Sixteenth Century." In R. Robertson and D. Buhari (eds.), *Global Culture*. New York: Routledge.

Chabbott, C. 2003. *Constructing Education for Development: International Organizations and Education for All*. New York: Routledge.

Chase-Dunn, C. 1989. *Global Formation: Structures of the World-Economy*. Cambridge: Blackwell.

Crosby, A. 2003. *The Columbian Exchange: Biological and Cultural Consequences of 1492*, 30th anniversary edition. Westport: Praeger.

Diamond, J. 2005. *Collapse: How Societies Choose to Fail or Succeed*. New York: Penguin.

Drori, G. S., Meyer, J. W., Ramirez, F. O., and Schofer, E. 2003. *Science in the Modern World Polity: Institutionalization and Globalization*. Stanford, CA: Stanford University Press.

Drori, G. S. and Moon, H. 2006. "The Changing Nature of Tertiary Education." In D. Baker and A. Wiseman (eds.), *The Impact of Comparative Education Research on Institutional Theory*. Bingley, UK: Emerald Group Publishing, 157–85.

Elliott, M. 2007. "Human Rights and the Triumph of the Individual in World Culture." *Cultural Sociology* 1(3): 353–63.

Findley, R. and O'Rourke, K. 2007. *Power and Plenty: Trade, War, and the World Economy in the Second Millennium*. Princeton: Princeton University Press.

Frank, D. J. 1999. "The Social Bases of Environmental Treaty Ratification, 1900–1990." *Sociological Inquiry* 69(4): 523–50.

Frank, D. J., Camp, B. J., and Boutcher, S. A. 2010. "Worldwide Trends in the Criminal Regulation of Sex." *American Sociological Review* 75(6): 867–93.

Frank, D. J. and Gabler, J. 2006. *Reconstructing the University: Worldwide Shifts in Academia in the 20th Century*. Stanford, CA: Stanford University Press.

Frank, D. J., Hironaka, A., and Schofer, E. 2000. "The Nation-State and the Natural Environment over the Twentieth Century." *American Sociological Review* 65(1): 96–116.

Frank, D. and Meyer, J. W. 2002. "The Profusion of Individual Roles and Identities in the Postwar Period." *Sociological Theory* 20(1): 86–105.

Frank, D. J., Meyer, J. W., and Miyahara, D. 1995. "The Individualist Polity and the Centrality of Professionalized Psychology." *American Sociological Review* 60(3): 360–77.

Giddens, A. 1984. *The Constitution of Society*. Cambridge: Polity Press.

Gilpin, R. 2001. *Global Political Economy: Understanding the International Economic Order*. Princeton: Princeton University Press.

Heater, D. 1996. *World Citizenship and Government: Cosmopolitan Ideas in the History of Western Political Thought*. Houndmills: Macmillan.

Heintz, P. 1982. "A Sociological Code for the Description of World Society and Its Change." *International Social Science Journal* 34(1): 11–21.

Heintz, B. and Greve, J. 2005. "Die 'Entdeckung' der Weltgesellschaft. Entstehung und Grenzen der Weltgesellschaftstheorie." In B. Heintz, et al. (eds.), *Weltgesellschaft*. Stuttgart: Lucius & Lucius, 89–119.

Held, D. 2004. *Global Covenant: The Social Democratic Alternative to the Washington Consensus*. Malden, MA: Polity Press.

Hwang, H. 2006. "Planning Development: Globalization and the Shifting Locus of Planning." In G. Drori, et al. (eds.), *Globalization and Organization*. Oxford: Oxford University Press, 69–90.

Inoue, K. and Drori, G. 2006. "The Global Institutionalization of Health as a Social Concern: Organizational and Discursive Trends." *International Sociology* 21(2): 199–219.

Jepperson, R. 2002. "Political Modernities: Disentangling Two Underlying Dimensions of International Differentiation." *Sociological Theory* 20: 61–85.

Kant, I. 1991. "On Perpetual Peace." In H. Reiss (ed.), *Kant: Political Writings*. Cambridge: Cambridge University Press.

Kleingeld, P. and Brown, E. 2013. "Cosmopolitanism." *Stanford Encyclopedia of Philosophy*.

Konstan, D. 2009. "Cosmopolitan Traditions." In Ryan Balot (ed.), *A Companion to Greek and Roman Political Thought*. Oxford: Blackwell, 473–84.

Koskenniemi, M. 2002. *The Gentle Civilizer of Nations: The Rise and Fall of International Law 1870–1960*. Cambridge: Cambridge University Press.

Krasner, S. 1999. *Sovereignty: Organized Hypocrisy*. Princeton: Princeton University Press.

Lauren, P. G. 2011. *The Evolution of International Human Rights: Visions Seen*. Philadelphia: University of Pennsylvania Press.

Luhmann, N. 1982. "The World Society as a Social System." *International Journal of General Systems* 8(3): 131–8.

Meyer, J. 1980. "The World Polity and the Authority of the Nation-State." In A. Bergesen (ed.), *Studies of the Modern World-System*. New York: Academic Press, 109–37.

Meyer, J. W., Boli, J., Thomas, G. M., and Ramirez, F. O. 1997. "World Society and the Nation-State." *American Journal of Sociology* 103(1): 144–81.

Meyer, J. W. and Jepperson, R. 2000. "The 'Actors' of Modern Society: The Cultural Construction of Social Agency." *Sociological Theory* 18(1): 100–20.

Meyer, J., Kamens, D., and Benavot, A. 1992. *School Knowledge for the Masses: World Models and National Curricula in the Twentieth Century.* London: Falmer.

Moles, J. 2000. "The Cynics." In C. Rowe and M. Schofield (eds.), *The Cambridge History of Greek and Roman Political Thought.* Cambridge: Cambridge University Press, 415–34.

Moon, H. and Wotipka, C. M. 2006. "The Worldwide Diffusion of Business Education, 1881–1999." In G. Drori, J. Meyer, and H. Hwang (eds.), *Globalization and Organization.* Oxford: Oxford University Press, 121–36.

Nussbaum, A. 1954. *A Concise History of the Law of Nations.* New York: Macmillan.

Pagden, A. 2015. *The Burdens of Empire: 1539 to the Present.* Cambridge: Cambridge University Press.

Parry, R. 2014. "Ancient Ethical Theory." *Stanford Encyclopedia of Philosophy.*

Parsons, T. and Platt, G. 1973. *The American University.* Cambridge, MA: Harvard University Press.

Pogge, T. 2006. *World Poverty and Human Rights.* Malden, MA: Polity.

Pogge, T. 1989. *Realizing Rawls.* Ithaca, NY: Cornell University Press.

Pomeranz, K. and Topik, S. 2006. *The World that Trade Created: Society, Culture, and the World Economy, 1400 to the Present.* London: Sharpe.

Ramirez, F. and Boli, J. 1987. "The Political Construction of Mass Education: European Origins and Worldwide Institutionalization." *Sociology of Education* 60: 2–17.

Rawls, J. 1993. *Political Liberalism.* New York: Columbia University Press.

Riddle, P. 1990. "University and State: Political Competition and the Rise of Universities, 1200–1985." Doctoral dissertation, Stanford University, Stanford, CA.

Robertson, R. 1992. *Globalization: Social Theory and Global Culture.* London: Sage.

Romm, J. 1992. *The Edges of the Earth in Ancient Thought: Geography, Exploration and Fiction.* Princeton: Princeton University Press.

Ryan, A. 2012. *On Politics.* New York: Norton.

Schmitt, C. 1963. *Der Begriff des Politischen: Text von 1932 mit einem Vorwort und drei Corollarien.* Berlin: Duncker & Humblot.

Schmitt, C. 1950. *Der Nomos der Erde im Völkerrecht des Jus Publicum Europaeum.* Berlin: Duncker & Humblot.

Schofield, M. 1991. *The Stoic Idea of the City.* Cambridge: Cambridge University Press.

Shils, E. 1971. "No Salvation Outside Higher Education." *Minerva* 6: 313–21.

Simmel, G. 1976 [1903]. *The Metropolis and Mental Life.* New York: Free Press.

Simmons, B., Dobbin, F., and Garrett, G. (eds.) 2008. *The Global Diffusion of Markets and Democracy.* Cambridge: Cambridge University Press.

Singer, P. 2011. *The Expanding Circle: Ethics, Evolution, and Moral Progress.* Princeton: Princeton University Press.

Spencer, H. 1896. *The Study of Sociology.* New York: D. Appleton.

Strang, D. 1991. "Global Patterns of Decolonization: 1500–1987." *International Studies Quarterly* 35: 429–54.

Thornton, A., Dorius, S., and Swindle, J. 2015. "Developmental Idealism." *Sociology of Development* 1(2): 277–320.

Tilly, C. (ed.) 1975. *The Formation of National States in Western Europe*. Princeton: Princeton University Press.

Toulmin, S. 1990. *Cosmopolis*. Chicago: University of Chicago Press.

Tuck, R. 2001. *The Rights of War and Peace: Political Thought and the International Order from Grotius to Kant*. Oxford: Oxford University Press.

Wallerstein, I. M. 1974. *The Modern World-System*. New York: Academic Press.

Waltz, K. 1979. *Theory of International Politics*. New York: McGraw-Hill.

Williams, B. 2005. "In the Beginning was the Deed." In B. Williams, *In the Beginning was the Deed: Realism and Moralism in Political Argument*. Edited by Geoffrey Hawthorn. Princeton: Princeton University Press.

Woodberry, R. 2012. "The Missionary Roots of Liberal Democracy." *American Political Science Review* 106(2): 244–74.

Ypi, L. 2012. *Global Justice and Avant-Garde Political Agency*. Oxford: Oxford University Press.

CHAPTER 3

....

A DIALOGUE BETWEEN
BUSINESS AND PHILOSOPHY

....

BERTRAND COLLOMB AND SUSAN NEIMAN

Abstract

Is there a way of doing business that can sustain material progress without displacing other values that are the essence of the good life? This chapter is a dialogue on this and related questions. Has the present economic system reversed the means–end relation between markets and life? What forms of reasoning and value might redress this? Given our growing awareness and relations, what responsibilities do we have toward people in other parts of the planet? Will enterprises face a sunset on the notion of limited liability? The chapter discusses the marketing economy's manufacture of needs and the seeming overfinancialization of the economy. It concludes by proposing that if something is necessary to act morally, it is rational for us to believe in it. The spontaneous outcomes of the free market have to be evaluated against our societal goals, and the process reshaped via education and not only regulation.

Philosophy begins in dialogue. This is as true if you place the beginning, as most do, in Plato, or less conventionally, as Susan Neiman has done, in the Book of Job. It's the dialogues in the latter—between God and Satan, between Job and his friends, between Job and God—that raise questions about life, evil, and suffering that lead philosophy on. Amartya Sen has made a convincing case for placing a beginning of philosophy in the ethical debate between Arjuna and Krishna in the Bhagavad Gita.

Neither of the present authors wishes to identify with Socrates, still less with God, Krishna, or Satan. We believe, however, that the differences between us are most fruitfully explored through dialogue, rather than buried in an attempt at consensus that a more conventional essay would require. One of us is a man, a Catholic, a Frenchman, a business leader; the other is a woman, a Jew, an American, a philosopher. Though the other differences matter, it's the differences between our professions that are the most significant. For one of us lives in a culture expressed by the statement "business is everything"; the other in a culture that views business as purely instrumental. It's necessary for producing the goods that are the material basis for realizing a good life, but the goodness of that life is determined by other values. Among other matters, we will explore the question of whether there is a way of doing business that allows these two standpoints to meet without conflict, but we do not presuppose that it's possible.

When David Hume used the form to create his masterpiece, *Dialogues Concerning Natural Religion*, he gave his characters Greek names as a nod to the great tradition he sought to tap. The authors of this text are less ambitious, and will retain their proper names.

Is Business Everything in Our World?

Susan. At the December 2015 meeting of the Society for Progress in Princeton, a distinguished European business leader spoke of the profit he'd received from the dialogue with philosophers and social scientists: before, he said, he'd believed that business was everything; now he experienced another world. The philosophers present were dumbfounded, having never been exposed to the view that business is everything. Where do you stand? What is the place of business in the set of things that make up your life: family, religion, political concerns, artistic interests? Do you consider any of these primary, any derivative? Have you been faced with dilemmas in which one had to take priority? How were the dilemmas resolved?

Bertrand. I am surprised it was a European, not an American businessman who said that! But this might reflect the zeal of the new converts. Twenty years ago, no European businessman would have said that business was everything. A study we did in 1993 for the European Round Table of Industrialists on "European management"[1] was clearly showing that European managers were more concerned by society at large than the American (but less than the Japanese). In the last twenty years the pressure of the globalized financial markets, and the globalization of companies as well, has changed the perspective. And, after all, if you read only the *Wall Street Journal* and the *Financial Times* (because you must read them, and have no time in a hectic schedule to read anything else) and if most people you meet—including shareholders, media, and political people—want you to talk only about business, it is not surprising that your universe shrinks a bit! Not to mention the famous mantra of Milton Friedman: "The business of business is business"! I belong to the older generation, I had started my professional life in government, and I have always been interested in sociology, if not pure philosophy. So I have not suffered from this syndrome.

---

[1] Roland Calori and Philippe de Woot, 1994. *A European Management Model: Beyond Diversity.* London and New York: Prentice Hall.

Susan. I would not have expected you to agree with that business leader's comment, since you introduced me to the work of Jean-Pierre Dupuy.[2] I'm grateful to you for sending me several of his papers, which indeed resonated deeply with many of my own interests, going so far as to be fascinated with the Lisbon earthquake and the problem of theodicy, on which I have written extensively. But it's not quite the sort of philosophy of economics I would have expected a business leader to recommend. His criticisms of capitalism are quite extreme. May I ask you to comment on the following of his statements?

(1) What needs to be questioned is not capitalism per se but the place of economy in our lives.[3]
(2) "A chief of state who thinks and behaves like an economist can only be a wicked person"[4]

In general, Dupuy argues that economics has taken the place of religion: "Economy is the continuation of the sacred by other means"[5] Do you agree? If so, what are the consequences?

MARKET IDEOLOGY AS A RELIGION?

Bertrand. I very much like Jean-Pierre Dupuy, who was a classmate, and his provocative thinking. But we are not always in agreement. On the fact that the economists, and the economic theory, have taken too much of a place in our world, I totally agree. But that does not mean that we should see the economy, the material and immaterial goods that it produces, but also the opportunity it gives to human intelligence and ingenuity to realize things, as a negligible factor in mankind's objectives. As the Gospel says, "man does not live by bread alone," but he does require bread to live (at least when he is French!).

Jean-Pierre Dupuy is also an active pessimist, and thinks it almost certain that mankind will eventually create its own demise (but he explains cleverly that his

---

[2] Jean-Pierre Dupuy is a French engineering graduate and an economist turned philosopher. He was a professor of social and political philosophy at the École Polytechnique in Paris, where he founded the Centre de recherches en Epistémologie Appliquée. He is also a researcher at the Center for the Study of Language and Information at Stanford University. In France he helped to promote the ideas of Ivan Illich and René Girard. Among his many books are Jean-Pierre Dupuy, 2004. *Pour un catastrophisme éclairé*. Seuil; Jean-Pierre Dupuy, 2009. *The Mark of the Sacred*. Stanford: Stanford University Press; Jean-Pierre Dupuy, 2012. *Economy and the Future: A Crisis of Faith*. East Lansing: Michigan State University Press; Jean-Pierre Dupuy, 2013. "Crisis and the Sacred." Paper presented at the Institute for New Economic Thinking Annual Plenary Conference, Hong Kong.
[3] Dupuy, "Crisis and the Sacred," p. 1.   [4] Dupuy, *Economy and the Future*, p. 34.
[5] Dupuy, "Crisis and the Sacred," p. 10.

approach is the best way to avoid it if at all possible). On that I differ from him. I am an optimist, and I do not believe in doomsday.

Susan. I would say the same of myself, constitutionally. But the last five years or so have sorely tested any kind of optimism.

Bertrand. I do not always follow Dupuy in the role of the sacred in our world. What is certain is that any strong ideology is akin to a religion. So was communism in its heyday. So was—and still is, for the republican right in the US, or for some economic Nobel laureates—the ideology of the market, that has permeated everything in the last twenty years.

Susan. Dupuy's critique in many ways echoes Karl Marx, who wrote in the *Communist Manifesto* that market value had usurped every other value, including that of religion:

> The bourgeois drowned the most heavenly ecstasies of religious fervor in the icy water of egotistical calculation. It has resolved personal worth into exchange value, and in place of the numberless indefeasible chartered freedoms has set up that single, unconscionable freedom—free trade. All that is solid, melts into air, all that is holy is profaned.[6]

Is Dupuy's critique different? Can a market economy avoid sacralizing itself?

HAS THE MARKET OUTLIVED ITS USEFULNESS?

Bertrand. Let us not forget why most early economists, and some philosophers, supported the market economy. Friedrich Hayek, the Austrian economist and philosopher, whose life spanned most of the twentieth century, thought there was evil when men were dependent on the capricious will of somebody else.[7] For him, to be free requires that one be submitted to an abstract, impersonal, and universal rule that one cannot alter. This is embodied in the market laws that are undecipherable for individuals, for whom they are forces leading them in a direction that they can neither change nor even predict.

And fortunately, theoretical economists have shown with Pareto that—under some assumptions—the economic outcome of these market rules is the best that can be achieved, in the Pareto sense, meaning the welfare of some cannot be improved without reducing the welfare of others. So freedom and efficiency—in these definitions—are the two qualities of the market economy. Of course, we know that the theoretical conditions for reaching the economic optimum are practically never met, but we rely on the

---

[6] Karl Marx and F. Engels, 2010 [1848]. *Communist Manifesto*. In Marx/Engels Internet Archive, pp. 15–16. <https://www.marxists.org/archive/marx/works/download/pdf/Manifesto.pdf>.

[7] Jean-Pierre Dupuy, 2013. "La France et le marché: Les sources philosophiques d'une incompatibilité d'humeur." Presented at the Académie des sciences morales et politiques, June.

experimental fact that a market, however imperfect, is a better way to allocate resources than a centralized command and control system.

I believe the usefulness of the market, and therefore of capitalism, has not changed in the last thirty years. What changed was the degree to which everybody was led to believe the market was perfect and had the only answer to all issues. And by letting the market play an excessive and unconstrained role, its potential for excess and abuse has been increased. Because the market, as we see it more clearly now, is—in the words of Dupuy again—"self-transcendent."

That means it leads the economy in a direction of its own, one that is not necessarily desired by the market participants (although resulting from their aggregated behavior) and not necessarily consistent with the political objectives of our societies (if they have some!). This has been clearly evidenced, for example, by the impact of the globalized, financially driven market system in the last thirty years on the evolution of inequality. In this situation I agree that some may see the free market system as a religion, but I am not sure this is the result of an absolute need to find new sacred beliefs.

Susan. I agree with that. While we are thinking about the general relations between religion and economy, I wonder what you think of Pope Francis' recent use of the quote that money is the dung of the devil. There are many ways to view that claim. I suspect that Nietzsche would find it an expression of resentment—part of the way in which, on his view, Christianity is a slave morality which condemns power and wealth out of weakness; the meek dream of inheriting a future world as compensation for the deprivations in this one. But most philosophers view money and wealth neither as dung nor as goal but as means. For all the differences between, for example, Rawls' theory of justice and Sen's capabilities approach, both view wealth as merely a means to a good life, rather than an end, and this has been true of philosophers since Plato. Is there something we don't understand about wealth, since few of us have much experience of it?

IS MONEY EVIL?

Bertrand. The Catholic Church has always had problems with economic issues. Jesus Christ in the Gospel shows the head of the emperor on a coin to say "Give therefore to Caesar the things that are Caesar's," establishing a separation between political society and religion (a teaching not well followed by the popes themselves in their later fights with the emperors); but it also says that it is more difficult for a rich man to go to heaven than for a camel to go through the eye of a needle. A pretty strong statement, which all casuistry about being rich or poor "in spirit" has difficulty sweetening!

Only recently has the Church made efforts to really understand the challenges of the economy. When we needed to close a plant, the local bishop would typically chastise us for creating hardship for people. We would need to explain that keeping an uneconomical plant open was not a service to the people, and that the real issue was to help them into the change that was unavoidable. In his encyclical "Caritas in veritate,"

Benoit XVI made a great effort to understand the market economy, and distinguish its positive and negative elements. However, he could not accept that everything be based on material interest, and asked that some element of gratuity be included in the merchant economy. He did not say how, and the idea puzzled many Catholic business-people, who understand and practice corporate social responsibility, but do not see how market transactions could include an "element of gratuity."

Of course, everything in the practical economy—whatever Milton Friedman may say—is a trade-off. Social issues need to be taken into consideration as well as economic ones. And I prefer to see Pope Francis on the side of the underprivileged rather than—as it was sometimes the case in the past—on the side of the rich and powerful.

That money can be evil unfortunately remains true. The addiction to being rich is very easy, and can obscure one's point of view. I have lived through the period when the compensation of CEOs of large companies has changed, from being determined by a reasonable distance with that of the other managers, to being set in comparison to the profit generated for the shareholders, and therefore at a much higher level.

Susan. It is clear the gap between the compensation of CEOs of large companies and that of the average worker in those companies, whatever the estimations of this gap, has risen enormously in the past decades.

INEQUALITIES CREATED BY
THE MARKET ECONOMY

Bertrand. I can testify that, without asking for more, and even sometimes resisting the desire of the board compensation committee to bring you "in line with the market," one gets easily used to making more money, and spending it.

Even more when most people you meet—bankers, lawyers, foreign partners, American colleagues—are making much more money than you, flying in private jets on a whim, and using only the best of everything everywhere!

Susan. Yes, Robert Frank has shown how the feeling of wealth is relative to one's surroundings: if everyone is building a larger house than they need, one begins to see normal-sized houses as small, if everyone throws an obscenely expensive party for their child's bat mitzvah or confirmation, anything smaller will seem to be inadequate. Do you think this is a good argument for reducing the amount we consume? I am not suggesting that governments confiscate luxury objects, but what would the world look like if (many of) those objects were not seen as a source of pride and status but a source of shame? Surely the amount of prestige attached to conspicuous wealth varies across cultures. Do you think we could and should change the role of luxury in ours?

Bertrand. I was born in Lyon, where the richest and most beautiful apartments were hidden in nondescript buildings, and where showing your wealth was in bad taste. The French *ancien régime* kept trying, through "luxury ordinances," to limit the display of wealth in clothing! And now you made me discover the craziness of the social media about the extravagant fiestas of some pop stars—Kardashian and the like! The display of wealth inequality is certainly much wider, and much more visible, than before. It could lead to a revolt of the less favored, but surprisingly they are the ones enjoying the extravaganzas!

Susan. Less fortunate people are easily diverted by watching the spectacles of the more fortunate. After all, they cannot afford to go to the theater or the opera; if they have to hire a babysitter, even a movie may be out of the question. So yes, without a lot to enjoy in their own lives they take vicarious pleasure in watching other people's extravagance. This is a phenomenon that has often helped royalties to maintain power; think how many people turn out to watch royal displays. But like you, I think this could lead to a revolt of the less favored; I do not believe they will be content to watch other people's spectacles forever.

Bertrand. More seriously, a culture where a US presidential candidate can say "I am the richest, therefore I am the best" will not appeal to either you or me. This sort of culture certainly creates an incentive to break any ethical rules when a monetary profit is possible. Among the different countries who have adopted more or less the same free market economy system, the differences are large.

Finland, one of the richest European countries in terms of GDP per capita, does not have many signs of wealth—current or even historical—on display. But that also makes it a little dull, at least for the tourist!

Susan. Is that really the criterion by which we should judge the health of a society? Haven't we gotten addicted to the kind of excitement that makes a decent society seem dull—what Pope Francis calls a culture of waste? The rise of neoliberalism has coincided with a rise in fundamentalism across all major religions. I don't believe that it's a coincidence; rather, I believe it is a protest against market fundamentalism, i.e. a global ideology that recognizes no values but market values. Needless to say, I reject fundamentalism in all its guises, whether in the Islamic State, the West Bank of Palestine, the American Tea Party, or Wall Street. However: as a non-Catholic I have never been particularly interested in news from the Vatican, but Pope Francis has me riveted. He is certainly not a fundamentalist, but some of his writings suggest a fundamental incompatibility between religious and economic values. What do you think of his critique, and why is it taking place now? What forms of practice could be developed to avoid it?

FUNDAMENTALISM AS A REACTION TO MARKET RELIGION?

Bertrand. Are you sure? It may not be a coincidence, but I would rather see the reason for the rise of fundamentalism in the demise of the communist ideal. I would agree that many people, especially when their life is dull and difficult, need an ideal to strive for.

Susan. I can agree with this if we can put it a bit more clearly. The communist ideal had many flaws but it was an ideal in two ways: an ideal of equality, and a belief that the meaning of life was found in something higher than individual consumption. Many who turn to fundamentalism are looking for some ideology which approaches those ideals, in response to neoliberalism. Since the collapse of communism, neoliberalism and globalization have created some benefits, especially in places like China, but they have also created a growing gulf between extreme wealth and poverty. And thanks to globalization, the world's poor are far more aware of this gulf than they would have been before. This is surely why Pope Francis is so beloved all over the world, even among non-Catholics. But it is also, unfortunately, a reason that some will turn to fundamentalism rather than a more rational religion.

Bertrand. The eighteenth century was the century of the Enlightenment; the nineteenth century was a time of technological progress and of social idealism. In the twentieth century, for a large part of the world, especially the developing world, communism and the socialist model were a powerful ideal. In India, for example, intellectuals had been taught socialism in British universities and Indira Gandhi, after Nehru, was still sticking to the socialist view of the world. An ideal that will supposedly deliver both material progress and social justice in this world is even better than a religious ideal that promises a better life only in the afterworld!

The free market economy does not generate that type of expectation. Actually Joseph Schumpeter, one of the best economic thinkers, wrote in 1942 that capitalism, contrary to communism and corporatism, had never been liked by intellectuals, and was afraid that, because of this lack of adhesion, capitalism would not survive.[8]

In fact, over the years, the practical comparison between the outcome of capitalism and that of communism was overwhelming and led to a rational acceptance of capitalism. But at the same time, capitalism started, at least in the industrialized countries, to deliver less growth, more unemployment, and rising inequality. And it became increasingly difficult to give a tangible vision of what a free market economy would produce. People were asked to believe in a process that is, as we said, fairly opaque and largely denies political choices, instead of creating a concrete utopia. The fundamentalism we see developing in different religions, for me, is filling a void rather than being a reaction against market liberalism. In the US, Christian fundamentalism developed against the scientific view of the world, but seems to be compatible with a strong belief in the market (as an alternative against evil government). In other parts of the world, rather than a reaction against a particular economic system, it is the inability of some sectors of society to participate effectively in the modern world that leads to going back to absolute beliefs.

Susan. I think this is too simple an explanation, because we have seen how many successful, or potentially successful people turn to Salafism. There is a great deal of evidence about this: the people who are going to ISIS (the Islamic State of Iraq and

---

[8] Joseph Schumpeter, 1942. *Capitalism, Socialism and Democracy*. New York: Harper and Brothers.

Syria), for example, are not those who are unable to participate effectively in the modern world but those who do not want to do so. I began thinking about this most seriously when wondering how young Western women could go to ISIS; I can understand why young men do, but it's harder to understand how a young woman could voluntarily take on what is in many ways a form of slavery. But looking at videos and photos of young women who are internationally famous and successful—Kim Kardashian, Nicki Minaj—it becomes easier to understand how a young woman might reject that. Our generation manages to avoid much contact with it, but young people live in a world that is hypersexualized—very raw sex is used to sell just about anything, as well as itself. I can actually understand a young woman who decides: if this is what success means in contemporary Western culture, I'd rather put on a burka. Now one might argue that Western consumer capitalism need not entail the pornographic culture we live in, but I think the logic of the market demands it. You could reinstitute censorship, as they did in the days when Ulysses—ach, for the good old days—was deemed pornographic. But this would be an artificial imposition on a system in which things that are sold—from arms to pornography—are neutral, and the maximization of profit is the main commandment.

Bertrand. May I suggest that the deluge of pornography in our societies is not the result of the free market, but of US Supreme Court decisions that were based, not on the free commerce clause of the US Constitution, but on the First Amendment freedom of speech? From the US, and of course thanks to the Internet, it went everywhere.

Susan. This is just the legal right to say (or show) anything, and the US Supreme Court, as the Citizens United decision shows so blatantly, is not exactly independent of basic assumptions that are heavily influenced by our economic system. So your reply doesn't solve my problem: that because markets are by definition ethically neutral and have but one goal, the maximization of profit, the means to that profit, however degrading or lethal, are unimportant. Our present economic system has reversed the means–ends relation: instead of viewing markets as (perhaps) the best means to a good life, all the other things that are part of a good life are subordinate to the market.

We both agree that rational choice theory is wrong about human motivation; our own experience, not to mention the work of many scholars, shows that human beings are motivated, for better and worse, by many things apart from maximizing utility. Dupuy goes so far as to call economic rationality a form of torture (*Economy and the Future*, p. 67). How is a multidimensional conception of reason possible in a culture that seeks to measure everything in quantitative terms? It's clear that even hardliners who speak of the need to placate shareholders are not willing to do anything to maximize profit. Even were it not illegal, few would advocate returning to slave labor in order to provide shareholders with better returns. Still, we live in a culture that presupposes an economic conception of reason, in which the bottom line is the bottom line. (The very expression "bottom line" to mean "what is most important in the final analysis" is an expression of that attitude.) In such a culture, what must be undertaken so that other forms of reasoning, and value, are not merely viewed as secondary?

Bertrand. If business is not everything, it is indeed striking that the concepts and the vocabulary of business and economic theory are everywhere, even in the social sciences. It should have been taken as a scandal, or a joke, when somebody received a Nobel Prize for analyzing the relationships of married couples using the concepts of economic theory![9] As you say, we do not need to argue very much to see that *homo economicus* is a gross simplification of the behavior of human beings. Lately, that has been discovered by the so-called "behavioral economists." But I was struck recently to hear a very respected economist, speaking about behavioral economy, still calling "irrational" those behaviors he was willing to take into consideration, but that were not fitting into the definition of *homo economicus*.

Susan. Yes, that's the crazy part. The behavioral economists still accept the premise that we are rational insofar as we conform to the paradigm of *homo economicus*, they just like to point out all the ways in which we're irrational. It doesn't seem to occur to them to question the premise.

Is There a Business Ethics?

Bertrand. More interesting is the issue of the role of ethics in the behavior of economic players. Adam Smith, who had published *The Theory of Moral Sentiments* before *The Wealth of Nations*, assumed that moral standards were necessary for a well-functioning market economy. Not everybody agrees, and the French philosopher André Comte-Sponville, in a debate organized by a business school, argued with me that, as CEO of a widely held company, I had the duty to do anything that could benefit my shareholders, provided it was legal, even if I thought some action was unethical. I disagreed, as I did not see why my shareholders, who are individuals with ethical standards, would expect me to do, as the CEO, something they would not do themselves. This led us to a debate on the moral conscience of a company, which the philosopher, apparently not very attuned to sociology, wanted to negate.

Susan. I would say he wasn't very attuned to philosophy either! In any case I wish your behavior in this case were more common. I gather that in most companies, shareholders' profits are the only thing that matters.

Bertrand. In the case of the 2007–8 financial crisis, for example, we could wonder whether the excesses leading to it were created only by deficient control systems and perverse incentives, or also by the breakdown of ethical standards among, principally but not exclusively, financial players. Initially the focus was on blaming the systems, but the discovery of practices in several markets and the ensuing fines against the largest and most successful banks seem to indicate that the breach of elementary ethical

---

[9] Gary Becker, and the so-called "home economics."

standards played a significant role. And the recent Volkswagen scandal shows that the problem is not limited to banks. How to re-establish ethical standards in our current world is not an easy question.

The business schools, and also the economists, obviously have a role to play. But who will write the code of ethics of the free market economy?

Susan. I am not sure it can be done, but perhaps this is the role of the Society for Progress. Or is that too ambitious a goal?

Bertrand. And what does the philosopher think about the role of ethics in the market economy and the way to make it evolve?

Susan. If I had to choose between ethics and the free market, I would give up the free market. I am not arguing for giving it up entirely, but I would only support a market that is far better regulated, internationally, than anything we now have. John Rawls argued that we no more deserve our talents than we deserve the good fortune of having been born into an intact extended family than a broken one, into wealth rather than poverty, in Berlin rather than Burundi—all accidents that deeply affect the rest of our lives. Our intelligence is no more due to merit than our ability to sing on-key or our possession of a face that meets the golden triangle criteria of beauty. Most crucially, he includes the capacity to take risks—often seen as a major business virtue—among the qualities that simply differ between people, whether due to inheritance or environment, and hence cannot be a matter of merit. All these qualities are gifts, whether or not we regard them as gifts of God; we no more deserve them than a child born blind or disabled deserves her fate. Hence, according to Rawls, we do not deserve their fruits either. I find his arguments increasingly compelling, particularly as I observe vast differences between people regarding risk taking and energy levels. (Freud called the latter "the constitutional factor.") This view seems to undermine any attempt to (justly) maintain a meritocracy, but it's also very troubling. If I lived by it, I would have to donate all my royalties to those who were born in circumstances less favorable to developing discipline and literary talent. I should add that those royalties are not particularly large, but since they enable me to meet more than my family's most basic needs, the contradiction with my belief that talent is not deserved leaves me troubled. Do you see a contradiction? Do we deserve the fruit of our talents?

Bertrand. I said earlier that the value and importance of the economy—in which business plays a major role—was not only in the supply of goods and services, some of which we could very well live without. There is for me a value in harnessing the energy, the intelligence, and the will of people to work together to take on new challenges. I believe that, after we have experienced scientific discovery, technological progress, and expansion of our capabilities as men, a static life where we would have chosen to have no economic growth and no disturbing change—and change is always disturbing—would be pretty dull.

Susan. I agree with you entirely. I think we are fundamentally active beings, who want to be challenged and to contribute something to the world. But the challenges that would arise if, for example, we followed Pope Francis' advice, are large enough, don't you think?

Bertrand. Even in an economy dedicated to growth or progress, there is some room for the social concerns the pope embodies. In the last few years, I have seen many young people who had a successful career deciding to dedicate themselves to improving society. Even more interestingly, some try to engage in ventures that serve a social purpose without losing the drive for effectiveness of a for-profit company: for example a consulting company that works on energy optimization, but with 25 percent of its consulting time given for free to non-profit organizations working in that area (with consultants being hired on the basis they will be paid only 75 percent of the prevailing rate).

This is akin to this new concept, created by a recent California law, of a company with a dual purpose, both economic and social. But I do not see a society where the ideas of growth and progress would be eliminated.

Perhaps mankind's energy could be redirected to nature contemplation, artistic experience, and loving relationships? Catholics—or Christians in general—believe in the original sin, a way to express that in man, evil is never very far from good. I would assume that societal problems would be as difficult—probably different, but as difficult, or actually more difficult—than those that we know in the free market, growth- and progress-oriented economy.

This importance of the dynamic dimension leads me to an answer to your question. Whether we deserve a reward for our talents or not is an interesting theoretical question, but I am more interested in the kind of society that would be produced by an absolute answer to the question. To continue the debate, one could first argue whether the capability to utilize and develop one's talents, which is obviously different between different people, is also an innate gift for which we do not deserve a reward!

Susan. This is actually Rawls' most disturbing point. The capacity to utilize and develop our talents is not entirely in our control. Aside from the fact that our educational prospects depend radically (statistically, if not absolutely) on where we were born and to whom, we are born with unequal amounts of energy, the desire to take risks, and so on—all the things that make it possible for one person to develop talents that in others lie dormant. We can all cite cases of people who rose above difficult circumstances thanks to hard work and strength of will, and these are certainly things one can cultivate. The question is to what extent even these things are deserved.

THE DREAM OF AN EGALITARIAN SOCIETY

Bertrand. But what is clear for me is that a totally egalitarian society, according to the motto proposed by Louis Blanc, and later used by Marx—"From each according to his ability, to each according to his needs"—would be a nightmare.

Susan. Because you think it wouldn't work? Or would it be a nightmare in itself? I find Marx's thought here utopian but quite beautiful. It's based on his idea that work is the key to being human. We want to produce, just as you said: we are active not passive creatures. We're not just a bunch of lazy bastards who would lie in the sun all day if we didn't have to earn a living. So I take the idea to be that we would all work anyway, but some of us would naturally produce more than others, whether we had a large family to feed or not; surely you and I do plenty of work in the evening, or on weekends and holidays, which isn't necessary except for goals that we have set for ourselves? Those people who are less gifted or more numerous would then share in the fruits of the work of those who just happen to produce more, and don't need it. Now this is a utopian vision, and it's based on an anthropology that doesn't take account of envy, for example. So it may well be unrealizable. But I don't understand why it's a nightmare.

Bertrand. I do not believe we are a bunch of lazy people, or that greed is always the main motivation. But the idea that we are, in a way, programmed by a mysterious gift of talents and therefore have no merits in whatever we achieve, cannot lead to a dynamic society, compared to one where we are being asked to develop our talents and are rewarded for it. Rewards are not necessarily only monetary, but I cannot follow Rawls if he says we should not be rewarded in any way, as we do not deserve it.

In fact, all the surveys show that, even in France, where "Egalité" is prominently written on each public building, people do not expect or desire total equality. They accept very well inequalities related to efforts and successes, within some limits. And when discussing the compensation of CEOs, the lack of relation between real performance (as seen by the public, with sometimes different criteria from the shareholders) and remuneration is the first target for criticism, followed by absolute levels that cannot be understood— although they are better understood for football players, who are seen as having unique skills, than for CEOs, who are not seen as particularly different from other managers.

Susan. I was a student of John Rawls but I too am very troubled by this doctrine.

Unfortunately, I was too young to formulate many of the questions I now wish I had asked my teachers before they died. This wasn't the part of Rawls' work that interested me as a student; now I don't accept it entirely, but it leaves me troubled. Most philosophers have allowed for differences in our obligations to others based on our relations to them. I have, for example, different obligations to my children than I do to others. In a world in which both business and communication are increasingly global, how much of a distinction can we maintain? What responsibilities do we have toward people in other parts of the planet?

SELF-INTEREST OR SOLIDARITY IN THE WORLD?

Bertrand. This is actually an area where business and the free market economy have had enormous consequences. The second commandment, "You shall love your neighbor as yourself," leads to the question: Who is my neighbor? There has always been a concern for "remote neighbors," sometimes expressed in outdated forms. In the colonial era, France was the center of enormous missionary activity (in 1920, 80 percent of the Catholic nuns in the world were French) that expressed a certain form of solidarity. At the same time, colonial exploitation was sometimes brutal, more than our history books teach us, but not without some internal opposition within the colonial powers themselves.

The current situation is somewhat paradoxical. Never has the dire situation of many people in the world been known and described so well, and never has the need for solidarity with others been expressed, discussed, and implemented so strongly in NGOs' programs. It is not unusual for university students, in the US or elsewhere, to go and work in solidarity programs after college for a year or more. Within the company I used to manage, the loss of 300 lives in our Indonesian plant to the 2004 tsunami was followed by a spontaneous and strong worldwide expression of concrete financial solidarity.

At the same time, knowing and seeing the plight of others can reinforce the will to protect oneself. "We cannot bear alone the misery of the world!" The worldwide reaction against immigration, at a time when some populations are desperate to live outside of countries which are torn by conflict, and when the demographics of many countries would require more immigration, is a striking example.

For business there is clearly an expansion of responsibilities. When a building collapsed in Bangladesh, there was hardly any discussion about bad construction and the responsibility of the builder. Every comment was focused on the Western international companies, whose sub-sub-contractors were employing workers in this unsafe environment. Far beyond their formal legal responsibilities, companies will be more and more held to a standard of care for everybody involved in dealing with them. Even though it is tough for some companies, and flies in the face of the concept of limited liability that was basic in building corporate law, I believe this is a positive evolution. But it does not answer your question about the level of solidarity between countries and societies themselves.

Susan. I think the concept of limited liability is legalistic, and ignores the fact that enormous profits are made by the companies who outsourced their building projects. So I don't think it's largesse, but simple justice, when those countries take on more than the law would require. And these problems are clearly only going to get worse, probably very soon. The current refugee crisis in Europe is probably the tip of the iceberg. Even without climate migration in the face of worsening climate conditions, we need to see this as the fruit of globalization. It was unreasonable to expect that everyone in the world would buy a cellphone, or get an Internet connection, without raising the question: Why can't I live like those in Western Europe or the US?

BUSINESS CAUGHT BETWEEN SUSTAINABLE DEVELOPMENT AND QUARTERLY EARNINGS

Bertrand. Maybe at this point I should address the issue of business behavior, that you have touched upon several times. When Volkswagen's CEO promotes his company as a champion of social responsibility and sustainable development, and a few weeks later we discover their major cheating on nitrogen oxide emission standards, it is easy to conclude that business is totally hypocritical on societal issues.

You said earlier that you believed that profit objectives were in any case taking precedence for business. This is not wrong, but the situation is a little more complicated than that. The traditional view of companies was that creating value (we used to say creating wealth, or in other words being efficient) was their *raison d'être* (they are not charitable operations or employment reservations), but that this value was shared among their different stakeholders: customers, employees, local communities, shareholders. In the early 1980s in the US, that had led to companies becoming somewhat complacent, with an informal consensus between unions and management not to rock the boat. Japanese competition, the Reagan revolution, and the Chicago economists destroyed that consensus. And financial globalization gave more and more power to the shareholders (or the professional asset managers representing them) who claimed to be the ultimate owners of companies, and created financial incentives to managers to be aligned only with the shareholders' interests.

However, the reality is that a company cannot be successful without faithful customers, committed employees, and friendly local communities, i.e. without catering to the stakeholders' needs. Responsible managers—those who do not only want to get rich and bail out—recognize that need and want their companies to be socially responsible and accept their share of responsibility for the well-being of the planet. But they are under enormous quarterly pressure from the financial markets. Among the shareholders, some have long-term interests and can understand these strategies. But a lot of asset managers are themselves under short-term evaluation constraints, and some shareholders are only interested in short-term speculation. As a result, the pressure to forget everything but quarterly earnings does exist, and is stronger if the company is not successful enough to build the buffer that might protect it from activist shareholders. For most companies this is not a hypocritical and cynical game, but a life of contradictory pressures that is difficult to survive. To avoid the negative consequences of that situation would require reinforcing the "buffers" between shareholders' pressure and companies, but this is another issue!

MARKETING AND CONSUMER CHOICES

Susan. Along with those changes in corporate self-understanding, I think we have to address the role of marketing. A number of critics have argued that capitalism itself has changed from a system concerned with the manufacture of goods to a system concerned with the manufacture of needs. This has to do with the importance of marketing. (In 2013 the US spent $23 billion in foreign aid and $190 billion on advertising within the US alone—that is, the smaller number is devoted to fulfilling basic and often desperate needs, whereas the larger number is devoted to creating new ones.) Here is a quote from Benjamin Barber's 2007 book *Consumed*:

> Inequality leaves capitalism with a dilemma: the overproducing capitalist market must either grow or expire. If the poor cannot be enriched enough to become consumers, then grownups in the First World who are currently responsible for 60 percent of the world's consumption, and with vast disposable income but few needs, will have to be enticed into shopping. Inducing them to remain childish and impetuous in their taste helps insure they will buy the global market goods designed for indolent and prosperous youth.[10]

Barber argues that while early capitalism may well have fostered adult virtues like the discipline, hard work, individual responsibility, and delayed gratification described by Weber, contemporary capitalism does just the opposite, contributing to—even demanding—our infantilization. I find his diagnosis very plausible. What do you think?

Bertrand. We are back to the issue of the value of the goods—tangible or intangible— that we consume. I do not personally find it very convincing that, beyond the satisfaction of basic needs, all consumption is a waste of our time and energy. First, because the concept of basic needs is fairly relative, and will change over time. Second, because a lot of what is beyond the basic may be very important, very gratifying, and enriches the life of people.

Why should food, for example, be restricted to the "basic" minimum, and why not be able to take personal pleasure in having a variety of tastes, in having access to food of other cultures? Now this very example will call for the criticism that capitalism leads to everybody in the world eating terrible and fattening McDonald's hamburgers! But actually this is not true. What we see in our economy is both the development of standardized mass products—with the guarantee that a standard gives you, but with associated limitations—and the growth of specialty products or services that have an infinite diversity.

Susan. I'm not an ascetic, and I agree that our lives are enriched by food or clothing or housing that goes beyond the basic needs needed to sustain life. It's a question of balance. Yes, the concept of basic needs is somewhat relative, but not entirely; both Rawls and Sen have tried to specify it, and I think common sense can also play a role here. In a world where thousands of people die daily of hunger while food is a major commodity for speculation, I fear there is something wrong about worrying whether we're eating from McDonald's or the latest Michelin-starred restaurant or health food discovery. You are right that we are moving toward infinite diversity in some areas— though you wouldn't know it when you see the same chains of stores all over the world. But how much diversity is really a good, and how much of it is a distraction? Do we

---

[10] Benjamin Barber, 2008. *Consumed: How Markets Corrupt Children, Infantilize Adults, and Swallow Citizens Whole.* New York: W.W. Norton & Company, pp. 10–11.

really need to spend our time choosing between hundreds of cereals or toothpaste or whatever—which leaves us little time and energy to make more important choices?

Bertrand. Who will decide what is a distraction, and what the more important things are? The development of marketing techniques may give the feeling that consumers are at the mercy of producers. Advertising has never been well accepted by intellectuals, and one French TV executive was provocative enough to say that his role was to "deliver empty available brains" to the advertisers! But my experience as a director of Unilever showed me that companies are never sure, even with the best advertising campaign, of the way a new product will be accepted or refused. So consumers do have a choice.

More importantly, this issue is not about capitalism itself. Assume we were in a more state-directed system, efficient enough to be able to produce diversified goods beyond the basics. How would such a system decide what it should produce: opera shows or cloth pins? How would the possible choices be communicated to the public? If there is competition—and of course competition is the cornerstone of a free market economy, always threatened by the desire of business to reduce it—the choices of the consumers will ultimately decide the direction in which the economy will evolve.

Now the issue of deciding whether the result of consumers' choices is globally desirable is something else. Here again we need to decide whether the market is a god, or a tool. Even in a free market economy, there are several tools—tax incentives, standards—to direct consumers' choices, some would say to distort them. Tobacco is one example of such bending of natural and well-established preferences. The fight against climate change requires a similar obligation for consumers to do the right thing. I very much surprised a car industry executive, who was repeating the mantra of answering the desires of his customers, by telling him that the Environmental Protection Agency's requirement for each manufacturer to reduce the gas consumption of the average car they sell will require them to bend the choices of the consumers toward lighters cars and fewer SUVs, even if SUV are not outlawed!

Susan. His surprise reflects a set of unquestioned assumptions that are frighteningly naïve.

DOES SOCIETY HAVE A CHOICE OR ARE WE DOMINATED BY MARKETING CAMPAIGNS?

Bertrand. How many political choices should a society make against the market is an open question, and it does not always work, as the history of the prohibition in the US shows! But I do not believe that society is powerless to decide what it will accept or refuse.

Susan. For a start, I think we'll agree that if society does not make some pretty serious political choices in the realm of energy consumption, our grandchildren will have very few choices to make at all. But I still think you underestimate the power of marketing. The consumer choices you mention are conscious choices, and of course it is possible to make some. But marketing is designed to affect our unconscious. Here I strongly recommend the film series *The Century of the Self* by Adam Curtis, which documents just how consciously the marketing industry used different forms of psychology—beginning with Freud, as presented to the US by his nephew—in order to work on our unconscious. I think if we're honest, we have to acknowledge how vulnerable we all are; we are not as autonomous as you make us out to be. Or rather: our only chance of becoming truly autonomous is to recognize our vulnerability.

Here's one rather old-fashioned example: when the *New York Times*, the most serious paper in the US, runs three-quarter-page ads announcing, let's say, the latest sale at Bloomingdale's underneath news of the latest slaughter in Syria, it conveys the message that one of these events looms much larger than the other, simply through sheer spatial relations. Of course, I don't *think* the sale is more important than the slaughter; but when I see that message every morning, I know I'm affected by it. I once had a long argument about this with the economist Eric Maskin, who argued that we can simply choose not to look at the ads. Indeed we can, and we do. But we are not simply cognitive beings, and I think it's naïve to suppose that we remain unaffected by the constant barrage of marketing suggestions about what the real priorities of our society are. And the example is old-fashioned because print advertising is old-fashioned; the Internet targets us in far more subtle, invasive, and ubiquitous ways.

The priority of marketing for business was dramatically expressed by founding Nike CEO Phil Knight:

> For years we thought of ourselves as a production-oriented company, meaning we put all our emphasis on designing and manufacturing the products. But now we understand that the most important thing we do is market the product...Nike is a marketing-oriented company, and *the product is our most important marketing tool.*[11]

In your experience, has marketing come to overshadow production? How has marketing changed so as to be divorced from the object being marketed? (It is clear that auto companies no longer sell a way to get from one place to another, but a set of emotions involving power, control, sex, and envy. And if you'll excuse a rather vulgar example, I wrote the first draft of my part of this paper on Naxos, where a brand of toilet paper is called "Dream." This is Greece, mind you, where dreams were the messages sent by gods.) In light of the billions spent by scientifically based marketing divisions in order to create our preferences, what does it mean to talk of free preference?

Bertrand. Would you rather have been contaminated by the *homo rationalis* syndrome? Why should emotions, or the desire for power, play no roles in our relations with the economy? Yes, I may want to have a nice car not only because I like it, but also because it

---

[11] Quoted in Barber, *Consumed*, p. 179, my emphasis.

flatters my ego. Or I might go to see a Wagner opera because it is fashionable, even though I am not a Wagner fan, and I suspect it may be too long and too boring. What makes a human life interesting if it is not this mix of satisfaction, relationships, and emotions? Not everybody can be a wise philosopher that has realized everything is illusion, and I am not sure I would like to live in a society where there would be too many wise philosophers!

Susan. Believe me, neither would I. And I certainly don't think everything is an illusion! But your car and opera examples strike me as problematic. I know lots of people who go to Wagner operas because they genuinely love the music. (For me, it would have to be Mozart, but that's another story.) To go if you find it boring, just because it's fashionable, is to do something you don't choose only because others have chosen it, and that is not really self-determined. Similarly, I don't understand why buying a certain car flatters the ego. I know this is truer for men than for women, but still, Rousseau would have quite a lot to say about how buying a car because it flatters the ego—rather than, say, because it's great fun to drive—is a problem. Even if you skip Rousseau and look to the psychologists who are researching happiness, you will find that experiences make people happier than possessions. So spending money on going to a concert you really enjoy—whatever it is, opera or jazz or rock 'n' roll—brings much more real happiness than going to one for the sake of fashion, or buying something in order to impress someone else.

Bertrand. I am critical enough of the excesses and the deviations of capitalism in the last thirty years, but I still believe in its fundamental value. It does unleash, as I said earlier, the potential of mankind to go for new things: new discoveries, new products, new relationships, new understandings of the surrounding world. It unleashes Prometheus, who I take as a much better model than his stupid brother Epimetheus!

This potential has been used in different directions: progress of knowledge and better understanding of the world, consumer satisfactions, more recently development of a variety of communication modes, but also development of art and culture.

Hayek's idea was that the free market model would release mankind from any particular ideology or dominant group. The reality looks somewhat different. You point out that the amount of money spent on marketing campaigns does not correspond to "free consumer choice," but this is not really certain. If somebody spends a lot of time, energy, and money finding out what my preference is for a car, and then offers me the exact car of my dreams, has my freedom of choice been denied?

I agree that some marketing campaigns, with the level of psychological sophistication you mention, can overwhelm individual freedom of choice and create entirely new "needs." Or more simply business can decide what to offer, like when Henry Ford decided people only needed to buy black cars. But even in that case, over time competition is likely to restore a more reasonable balance between different "needs." And, like we said about tobacco, all the marketing campaigns have eventually been powerless in the face of societal reaction.

I am not sure how the excesses of marketing can be avoided, but I am less worried than you about their long-term consequences.

It is clear (except for a majority of the US Supreme Court) that the power of money in political campaigns is creating an issue of freedom. Is it the case for business marketing and advertising campaigns? I am not sure for the majority of them, but I am prepared to be challenged.

Susan. I'm happy to challenge you, because the majority of consumers are less thoughtful than you are. From the fairly trivial example of young children demanding sugary cereal to the more serious one of young men seeking weapons, advertising helps persuade people to buy things that are no good for them or the culture they live in. Even more importantly, the plethora of choices available is a problem in itself. Barry Schwartz's book *The Paradox of Choice* shows that people become less satisfied the more choice they have, and his experiments are convincing, even though he is writing from the perspective of behavioral economics, which, as we agreed, takes a lot of questionable assumptions for granted.[12] I am more worried about the fact that we are forced to spend so much time on trivial choices—which smartphone or printer to buy when the last one breaks down, as it is programmed to do shortly after the guarantee expires, and even more time figuring out how to operate them—that we barely realize how many important choices are out of our hands. So I don't think the heroic model of Prometheus is as relevant to contemporary capitalism as you do.

Again, I think this development is related to the finance economy in which goods are bought less for their own sake than in order to sell to others who want them more than you do and are hence willing to pay more. Is this a similar divorce of desire from product that we see in marketing?

Too Much Finance?

Bertrand. I am not too worried by the development or the influence of marketing, but the role of the financial world worries me much more. Trading goods not for the utility or the satisfaction they provide to you, but for the expectation that they will be more valuable for somebody else, can be called either "arbitrage" (a positive word) or "speculation" (a negative one). Some degree of speculation is a necessary part of a market. But a market that works mainly on speculation necessarily goes from bubble to crash. A financial market needs arbitrageurs to function properly, but a financial market where speculation has taken over and nobody cares about the utility value of the goods is in trouble—more likely in a bubble!

The fundamental theorem justifying the efficiency of markets assumes that players act independently from each other. What happens when everyone is moving with the herd? This problem is being exacerbated by the professionalization of asset management, and the way asset managers are evaluated quarterly. Being wrong with everybody

[12] Barry Schwartz, 2004. *The Paradox of Choice: Why More is Less.* New York: Ecco.

else becomes a better option than being right alone. If two or three years are necessary to prove you right, you will likely have lost your clients in the meantime! Then there is no counterbalancing effect to the collective excitement any more, and the markets go from bubble to bubble.

Many asset managers recognize the problem, but it is not easy to find a solution. And this is the same for derivatives products, which allow you to play on the rise or the decrease of a stock or of an indicator without being obliged to buy the product itself, with a much lower investment, and therefore a high leverage. Derivatives are a good way to reduce risk for companies when they are associated with a physical transaction, but they are also a way to "speculate," to play on an asset without any connection to your business. And, to cover its risk, a hedging firm, if there is not another firm having exactly the contrary profile, needs to find a counter-party, who is precisely the financial speculator.

Even though it is difficult to prove it conclusively, it is likely that an excess of derivative products has a negative impact on the stability and efficiency of markets. A product that is useful in small amounts becomes "toxic" in large quantities! But, where to draw the line? This is a difficult question for regulators.

More generally, the financial world is probably the sector where the breakdown of ethical values we have already discussed has been the strongest. The "religion" of the market, and the belief that anything providing liquidity to the market is good, has led some players to forget common sense—like when Goldman Sachs packaged a failing product to allow a client to play against it, and then proceeded to sell it to other unsuspecting customers—or to commit outright frauds—like in the manipulation of interest rates or exchange rate fixing.

I do not believe that we can deal with this problem only through regulation. We need to have a better understanding of the problems with markets, and restore ethical standards for players. Also, even if the difference between normal business and dangerous specula-tion will never be clear, it is possible to penalize—through the tax system or otherwise—short-term gains versus benefits received from long-term investments. Such an evolution would obviously curtail the profit potential of the players, and would therefore be strongly opposed by them. Most of the debate on control and regulation takes place in New York, still the center of the financial world, and the control of financial powers over political campaigns in the US limits the independence of the legislators.

Susan. I was recently shocked to see the numbers that show the disparity between profits in the financial markets and those in the real economy that actually produces things, as Prometheus produced fire. (We won't look too closely about how he actually got it.) But you know a great deal more about this world than I do, and if you are worried about it, we all should be.

Still, I want to turn to an even greater worry. In "Rational Choice Before the Apocalypse," Jean-Pierre Dupuy gives a set of chilling arguments for the idea that the apocalypse is near.[13]

---

[13] Jean-Pierre Dupuy, 2008. "Rational Choice Before the Apocalypse." *Anthropoetics: The Journal of Generative Anthropology* 13: 3.

Even if one is less pessimistic than those two major scientists, it remains that our way of life is, in the long run, irremediably doomed. One would be hard-pressed to imagine how it could last more than another half-century. Many of us will no longer be here, but our children will. If we care about them, it is high time that we open our eyes to what awaits them.[14] Dupuy argues that several factors, but especially climate change, make action imperative. In view of this, what is the point of this kind of theoretical discussion? What can we do?

IS MANKIND GOING TO ITS DOOM?

Bertrand. Here the debate is not about the economic system, but about our way of life. The Club of Rome in the 1960s argued that economic growth could not last because of raw materials limitations. That proved to be both right and wrong.

Right because resources of a particular material are obviously finite, and we could well hit such limits. Wrong because new resources were found, but even more because the economy is not only growing but changing, and needs ever-changing resources. The development of physical goods is obviously constrained by the limited resources of the planet—unless some disappearing and very essential elements could be found in asteroids, which probably will be possible, although at a much higher cost. But the development of services and intangible goods has no physical limit. The switch of our economies toward services may make the forecasts of the Club of Rome irrelevant.

Another obstacle for mankind could be its own negative impact on the environment. The local pollution issues are well known, and horrific stories abound about China. In fact Beijing currently has fairly bad air quality, but not much worse than Pittsburg in the 1950s, or even London at some time. The Chinese should be able to solve them at some point, though it looks politically difficult to impose strict standards centrally, even in China.

Susan. I gather the problem in India is even worse.

Bertrand. And global issues like the ozone layer, the quality of the oceans, or of course climate change are much more difficult to solve, mainly because the world is not organized to deal with global issues. It is clear that the target of limiting global warming to 2°C will not be met. Mankind globally has the knowledge and the technological resources necessary to face such a warming. Bangladesh could very well survive if it adopted the polders technique of the Netherlands. But most likely, in the next forty years Bangladesh will have neither the financial resources nor the organizational and political skills necessary to face that challenge. So climatic migrations will probably be an issue, and we know that our modern world is—paradoxically—not very good at handling migrations.

The risk of the destruction of our planet by nuclear wars does exist, even if the nuclear dissuasion mechanism has functioned well for seventy years.

---

[14] Dupuy, "Rational Choice Before the Apocalypse," p. 2.

Susan. For sixty of those years we were dealing with instrumentally rational agents. I worry about those apocalyptic fundamentalists, and they are not all Salafists—there are quite a few (predominantly American) Christians among them.

Bertrand. Finally, the capability of mankind to control its own genetic evolution will be there in less than a century. Could that be put to wise usage, or will it trigger biological catastrophes?

Similarly, some scientists forecast that the computing capability of machines will reach the level of the brain in a few decades, and that real artificial intelligence—one that can train and develop itself—could become both a tool and a threat to mankind. All these elements warrant some degree of concern, and even anxiety about the future of the human race. But none should automatically result in an apocalypse. When Jean-Pierre Dupuy thinks that taking the catastrophe to be certain is the only way to avoid it, I have the opposite view. Outlining the challenges and the extraordinary potential that mankind has at hand, but also the very critical risks and responsibilities this entails, is for me a better approach.

Susan. I agree with you there. Kant has a doctrine of rational faith that argues that if something is necessary for us to act morally, it is rational for us to believe in it. I do not see how we can act morally—in this case, to prevent catastrophe—if we hold the catastrophe to be certain. So I don't.

Bertrand. There is obviously a choice to be made by our societies when we look at the future: either take a "prudent man" approach that tries to avoid any risk of being overwhelmed by our success, or a "risk-conscious entrepreneur" approach that bets on our ability to deal with this risk. The debate about the "precautionary principle" is about this choice. There are several ways to be cautious, either by drawing a map of forbidden territories, or by deciding to continue to explore everything while anticipating and addressing risks where they may appear.

History is never a guarantee for the future—as investment prospectuses say!—and there are different ways to look at our history. Many philosophers—including Dupuy—are seeing the Shoah as proof that there has not been any human progress, and that the human adventure is producing evil rather than good. I do not agree, but I accept the fact that science, technology, knowledge, and communication have not abolished the evil part of man, or guaranteed the success of good over evil.

Susan. I don't agree with Dupuy on that either; in fact, I think it is a blind and foolish argument. The Holocaust used modern technology in service of a pre-modern ideology. It's easy to list real, moral progress that has been made since the Enlightenment—starting with the abolition of torture and slavery, continuing to the emancipation of women, and so on. Obviously, this doesn't mean progress is inevitable; it lies in our hands. And it certainly doesn't mean we've abolished human evil.

Bertrand. Dupuy said that the religious and the sacred are never very far from our modern debates. I might prove him right if I confess that my preferred philosopher is the French Jesuit and anthropologist, Pierre Teilhard de Chardin. Writing in the 1940s and the 1950s, he was probably the best at merging the Christian faith with a very advanced view of modern science, including of course the theory of evolution, but also forecasting the potential of modern biology and the explosion of communication. His intuition is that, by establishing increasingly strong links between themselves, in the way individual cells cooperate (or fight) in the body, human beings are forming a new collective organism, that he calls the Noosphere, and he identifies this new ultimate unity with Christ.

I personally, in my years managing a large international company with 70,000 employees in seventy countries at the turn of the century, had the feeling that this Noosphere was really being built before my eyes, beyond all the difficulties and problems we have discussed. And that leads me to be more optimistic for our future.

But it may be time to go back to the main issue of our debate: Can free markets and ethical values live together? My answer is clearly: yes, but not without major efforts. We first have to refuse to take free markets as the idols of a new religion, and to view them only as necessary and useful tools. The spontaneous outcome of the market system has to be evaluated against our societal goals, and we must streamline the market process to try and avoid blatant contradictions.

Market regulation, business governance, as well as the tax system or other redistribution mechanisms, are ways to achieve this streamlining. They have to be carefully weighed against the loss of effectiveness created by heavy regulation, and should not stifle the uniquely dynamic thrust of a market economy. But regulation alone is not likely to do the job. It should be complemented by a societal effort to establish—or reestablish, if needed—ethical standards. We should not let complexity, technicalities, or an excessively legalistic attitude obfuscate the common sense ethics that should be the basis for a free and effective economic system. That may be our challenge—one that is even more difficult than achieving a balanced regulatory system.

Susan. We both agree that free markets create values, including values that neither of us want to embrace. Your solution, as I understand it, is that the market should retreat from being the religion it has become since the fall of communism, at the latest, and return to being simply the most efficient way of organizing commerce; then we can add on other, ethical views from different sources. The main difference between us is that I worry that the implicit value inherent in the allegedly neutral market—economic growth *über alles*—is simply more powerful at the moment than any of the other sources of value. Whatever messages children learn in schools, for example, pale before the messages they get from a popular culture that idolizes extravagant consumption. I don't think teachers, or university professors, if we're honest, stand a chance against that competition. I never, ever thought I would say this, but the greatest chance I see for a revitalization and propagation of ethical standards is coming from the present Vatican. But then I take Pope Francis' claim very seriously, that if we are to save the planet, and our souls at the same time, we will need to make very significant changes.

. . . .

COMMENTS AND DISCUSSION

In a classical philosophical spirit, Collomb and Neiman have produced a dialogue exploring their differences, and commonalities, on the ethos of the free market and its effects on public life. Though both lament the excessive narrowness and dominance of market values and priorities at present, Collomb tends to be more of a reformist about the free market, while Neiman is more deeply skeptical of its basic role in society and the norms governing it.

> *In what ways do free markets contribute to the prevalence of socially wasteful or otherwise harmful desires? How should we think about the idea of morally good consumer desires? And what kinds of legal, economic, and political measures might enable the market to better create and satisfy such desires?*

At the Society for Progress' second assembly, Frank observed that, in many cases, economists can offer us straightforward measures (e.g. taxing externalities) when the market fails to produce what we want it to produce. The deeper question, he suggests, arises when we think more fundamentally about why the market produces a particular profile of consumer desires in the first place, and what measures are available to change that profile. How do we shift consumer desires away from frivolous private consumption toward more socially valuable goods? Anderson observes here that the tendency of the market to indulge consumer fantasies is not objectionable in itself; the question is "What kind of imagination do people have? What kinds of things are they staking their happiness on? What kinds of dreams or ideals?" Anderson suggested that we ought to encourage preferences that are better shaped by relevant information about social consequences.

In thinking about a moral model of desires, Kitcher suggested that we might draw on Adam Smith's impartial spectator, seeking preferences that are better informed by a deep regard for diverse perspectives: "to see how my preferences *would* have been formed *if* I'd had more information, *if* I'd engaged more thoroughly with more points of view, and if I had used those as stimuli to imagination." On the subject of information, Mendiola and Rangan observed that firms themselves tend to be well positioned to educate consumers, given intimate knowledge of their products. But that requires marketing goods in a way that genuinely leverages relevant information. At the same time, Frank cautioned that the social failures of the free market are not only information problems; they are also collective action problems. The preference of individuals for expensive, status-promoting private goods over public investment requires interventions that realign private and public incentives.

Some contributors emphasized the importance of thinking about factors outside the market in shaping the values guiding market behavior. Pettit observed, for example, that the growing attention of companies to environmental values was the result of a grassroots, democratic movement rather than the reflections of companies about how to conduct their business. Perhaps one of the keys to checking an overly narrow market ethos is a robust democratic and civil sphere? Schmidtz observed, however, that one crucial virtue of markets is their capacity to create and satisfy many different kinds of desires. Thus, we should encourage the development of a critical public perspective on those desires rather than interventions that constrain the marketplace itself. We should exercise caution in pursuing government solutions even if the development of a public consciousness is important.

CHAPTER 4

DECISION PROCESSES AND VALUE ENDOGENEITY

JAMES G. MARCH

Abstract

Humans use reasons to shape and justify choices. In the process, trade-offs seem essential and often inevitable. But trade-offs involve comparisons, which are problematic both across values and especially over time. Reducing disparate values to a common metric (especially if that metric is money) is often problematic and unsatisfactory. Critically, it is not that values just shape choices, but that choices themselves shape values. This endogeneity of values makes an unconditional normative endorsement of modern decision-theoretic rationality unwise. This is a hard problem and there is no escaping the definition of good values, that is, those that make humans better. This removes the wall between economics and philosophy. If we are to adopt and enact this perspective, then greater discourse and debate on what matters and not just what counts will be useful and even indispensable.

I wish to anticipate and add to Kwame Anthony Appiah's excellent observations (in Chapter 5) about the complications of human action when confronted with what he so evocatively describes as a forest of reasons.

Human beings do many things rather automatically, hardly thinking at all; but most of the angst and difficulty of human life surrounds choice, situations in which the human actor sees multiple options available, any one of which is imaginable, but among which a choice must be made and justified. To carry out this task, humans use reasons that shape choices. These reasons, however, come in a bewildering mix of precepts involving innumerable conflicting or ambiguous values.

MAKING TRADE-OFFS

Modern decision theory seeks to bring order to this forest of reasons by associating consequences to actions (often only up to a probability function) and by associating values to consequences. The values are compared by making trade-offs, that is by determining how much of one consequence (or good) one would exchange for one unit of another consequence (or good). At the limit, this means establishing a cardinal utility function over consequences, but the rudimentary mechanism is the trade-off.

The difficulties in establishing sensible trade-offs are legendary. Markets, where they exist, help; but many important trade-offs do not find places in markets. How, for example, does an individual or a society make trades between the desire for years of life and the cost of medical care? When comparisons are between consequences now and consequences a hundred years from now, how can they be made? When comparisons are between consequences to oneself and consequences to a valued social institution, how can they be made? Although these difficulties can be imagined to be dealt with theoretically by heroic extensions of the maximize expected utility credo, it is hard to see such solutions as providing much immediate help to real human beings in real situations.

Since typical choices by humans involve many such trade-offs, the requirements for rational intelligence quickly swamp human capabilities. The issue becomes not what would be good in a perfect world but what would be good in ours? The most common criticisms of trade-off strategies in practice turn on the difficulties of making such calculations and on their presumed prejudice in favor of numbers, particularly money. Reducing disparate values to a common metric often seems impossible. And many of the more strongly held human values cannot easily be given monetary value and, as a result, tend to become inconsequential in trade-off calculations.

ENDOGENOUS VALUES

I share Appiah's skepticism about the feasibility of making trade-offs in real-world situations, but my immediate concern is somewhat different. Standard decision theory requires values that are not only comparable but are also exogenous to the process of choice. Action is taken in pursuit of values that are given by some unspecified prior process. Decision makers act upon values in making choices, but the decision-making process itself does not affect the values, only their realizations.

This exogeneity of values is a feature of the theory that seems manifestly inaccurate. The way we choose and the choices we make affect the values we have. I have often found myself talking to undergraduates about their future plans. A very common plan involves first getting an MBA, then becoming rich, and then dedicating oneself to doing good (e.g. helping the poor). After commending the thought, I often found myself commenting that the plan seriously underestimated the effect of getting an MBA and becoming rich on the urge toward, and definition of, doing good. It is nearly impossible to study economics or pursue wealth without affecting one's values. In particular, the socialization involved in pursuing an MBA and wealth almost certainly makes one less concerned with disparities in income and wealth.

Decision making shapes values as well as acts upon them; and thoughtful normative students of decision making are acutely conscious of the role of decision processes in determining desires. There are at least three distinct ways in which values are endogenous to decision process. First, values are affected by the difficulty in achieving them. Difficulty affects values as well as prices; and prices affect values as well as being affected by them. The process is not simple. The difficulty in achieving a value sometimes seems to increase the value, sometimes to decrease it. Competition sometimes stimulates humans to greater effort, sometimes leads them to devalue victory.

Second, values are affected by the process of choosing among them. For example, if we make explicit the de facto conflict between two strongly held values by trying to compare the relative importance of the two, we compromise the purity of each. If we convert the maxim that "thou shalt not kill" to the maxim "thou shall kill only when the expected value of doing so is greater than the alternative," we are likely to undermine the force of the feelings against killing.

Third, values are affected by the choices themselves. The choice of an alternative normally alters the perceived value of that alternative, particularly if the choice is difficult. In parallel, of course, choices may perturb the estimates of future consequences, much as a decision maker may adjust the estimates in defending a choice publicly. The choice of an action leads to increases both in the perceived likelihood of good consequences and also in the values associated with likely consequences. Thus, as a general rule, a posteriori assessments of an action will be more positive than a priori assessments, a phenomenon that not only should be anticipated in making choices but also affects considerably learning from experience.

The rationality that is encapsulated in modern decision theory and the economic theory of choice is, *prima facie*, value-neutral, an instrument of intelligence in the pursuit of any arbitrary values; and it would be blind not to acknowledge the various substantial contributions that have been made from that perspective. However, it would be foolish not to recognize that the endogeneity of values makes an unconditional normative endorsement of that rationality unwise.

ALTERNATIVE CHOICE MAKING

But is there any alternative? If I know that my values will be changed by making choices, how do I choose? How do I choose my values? The most obvious answer is that we specify a set of higher-level values in the names of which we choose our values, perhaps using the same techniques of rationality. It is not a bad answer, and much of the criticism of rational choice has come from advocates of various religious or social moral codes that might be seen as higher-level values.

A second possible answer is to choose an action such that the changes in values resulting from the choice and the process of making it confirm the action. For example, it is sometimes easy to anticipate that taking a particular action will transform values in such a way that the decision to go that route will be confirmed.

A third possible answer is to abandon the idea of trade-offs and maximizing expected value. It is reasonably well established that human beings are not reliably rational in a decision theory sense, and considerable contemporary effort is devoted to identifying situations in which they are and clarifying the ways in which they are not. So, the proposition that human beings make decisions in a decision-theoretic way is not, in general, true. What is less commonly discussed is whether human beings *ought* to make decisions that way. In most of the literature on decision making, it is taken as self-evident that the pursuit of a maximum expected value return constitutes optimal behavior. Such a posture is consistent with a long philosophic tradition, but it is by no means obvious. First, it is not clear that the *pursuit* of maximum expected value is the best way of *achieving* it. Second, it is not clear that making trade-offs among values is the best way of resolving conflicts among them. Rather conspicuously, humans make some choices by considering values sequentially, rather than simultaneously. They shift attention from one set of values to another, considering conflict only among evoked values. Rather than resolving conflict in values through some kind of analysis, they are likely to experience torment that is not reduced by making a choice. They engage in intrapersonal or interpersonal discourse and debate.

CHOICES AS SHAPING VALUES

Each of these answers is conceivable, but none of them truly confronts the reality of value endogeneity. You cannot choose a process for making a value-based choice without choosing among values. Once it is recognized that values are shaped by the process of pursuing them, it is no longer easy to imagine a value-neutral theory of choice. The endogeneity of values makes the design of decision processes and institutions inescapably concerned with the construction of values, and thereby with definitions of good values. Such a recognition is inimical to modern thinking, which vociferously maintains that the evaluation of values is outside the purview of theories of choice, that the proper role of economics is to facilitate the achievement of subjectively valued states, neither to question nor to affect the values. *De gustibus non est disputandum.*

Insofar as values are shaped by the decision-making process and by its outcomes, the process of choice must be evaluated, in part, by its contribution to the emergence of good values, by the extent to which it helps make humans better. Decision processes comprise elementary components of the institutional foundation of human character.

It is, consequently, irresponsible to advocate a decision process without attending to its value-shaping consequences. The idea is terrifying, for it removes the wall constructed by modern thinking between economics and philosophy; but it might possibly lead to approaching choices in ways that would make the world and the individuals inhabiting it better—if, of course, we can come to an understanding of what is "better."

It is a thought particularly relevant to the design of contemporary political institutions, which might come to be seen not simply as instruments for aggregating citizen desires, but also as mechanisms for creating better desires. It is a perspective that traces its origins at least as far back as Aristotle and has persistently been abandoned as intractable or impossibly authoritarian.

ASSESSING VALUES

All value systems are embedded in social norms, practices, and institutions from which they gain their commitments, legitimacy, and authority; and those norms, practices, and institutions determine the characters and values of a society and its members. But can we legitimately distinguish among such value systems in terms of their virtues? Alternatively, can we discover ways of making individuals and societies better without knowing precisely what "better" is? And if we cannot, can we legitimately choose among decision processes that shape the values?

It is clear that all societies do so, but modern democratic societies do so gingerly. They endorse variety in values but seek to establish a changing and often ambiguous set of central tendencies that define "goodness." The central, classical decision processes for simultaneously shaping values and acting on them in a democracy or among independent adults are discourse and debate around the forest of reasons that Appiah identifies, as well as the personal and institutional torment associated with them. Discourse and debate (and political processes built around them) manifestly have their own weaknesses as instruments of value construction and choice; and it is certainly possible to conclude that in some situations processes involving maximum expected value rationality have value consequences preferable to other processes. Such a conclusion is possible, but it is not axiomatic; and it clearly involves assessing the value-shaping consequences of the process as well as its value realization.[1]

---

[1] I am grateful for conversations with Kwame Anthony Appiah and Johan P. Olsen. Comments and discussion related to this essay, which is a companion to the one by Kwame Anthony Appiah, appear at the end of Chapter 5.

CHAPTER 5

···

THE FOREST OF REASONS

···

KWAME ANTHONY APPIAH

Abstract

As business decisions and actions spill over into society in ways that arouse our concern, it is useful to explore how philosophy might offer an alternative perspective to consequentialism. This chapter reviews the conventional approach and the risks of "maximizing." It submits that the narrowly consequential approach provides us with practical reasons for action but neglects normative or moral reasoning. Reasons for doing might be based on rational choice, but reasons for being (existential reasons) and feeling (sentimental reasons) are guided by moral choice. That these last two may not be "commensurable" does not make them less important. Treating everything as tradable with everything else may be bad for the soul and society. We have moral reasons to feel and to be certain ways, as well as to do certain things. It is time to pay greater heed to Jim March's long-standing challenge to consequentialist decision theories.

If I ask you whether you prefer that it rains or that it snows tomorrow, the likelihood is that you will either rank one of these possibilities above the other or be indifferent between them. If you refuse to say either that you prefer one to the other or that you don't mind, it will probably be because you are waiting for information about something else. For how you rank these possibilities—snow versus rain—will reasonably depend on what else you think is going to happen tomorrow. You might be indifferent between rain and snow in London if you thought you were going to be in the Bahamas tomorrow, but prefer the snow, because it's less drenching, if you thought you were going to be walking around in the city. So creating a fuller and fuller picture of the outcomes I ask you to consider, I can get a richer and richer picture of the structure of your preferences.

It is possible, I suppose, but surely unlikely, that you prefer rain to snow intrinsically (though Emerson admired "the frolic architecture of the snow" and Whitman channeled "The Voice of the Rain," so I cannot be sure).[1] The main reasons people care

---

[1] Ralph Waldo Emerson, "The Snow Storm," <http://www.poetryfoundation.org/poem/175142>; Walt Whitman, "The Voice of the Rain," <http://www.whitmanarchive.org/published/LG/1891/poems/349>.

about such things have to do with their consequences. Rain cleans the sidewalks, clears the air; that gentle susurration helps you sleep. Snow sullies the sidewalks, looks pretty until it turns to muck; when you walk on it, your steps make a pleasant crunching sound. And some of these consequences you care about intrinsically—in a small way, the pleasant crunch, the pretty look—others, again (the sleep, the clear air) because they contribute to your health, which you may care about intrinsically. It's natural, in other words, to think of your preferences as reflecting the product of two factors: your ranking of certain fundamental features of the world and your beliefs about whether they obtain in a certain situation.

It is natural, too, to think that some of your beliefs are stronger than others. So that what goes into your evaluation of the question "Snow versus rain?" is not just whether you think you will be in the Bahamas or in New York, but how likely these possibilities are.

By radically idealizing and extending these thoughts, you can come to the picture of human psychology that underlies modern decision theory. You may not think you can rank any two states of the world right now, but by analyzing each state of the world in terms of the features you care about, we should, in the ideal, be able to complete your preference ranking, assigning to every proposition its proper place, above, below, or alongside each other proposition. By that route we can find a utility function that reflects your complete preferences and a subjective probability function that represents the relative strengths of your beliefs. Among your options for action you will pick the one that has the highest expected utility, which is the sum of the utilities of its outcomes, weighted by their probabilities: this is the available action that is most preferred.

Both the utility and the probability functions must obey certain formal constraints. So far as form goes, intuitive constraints on the coherence of our preferences—such as that they be transitive—along with a number of technical demands, allow one to prove representation theorems that show that a person with rational preferences can be represented as having degrees of belief that have the shape of a probability function. But the standard decision-theoretic picture says nothing about what our utilities and subjective probabilities should be, except that they should be coherent: representable, that is, by a utility function and a probability function that satisfy certain structural demands. There are many controversies about exactly what the right formal constraints are—for example, should we or should we not allow for risk-aversion?—and in settling these controversies for ourselves we settle upon a particular idealized model of decision.

But reasonableness demands more than mere coherence. If you're standing in front of a red screen with your eyes open, it can hardly be reasonable to believe that you are looking at something green—unless you also believe that there is something currently wrong with your color perception. Someone, in such circumstances, who says, "Yes, it looks red, and there's nothing wrong with my eyes, so far as I know, but why should I think it *is* red?" is as irrational as someone who prefers eating this apple to eating that orange and eating that orange to eating this banana, but prefers eating this banana to that apple—which is ruled out by the formal demand for transitivity of preferences. Experience and argument provide reasons to believe things that it would, therefore, be unreasonable to ignore.

This is all quite familiar. What is less familiar is the thought that our subjective preferences—preferences that are subjective in the sense that they are the preferences of a particular subject—can also be irrational even if they meet the structural demands of coherence. But there are philosophical arguments, going back at least to Plato, for the view that desires are only reasonable if they are responses to things worth wanting: things, that is, that there is some reason to want. Or, as Elizabeth Anscombe put it, in *Intention*, when someone says they desire something, "the question 'What do you want that for?' arises—until at last we reach the desirability characterization, about which 'What do you want that for?' does not arise."[2] A desire that can't meet this test is one we shouldn't act on. It is not one that gives us a reason to do anything. And, if that is so, it is one we should both seek to eradicate, if we can, and, in any case, seek not to act on.

Reading David Hume and some of his successors has persuaded many people this cannot be right. They interpret his observation that "reason is and ought only to be the slave of the passions" as entailing that reasons have no place in shaping our fundamental desires.[3] A reasonable person, many modern thinkers believe, can desire anything at all, provided the pattern of her desires meets the structural constraints. That view has been the subject of a good deal of critique recently, and there are theories around now that treat desire, as Anscombe did, as something constrained by reasons in the sort of way that epistemologists conceive of belief as constrained by evidence, that is, by reasons for belief.

For example: if something is valuable, Tim Scanlon has argued, it must have other properties that give you reasons to adopt certain attitudes toward it. He calls this a "buck-passing" account of value because it passes the buck in the explanation of value to those "other properties."[4] On such a view, things are valuable because of the reasons they provide: reasons for wanting to do things, reasons, that is, for desires of exactly the sort that Humeans have thought impossible. But values can give us reasons not just for desires—for wanting to do and to have things—but also for feelings and for other states as well. I promise to meet you at the café. That I promised you gives me a reason to do what I promised. That makes my showing up a good thing to do. The novel is interesting. That gives me a reason to read it. It makes it a good novel, good, that is, for doing what we do with novels, good for reading. Courage is admirable. That gives me a reason to respect the courageous, perhaps to be or become courageous myself. It makes being courageous good. The buck-passing view is one that makes value derive from something deontic: having a reason. So, to

    [2] G. E. M. Anscombe, 2000. *Intention*, 2nd edition. Cambridge, MA: Harvard University Press, 78.
    [3] David Hume, 1896. *A Treatise of Human Nature*. Edited by L. A. Selby-Bigge. Oxford: Clarendon Press. <http://oll.libertyfund.org/titles/342#Hume_0213_877>.
    [4] Tim M. Scanlon, 1998. *What We Owe to Each Other*. Cambridge, MA: Harvard University Press.

put the matter in an older idiom, the right here is prior to the good. I will call the large family of views that claim, instead, that the good comes first, so that action aims at the good, consequentialist.

The buck-passing account appears to have some virtues. (That is, it seems to have features that provide reasons for adopting it.) One, it has been argued, is that it solves a problem that consequentialists should find challenging. If actions aim at the good—so that it is value that gives rise to reasons, not the other way round—then it seems that we always have reason to seek as much good as possible. How could we have reason to seek more value rather than less? This commitment to maximization seems to have unpalatable consequences, however. If friendship is a good, then shouldn't we be happy to sacrifice one friend to get more friendship from others? But on the buck-passing view, as Jussi Suikkanen has argued, we start with the reasons

> a particular friend . . . provides us with. If these are not reasons for bringing about as many of these relations with alike objects as possible, and yet are strong enough reasons to act in certain ways, the object can indeed be valuable, yet not one that is valued by maximization.[5]

The underlying thought here, though, is one that the consequentialist can absorb. There is no reason to think that the good of friendship must be conceived in a way that generates this problem. Perhaps what is good is to have a manageable number of friends, whose friendship you can nurture and sustain. And to have a friend is to be committed to someone in such a way that their good matters for you more than it otherwise would: so that, unless you have some other reason for favoring someone else (she might be a member of your family), it will be good to attend to the friend's welfare over that of the stranger. This is part of the more complex truth that we expressed misleadingly by saying that friendship was a good. On this view it can be very bad to dump a friend, even if the result will be to acquire two new friends: for, before they are your friends, they matter less to you than your existing friend does. So it will be explicable in terms of the goods of friendship why you cannot dump one friend to get two; and also why it is not good to have more than a manageable number of friends. (A fact that should probably be explained to the programmers at Facebook, who appear to be tempted by a maximizing view.)

The maximizing character of consequentialism has other results that are not so easy to escape, however. In general, in our actual lives, we do not think that we ought always to be about maximizing *anything*. Can I be maximizing the good by sitting here writing this essay? (Even if it were going to turn out to be a very fine one, once improved by more conversation with Jim March.) There are, after all, other things that I could be doing that would surely do more good: I could be down in the inner city working at a food kitchen, writing checks to Oxfam, vaccinating children in Peru. It is precisely such

---

[5] Jussi Suikkanen, 2005. "Reasons and Value: In Defence of the Buck-Passing Account." *Ethical Theory and Moral Practice* 7(5): 530. He raises the problem for consequentialism at p. 520.

consequences of one member of the class of consequentialisms—the utilitarianisms—that had led their exponents, such as Peter Singer and Peter Unger, to complain that most of us are simply not doing most, if any, of the acts we ought to be doing. And part of what they are drawing our attention to is that we could set out to open up to ourselves options for doing more good than most of us allow ourselves in our ordinary lives. I do not think the fact that these claims offend common sense rules them out. And there might, in any case, be other substantial goods that weigh in a consequentialist balance in ways that would allow us to reject them. So I mention these disputes not to try to settle them, but for two other motives.

First, to show that the question of whether reasons or goods have explanatory priority is not easily settled. And second, to bring out, as these two examples do, some of the difficulties of framing the right questions.

The first challenge, for example, shows that identifying a practical value—something the achievement of which give us a reason to perform an act that realizes that value—often requires some care. Friendship is not some substance whose quantity we are trying to increase. We were misled there by an unhelpful abstraction. The same sort of error occurs, perhaps, when someone argues that we should create more people in order to create more total utility. Utility is not a substance we are trying to maximize, either. It is a feature of people—actually existing people—we should take into account in our treatment of them.

The second challenge reminds us that, in many situations, it will be hard to be sure both whether we have considered all the relevant goods or all the available options and whether we have correctly identified what all the consequences will be. But this is not a problem unique to the consequentialist. For it will generally be hard to assure ourselves that we have identified and weighed correctly all the relevant reasons; and the buck-passer needs to identify her options with as much care as the consequentialist.

Whether you think goods account for reasons or reasons account for goods (or hold, as Joseph Raz does, that both reasons and values can be explanatorily fundamental), I will assume that we can generally restate claims made in one vocabulary—reasons, values—in the other. So in this essay I will feel free to use both ways of speaking. On either view, we should view our ethical lives as fundamentally a matter of responding to the many reasons that there are for doing, feeling, and being this that or the other.

When it comes to moral action the relevant reasons are reasons for doing things, of course. But if there are so many sources of reasons, so many values, you might wonder how they all come together. Here is one possibility: each reason addresses the will. And it either weighs for or weighs against an available option for action. There are two features of a reason for action then: its weight and its direction. If that were all there was to it, then there would be some reason for supposing our reasons for action were guaranteed to be coherent. Take weights against as negative numbers and weights in favor as positive numbers. Sum the weights of all the relevant reasons for doing A. You would have the all-things-considered strength of the reasons to do it (if the sum is positive) or to abstain (if it is not). (At net zero you are rationally free to do as you please—or perhaps, like Buridan's ass, you will dither.)

Weight, of course, is only one possible metaphor. A consideration in favor of an action might not exert a determinate pressure. And reasons can relate to action in more than one way. Joseph Raz has argued that some reasons exclude others, rather than outweighing them: he calls them "exclusionary reasons." (His example: if I am tired I can decide not to review the considerations pro and con making a certain investment, the opportunity for which will disappear in a few hours. That I am too tired to make a reasonable decision excludes these other reasons from consideration. If this is rational, then a reason can rule another one out as a basis of action without outweighing it.)[6] Or we can consider that in a certain factual situation, one duty overrides another, without giving weights to either of them.[7]

That my promise to meet you for dinner loses out to the fact that I can save a child from drowning doesn't entail that each has a weight and the second weighs more: after all, the metaphor of weight might suggest that we could always ask how many times a certain consideration weighs more than another, and cases like this suggest that that question often doesn't make sense. Of course, it would be natural to say that saving the child is more important than keeping the promise. That requires that we can at least order reasons for action, some being more important than (or equally important as) others. But since reasons can operate together, we will need not only to rank reasons, we will need also to know how to combine them: and knowing that reasons rank in order A, B, C, D doesn't tell you what to do when the choice is between A and D and B and C. Assigning them weights—a real number function unique up to a linear transformation—would indeed solve this problem, but so could a variety of other formal devices.

But what we feel and what we are is not something we do. Our sentiments and our characters are certainly profoundly *shaped* by what we do. And we may have reasons for wanting to feel and be a certain way. But that doesn't get you to doing anything yet, since you will not in general know how to affect your emotional responses and your character. Neither, unlike our actions, is directly subject to the will. Elizabeth Anderson once wrote:

> My provisional account of how goods differ in kind is ... that they differ in kind if they are properly valued in different ways.... Ideals tell individuals how they should value different things ... beautiful things are worthy of appreciation, rational beings of respect, sentient beings of consideration, virtuous ones of admiration, convenient things of use.[8]

---

[6] Joseph Raz, 1975. *Practical Reason and Norms*. Oxford: Oxford University Press, 37.

[7] English idiom may mislead here: we speak of "weighing a reason" whenever we consider one. It does not follow that weighing a reason is literally a matter of assessing its relative weight.

[8] Elizabeth Anderson, 1993. *Value in Ethics and Economics*. Cambridge, MA: Harvard University Press, 10–11.

Perhaps we would want coherence among the values aimed at the same thing. But there's no obvious reason why we should have coherence among the values (or dimensions of value) that address, say, our feelings and our actions. For, to put the matter in a way more suitable for a buck-passing view, beauty gives us reasons to attend to things, perhaps to protect things worth attending to. But that rarely brings it into conflict with kindness, which directs us to treat people in ways attentive to their well-being. Perhaps beautiful things can be used unkindly; perhaps kindness is itself beautiful. But there is no general argument for thinking that beauty and kindness need to compete in the space of action, because beauty is not primarily directed at action at all. Similarly, if "respect" is an attitude toward people, it will not generally itself entail that we do anything in particular to them. Respect is a matter of taking into account practically salient facts about someone. It is, therefore, most likely to require us to be attentive to certain features of other people. It will be facts about those features that give us reasons to act—facts, say, about pleasure and pain, desire and aversion, ambitions and interests. But what we do will reflect our respect not constitute it. So even if there is reason to hope that our practical reasons fit together like weights, because not all reasons are reasons for action, we do not have an immediate argument that practical reasons—reasons for doing things—will fit together for the same reason with sentimental reasons—reasons for feeling things.

By "objectivism" about normative questions I will mean the view that they have right and wrong answers. Objectivism entails that it is possible for someone to be fully convinced that something that is, in fact, right is wrong, and vice versa. Objectivists believe their practical values are coherent in the sense that there is always at least one thing that one is permitted to do (including, of course, just doing nothing). Practical values— moral, prudential, personal—are meant to guide action. They wouldn't be much use for that if they sometimes told us that there was nothing we could permissibly do. For, in general (and counting what we call "doing nothing" as always one of the options) what we face in a situation of choice is a set of options one of which we must perform. But there need not be just one thing a person is required to do: indeed, we would not be in difficulty if we were required to do one but no particular one of a large class of possible actions. That would leave us open options, consistent with all the practical values, and we could make our own choices, in whatever way Buridan's ass should have done. There is no need for practical reason to give us all the answers. Equally, we could deal with many situations in which there is nothing one is forbidden to do, in particular when one has a very limited range of options, all of which are permissible. A system of values with that feature is no obstacle to action. What *would* be impractical is a system that sometimes (or, even worse, always) said that all paths were forbidden.

Still, we might be able to work pretty well with a system of reasons that mostly gave us guidance in the form of permitting us a number of actions, requiring a few, forbidding others, but occasionally led us to a rational impasse: declaring nothing permissible or forbidding and requiring the same thing. On anti-objectivist views, in which there is, in general, no guarantee of a right or wrong answer to normative questions, this will always be a possibility. I favor approaches that are not anti-objectivist in this way, but I do not want to discuss this issue here. I will proceed, without argument, in a broadly objectivist way, while remaining agnostic about the metaphysics of morals and the question why objectivism is the better option. And much of what I have to say would, I suspect, survive some moderate forms of anti-objectivism.

THE DIVERSITY OF REASONS

In making our choices we respond to what we take to be valuable, to the practical reasons of which we are aware. What is valuable need not be very grand. Scratching an itch. Satisfying your hunger. Enjoying a book. Meeting a friend. But not all reasons are practical. Normative reasons are, as I said, reasons not just for doing, but also for being and feeling things. (Typical examples. Doing: a reason for action, say, to return a loan. Being: an existential reason, say, not to be a bigot. Feeling: a sentimental reason, say, to resent an act of cruelty.) And they have strengths. The stronger a reason for action the more firmly it directs the will toward doing that action. So too, *mutatis mutandis*, for what I am calling existential and sentimental reasons.

In cataloging the reasons people offer for doing what they do—their practical reasons—Tom Nagel has argued that there are "five fundamental types of value."[9] First, there are obligations to others that derive from a "special relation" or a "deliberate undertaking." These are exemplified in the mutual (if distinct) obligations of parents to children, doctors to patients, citizens to their countries. These are usually agent-relative reasons, in the technical sense that the principles that underlie them make essential reference to facts about the agent. A doctor's obligations are to *her* patients.

Second, there are general rights that "restrict what others may do to their possessor." Each of us has general duties that derive from rights of this kind, such as our obligation not to assault others. This is a negative duty. But some of these duties are positive—to return to someone what's hers—and the restrictions here limit what we can abstain from doing for someone.

A third sort of value derives from the welfare of human beings, something that has come to be expressed by technical notions of utility in economics. That I can make many others better off by doing something counts in its favor, even if these others are people to whom I have no special obligations, even if I am not duty bound to do so. And, it's worth observing, considerations of my own welfare or the welfare for those to whom I am connected, may matter for me in a special agent-relative way.

---

[9] Thomas Nagel, 1979. "The Fragmentation of Value." In *Mortal Questions*. New York: Cambridge University Press, 129–30. Though he doesn't mention it, I'd like to relativize this categorical system to people of our own and similar cultural backgrounds; by which I mean only to say that there may be considerations brought to bear in other cultures that do not fit naturally on this list. I do not mean to be suggesting that these considerations only matter for people of our cultural background. Either our way of thinking is correct, in which case it would be correct for others; or, if it is not correct for others, it needs supplementation or revision. Or so I believe.

Fourth, there are what Nagel calls "perfectionist ends or values." For these he offers by way of example, "the intrinsic value of scientific discovery, of artistic creation, of space exploration, perhaps." And the final source of value he mentions is "commitment to one's own projects or undertakings."[10]

These different sources of reasons for action can each raise complex issues. Our commitments, to begin with the last of the five kinds of value, do not naturally seem to fit into a single plan. Perhaps I am a novelist *and* a philosopher. These projects require different things of me, and it seems odd to claim that I must have some way of fixing standards for deciding which of them is most pressing when. Of course, in the end, I will be doing things at any time that contribute to one or the other or neither of them. But why should we insist that I have at every moment judged one or the other more important? Nor, to turn to perfectionist ends, is it reasonable to assume that there is some sensible way of deciding whether science or art is at any moment the more demanding mistress or master.

Similar difficulties attend the project of rationally balancing the other sources of value. Obligations can conflict in particular situations, whether they derive from general rights or special relations. Each of us has rights to privacy and to security: plausibly, one cannot secure complete privacy for people, in the modern world of terrorism and other forms of criminality, while also keeping them safe from wrongful harm. My psychiatrist owes me confidentiality but has a duty of care to everyone my actions threaten with wrongful harm. That these values conflict in particular situations doesn't entail that we cannot weigh them against each other and decide that one or the other is more important in this situation or that. Conflict is compatible with comparability.

But in many cases people think they know what they need to know to bring confidentiality or harm to bear and they still don't know what to do. Neither is more important than the other, in these circumstances, but that doesn't make it okay that we should just choose one. How can that be? If there was simply a scale of overall value and each good was relevant because it weighed on that single scale, then, if we had enough information about the particular situation, we should always be able to identify what we must do: namely something that weighs at least as high as anything else on that single scale. This thought—that, once the facts are in, reason always determines just what we may do—would offend both those who think that our values are not always commensurable and those who think that reason requires us to do the best thing we can. For if there are any supererogatory acts, then sometimes there is a better thing to do and we are not morally bound to do it.

As for utility, human welfare has many dimensions, and it is not obvious that they can all be weighed with a single measure. The "capabilities" approach, developed by Amartya Sen and Martha Nussbaum, suggests that what is of fundamental importance in the moral domain is our ability to engage in the wide range of human functionings,

---

[10] Thomas Nagel, 1979. *Mortal Questions*. Cambridge: Cambridge University Press.

defined as: "the achieved states of being and activities of an individual, such as being in good health, being well-sheltered, moving about freely, being employed, or being educated."[11] As its proponents concede, these different functionings are not easily traded for each other, so that a theory of this sort will produce only partial orderings of individual or collective welfare. Nor, once we have weighed my welfare, is it obvious generally how to integrate it with other considerations.

Let me add, finally, in this list of challenges we face in making our choices, that most actual people are motivated by a concern for self-respect, for honor and the respect of others, in ways that can conflict with virtue, welfare, and moral duty. Many, of course, are also actuated by malice or envy or vengeance or forms of irrational hostility or unjustified contempt. There are, that is, considerations that actually motivate people other than value, and the challenge of escaping them, if we think we should, does not seem to be met by simply attending to the values on Nagel's list.

WHY INCOMMENSURABILITY APPEARS

Kant argued at the beginning of modern moral philosophy that

> In the kingdom of ends everything has either a *price* or a *dignity*. What has a price can be replaced by something else as its *equivalent*; what on the other hand is above all price and therefore admits of no equivalent has a dignity.[12]

This idea has been subjected to a couple of centuries of commentary, and remains difficult to understand. But it can seem to follow from ideas like these that if each human being is beyond price, then nothing could weigh in the balance against the welfare of one such being, save, perhaps, the welfare of others.

This thought leads to a different way of thinking about the relations among reasons. They can be, in a formulation made familiar by Rawls, lexically ordered. That is, we can think that reasons of one kind—the dignity-regarding reasons, for example—must all be satisfied before we even begin to think about those of another—pleasure-regarding reasons, say. This gives us reason to suppose that some classes of reasons matter more than others not because they weigh more, but because they should be considered first. The view that rights must first be satisfied, before we turn to considerations of welfare, for example, need not be the view that rights have infinite weight: it can be the view that you do not have to consider utility if rights settle the matter. Elizabeth Anscombe once said, apropos of murder, that "the strictness of the prohibition has as its point *that you are not to be tempted by fear or hope of consequences*."[13] Her thought was that, granted

---

[11]   Wiebke Kuklys, 2005. *Amartya Sen's Capabilities Approach.* New York: Springer, 21.

[12]   Immanuel Kant, 1998. *Groundwork of the Metaphysics of Morals.* Edited and translated by Mary Gregor. New York: Cambridge University Press, 42.

[13]   G. E. M. Anscombe, 1958. "Modern Moral Philosophy." *Philosophy* 33(124): 1–19.

that shooting someone would be murder, it is settled that you must not do it. You can stop thinking about all the other reasons for and against the shooting. The case is closed.

I am not endorsing this thought. I am just offering the first of a number of grounds that have been offered for doubting the view that all considerations relate to one another as weights do, that they are commensurable.

Here is a second. Nagel's anatomy of values focuses more on what we do than on what we are: but, as I have said, many of us think that a decent life requires attention to the virtues, to being a person of a certain kind in ways that go beyond our actions. A virtuous person thinks and feels in a certain way as well as doing what is right and avoiding what is wrong. We thought that if the practical reasons worked like weights they would help us in the way we need them to: they would fix what we should do. But there could be a separate system of reasons that determined what we should feel, and while what we do and we feel must fit together to some extent, as we shall see, sentimental reasons need only, in the first instance, cohere with one another in a certain way. What I mean by this is best explained by way of cases.

The fact that you have deliberately stepped on my toe counts in favor of my resenting you. That you have apologized counts against. So should I resent you? One way of settling the matter would be to say that the strength of the reason for resenting you determines the level of resentment that is appropriate, and the strength of the reason against reduces that level by some amount. So reasons for and against resentment could have positive and negative weights, too, addressing our sentiments as practical reasons address the will. I pick this case because it is one where the thought is not especially plausible. It would be more natural, I think, to suppose that your apology cancels the reason I had for resentment, rather than outweighing it. But a system of reasons for resentment in which some cancel others is coherent, in the relevant sense, if it fixes whether or not and how much you should resent someone. It doesn't need to do so by providing weights.

We have many sentiments—resentment, but also fear, love, amusement, respect and self-respect, and many more—and our sentimental responses are, indeed, responses: we have reasons for them. There are constraints of coherence among the reasons for any particular sentiment, but also surely constraints on the rational relations of the sentiments with one another. Perhaps love requires respect or resentment is incompatible with liking. But I do not think we need to suppose that a person who has the best practical reason, say, to help you in trouble, cannot also have the best reason to resent you, and some reasons to dislike you as well. So one way in which values can be incommensurable, in a sense, is that they are addressed to different kinds of response.

I want to mention a final source of the appearance of incommensurability, which is epistemic. As our discussion so far has suggested, we dwell in a forest of reasons. They are multiple, diverse, and addressed to different aspects of our responsiveness to the human world. Given this richness it is not surprising that we do not see what reasons require, because assembling and then weighing, or prioritizing or cancelling the relevant reasons, and the like, is a massively complex task. Sometimes we will misjudge the weights of reasons, fail to see which are lexically prior, forget that some have been cancelled or overridden, ignore some altogether. As we struggle with these problems it may strike us at one moment that we should do or feel one thing, and then, at another, that we should feel or do something else, and then it may feel that we cannot see what to do at all. We might come in such a case to misdescribe a situation in which the reasons we have do in fact determine an answer that we cannot discern for a situation in which there is no answer.

Almost everything I have said so far is controversial. But if, like me, you have a picture of our normative situation something like this, you will be skeptical that a reasonable person would be able to come to have a set of preferences that takes account of all the relevant considerations of value and that ranks all her options in every possible situation so that each of them is, all things considered, better, worse, or of the same value as every other. For as we saw, one might doubt that any of these sources of value has an algorithm for mapping considerations of its kind into its domain, or for supposing that, were it possible, we could then adjudicate competing claims between one domain and another.

That might be true, even given infinite time or computational resources, so far as I can see. But it is obviously true in the actual circumstances of human beings, where decisions need to be made in real time, in response to limited evidence, and with modest rational capacities. I think it is clear that the domain of value has a great deal of structure and that we can often produce partial rankings that are sufficient, when we face actual choices, to guide us to a satisfactory resolution. When the range of relevant considerations is narrow, our information relatively solid, and our options few, we can no doubt sometimes assimilate all the relevant value considerations and bring them appropriately to bear. Let me call situations like these occasions of manageable judgment.

But getting to a manageable occasion is usually, itself, an achievement. You don't just happen to have solid information. You went looking for it. You avoided making promises that would have burdened you with further considerations. You picked friends and associates who do not require you to choose between loyalty and the law. You developed habits of feeling that keep you from wanting to do what is, for one reason or another, wrong. You avoided temptation by deciding not to own a gun or wander into the red light district. You paid your taxes, and helped elect a government that would discharge some of your obligations to the world's poor. And you trained yourself to recognize the morally relevant features of the situation.

And yet the dominant models of rational choice in the contemporary social sciences—the decision-theoretic picture—have long supposed a very different picture. Here is Jim March's apt description of it:

Rational Choice

Almost all modern theories of rational choice associate proper choice with two major foundations:

(1) Some assessment of the likely future consequences of a particular choice.
(2) Some assessment of the subjective values associated with possible future consequences.

The idea is to pursue choices that are expected to have good consequences in terms of the subjective values. The values are presumed to be held by the actor and to be exogenous to the process of decision making. In conventional economic theories of choice, an actor is enjoined to assign a cardinal value (utility) and a probability or likelihood to each possible outcome, and to act by maximizing expected value.

Ways of using such a framework to make decisions have been considerably refined and extended in the past 100 years, and it has become a central part of decision-making litany. In practice, neither the utility nor the likelihood of a possible outcome is trivial to establish. Considerable effort has been devoted to improving the probability estimates of the likelihood of possible outcomes, with substantial success in some domains.

There has been less energy devoted to determining utilities. Commonly, theorists of choice take preferences as given and explicitly leave any discussion of values to moral philosophers. The division of labor is not complete, however, since most forms of decision theory presume values that are consistent and comparable; and useful techniques have been developed for establishing consistency and comparability.

In particular, decision makers are advised to determine the "trade-offs" among values. Thus, they ask: "How much of Value A would I be willing to give up in order to gain one unit of Value B?" They are encouraged to determine the relative importance of alternative values, as much as possible to rate outcomes by some metric that sustains consistent choices.[14]

If the story I began with is anything like correct, the process of producing the subjective values associated with outcomes—the process that these theorists have often left to the philosophers—is one that some philosophers think they have reason to deny that they can complete. This will be for many reasons, but one of them is that they believe certain values are incommensurable. In a familiar example, a person can face a *Sophie's choice*. She can find herself in a situation where two powerful duties—to secure the lives of one's children and to treat them equally—cannot be satisfied together. And she can think, rightly, that there is no ranking of these duties that determines what she should do, nor any reason to think that they are equally important in the circumstances, so that she can opt rationally, without moral loss, to do what is required by one or to do what is required by the other. You might think that Sophie is faced with the sort of situation that I said at the start no usable theory of practical reason could accept: one where every path is forbidden.

Sartre famously discussed a case where one of his students had to choose between his duty to his mother and his duty to his country in wartime. The man came to ask his philosopher professor for advice. After filling in many of the details of the situation, Sartre says that he could only tell him, "You are free, so choose; in other words, invent. No general code of ethics can tell you what you ought to do; there are no signs in the world."[15]

---

[14] Personal communication with Jim March, August 2015.

[15] Jean Paul Sartre, 2007. *Existentialism is a Humanism*. Edited by John Kulka, translated by Carol Macomber. New Haven, CT: Yale University Press, 33.

Part of the difficulty that the student faced was that he wasn't sure about whether joining the resistance would do any good. But even if that had been clear, Sartre could have told him the same thing. For Sartre had a picture in which deciding for one option could *make* it the right option. This is something I am inclined to deny.

But even if all values were commensurable—so that a magical algorithm resolved all the relevant considerations—or there was no magic algorithm but we could always make a choice the right one by opting for it, there would still be cases where we cannot satisfy both of two values that are in conflict in the particular situation. And when that happened, even if there were such a rational mechanism for resolving the tension, it might be right to say that the decent person would feel the moral pressure of regret at not having been able to meet both values or even of guilt at having done what was, all things considered, the right thing.

The point, more abstractly, is that even if reasons for action cohere, we have reasons for things other than action. And we can, like Sophie, have reasons, even the best reason, for doing something that we also have reasons, the best reasons, for regretting.

Given that this is so, there is a further problem we might consider about the rational choice paradigm Jim March has laid out so elegantly. Here is how he puts that problem:

> Our problem
>
> The remarkable thing, however, is that almost no attention has been devoted to a parallel question: How does expected value decision making affect the values associated with possible future consequences? The present essay examines some aspects of that question. It proceeds from the assumption that decision making is not simply an opportunity to pursue prior values. It is also an occasion for shaping values. Thus, values are not only the premises of action but also one of its products. Insofar as decision procedures are evaluated normatively, they should be assessed partly in terms of their impact on values.
>
> More specifically, this essay argues that making explicit trade-offs among values can compromise the values over time. The argument depends on a simple assertion: The deep values of human life are inconsistent absolutes and commitment to them suffers from efforts to make comparisons among them. Behavior in the face of conflicting absolute values may be interpreted as reflecting implicit imputed trade-offs among them, but conscious attempts to specify explicitly calculated trade-offs transform the values in ways that undermine their fundamental nature.
>
> The moral absolutes of human understanding are often inconsistent. They pose dilemmas. Although it is possible in some cases to deal with these dilemmas by determining trade-offs, humans more commonly deal with them by torment and anguish, by denial, and by the sequential attention to values. They experience the subordination of one absolute to another as a troubling symptom of moral inadequacy that leads to a confession of weakness and a reaffirmation of commitment to the violated values.[16]

---

[16] Personal communication with Jim March, August 2015.

I am not as sure as Jim that the deep values of human life are "inconsistent absolutes." As I said at the start, the fact that values compete in a particular situation doesn't make them inconsistent: that we can *sometimes* not do both what value A requires and what value B requires does not entail that we *never* can, which I take it is what would be required for them to be inconsistent. But I've already explained why we might expect that even if, in the end, we settle on a path of action, it need not be the case that we do so without regret (or, let me add, a host of other negative feelings). Still, the problem he identifies strikes me as a real one even if there are no inconsistent absolutes: rational choice, calculating profit and loss in all their many dimensions, could undermine our attachment to some of our values; deciding this way explicitly could make us worse people, by dulling our responses, or even by reducing the power of certain practical reasons to engage our wills. Making Sophie's choice by a rational calculation of the pros and cons might leave you unable to love anyone at all, or deprive you of the proper sense of the value of human life. It might also lead you to take notice only of the sorts of reason that fit easily onto such a framework, leading you to ignore entirely considerations that matter, or to take them into account in the wrong way. If that were so, it might be better not to deal with the matter by weighing the pros and cons in a decision-theoretic way.

Jim puts this issue in terms of a challenge to decision theory. But, in fact, any theory at all about how we ought to come to decide what to do might have to respond to the fact—if it is a fact—that using that very theory can change what we value: for it is natural to suppose that what is actually valuable—what we have the best reasons to care about—should not depend on the ways we choose to decide what to do.

A familiar example is the claim that the Ford Motor Company deliberately avoided making changes to the design of the Ford Pinto because they calculated that the cost of settling lawsuits for loss of life in avoidable accidents would be less than the cost of making the change. As it happens, a careful analysis many years ago revealed that what people remember from coverage of lawsuits brought against Ford is almost entirely wrong.[17] The Pinto doesn't seem to have been more dangerous than most cars of its size and the calculations in question played no role in decisions about the design and location of the gas tank. Still, the events as misremembered provide a useful model for what we are talking about. Suppose a company were to make such a calculation. What would be wrong with that?

After all, the compensation for loss of life presumably reflects a social judgment as to the monetary value of the life lost. If it would be wrong not to make the changes to reduce avoidable loss of life, wouldn't that be because the lives were worth more than the calculation suggested, so that the error here is not the company's but the social judgment? Analogously, if a company decides whether to reduce some toxic externality by calculating whether it is more profitable to make changes or to accept penalties from

---

[17] Gary T. Schwartz, 1991. "The Myth of the Ford Pinto Case," *Rutgers Law Review* 43(1): 1013–68.

environmental regulators, isn't it the task of the regulators to set the price in a way that makes reduction in outputs the right decision, when it is the right decision?

I think we can see in Jim March's question the beginnings of a different answer.

We should be clear that there are lots of reasons to doubt that this is the right way to make the decision that have nothing to do with the worry Jim March has raised. Companies should aim to make profits subject to constraints of morality and legality. Measuring the significance of a breach of law or morality by calculating the expected financial cost to the company of the breach is evidently not to treat these considerations as reasons in the right way. Different approaches will give different explanations here. But many will agree that if I have a strong moral reason to reduce avoidable deaths, the financial costs of the breach are simply the wrong thing to think about. For one thing, the effect here is to outsource to courts and regulators the task of weighing the cost of the deaths to those who die and their associates. But you are required to respond to the moral reasons themselves, not to some surrogate. Furthermore, nobody thinks that the compensation substitutes for the lost life: we shouldn't be indifferent between a world in which a person dies and their family is compensated and one in which they live. The violation of a person's right to life is not a tradable commodity. This is part of what is meant by the Kantian thought I mentioned earlier that human beings have dignity and should be treated as ends.

But suppose the company takes these considerations properly into account, giving them the appropriate weight in its calculations, you might still worry for two reasons. One is that it isn't obvious that this calculation can be represented in the decision-theoretic way. That's because the fact that a decision will lead to deaths that are avoidable might provide a reason that is lexically prior to considerations of profit. Once you see that there are avoidable deaths associated with a path of action, the right thing to do, you might think, is to start looking for affordable ways to avoid them, not to assign some weight to the deaths and proceed with the calculation. With sufficient ingenuity, you might be able to rejig this approach within the decision-theoretic framework. That would take more argument to settle. But you would still be left with Jim March's worry.

For people who proceeded in this way, and not just once but regularly, might dull their moral responses to the deaths and injuries they were contemplating, not by failing to give them the proper practical weight, but by becoming emotionally inured to these harms that are under their control. We have moral reasons, I said at the start, to feel and to be certain ways, as well as to do certain things. The worry here is that in settling on this way of deciding what to do, one would end up being a morally undesirable kind of person and lacking morally desirable sentiments.

So there are grounds for skepticism about the moral appropriateness of deciding in the way many standard formal models of rational decision making taught in business schools suggest. Oscar Wilde's Lord Darlington (in *Lady Windermere's Fan*) says a cynic "knows the price of everything, and the value of nothing." Treating everything as tradable with everything else may be bad for the soul. And, of course, if people find out that you are a cynic, it may also end up being bad for the bottom line.

. . . .

COMMENTS AND DISCUSSION

March and Appiah in their respective essays consider a cluster of problems and questions surrounding the decision-theoretic framework so often deployed in accounts of our economic pursuits. To what extent does this framework provide a useful account of, and/or a basis for, decision making in businesses? In what ways, they ask, does using the framework itself shape the values that it is supposed to represent?

What are the limits and presuppositions of a decision-theoretic framework on questions of value?

Many decisions seem to require in some way making comparative judgments of incommensurable values. At the Society for Progress' second assembly, Sen suggested, however, that the problem typically associated with incommensurability is overblown: we routinely make ordinal comparisons of goods without measuring them in common terms. Drawing on Dewey, Anderson pointed out that we often bring multiple evaluative perspectives to a given question. We can frame a question in terms of a third-personal assessment of virtue: Does this person merit my admiration? Or in first-personal terms of the good: Is this particular outcome appealing? It is hard to see how this kind of plurality could be reduced to some common type of concern, though it may still permit us to deliberate effectively about comparative merits. In some cases, however, we may overstate the extent of incommensurability. It may seem like the safety of consumers, for example, is incommensurable with economic measures of cost. As Frank noted, however, we accept some measure of risk associated with cost reductions in our products (a perfectly safe car would be infinitely expensive). However we think about the problem of incommensurability, Pettit and Anderson both observed a fundamental limitation of the decision-theoretic framework: it only tells you what to do given a function that ranks possibilities. We need independent deliberation to make the requisite rankings appropriately.

What is the role of maximization versus optimization in decision making?

As Sen observes, we routinely make comparative judgments of outcomes without knowing what the optimal outcome would be and, indeed, the effort required to decide the optimal outcome would in fact be counterproductive. In the classic parable, Buridan's ass dies because it cannot effectively decide which outcome is superior to the other. Thus, in practical decision contexts, we typically need a framework for comparative judgment (a maximization framework) rather than optimization. As Snabe noted, this is particularly crucial in the business context, where decisions must be made under heavy time constraints. At the same time, he observed, a business can get trapped in this comparative framework if it fails to think about the long term: often, one must accept comparatively worse outcomes in the short term in order to achieve superior outcomes in the long term.

To what extent does the decision-theoretic model distort our conception of agency?

Both Meyer and Anderson observed that a large share of what we do is not a function of decisions but is, instead, a consequence of habit. Thus, Meyer pointed out, undergraduates who go to college rarely decide on going to college: it is more or less predetermined by their social background and upbringing. Nonetheless, if one asks them why they went to college, they can give a well worked out answer. Representing actions as decisions in this way can sometimes have odd consequences, and in many cases important institutional ramifications. Institutions such as the Federal Reserve Board, Meyer suggested, have an enormous apparatus of staff built up on the premise of rational decision making though—arguably—that apparatus adds little to the quality of the decisions. It is there strictly as a "performance ritual" that the outcome is legitimated as a decision.[18]

---

[18] This essay arose out of a series of discussions I had with James G. March in the summer of 2015. He identified a problem that struck me as very interesting and worth trying to understand, which I state during the course of the chapter.

CHAPTER 6

INTERGENERATIONAL EQUITY AND RESPONSIBILITY FOR FUTURE GENERATIONS

KOTARO SUZUMURA

"We are always doing", says he, "something for Posterity, but I would fain see Posterity do something for us."

Joseph Addison, *The Spectator*, August 20, 1714

Any man's death diminishes me, because I am involved in Mankind; And therefore never send to know for whom the bell tolls; it tolls for thee.

John Donne, *Devotions Upon Emergent Occasions, Meditation* XVII, 1624

Abstract
Why should the present generation be held responsible for the sustainable well-being of future generations, especially since past generations must bear some large share of the cause of global warming? This chapter describes the principle that all generations irrespective of when they emerged in the past or will emerge in the future should have equal opportunity to lead worthwhile lives of their choice. It assesses several alternatives including assigning voting rights to the very young and setting aside these alternatives as on balance unsatisfactory or unworkable. On the principle of responsibility and compensation, the chapter proposes that the present generation must either abate global warming or compensate future generations. It explains and defends why this one-sided, external, and irrevocable choice of the present generation is the only sensible and moral alternative for addressing intergenerational equity.

INTRODUCTION

From time immemorial, human beings live in society.

> Before the first "syllable of recorded time", [human beings] had to make decisions which bind an entire group. Hunting frequently pitted physically weak men against stronger animals; it was only by agreeing on a division of functions that human hunters could kill or capture mammoths or bison or elephants or lions. As society became more complex, especially after the development of agriculture, social decisions covered a wider and wider range: the development of irrigation works, the administration of cities, and, of course and alas, the fighting of wars[1]

We may also remind ourselves of the famous passage from Karl Marx (1904) to the effect that

> it is but in the eighteenth century, in "bourgeois society," that the different forms of social union confront the individual as a mere means to his private ends, as an outward necessity. But the period in which this view of the isolated individual becomes prevalent, is the very one in which the interrelations of society have reached the highest state of development. Man is in the most literal sense of the word a *zoon politikon*, not only a social animal, but an animal which can develop into an individual only in society.[2]

The ties that bind individuals with each other in a society may be either *tangible* or *intangible*. Individuals may be connected through the complex network of exchange contracts, employment contracts, extended family relationships, alumni associations, viz. tangible nexuses of interpersonal relationships. Individuals may also be tied by means of compassions one may feel toward the miserable plights of others as well as fellow feelings one may find within him/herself when he/she faces the rapture of others, viz. intangible nexuses of interpersonal relationships. It was Adam Smith (1759) who noticed the importance of *sympathy* or *compassion* as a tie that is intangible, yet strongly binds individuals in human society.

In the age of globalization, not only tangible, but also intangible interpersonal ties became so widespread and intertwined that the causes and consequences of an increase or decrease of material wealth as well as the subjective well-being of individuals could be analyzed only by going beyond national boundaries and taking past, present, and future generations into account. It is in this context that I aspire to crystallize a few relevant observations on the *equitable treatment* of individuals belonging to future generations vis-à-vis those belonging to the present generation. My analysis will be mainly focused on the ethical basis of the reason why the present generation should be held responsible for the sustainable well-being of future generations.

---

[1] This is an excerpt from Arrow's "Introduction" to Arrow et al. (1996/1997: xvi).
[2] Marx (1904: 267–8).

To divide the broad task into tractable pieces, the next section devotes itself to the equitable treatment of the *adjacent future generation* vis-à-vis the present generation, whereas in section three I turn to the equitable treatment of *far-distant future generations* vis-à-vis the present generation. While the analysis in section three turns out to be largely negative and skeptical, section four tries to go beyond agnosticism by making use of the basic concept of responsibility and compensation in the choice of a future path of history. Section five concludes this essay with a few final observations.

Equitable Treatment of the Adjacent Future Generation

The Adjacent Future Generation versus Far-Distant Future Generations

Time flows in one direction from the immemorial past, through the present, and into the indefinite future. The further we go backward along the time axis, the more our ancestors recede behind the veil of fuzzy individual and collective memories. Even when we seriously feel that we owe much to what our ancestors had done for us, there is very little, if anything, we can do in concrete terms to remunerate our ancestors other than to keep our grateful sentiment toward them. Likewise, the further we go forward along the time axis, the more uncertain we cannot but feel about personal identities, social and economic status, and the composition and size of the population of our distant descendants. We may bequeath tangible and intangible assets to far-distant descendants, but we are keenly aware that there would be nothing they could do to remunerate us in token of their gratitude. Indeed, there is no way for the present generation to communicate directly with far-distant future generations. In-between the present generation and far-distant future generations lie the adjacent future generation, viz. children of the present generation, with whom people in the present generation have many channels through which to know their personal idiosyncrasies and exchange views directly. Keeping this clear contrast in mind, I devote the rest of this section to the issue of equitable treatment of the adjacent future generation vis-à-vis the present generation.

Equitable Treatment of the Adjacent Future Generation vis-à-vis the Present Generation: Some Demographic Backgrounds

One of the remarkable features of the globalized world is the conspicuous contrast in population dynamics of countries and regions. According to the World Development Indicators published by the World Bank, the *total fertility rate* (TFR)—viz. the number of children that would be born to a woman if she were to live to the end of her childbearing years and bear children in accordance with current age-specific fertility rates, as of 2013—ranges from Niger with 7.6, Mali with 6.8, through the United Kingdom and the United States with 1.9, Japan and Germany with 1.4, to Singapore and Korea with 1.2. To be contrasted with the TFR is a *replacement fertility rate* (RFR), viz. the TFR at which women give birth to enough babies to sustain the population level. If there were no mortality in the female population until the end of the childbearing years, an RFR would be close to 2.0. For most industrial countries, an RFR would be close to 2.1 births per woman, and it varies from 2.5 to 3.3 in developing countries due to higher mortality rates.[3] Those countries or regions with the TFR more than (respectively less than) an RFR are going to experience an increase (respectively a decrease) in total population. For example, Japan at present has an RFR of 2.07, which far exceeds the TFR of 1.4. An RFR varies from one country or region to the other, depending on the medical treatment level, which by and large regulates the mortality rate of the country or region. Countries or regions having low TFRs and high medical treatment system tend to have rapidly aging populations.[4]

With this background in mind, the core of the general issue we are going to confront may be stated as follows. In the political system of representative democracy, the old generation, which is going to weigh heavier in total population, has stronger voting power vis-à-vis the young generation, which is going to weigh lighter in total population. The burden imposed on the young generation is becoming too heavy in the face of increasing numbers of the elderly, who are socially supported by the prime-of-life generation and the young generation, whereas the voting rights of the young generation are tightly handcuffed by an age limit of, say, 18 years and over, so that desires of the young generation are hardly reflected in political decision making. It deserves emphasis that the problem of inequitable treatment of the young generation vis-à-vis the old generation is already conspicuous in some countries, including Japan, and it is latent in many industrialized countries in the global world.[5]

---

[3] See Espenshade et al. (2003).

[4] To exemplify the seriousness of this problem by means of Japan's historical experience, let α (t) and β (t) be the percentage in the population of those over 60 years of age and of those below 15 years of age, respectively, in the year t. In 1950, α (1950) < 9 percent, β (1950) > 5 percent, whereas in the year 2010, α (2010) > 30 percent and β (2010) $\cong$ 13 percent. If we add to these historical records a predicted value of α (2050) that exceeds 44 percent, the demographic transition in Japan since 1950 is truly remarkable. No wonder, the equitable treatment of the old generation vis-à-vis the young generation is one of the focal political issues in Japan.

[5] In some European countries and elsewhere, this problem is partly coped with by means of immigration from countries or regions with high TFRs. This essay is not concerned with the problem of immigration in the context of intergenerational equity. The reason is not that the problem of immigration is unimportant. Quite to the contrary, it poses distinct problems of its own including the problem of refugees. It seems sensible to avoid cursory and fragmentary treatment of this multifaceted problem, and leave its discussion for a future occasion.

To cope with this problem, some radical proposals have been made with the purpose of revising the assignation scheme of voting rights with the purpose of relaxing the problem of inequitable treatment of the young generation vis-à-vis the old generation.[6] In essence, it consists of assigning more voting rights to the young generation, and assigning fewer voting rights to the old generation.

Pros and Cons of the Revised Assignation of Voting Rights

The essence of the proposed assignation scheme may be summarized by the following two claims: (a) the *disfranchisement of the elderly*, and (b) the *enfranchisement of the minors*.

One of the early statements of the claim (a) can be found in Douglas Stewart (1970: 20–2), according to whom

> there are simply too many senile voters and their number is growing. The vote should not be a privilege in perpetuity, guaranteed by minimal physical survival, but a share in the continuing fate of the political community, both in its benefits and its risks. The old, having no future, are dangerously free from the consequences of their own political acts, and it makes no sense to allow the vote to someone who is actuarially unlikely to survive.

He went on to "advocate that all persons lose the vote at retirement or age 70, whichever is earlier."

The claim (b) may be in the *weak form*, viz. to lower the age limit below the current level, or in the *strong form*, viz. to assign voting rights to all minors, irrespective of their actual ages. As Van Parijs (1998: 309) aptly points out, the origin of the claim (b) in the strong form is attributable to the introduction of *genuine universal suffrage* to the effect that every member of the population is given the right to vote from the very first day of his/her life.

Van Parijs is well aware that an immediate criticism would be raised against the claim (b) in the strong form, which says that it is absurd to imagine that infants, kindergartners, and schoolchildren read the election bulletin, and cast their votes on their own judgments and responsibility. To defend claim (b) in the strong form from the criticism to this effect, Van Parijs asserts that "this can easily be achieved without requiring minor children to cast votes themselves. One can simply entrust their parents with the responsibility of doing so on their behalf, by granting them proxy votes."[7]

---

[6] See, among others, Acemoglu and Robinson (2000), Aoki (2012), Bossert and Suzumura (2014), Campiglio (2009), Carballo (1981), Demeny (1986, 2011a, 2011b), Herche (2011), Ringen (1996), and Van Parijs (1998) for some proposed schemes and their critical scrutiny.

[7] One may be reminded that the conferred right of an individual may be entrusted to somebody else if the right-holder is not in the position to exercise his/her own right by him/herself. Suppose that the holder of a libertarian right in the sense of J. S. Mill (1859) can choose either to be buried or cremated after his/her death. It is clear that nobody can *directly* exercise this right, but anybody can *indirectly* exercise this right by entrusting somebody else to follow his/her instruction after his/her death. Observe

He refers to several writers who expressed strong arguments in favor of conferring voting rights to children, including Manuel Carballo (1981):[8]

> I am left with an uncomfortable sense of imbalance in our political system. In a society all too ready to live for the present, how do we create a political force for our children's pensions? My proposal is quite simple. Give parents a vote weighted by their number of minor children. Two parents with two children get four votes. One parent with one child gets two votes.[9]

To safeguard the claim (a) and the claim (b) against the charge of using a single measure of physical and mental aptitude, viz. age, for depriving or conferring voting rights, it is stipulated that both disfranchising the old and enfranchising the young should be subject to a certain competence test. In the presence of such a safeguard device, should we be resigned to accept the proposed assignation of voting rights in the name of treating the young generation and the old generation equitably?

We fall far short of thinking that we should accept such a proposal offhandedly. It is true that the urgent plea for restoring equitable treatment of the young generation and the old generation in the assignation of voting rights is legitimate, pressing, and appealing, but the proposed scheme for implementing equitable treatment between generations seems to be surrounded by several logical and ethical difficulties.

In the first place, the disfranchisement of the old generation by making all elderly individuals lose their voting rights at retirement or age 70, whichever is earlier, may create another problem of intergenerational inequity of its own. Observe that the old generation, for all that they have contributed to the current state of the country and the current well-being of the whole population, are going to be deprived of their voting rights, viz. rights to participate in the process through which public decisions are going to be made, by one stroke and all at once. One may ask: How can we nullify our indebtedness to the old generation in the proposed mechanism design for restoring intergenerational equity? What about the wisdom and experience that they have accumulated throughout their lives, which could play an active role for future society through their introspective voting behavior? After all, political decision making is not just for aggregating individuals' *private interests*; it is for aggregating individuals' *public judgments* as well.[10] The exclusion of elderly individuals might deprive the political

---

that this indirect exercise of the right presupposes that the right-holders are able to express what they would choose if they were in the position to make their own choice. On the concept of libertarian rights, see the exchange of views between Sen (1982) and Gaertner et al. (1992). Note, however, that this scenario does *not* apply to the case of proxy voting rights proposed by Van Parijs and many others, for the obvious reason that the original right-holders, viz. minors, are not in the position to instruct the entrusted agents, viz. their parents, how to exercise the proxy voting rights on their behalf.

[8] I owe this citation from Carballo (1981) to Van Parijs (1998: 311, n. 49).

[9] Carballo's brief proposal was succeeded by an American demographer, Paul Demeny. In a short article that he contributed to the *Japan Economic Newspaper*, viz. Demeny (2011a), he essentially proposed Carballo's scheme of giving parents a vote weighted by their number of minor children as a measure to cope with the aging population problem in Japan.

[10] Suppose that elderly individuals are deprived of their voting rights *subject to their failure to pass a certain competence test*. This contingent disfranchisement of elderly individuals may narrow down the

system of the services that could be rendered by experienced and disinterested individuals who are capable of offering something valuable to society.[11]

In the second place, and turning to the enfranchisement of the young generation, the focus of the debate should be on the idea of granting parents proxy votes on behalf of their children. The exact details of implementing such a scheme, viz. how many additional votes should be granted to parents, whether fathers or mothers or both should be entitled to exercise these votes, whether these votes should be granted in perpetuity as opposed to the period until their children reach the voting age, and so forth do not seem to be universally agreed on. In essence, however, these proposals seem to be based on the common belief that parents are entitled to be favorably treated vis-à-vis non-parents in providing someone with proxy voting rights for enfranchising the young generation. In what follows, let us enumerate several reasons why we must feel rather skeptical about this common belief.[12]

To begin with, parents are often looked upon as better judges than non-parents about the circumstances that the young generation will confront in the pursuit of their future self-interest. This argument may have some appeal to the extent that parents care more about the interests of their own children than parents of other children or, for that matter, persons with no children. However, in discussing the assignation scheme of proxy voting rights, what is indeed at stake is not what individuals think will promote their *dynastic self-interests*, but what individuals judge will be conducive to a *better social mechanism* for successive future generations. Thus, there seems to be very little, if any at all, reason to justify the asymmetric treatment of parents vis-à-vis individuals with no children in the context of assigning proxy voting rights. Note in passing that, in some countries at least, the proportion of adults who never have children is increasing even when average family size is stable. Although we do not dare to dispute that parents care strongly about their children—indeed, we wish them to do so—unfavorable treatment of individuals with no children vis-à-vis individuals with children seems to be unforgivable, particularly when the childlessness of an individual is not due to his/her voluntary choice, but due to an involuntary misfortune that had fallen upon him/her.

From the viewpoint of theories of political decision making, there exist at least two basic reasons to be skeptical about the scheme of conferring proxy votes to parents. In the first place, this is an outright infringement of the *one-man one-vote principle* that is the basic idea of democracy. Are we determined on deliberation to sacrifice this fundamental principle for the sake of restoring intergenerational equity?

---

possible room for our objection. Even in this case, however, it may be more appealing if we provide elderly individuals with the freedom to choose voluntarily to discontinue their rights if and when they find themselves to be ineligible due to their advanced age, rather than by the forced renouncement of their universal suffrage. Such a scheme of voluntary annulment of voting rights reminds us of the scheme of voluntary annulment of driving licenses of elderly individuals due to their advanced age and deteriorating driving skill.

[11] It seems apt to remind ourselves of Sen's (1977) contrast between the *interests aggregation* and the *judgments aggregation* in the theory of social choice.

[12] The following discussion capitalizes heavily on Bossert and Suzumura (2014).

At the very least, there seems to be no social consensus on how to resolve the conflict between the respect for the basic principle of democracy, on the one hand, and the restoration of intergenerational inequity, on the other. In the second place, there is a basic contradiction in the very idea of proxy votes entrusted to somebody else. If the entrusted agent *does* discuss with the minor principal how to exercise his/her vote in the polling booth, this act infringes upon the *principle of secret voting*. If the agent *does not* consult the intention of the minor principal, however, it is difficult to call the proposed scheme proxy voting for the sake of the minor principal. Indeed, it then becomes close to outright paternalism, which may well be the worst form of despotism imaginable.

Those who are keenly advocating the enfranchisement of the young generation by means of providing parents with proxy votes consist not only of economists, political scientists, sociologists, and philosophers, but also of demographers. This last class of advocates emphasize the pronatalist aspect of the scheme of proxy votes, according to which the proxy votes conferred to natural parents will provide them with an incentive to have more children than otherwise. In Demeny's (2011b: 270) own words, "the very young constitute a completely disenfranchised group. They could, however, be granted full voting power, to be exercised by their parents or caregivers." If such an electoral reform is implemented, it "could create a more hospitable reception for effective pronatalist measures in democratically elected legislatures." Whether the scheme of proxy votes provides a sufficiently strong natalist incentive as to be effective in coping with the adverse population dynamics in some democratic countries can be answered only by means of empirical studies, which is beyond the reach of the present essay.

Throughout this section, we have argued against several proposals to change the assignation of voting rights so as to enfranchise the young generation by conferring proxy votes to their parents, thereby reducing the relative voting power of the old generation. We have also argued against the mechanical disfranchisement of the old generation by depriving their voting rights "at retirement or age 70, whichever is earlier." Such an abrupt declaration of the "political death" of the elderly creates the problem of intergenerational inequity of its own. Having said this, let us conclude this section with a few observations.

In the first place, I am in full agreement with previous studies on the necessity of carefully re-examining the current assignation of voting rights between generations. It is true that we are not yet in the position of proposing an alternative assignation scheme of our own. However, this should not preclude the critical examination of the performance characteristics of existing proposals for the sake of knowing the precise content of the problem to be faced. In the second place, lowering the voting age below the current level subject to a certain competence test is an agreeable step for improving the representation of the young generation in current political decision making. In the case of disfranchising the old generation, I have argued against the mechanical imposition of the age limit even under certain competence tests. The reason for this objection boils down to the procedural injustice involved in the proposed scheme of disfranchisement. In the third place, in order to safeguard the proper representation of the young generation, the appointment of a committee of "guardians" may be in order. It may be asked: Why can we trust guardians if we are unable to trust parents in the exercise of proxy votes? Our plea is twofold: (a) parents are likely to be guided by dynastic self-interests rather than impersonal concern about the just procedure for equitable treatment between generations; and (b) parents are not capable of gathering, processing, and making use of relevant information, which is necessary for services to be rendered by the committee of guardians.[13] In the fourth and last place, to increase fertility in a society, support programs such as low-cost daycare facilities may well be a more dependable incentive scheme for working couples to have any offspring at all, or to have a larger number of children than they would otherwise have, than the scheme of conferring dubious proxy votes to natural parents.

It is true that the alternative measures suggested here are uneventful tools and not at all revolutionary. However, there is nothing wrong with being uneventful and non-revolutionary to the extent that these measures do not generate the problem of intergenerational inequity of their own.

EQUITABLE TREATMENT OF FAR-DISTANT FUTURE GENERATIONS

Let us now turn to the problem of treating far-distant future generations equitably vis-à-vis the present generation. The problem to be tackled may be decomposed into the following two related but distinct sub-problems:

Problem A.   Why should the present generation be held responsible for the well-being of far-distant future generations, with whom individuals in the present generation have no opportunity to encounter during their finite lifespan?

---

[13] It may be asked why we can trust a "guardian" to act faithfully on behalf of the young generation when we do not trust offhandedly the sincerity of parents to cast a proxy vote for the sake of their children. To answer this natural question, let us remind ourselves of the following passage from John Harsanyi (1977: 315): "Each individual is supposed to have a social welfare function of his own, expressing his own individual value—in the same way as each individual has a utility function of his own, expressing his own individual taste. Even if both an individual's social welfare function and his utility function in a sense express his own individual preferences, they must express preferences of different sorts: the former must express what this individual prefers (or, rather, would prefer) on the basis of impersonal social considerations alone, and the latter must express what he actually prefers, whether on the basis of his personal interests or any other basis. The former may be called his 'ethical' preferences, the latter his 'subjective' preferences." Our scenario is that nothing prevents parents from using their subjective preferences in exercising proxy votes for the sake of maximizing their dynastic self-interests, whereas a guardian is a human incarnation of what society entrusts him/her to do on behalf of minors and youths by following his/her ethical preferences.

Problem B.   Granting that there is a persuasive reason for imposing on the present generation the responsibility for the well-being of far-distant future generations, why should this responsibility be unilaterally and single-handedly imposed on the present generation even when there are other agents who should be equally held responsible?

The Problem of Global Warming and Malleability of Future Generations

Before tackling these crucial sub-problems, let us shed further light on the nature of our task by means of an example, viz. the problem of *global warming*.[14]

The accumulation of greenhouse gases generated by human activities exerts an influence on the global environment at a historically unprecedented scale. Since greenhouse gases may stay in the air for a long time, the current emission of greenhouse gases may affect many generations, even generations in the far-distant future. Besides, everyone leading a normal economic life cannot avoid generating greenhouse gases, so everyone should be partly held responsible for causing the problem of global warming. Furthermore, not only present, but also past human activities, at least since the Industrial Revolution, have contributed to the accumulation of greenhouse gases. However, most of the past generations no longer exist. If we look ahead along the time axis into the indefinite future, those generations that would be most severely affected by aggravating global climate would likely be born in the far-distant future. These future generations simply do not yet exist, so that the present generation is not in the position of knowing anything about the personal characteristics, population size, and composition of far-distant future generations. To sum up, the problem of global warming is such that a large part of the "culprits" do not exist any longer, and a large part of the "victims" do not yet exist. In-between these non-existing parties lies the present generation, which is only partly responsible for the problem. We should also observe that the simile of "culprits and victims" might be misleading. Everyone who lives on earth cannot but be a culprit of the problem of global warming because of his/her very existence, irrespective of whether he/she is a producer, or a consumer, and nobody can hide him/herself behind the shield of innocent victims.

As if these intricacies are not enough, the problem of global warming is made more complex by the so-called *non-identity problem* à la Derek Parfit (1984). Note that, among potential historical paths of human evolution, the one that describes the actual historical path from the past to the present is uniquely fixed, and so are individuals who had existed and at present exist along the realized historical path. However, the type, size, and composition of individuals who will emerge in the future are *malleable*,

---

[14] The following analysis of the nature and consequence of global warming draws heavily on Suzumura and Tadenuma (2007). It can be applied not only to the problem of global climate change, but also to the problem of nuclear waste disposal, *mutatis mutandis*.

depending on the actions taken by the present generation. For instance, suppose that there are two alternative scenarios, viz. either to adopt policy measures that strictly constrain the use of petroleum in developed countries, or to impose no such constraint. The use of petroleum plays such a crucial role in all aspects of human life that the styles of food, clothes, and shelter, as well as convenience and opportunity to travel, would be substantially different depending on choices to be made by the present generation. Accordingly, individuals would meet and marry different partners, which would lead to different families and lifestyles, and would accumulate different life experiences. Thus, the personality characteristics, size, and composition of far-distant future generations would be substantially different in accordance with the choice that the present generation would make between these two alternative policy measures. Observe that the total emission of greenhouse gases depends not only on the total population, but also on the per head emission, so that there would be very different culmination outcomes in response to whether the present generation would choose the former policy measure, or the latter policy measure. The problem of the personality characteristics of future generations being malleable in accordance with the choices made by the present generation is called the *non-identity problem*. It was Derek Parfit (1984) who discussed some philosophical implications of the non-identity problem and caused a stir in the profession. Since this is a controversial issue, I will try to make it explicit if and when our subsequent discussions hinge squarely on human malleability due to the non-identity problem.

This is the illustration of the structure that underlies Problem A and Problem B. Although the subsequent analysis is not contingent on the specific features of the problem of global warming, we will maintain the context of global warming for the sake of emphasis and mnemonic convenience.

How Much Help do Conventional Wisdoms Offer?

Back, then, to the crucial Problem A. Why should the present generation be held responsible for the well-being of far-distant future generations? Recollect that the present generation has virtually no chance of encountering far-distant future generations, neither is there any reason to expect that far-distant future generations will reciprocate the courtesy extended to them by the present generation.

To begin with, let us examine the extent to which we can learn lessons from such well-known conventional wisdoms as the Golden Rule in the Gospel of Luke, the scheme of conferring rights to "victims" and to require "culprits" to take actions to abate greenhouse gases, and the utilitarian principle of equity à la Henry Sidgwick (1907).

The "Golden Rule" in the Gospel of Luke

Recollect that the "Golden Rule" in the Gospel of Luke is an expression of interpersonal compassion in the Holy Bible: "So whatever you wish that others do to you, do also to them, for this is the Law and the Prophets."[15] Similar maxims for right behavior abound throughout recorded history, and in distinct cultures in the world. Suffice it to quote just one salient example. When Tzu-hung asked Confucius for "one word which can serve as the guiding principle for conduct throughout life," Confucius reportedly answered as follows: "It is the word altruism. Do not do to others what you do not want them to do to you."[16]

However appealing this maxim may seem to many, it is worthwhile to remind ourselves that an insidious feature of this code of behavior was acutely pointed out by George Bernard Shaw (1903): "Do not do unto others as you would that they should do unto you. Their tastes may not be the same." Shaw added a remark that "the golden rule is that there are no golden rules." Although we are not willing to swallow Shaw's sweeping cynicism in one draft, it is undeniable that his cynical remark has strong relevance in the context of obligation of the present generation to far-distant future generations in the presence of global warming, with or without taking the malleability of human personality and many other idiosyncrasies seriously. No magic wand seems to be available here.

Conferment of Rights to "Victims" and Imposition of Duties to "Culprits"

Social justice is often expressed in terms of rights and duties. A common argument about "rights and duties between generations" in the context of global warming goes as follows: "Future generations have the right to claim that the present generation should abate greenhouse gases, whereas the present generation has the corresponding duty owed to future generations." However, there seem to be logical difficulties in articulating the relation between future generations and the present generation in terms of such a right–duty relationship if we take the non-identity problem seriously.

As an auxiliary step, let the policy a^{t^*} (respectively b^{t^*}) mean "to implement policy measures against global warming at t^*" (respectively "not to implement any policy measure against global warming at t^*"). In each case, the sets of individuals who exist in the future, viz. $N(a^{t^*})$ and $N(b^{t^*})$, have few, if any at all, individuals in common. Let us now ask: To which group of people, $N(a^{t^*})$ or $N(b^{t^*})$, should the right to request the present generation to restrain the emission of greenhouse gases belong? Or, to which group of people does the present generation owe the duty?

First, suppose that the group of individuals $N(b^{t^*})$ who would live in the world with worsened global warming, has the right. However, once the present generation fulfills the duty corresponding to the right-exercising by the group $N(b^{t^*})$ the set of individuals who would exist in the future is the group $N(a^{t^*})$, and not the group $N(b^{t^*})$ any more. Thus, the exercise of the right conferred to the group $N(b^{t^*})$ results in the outcome that the group of individuals in $N(b^{t^*})$ is deprived of its own existence on the earth. J. S. Mill (1859) once insisted that one cannot justify the slave contract to sell his

---

[15] See the Holy Bible, English Standard Version, Matthew 7:12.
[16] Confucius, *Analects*, chapter 15, v. 23.

own freedom under the name of freedom of choice. Likewise, when one agrees on the assignment of rights that decides one's own circumstances, it is irrational to agree on the right including the right to deny one's own existence.

On the other hand, there is no rational ground that the group $N(a^{t^*})$ who would exist only in the world with restrained global warming, should be conferred the right to require that the present generation should restrain the emission of warming gases. If the present generation in fact refrains from emitting greenhouse gases, the group of individuals $N(a^{t^*})$ has no incentive to exercise the conferred right. In view of the non-exercising of this right, the present generation may be motivated not to restrain the emission of greenhouse gases, so that it is the group $N(b^{t^*})$ who will exist, and the group $N(a^{t^*})$ will disappear. It follows that the conferment of the right to the group of individuals $N(a^{t^*})$ is also vacuous. In any case, the conferment of the right to far-distant future generations does not seem to make any rational sense if we take the malleability of personality characteristics of future generations seriously.

The inevitable conclusion seems to be that the paradigm of "rights and duties" cannot capture the reason for the present generation to be held responsible for the well-being of far-distant future generations as far as we take the malleability of human personality seriously. We must explore somewhere else in order to find an answer to our problem.

Sidgwick's Utilitarian Principle of Equity as Anonymity

Although human malleability over time is not a fiction, but a real possibility, it may be doubted whether the non-identity problem deserves such a preponderance as to annihilate all possibilities of intergenerational normative judgments in one stroke. Let us see if a standard normative approach such as utilitarianism, where no attention is given to the non-identity problem, can help us solve the problem of intergenerational equity.

Since the advent of modern normative economics, the problem of intergenerational equity has been receiving close attention. According to Henry Sidgwick, there is a strong utilitarian tradition of treating otherwise equal generations equally. This tradition can be neatly summarized as follows:

> How far [should we] consider the interests of posterity when they seem to conflict with those of existing human beings? It seems clear that the time at which a man exists cannot affect the value of his happiness from a universal point of view; and that the interests of posterity must concern a utilitarian as much as those of his contemporaries.   (Sidgwick 1907: 414)

If we follow this traditional way of reasoning, the intergenerational normative judgments should treat otherwise equal generations equally irrespective of the places they occupy along the historical time axis. From this viewpoint, the widespread convention of discounting future utilities vis-à-vis the present utility is ethically indefensible. It is nothing other than the outcome of human irrationality and fallibility.[17]

---

[17] See, *inter alia*, Arthur Pigou (1920: 24–5), Frank Ramsey (1928: 543), and Roy Harrod (1948: 37).

A striking changeover took place in 1960 when Tjalling Koopmans (1960) proved a formal result that goes squarely counter to the Sidgwickean principle of treating otherwise equal individuals equally. Roughly speaking, what Koopmans proved is that the rational, continuous, and stationary evaluation of infinite utility streams, each term of which being the utility of each generation, cannot but exhibit the phenomenon of *impatience*, viz. the preference for an advancement along the time axis of a higher utility ahead of a lower utility. It should be clear that Koopmans' result goes squarely counter to Sidgwick's assertion to the effect that "the time at which a man exists cannot affect the value of his happiness from a universal point of view." This intriguing result was further polished by Peter Diamond (1965) into an impossibility theorem: there exists no social evaluation ordering over the set of infinite utility streams that satisfies the Pareto principle, the equity principle à la Sidgwick, and the continuity axiom. By now, there is a large literature that confirms the robustness of the Koopmans–Diamond theorem. It may safely be said that the essential conflict between the Pareto principle, which is a standard requirement of efficiency, and the Sidgwick-ean equity principle persists as long as the continuity axiom is maintained even in a weakened form.[18] In this sense, the equity–efficiency trade-off cannot be exorcized in the context of evaluating intergenerational utility streams.

Recollect that the general impossibility theorem in social choice theory, which kicked off the modern theory of rational social evaluations and exposed logical difficulties surrounding the formation of rational social choice, was founded on the informational basis of ordinal and interpersonally non-comparable utilities. It was Kenneth Arrow (1963: 109–10) who made a plea for this background of social choice theory as follows:

> The essential point of the modern insistence on ordinal utility is the application of Leibniz's principle of the identity of indiscernibles. Only observable differences can be used as a basis for explanation. In the field of consumers' demand theory, the ordinalist position turned out to create no problems; cardinal utility had no explanatory power above and beyond ordinal. It is the great merit of Bergson's 1938 paper to have carried the same principle into the analysis of social welfare. The social welfare function was to depend only on indifference maps; in other words, welfare judgments were to be based only on interpersonally observable behavior.

It was Arrow's ordinal and interpersonally non-comparable informational basis, coupled with the axiom of independence of irrelevant alternatives,[19] that precipitated his general impossibility theorem. In contrast, the conflict between the intergener-ational equity à la Sidgwick and Pareto efficiency, which is the essence of the Koopmans–Diamond impossibility theorem, remains true even if we are ready to use

---

[18] See, among many others, Basu and Mitra (2003, 2007), Bossert et al. (2007), Bossert and Suzumura (2011), Hara et al. (2008), Koopmans et al. (1964), and Roemer and Suzumura (2007).

[19] The independence of irrelevant alternatives requires that "the choice made by society from a given environment depend only on the orderings of individuals among the alternatives in that environment" (Arrow 1951/1963: 26).

cardinal and intergenerationally comparable utility information. In contrast with Arrovian impossibility theorems, the culprit of the Koopmans–Diamond impossibility theorem cannot be attributed to the informational parsimony of the framework of analysis.

Before leaving this ground, let us refer to the concept of *sustainable development*, which was first introduced in 1980 by the International Union for the Conservation of Nature and Natural Resources. Subsequently, it came to acquire worldwide recognition through the publication in 1987 of the so-called Brundtland Report by the World Commission on Environment and Development. It deserves emphasis that the essence of "sustainable development is development that meets the needs of the present [generation] without compromising the ability of future generations to meet their own needs" (World Commission on Environment and Development 1987: 43). This concept embodies the basic belief that the well-being of future generations is as important as the well-being of the present generation. It should be clear that sustainability echoes the equity concept due to Sidgwick, viz. all generations, irrespective of when they emerged in the past, or will emerge in the future, should have equal opportunity to lead worthwhile lives of their own choice.

Responsibility and Compensation in the Choice of a Future Path

I have shown that it is logically impossible to find the normative basis of policy evaluation in the context of global environmental externalities by means of the "Golden Rule" in the Gospel of Luke, and the paradigm of conferring rights to "victims" and imposing duties to "culprits" if only we accept the malleability of far-distant future generations. We have also seen that the classical utilitarian principle of equitable treatment of future generations vis-à-vis the present generation falls into an incompatibility with the Pareto efficiency principle if we ask for a *rational* and *continuous* evaluation ordering over the set of infinite sequences of generational utilities. In order not to resign ourselves to agnosticism on the issue of equitable treatment of the present and far-distant future generations, we must grope for an alternative scenario of normative judgments.

Principle of Responsibility and Compensation

As one of the possible candidates of such normative scenarios, let us focus on the *principle of responsibility and compensation*, which has been introduced into normative economics by Ronald Dworkin (1981a, 1981b, 2000), John Roemer (1985, 1986), and Marc Fleurbaey (1995, 1998). It was Fleurbaey (1998) who christened the principle to the effect that one should be held responsible for the outcome of one's own voluntary act, over which one has full of control, as the *principle of responsibility by control*. It follows from this principle that the voluntary exercise of freedom of choice accompanies a responsibility of the person in charge of that act of choice to rectify the detrimental effects thereby generated. Thus, a person who nourished special tastes for expensive champagne through his/her luxurious life has no justifiable reason to require his/her dying father to bequeath him/her more than his/her brother with modest tastes for the reason that he/she is unable to receive the same satisfaction as his/her brother from a pint of beer, if both are bequeathed the same amount of money from their father.[20]

Another implication of the same principle is that, if a person is suffering from severe handicap by birth, for which he/she has no reason to be held personally responsible, he/she deserves to be compensated for the misfortune, which was caused by external factors. The same argument applies to a victim of a traffic accident that was caused by someone else's reckless drunken driving. Needless to say, the primary responsibility for compensatory payment should fall on the reckless driver, but it is society that should assume responsibility for designing an institutional framework that sees to it that fair compensatory payments are paid to the unfortunate victim.

Let us have another look at the problem of global warming, keeping the principle of responsibility and compensation in mind. Observe that there is a basic difference between the theoretical structure envisaged by Dworkin, Roemer, and Fleurbaey, on the one hand, and the structure of the problem of global warming, which prevents us from applying their theory straightaway to the problem of global warming. Observe that one of the conspicuous features of the Dworkin–Roemer–Fleurbaey theory is that either the responsible subject and the affected subject are identical, or, if they are not the same, both subjects coexist at the same point of time. The "expensive champagne case" is one where the cause and the consequence are attributable to the same subject, whereas the "drunken driving case" is one where the culprit and the victim are not the same, but they coexist at the same point of time. Recollect that one of the crucial features of the problem of global warming is that the responsible subjects are the past and present generations, whereas the seriously affected subjects are far-distant future generations, and they do not yet exist at the time the present generation makes its choice of action. There is one further feature of the problem of global warming, which is missing from the Dworkin–Roemer–Fleurbaey theory, viz. depending on the choice of action by the present generation, individual characteristics of the far-distant future generations may be malleable. Despite these large differences, there still exists a crucial verdict that can be extracted from the principle of responsibility and compensation in the context of global warming. The economic activities of the present generation, which emit greenhouse gases and affect the personal characteristics of far-distant future generations, are under the exclusive

---

[20] This parable of Champagne taste is due to Dworkin (1981a).

control of the present generation. According to the principle of responsibility and compensation, therefore, the present generation should be held responsible for the problem of global warming in view of the fact that the present generation has full autonomy to control policy choices, thereby deciding on the path the future evolution of the world takes. Observe that this crucial verdict does not hinge on the non-identity problem à la Parfit.

An Equitable Future Path of Evolution

Let us reiterate the major point in the previous sub-section. The choice of policy measures by the present generation is nothing other than the choice of the future path of evolution from the present to the indefinite future, thereby deciding on the personal identity of far-distant future generations as well as their living standards. Potential future generations have no way of moving back along the historical time path and making a choice of their own from scratch. In this sense, the choice of the present generation is one-sided, external, and irrevocable. The primary meaning of responsibility, which the present generation owes to far-distant future generations, is nothing but the responsibility of choosing the historical path that is accountable as a socially rationalizable choice based on a clear standard of value judgments. Let us emphasize that, up to this point, our verdict on the responsibility of the present generation to far-distant future generations does not hinge on the specific standard of value judgments.

Going forward one step further, we now assume the principle of responsibility and compensation itself to be the standard of value judgments adopted by the present generation. What is the implication of this standard of value judgments for choosing a future path of evolution?

Suppose that there are three alternative policies that are available for choice by the present generation. The first alternative is the policy to abate global warming. The second alternative is the policy to leave global warming unhindered, but to improve the future level of social capital accumulation. The third alternative is the policy to leave global warming unhindered, and to take no measure to improve the future level of social capital accumulation. Depending on the choice of policy from among these three alternatives by the present generation, the identity of individuals who would exist in the far-distant future would be determined, and their living standards would also be determined. Regardless of which individuals would exist, far-distant future generations cannot be held responsible for the choice of policies by the present generation. If the third policy alternative is chosen by the present generation, far-distant future individuals would be forced to live under harsh natural environments with worsened global warming, which is the consequence of the external policy choice by the present generation, without being compensated for the imposed hardships. On the other hand, if the present generation chooses the second policy alternative, far-distant future generations, who would then emerge, would also be severely affected by global warming, but they would be receiving compensatory benefits through the medium of accumulated social capital.

It deserves emphasis that the basic implication of the principle of responsibility and compensation is that the initial opportunities open to individuals at the start of their lives should be equitable. In the context of global warming, the initial opportunities of far-distant future generations are determined by the actions of the present generation. If the choice of the present generation is the third policy alternative, future generations would have very poor opportunities vis-à-vis the present generation. Such an inequitable treatment of far-distant future generations vis-à-vis the present generation will never be endorsed as socially just by the principle of responsibility and compensation. If the choice of the present generation is either the first policy alternative or the second policy alternative, either path is accountable as socially just on the basis of the principle of responsibility and compensation.

We have thus identified one possible theoretical scenario that would help us solve the intergenerational equity problem in the face of severe environmental externalities.[21]

CONCLUDING REMARKS

A problem still remains. The cumulative effects of emitted greenhouse gases are causing global warming, yet its detrimental effect falls mostly upon far-distant future generations. It is true that present economic activities should be partially held responsible for this detrimental outcome. However, we must still ask: Why should the present generation be *single-handedly* and *unilaterally* held responsible in the presence of other culprits who can be traced at least as far back as the people in the era of the Industrial Revolution? I contend that the reasoning that we have pursued in section four implies the primary responsibility of the present generation even if past generations had also emitted greenhouse gases and escaped behind the thick veil of history.

To crystallize ideas, consider the following hypothetical scenario:

(1) If we leave global warming uncontrolled, the average temperature of the world will increase by three degrees in one hundred years;

(2) 50 percent of this global warming is caused by the emissions of greenhouse gases by the present generation, but the remaining 50 percent is due to the accumulation of greenhouse gases emitted by the past generations;

(3) If the temperature rises by 1.5 degrees, it is very likely that some catastrophic disaster will occur; and

(4) To avoid such catastrophe, the increase in the temperature must be at most one degree.

---

[21] Let us emphasize that there is no claim that this theoretical scenario based on the principle of responsibility and compensation is the uniquely qualified resolution scheme. There is room for further exploration of alternative schemes, but it cannot but be left for future investigations.

Assume that the present generation should bear responsibility to abate global warming only to the extent that they have contributed to its cause. Then, of the reduction of two degrees in world temperature, which is required for avoiding catastrophe, the part that the present generation should be held responsible for would be only a one-degree reduction. The remaining one-degree reduction will have to be accomplished by other culprits, viz. past generations, but they do not exist anymore and are not in the position to fulfill this assigned quota. Then, the future world will be thrown into a catastrophic environment, and the initial opportunities of future generations will have to be miserable to say the least. Such an inequitable future path can never be accountable as socially just according to the principle of responsibility and compensation. Thus, to accomplish the responsibility, which is accountable, the present generation must bear all the required reduction of two degrees in world temperature.

In conclusion, our primary responsibility for the choice of a future path should be accepted, single-handedly and unilaterally, irrespective of the actions of the past generations. It deserves emphasis that our answer to Problem A and Problem B by means of the principle of responsibility and compensation does not hinge on the stance we take in the non-identity problem.[22]

References

Acemoglu, D. and Robinson, J. A. 2000. "Why Did the West Extend the Franchise? Democracy, Inequality, and Growth in Historical Perspective." *Quarterly Journal of Economics* 115: 1167–99.

Aoki, R. 2012. "A Demographic Perspective on Japan's 'Lost Decade'." *Population and Development Review* 38 (Supplement): 103–12.

Arrow, K. J. 1951/1963. *Social Choice and Individual Values*. New York: John Wiley & Sons, 1st edition 1951, 2nd edition 1963.

Arrow, K. J., Sen, A. K., and Suzumura, K. (eds.) 1996/1997. *Social Choice Re-examined*, 2 vols. New York: St. Martin's Press.

Basu, K. and Mitra, T. 2003. "Aggregating Infinite Utility Streams with Intergenerational Equity: The Importance of Being Paretian." *Econometrica* 71: 1557–63.

Basu, K. and Mitra, T. 2007. "Utilitarianism for Infinite Utility Streams: A New Welfare Criterion and its Axiomatic Characterization." *Journal of Economic Theory* 133: 350–73.

Bergson, A. 1938. "A Reformulation of Certain Aspects of Welfare Economics." *Quarterly Journal of Economics* 52: 310–34.

Bossert, W., Sprumont, Y., and Suzumura, K. 2007. "Ordering Infinite Utility Streams." *Journal of Economic Theory* 135: 579–89. Reprinted in Suzumura (2016: essay 11).

[22] Comments and discussion related to this essay, which is a companion to the one by Amartya Sen, appear at the end of Chapter 7. Thanks are due to Kenneth Arrow and Amartya Sen, with whom I had several opportunities to discuss the central issue of this essay. I am also grateful to Walter Bossert, whose incisive comments on an earlier draft helped me avoid many ambiguities and inadequacies. Financial support from a Grant-in-Aid for Specially Promoted Research from the Ministry of Education, Culture, Sports, Science and Technology of Japan for the Project on Economic Analysis of Intergenerational Issues (grant number 22000001) is gratefully acknowledged.

Bossert, W. and Suzumura, K. 2011. "Multiprofile Intergenerational Social Choice." *Social Choice and Welfare* 37: 493–509. Reprinted in Suzumura (2016: essay 12).

Bossert, W. and Suzumura, K. 2014. "Parental Voting Weights: A Critical Examination." Working paper, School of Political Science and Economics, Waseda University.

Campiglio, L. 2009. "Children's Right to Vote: The Missing Link in Modern Democracies." *Sociological Studies of Children and Youth* 12: 221–47.

Carballo, M. 1981. "Extra Votes for Parents?" *Boston Globe*, December 17, p. 35.

Coase, R. 1960. "The Problem of Social Cost." *Journal of Law and Economics* 3: 1–44.

Demeny, P. 1986. "Pronatalist Policies in Low-Fertility Countries: Patterns, Performance, and Prospects." *Population and Development Review* 12 (Supplement): 335–58.

Demeny, P. 2011a. "Population Decrease and Intergenerational Disparity: Give Voting Rights to Children." *Japan Economic Newspaper*, March 11.

Demeny, P. 2011b. "Population Policy and the Demographic Transition: Performance, Prospects, and Options." *Population and Development Review* 37 (Supplement, S1): 249–74.

Diamond, P. 1965. "The Evaluation of Infinite Utility Streams." *Econometrica* 33: 170–7.

Dworkin, R. 1981a. "What is Equality? Part I: Equality of Welfare." *Philosophy and Public Affairs* 10: 185–246.

Dworkin, R. 1981b. "What is Equality? Part II: Equality of Resources." *Philosophy and Public Affairs* 10: 283–345.

Dworkin, R. 2000. *Sovereign Virtue: The Theory and Practice of Equity.* Cambridge, MA: Harvard University Press.

Espenshade, T. J., Guzman, J. C., and Westoff, C. F. 2003. "The Surprising Global Variation in Replacement Fertility." *Population Research and Policy Review* 22: 575.

Fleurbaey, M. 1995. "Equality and Responsibility." *European Economic Review* 39: 683–9.

Fleurbaey, M. 1998. "Equality among Responsible Individuals." In J.-J. Laslier, et al. (eds.), *Freedom in Economics: New Perspectives in Normative Analysis.* London: Routledge.

Gaertner, W., Pattanaik, P. K., and Suzumura, K. 1992. "Individual Rights Revisited." *Economica* 59: 161–77. Reprinted in Suzumura (2016: essay 15).

Hara, C., Shinotsuka, T., Suzumura, K., and Xu, Y. 2008. "Continuity and Egalitarianism in the Evaluation of Infinite Utility Streams." *Social Choice and Welfare* 31: 179–91.

Harrod, R. 1948. *Towards a Dynamic Economics.* London: Macmillan.

Harsanyi, J. C. 1977. *Rational Behavior and Bargaining Equilibrium in Games and Social Situations.* Cambridge: Cambridge University Press.

Herche, V. 2011. "Demographic Changes and Challenges in Europe: An Interview With Paul Demeny." *Demographic Change and the Family in Europe* 3: 8–17.

Koopmans, T. C. 1960. "Stationary Ordinal Utility and Impatience." *Econometrica* 28: 287–309.

Koopmans, T., Diamond, P., and Williamson, R. 1964. "Stationary Utility and Time Perspective." *Econometrica* 32: 82–100.

Marx, K. 1904. "Introduction to the Critique of Political Economy." In *A Contribution to the Critique of Political Economy.* Translated from the second German edition by N. I. Stone. Chicago: Charles H. Kerr.

Mill, J. S. 1859. *On Liberty.* London: Parker. Reprinted in Robsen (1977).

Parfit, D. 1984. *Reasons and Persons.* Oxford: Oxford University Press.

Pigou, A. C. 1912. *Wealth and Welfare.* London: Macmillan.

Pigou, A. C. 1920. *The Economics of Welfare.* London: Macmillan.

Ramsey, F. P. 1928. "A Mathematical Theory of Saving." *Economic Journal* 38: 543–59.

Ringen, S. 1996. "In a Democracy, Children Should Get the Vote." *International Herald Tribune*, December 14–15.

Robsen, J. M. (ed.) 1977. *The Collected Works of John Stuart Mill*. Toronto: University of Toronto Press.

Roemer, J. E. 1985. "Equality of Talent." *Economics and Philosophy* 1: 151–81.

Roemer, J. E. 1986. "Equality of Resources Implies Equality of Welfare." *Quarterly Journal of Economics* 101: 751–84.

Roemer, J. and Suzumura, K. (eds.) 2007. *Intergenerational Equity and Sustainability*. New York: Palgrave Macmillan.

Sen, A. K. 1970. *Collective Choice and Social Welfare*. San Francisco: Holden-Day.

Sen, A. K. 1977. "Social Choice Theory: A Re-examination." *Econometrica* 45: 53–89.

Sen, A. K. 1982. "Liberty as Control: An Appraisal." *Midwest Studies in Philosophy* 7: 207–21.

Shaw, G. B. 1903. "Maxims for Revolutionists." In *Man and Superman: A Comedy and a Philosophy*. Cambridge, MA: The University Press.

Sidgwick, H. 1907. *The Methods of Ethics*, 7th edition. London: Macmillan.

Smith, A. 1759. *The Theory of Moral Sentiments*. London: A. Millar and Edinburgh: A. Kincaid and J. Bell. Penguin Classics edition (2009) with an Introduction by A. K. Sen, edited with notes by R. P. Hanley. London: Penguin Books Ltd.

Stewart, D. J. 1970. "Disfranchise the Old." *New Republic* 29(8): 20–2.

Suzumura, K. 2016. *Choice, Preferences, and Procedures: A Rational Choice Theoretic Approach*. Cambridge, MA: Harvard University Press.

Suzumura, K. and Tadenuma, K. 2007. "Normative Approaches to the Issues of Global Warming: Responsibility and Compensation." In J. Roemer and K. Suzumura (eds.), *Intergenerational Equity and Sustainability*. New York: Palgrave/Macmillan, 320–36.

Van Parijs, P. 1998. "The Disfranchisement of the Elderly, and Other Attempts to Secure Intergenerational Justice." *Philosophy and Public Affairs* 27: 292–333.

World Commission on Environment and Development. 1987. *Our Common Future*. Oxford: Oxford University Press.

PART II

THE AGENCY
PROBLEM

CHAPTER 7

....

OUR OBLIGATION TO FUTURE GENERATIONS

....

AMARTYA SEN

Abstract

Our reasoned sense of obligations to others can arise from at least three possible sources: cooperation, having caused harm, and effective power to improve suffering. The last source, this chapter argues, is particularly important in considering our obligations to future generations. It draws on a line of reasoning that takes us well beyond contractarian motivations to the idea of the "impartial spectator" as developed by Adam Smith. The interests of future generations come into the story because they are important in our attempt to be impartial spectators. The obligation of power contrasts with the mutual obligations for cooperation at the basic plane of motivational justification. In the context of climate concerns and intergenerational justice, this asymmetry-embracing approach seems to allow an easier entry for understanding our obligations.

OBLIGATIONS OF POWER

....

Obligations can arise for different reasons. Let me begin by distinguishing between three possible sources of our reasoned sense of obligation to others:

(1) *Cooperation*: if we are working along with others to pursue some social objective, we owe it to each other to do "our bit," and that can yield obligations of what we should do to further our joint program.

(2) *Responsibility for having caused harm*: if the suffering or disadvantage of others have been caused by our actions or behavior, we may have reason to try to do what we can to remove those harms, on grounds of our agency responsibility.

(3) *Obligation of power*: if we have the effective power to improve the lives of suffering people, we may have reason to consider what we should do to help, whether or not we had any role in causing that suffering.

The first two lines of reasoning have received much more championing and attention than the third avenue has, which is particularly important to explore, I will argue, for considering our obligations to the future generations.

This note is intended to supplement Kotaro Suzumura's far-reaching essay for the Society for Progress' second assembly in November 2015.[1] I very much endorse the considerations he has placed before us. It is possible to argue that Suzumura's direct focus is mainly on "harm-correction" and "cooperation," and after accepting the reasonableness of what he says, I want to proceed further and try to propose a different way of approaching ethical reasoning, based on the "power to do good" in thinking about our responsibility toward future generations (which, as I will discuss, fits in very well with Suzumura's own ideas).

In particular, I want to draw on a kind of reasoning that would take us well beyond contractarian motivations, such as the impartiality embedded in "justice as fairness" involving the use of Rawlsian "original position" (an imagined state of primordial equality where no one knows who he or she is going to be in the actual world). Nor should we be restricted to arguments linked with "harm-correction" which dominates another way of diagnosing obligations, much used in the literature on the subject.[2] If the idea of contractual impartiality has Hobbsian–Kantian–Rawlsian antecedence, the approach I would like to consider has strong links with the thoughts of Condorcet, Adam Smith, and Mary Wollstonecraft—and going much further back, Gautama Buddha.

It is easy to understand that the idea of justice as well as our ethical sense of "responsibility" must invoke some kind of justifiable *impartiality*. The interests of the future generations need not get into the story through—at least not primarily through—how we may ourselves personally benefit from cooperation with future generations. As Ken Arrow pointed out in a note to Kotaro Suzumura and myself in the context of our joint work for this symposium, we must take into account the obvious but profound fact that the future generation cannot do anything for us. This elementary but forceful recognition may pose a huge problem for a contractual approach that has to invoke, in one way or another, mutual advantages from cooperation.

This consideration does not, however, pose a similar challenge when the ethical demands arise not from contractarian pursuit of mutual advantage but from the obligation of our power. In this broad perspective, the reasoning sought does not

---

[1] See Chapter 6.
[2] I have tried to outline such an approach in a broader context in my book, *The Idea of Justice* (London: Penguin, and Cambridge, MA: Harvard University Press, 2009), particularly in chapter 9 ("Plurality of Impartial Reasons").

have to be a self-interest-mediated contractarian argument (pioneered through the idea of a "social contract" by Thomas Hobbes), nor an argument that is confined to restituting the harm we tend to do to future generations.

THE DEMANDS OF IMPARTIAL REASONING

We must also note the fact that contractarian justice, if based on mutual advantage, is not in its origin an ethical argument with full demands of impartiality, but either a *prudential* argument supporting self-interest with an instrumental use of a contract, or the ethical reflection of a prudential argument based on an imagined contract (which we would have reason to sustain on self-interested grounds, had the circumstances been as they are postulated to be in the imaginary exercise).[3] It is not hard to see why the contractarian approach appeals to people who insist that we cannot look—in one way or another—beyond sophisticated pursuit of self-interest, and who want decent behavior to emerge ultimately from some direct or indirect consideration of personal advantage. While the Rawlsian theory of contractual justice can be justified in many different ways, there is a clear connection here with Rawls' desire to see "society as a fair system of cooperation." As Rawls puts it, the idea of cooperation "includes the idea of each participant's rational advantage, or good," and "the idea of rational advantage specifies what it is that those engaged in cooperation are seeking to advance from the standpoint of their own good."[4] There is something in common here with the self-interested perspective of "rational choice theory" except that it is used under the imagined conditions of the "original position," with a veil of ignorance about personal identities (so that no one knows exactly who he or she is going to be in the real world).

If this is social morality, it is undoubtedly a *self-interest-coated* social morality. Since the idea of mutually beneficial cooperation is so central to the conception of the Rawlsian original position, and since Rawls' invoking of the foundational idea of fairness is mainly through the device of the original position, there is a quintessentially advantage-based underpinning to the Rawlsian approach to "justice as fairness."

The advantage-based perspective is undoubtedly important for social rules and behavior, since there are many situations in which the joint interests of a group of people are much better served by everyone following rules of behavior that restrain each person from trying to snatch personal gain at the cost of making things worse for others. The real world is full of a great many problems of this kind, for example the

---

[3] Thomas Scanlon's "contractualist" approach—focusing on diagnoses of what others "cannot reasonably reject"—has some similarity with the power-to-do-good approach, despite the name that Scanlon has chosen for his theory. I am not referring to this class of theories as "contractarian." On this point, see *The Idea of Justice*, chapter 9.

[4] John Rawls, 2001. *Justice as Fairness: A Restatement.* Cambridge, MA: Harvard University Press, 5–8.

preservation of shared natural resources ("the commons"), or adherence to work ethics in production processes, or to mutually supportive civic behavior in urban living.

It must be acknowledged that this contractual understanding has extensive relevance in social analysis and political reasoning. There can be little doubt that prudential arguments, based ultimately on mutual benefit, are very important for social cooperation and through that for social morality and politics. In looking for a type of ethical reasoning that goes *beyond* that, there would obviously not be any attempt to deny the relevance of the cooperative perspective in practical reasoning, as far as it goes.

There is indeed plenty of scope for taking note of cooperative advantages of contractual behavior. This is not in dispute. The question that arises is whether moral or political reasoning must be confined to recognizing the relevance of cooperative advantages—without encouragement to go beyond that. If the cooperation-based approach were to define the limits or our concern, then questions of intergenerational justice must be inescapably in rough terrain, with temptations to "repair" the problem through some cleverly derived compromise, such as relying on a chain of interconnections through the overlap between every generation and the immediately next (even though that line of reasoning has serious problems of consistency and cogency).

Contrast that line of reasoning with the idea of the "impartial spectator" as developed by Adam Smith in his *Theory of Moral Sentiments* (1759). The "impartial spectator" is not working out a convenient contract, but insisting that we place ourselves in each other's positions, and then deciding what would be the right thing to do—or more particularly in the present context, the "responsible" thing to do. The interests of future generations come into the story because they are important in our attempt to be impartial spectators, and this concern does not have to be justified on some ground—real or imagined—that using our power to enhance their lives would somehow benefit us right now and right here. If we have the power to do good, and understand this connection, then that can itself be the basis of our obligations to future generations.

In this view of impartiality, the key factor is not each person's benefiting individually from cooperation with others (so powerfully identified by Thomas Hobbes), but rather how we can understand the demands of impartial reasoning, despite the inescapable asymmetry between the respective roles of different generations. The "impartial spectator" can be invoked precisely to address this question (though the idea has other uses as well). The "obligation of power" contrasts with the mutual obligation for cooperation, at the basic plane of motivational justification. The cooperative argument not only has the underpinning of one's own advantage, but also a conditionality on which its rationale depends: as Rawls acknowledges, these motivational reasons can work "provided that everyone else likewise accepts them."[5] The obligation of power does not share the foundation of self-advantage (even in the impartial form developed by Rawls through "the original position"), and need not have the conditionality requirement

---

[5] Rawls, *Justice as Fairness: A Restatement*, 6.

(except to the extent that the power involved is contingent on others joining in, particularly within a specific generation).

ASYMMETRY IN INTERGENERATIONAL JUSTICE

In my book *The Idea of Justice*, I also invoked an argument presented by Gautama Buddha to the effect that if we can recognize (on the basis of impartial reasoning) that some decision would bring about a better state of affairs, then that is an argument to consider doing just that. There is a clear similarity here with Smithian reasoning.

The perspective of obligations of power was presented powerfully by Gautama Buddha in *Sutta Nipata*. Buddha argues there that we have responsibility to animals precisely because of the asymmetry between us, not because of any symmetry that takes us to the need for cooperation. He argues instead that since we are enormously more powerful than the other species, we have some responsibility toward other species that connects exactly with this asymmetry of power.

Buddha illustrated the point by an analogy with the responsibility of a mother toward her child, not because she has given birth to the child (that connection is not invoked in this particular argument—there is room for it elsewhere), but because she can do things to influence the child's life that the child itself cannot do. The mother's reason for helping the child, in this line of thinking, is not guided by the rewards of cooperation, but precisely from her recognition that she can, asymmetrically, do things for the child that will make a huge difference to the child's life and which the child itself cannot do. This is a part of the moral universe in which the mother—and more generally the parents—live. The mother does not have to seek any mutual benefit—real or imagined—nor seek any "as if" contract to understand her obligation to the child. That is the point that Gautama was making.

In the context of intergenerational justice and obligations, this approach, which allows asymmetry (and may even build on it constructively), seems to me to allow an easier entry than can be obtained through a contractual approach with some underlying motivation of making justice foundationally dependent on "mutual advantage."

NORMATIVE REASONING BEYOND
RESPONSIBILITY AND COMPENSATION

Toward the end of his essay (in section five), Kotaro Suzumura considers a "hypothetical scenario" which involves, among other specifications, the assumption that "50 percent of this global warming is caused by the emissions of greenhouse gases by the present generation, but the remaining 50 percent is due to the accumulation of greenhouse gases emitted by the past generations." Suzumura then invokes what we have been calling "responsibility for having caused harm," and considers the ethical position that "the present generation should bear responsibility to abate global warming only to the extent that they have contributed to its cause." So for the two degrees of temperature reduction needed for avoiding catastrophe (worked out from Suzumura's other assumptions) the present generation "should be held responsible for … only a one-degree reduction."

But Suzumura rightly notes that the "other culprits, viz. past generations," who should be responsible for the "remaining one-degree reduction," cannot do this for "they do not exist anymore." So Suzumura extends the notion of "accountable responsibility" to require that "the present generation must bear all the required reduction of two degrees in world temperature." I take this to be an endorsement—if only implicit—of the obligation of power. The present generation has the power to do this to prevent the catastrophe in question in a way that past generations—no matter how much harm they have caused—cannot (since they are *no longer* here), nor can future generations (since they are *not yet* here). So we end up with what can be seen as a default obligation, which, in this case, coincides with the obligation of power.

I am not arguing that the obligation of power is the only way of thinking about our responsibility to future generations in the field of environmental security. The responsibility for causing harm has been brought into contemporary global ethics with some immediate appeal, for example in asking the richer countries, with a much longer history of industrialization, to take extra responsibility for accepting the relevance of their role as long-term polluters (making societal identity override generational identity). And the need for cooperation-based thinking is also quite important for environmental planning, since many of the proposed remedies can work only through joint efforts today.

What I am arguing for is to pay more direct attention to the ethics and politics of the obligation of power, which has received far less attention in the literature than the approach of social contract and that of responsibility for causing harm. Normative reasoning can take many different forms, and if a particular line of reasoning is both very important and has been much neglected, then the case for paying attention to it can be extraordinarily strong.

. . . .

Comments and Discussion

In Chapter 6, Suzumura seeks an appropriate moral framework for thinking about our obligations to future generations vis-à-vis climate change in light of a range of complications, such as the asymmetric vulnerability of future people to present actions, the impossibility of establishing any kind of contractual relationship between future and present people, Parfit's "non-identity" problem, and others. Drawing on the ideas of Dworkin, Roemer, and Fleurbaey, Suzumura suggests that the most promising route is a principle of responsibility and compensation: we should be held responsible for outcomes which result from actions over which we have full control.

Sen's essay, which he proposes as a supplement to Suzumura's, criticizes the tendency of contractarian thinking to dominate in issues of this nature. As an alternative, Sen suggests, Smith's impartiality standard provides us with a basis for thinking about moral obligations in cases like climate change, where contractual or mutualistic relationships are either non-existent or inadequate to capture the obligations in play.

What kinds of institutional measures might best motivate people to act in a way that serves the good of future people at some expense to themselves?

In his essay, Suzumura considers and dismisses as problematic some ways of tweaking our system of democratic representation so as to give better voice to future people. In response to such suggestions, at the Society for Progress' second assembly, Kitcher likewise expressed skepticism about alterations of conventional representational mechanisms and suggested that greater promise lies in measures to foster heightened engagement with information bearing on the interests and concerns of future people. Could we envision town hall-style meetings addressed to this purpose, for example? On this point, Anderson pointed to a body of research showing that people do not, in general, vote on the basis of self-interest. Perhaps, then, the primary issue is not getting people to subordinate their own good to future concerns, but rather, as Kitcher suggested, getting them to properly understand the weight of those concerns.

How should we think about our moral responsibility in the case of a large-scale, intergenerational problem like climate change?

One problem with climate change is that the present generation is burdened with taking action even though previous generations have contributed massively to the problem. In sympathy with Sen, Schmidtz and Anderson both made comments suggesting that there are good grounds for thinking we should take responsibility when action is urgent, independently of whether it's our fault. As Anderson put it, "at the point where the ship is sinking, bickering over who ought to do the bailing out, it's really irrelevant." One might suggest that justice simply isn't the primary or exclusive consideration. Alternatively, Anderson proposed, one might recognize that justice plausibly requires those with the most capacity—in this case the wealthy countries of the world—to bear the burden of action. Another way of thinking about justice in this case, Kitcher proposed, is in terms of an atmospheric carbon sink: those presently alive, and particularly the wealthy, have used up more than their fair share of this finite resource, and are therefore obliged to take measures to ensure the capacity of others to use it in the future.

How should the burdens of addressing climate change be distributed?

While Suzumura's essay focuses on intergenerational obligations, Fuerstein and Collomb separately emphasized that it is not only intergenerational justice at stake, but also intragenerational justice. In addressing climate challenges, we must also make sure that the burden of aiding future people does not fall disproportionately on the poor. This complicates an already complicated question of how to proceed. In thinking about the burdens of addressing climate change, Sen indicated his concern about the prospects of over-reliance on nuclear energy as a solution. Given the associated risks, this in effect replaces one kind of severe threat with another. On the other hand, Frank argued, given some already ominous estimates of the probability of a future large-scale climate disaster, we might be justified in subordinating even weighty concerns about nuclear risk for the sake of immediate action. Another set of issues here concerns distribution of the cost of addressing climate change intergenerationally. Discussions here tend to focus on the potentially high economic cost to the present generation. Anderson, however, noted John Broome's argument that we could mitigate this problem by taking out a long-term bond to pay for the necessary measures, in effect kicking some of the cost down to future people. Even if there is some unfairness in that solution, it might serve as an effective route around cost-based objections. There is yet a further question, though, of how much the present generation owes the future generation in the first place. Suzumura's scheme invokes a notion of compensation. Pettit, however, raised a question about how to conceptualize this: "Do we compensate just for what we might otherwise do, or for what past generations have also done? Against what benchmark do we compensate?"[6]

[6] I have benefited from conversations with Kenneth Arrow and Kotaro Suzumura, from the lively symposium in the Second Assembly in London in November 2015, and from discussions with Philip Kitcher, Philip Pettit, and Susan Neiman, among others at the assembly.

CHAPTER 8

AS YOU LIKE IT

Work, Life, and Satisfaction

DAVID AUTOR AND PHILIP KITCHER

Think over the men and women you know...you will find a comparatively small number of persons of greater moral energy than usual, in whom a conscious desire for service is evident, and another small group of greater economic energy than usual who are concerned with making pecuniary profit. In many ways the latter rule the roost and fix the conditions under which the mass, who are engaged in doing what conditions permit and require, live and work. But the mass does not think the game of profit making is worthwhile; unconsciously and in effect they do not think so. They want to get along, to support their families, to enjoy companionship with others. They regard these things as more important than making profit.[1]

John Dewey

Abstract

To what extent and how does economic work relate to life satisfaction? Over the past century, work or a job has become crucial to gaining a livelihood. Writers have also suggested that (at least some proportion of) individuals also have life goals or "life themes" that are central to their life fulfillment. This chapter explores the philosophical origins of these ideas and considers the (usually survey-based) research that attempts to sort out these complex issues. Integrating ideas from labor economics and social philosophy, it explores patterns in the historical survey data for the US, and presents reflections on why and for whom work matters, how it might and ought to relate to life satisfaction, and how one might ideally measure these links. The chapter also discusses an expanded role for education, and closes by outlining specific questions for future research on this topic.

---

[1] John Dewey, 1983. *John Dewey: The Middle Works, 1899–1922.* Carbondale: University of Southern Illinois Press, 282.

PRELIMINARIES

In a short essay, "Industry and Motives," published in 1922, John Dewey took up the question of how, in a capitalist or post-capitalist society, business might be induced to be more public-spirited, to emphasize "service" more and "profit" less. His response credited Adam Smith with an insight and charged him with an error. Smith perceived correctly that public good isn't always (or perhaps isn't often) achieved by preaching private virtue—it may be "no worse for society" that the collective good was no part of the entrepreneur's intention. Yet, Dewey contends, Smith's account of human motivation is incorrect. There's no universal, or even common, "propensity to truck and barter" with the goal of maximizing returns to oneself. The profit motive emerges as a distortion of natural human tendencies because the few people driven by it come to run the show. Once the capitalist emphasis on economic growth is in place, the masses are forced to conform. The poor become obsessed with the doings of the rich: the newspapers they read are those "that give most attention to the activities of millionaires."[2] Dewey proposes to correct the distorting system by fostering developments in education, in the practices of the sciences, and in the law.

We aren't concerned with Dewey's sketches of solutions, but with the predicament he hypothesized, on the basis, apparently, of anecdotal (or anthropological?) evidence ("Think over the men and women you know"). To what extent are the conditions of work today antithetical to the wants of the workers? With respect to workers in some parts of the world, those places that seem to replicate some of the conditions described by Engels and Orwell,[3] the answer seems straightforward. When the workers in a Chinese factory are required to live in dormitories at great distances from their families, or when the workers in a Bangladeshi sweatshop have to work long hours under dangerous conditions for very low pay, it's hard to resist the conclusion that the workers' situations are not exactly desirable, even if they are preferable to the available alternatives. Our interest, however, will be in the predicament of workers in affluent societies, particularly in North America and Europe.

Newspapers often paint a dismal picture of the plight of these workers, pointing out that real wages have stagnated for several decades, that employment is precarious, that many of those who work must take on two or more jobs to make ends meet, that workers' hours are often determined on very short notice, that manufacturing jobs (with dignity) give way to menial employment in the service sector, and other factors expected to decrease satisfaction. We want to go beyond the surface features, however. Economists and other social scientists have investigated the relations between work and welfare. We'll attempt an analysis of what they have found, using it as the basis for considering whether the conditions of work in the affluent world interfere with the lives and the happiness of workers.

---

[2] Dewey, *John Dewey: The Middle Works, 1899–1922*, 283.
[3] Friedrich Engels, 1993. *The Condition of the Working Class in England*. Oxford and New York: Oxford University Press; George Orwell, 1958. *The Road to Wigan Pier*. New York: Harcourt, Brace.

SOME FACTS

There is a considerable body of social science devoted to collecting and analyzing measures of so-called subjective well-being.[4] An often-used measure of subjective well-being is calculated from responses to a single survey question regarding global life satisfaction, such as "In general, how satisfied are you with your life?" or, alternatively, " . . . with the work you do?" (as it turns out, the answers to these questions are extremely highly correlated). There are numerous conceptual and empirical limitations to these measures, however.

As an empirical matter, it is widely recognized that reports of subjective well-being based on a single omnibus survey measure of global life satisfaction do not generally capture stable, long-term assessments of personal well-being. Instead, survey responses typically reflect transient judgments that are heavily influenced by temporal context, current mood, and the design of the survey questions themselves.

Responses to these questions are not entirely meaningless, however. A 2010 paper in *Science* by Oswald and Wu using US data confirms that, on average, people's subjective answers to personal well-being questions trace out approximately the same cross-state ranking of quality of life as do estimates based on purely objective measures of wages, housing costs, and a large set of amenities and disamenities (e.g. precipitation and humidity, sunshine, school quality, violence, vehicular congestion, pollution, and state and local taxes).[5]

In an effort to overcome the limitations of the omnibus attitudinal measurement approach, researchers have developed techniques for capturing moment-to-moment self-assessments of emotional well-being ("net affect").[6] Used in combination with time diaries, these tools capture the ebb and flow of transient emotional states more accurately than do the single survey question approach. Whether they do a better job of assessing any broader measure of personal welfare is open to debate.

---

[4] Richard Layard's 2005 book, *Happiness: Lessons from a New Science* (London: Allen Lane), presents a forceful argument that social science should focus on happiness rather than material well-being to quantify human welfare and societal progress. Philosophical accounts of welfare are often classified as *subjective* if they center on the satisfaction of desires, or *objective* if they offer a list of features found in lives that go well. In "Well-Being: Psychological Research for Philosophers" (*Philosophy Compass* 1(5), 2006: 493–505), Valerie Tiberius provides a valuable review of the major current positions.

[5] A. J. Oswald and S. Wu, 2010. "Objective Confirmation of Subjective Measures of Human Well-Being: Evidence from the U.S.A." *Science* 327(5965): 576–9. An interesting feature of the objective data is that the highest-ranked states are some of the least populous: Wyoming, South Dakota, Arkansas, etc. The canonical interpretation of this pattern would be that the high quality of life in these states is insufficient to compensate potential residents for the very low prevailing wage levels; thus, few people choose to live in these states, despite their high amenity value. We leave it to readers to draw their own conclusions about the plausibility of this argument.

[6] D. Kahneman, A. B. Krueger, D.A. Schkade, N. Schwarz, and A. A. Stone, 2006. "Would You Be Happier if You Were Richer? A Focusing Illusion." *Science* 312(5782): 1908–10.

A third approach recently employed in US survey data (specifically, the American Time Use Survey) is to ask respondents about the "meaningfulness" of the activities that occupy their time.[7] A recent working paper by Song finds that self-reported meaningfulness is substantially more positively correlated with "objective" state-level rankings of quality of life than either the omnibus global life satisfaction measure or the net affect scales used in conjunction with time diary data.[8]

At a conceptual level, these survey measures are also poorly grounded in a broader theory of well-being. This point was well articulated by economist Gary Becker:

> The big question that is not answered . . . is what happiness data tell us about well-being. That is, about lifetime "utility" of persons who differ by income and other characteristics? Virtually all economists who have written on happiness automatically assume that it is a quantitative measure of utility, and that this provides a way to make interpersonal comparisons of utility and well being. But I argue . . . that "happiness", even if accurately measured by these surveys, is not the same as utility or well being. Rather, happiness may be an important component of utility that often, but not always, moves in the same direction as utility.
>
> I use health as an analogy to happiness. Individuals generally get more utility when they expect to live longer and are in better health. However, they do not try to simply maximize how long they live and the quality of their health since they may trade off lower life expectancy for higher income by taking jobs with greater risks to their lives, or for pleasures of food, drink, driving fast, and other activities. The same is true for "happiness". Yes, individuals generally prefer to be happier, but sometimes they are willing to trade off happiness for other behavior that gives them greater utility.[9]

Despite our concerns about the conceptual underpinnings and empirical reliability of omnibus measures of subjective well-being, we suspected that it would be illuminating to see what these measures tell about job satisfaction. Using General Social Survey (GSS) data for US respondents from the years 1973 through 2014, one of us (Autor) estimated a set of descriptive ordinary least squares regression models for the relationship between self-reported job satisfaction (measured on an increasing ordinal scale from 0 to 3, where 0 means very dissatisfied and 3 means very satisfied). While GSS sample sizes are not enormous (roughly 1,000 observations from US workers per year), they have the advantage of providing a consistent time series over more than four decades.

---

[7] The specific question is, "From 0 to 6, how meaningful did you consider what you were doing? 0 means it was not meaningful at all to you and a 6 means it was very meaningful to you."

[8] Younghwan Song, 2015. "A Cross-State Comparison of Measures of Subjective Well-Being." IZA Discussion Paper No. 9396 (September). One striking but difficult-to-interpret pattern detected by Song's analysis is that self-reported meaningfulness is strongly *declining* in education and earnings, and is substantially lower among whites than Asians, Hispanics, or especially blacks. This odd pattern raises a concern that the strong positive correlation between "meaningfulness" and state quality-of-life rankings derives from the fact that highly ranked states have relatively few highly educated and high-income residents.

[9] Becker-Posner Blog, "Happiness and Wellbeing" by Gary Becker (January 10, 2010), <http://www.becker-posner-blog.com/2010/01/happiness-and-wellbeing--becker.html>.

The questions that we sought to explore empirically are:

- Is money the prime determinant of job satisfaction, as conventional economic models would suggest?
- Do valuations of job attributes differ by gender, race, occupation, or educational level?
- Has job satisfaction changed systematically in recent decades across gender, race, education, and occupation as income has diverged across these groups?

Our results are as follows:

1. Job satisfaction is considerably higher among whites than blacks (Figure 8.1), among more-educated than less-educated workers (Figure 8.2), and among higher-paid than lower-paid workers.
2. Job satisfaction differs considerably across occupations. Job satisfaction generally increases with the prestige or social standing of occupations. The most satisfying jobs (as self-reported) are mostly professions, especially those involving caring for, teaching, and protecting others, as well as creative pursuits. The least satisfying jobs are mostly low-skill, manual, and service occupations, especially involving customer service and food/beverage preparation and serving.
3. While the earnings measure in the GSS is quite crude, it is nevertheless clear that, *ceteris paribus*, workers with higher earnings report higher levels of satisfaction.

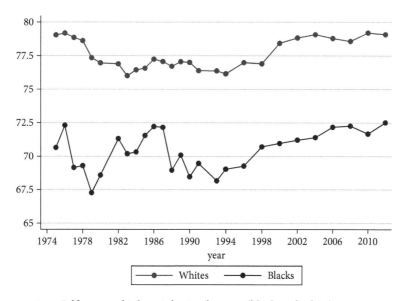

FIGURE **8.1.** Self-reported job satisfaction by race (black and white), 1974–2012

Source: Authors' tabulation of General Social Survey (various years). Sample is limited to self-reported white and black workers with non-missing data on age, earnings, and job satisfaction (n = 29,000). Categorical satisfaction responses are collapsed to continuous measure: "Very satisfied" = 1; "Moderately satisfied" = 0.67; "Moderately dissatisfied" = 0.33; and "Very dissatisfied" = 0.

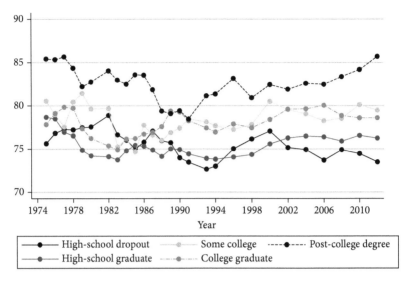

FIGURE **8.2.** Self-reported job satisfaction by educational attainment, 1974–2012

Source: Authors' tabulation of General Social Survey (various years). Categorical satisfaction responses are collapsed to continuous measure: "Very satisfied" = 1; "Moderately satisfied" = 0.67; "Moderately dissatisfied" = 0.33; and "Very dissatisfied" = 0. Sample restrictions are as per Figure 8.1.

4. Accounting for earnings differentials explains approximately half of the job satisfaction gaps across workers with different education levels, explains none of the black/white gap in job satisfaction, and modestly *increases* the apparent satisfaction levels of women relative to men (implying that if women earned the same as men, they'd be more satisfied than men, Figure 8.3).

5. Accounting for earnings differentials accounts for only a modest share of the differences in job satisfaction across occupations; the bulk of the raw occupational satisfaction differentials remain. It appears a robust fact that workers in service, clerking, elementary, and operative occupations are substantially less satisfied with their jobs than are workers in professional, technical, and managerial occupations.

6. While education is predictive of higher job satisfaction, dissatisfaction is extremely high among highly educated workers employed in normally low-education occupations (e.g. college-educated workers in elementary and operative positions). This remains the case even after accounting for earnings levels.

7. Perhaps the most surprising finding from our descriptive analysis is that the cross section of self-reported job satisfaction is extremely stable over time. We do not detect pronounced secular trends in satisfaction across education, race, gender, occupation, or pay categories over the four decades covered by our survey (Figure 8.4).

8. Yet, paradoxically, despite rising educational attainment and a growing share of workers employed in high-status occupations, there is only a very modest general upward trend in aggregate job satisfaction. This trend follows a modest U-shape over the four decades of our sample—declining from the early 1970s (when the sample starts) to the mid-1990s, then slowly rising throughout the 2000s (though falling in the Great Recession). (See Figure 8.5.)

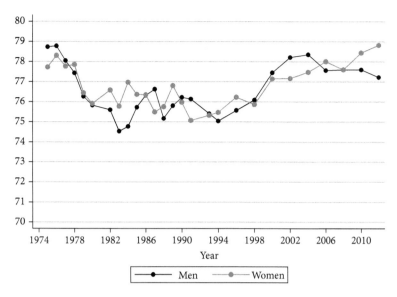

FIGURE **8.3.** Self-reported job satisfaction by sex, 1974–2012

Source: Authors' tabulation of General Social Survey (various years). Categorical satisfaction responses are collapsed to continuous measure: "Very satisfied" = 1; "Moderately satisfied" = 0.67; "Moderately dissatisfied" = 0.33; and "Very dissatisfied" = 0. Sample restrictions are as per Figure 8.1.

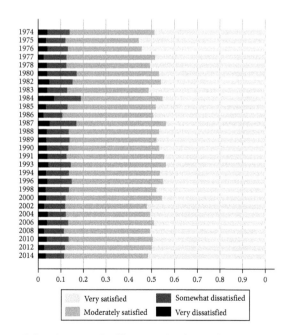

FIGURE **8.4.** Empirical distribution of self-reported job satisfaction, US workers, 1974–2014

Source: Authors' tabulation of General Social Survey (various years).

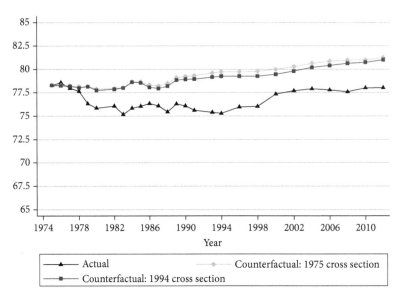

FIGURE **8.5.** Observed and counterfactual job satisfaction 1974–2012, holding constant the cross-sectional relationship between self-reported job satisfaction and individual covariates observed in 1974–6 and 1993–5

> *Source*: Authors' tabulation of General Social Survey (various years). Counterfactual series hold constant the
> distribution of sex, race (black/white), age (and its square), and education (high-school dropout,
> high-school graduate, some college, college graduate). Counterfactual series are calculated by regressing
> self-reported job satisfaction on sex, race, age (and its square), education, and a constant in the base period
> (1974–6, 1993–5), predicting mean satisfaction in all alternate years using the observed distribution
> of covariates in that year, and renormalizing the series to equal the base level in 1974.

In short, we conclude that education, income, occupational prestige, and race are each robust predictors of job satisfaction, and that it is unlikely that any one of these factors is fully explained by another (e.g. the direct relationship between occupational prestige and job satisfaction would probably not be eliminated by better measurement of income; the lower job satisfaction of black workers would probably not be eliminated by finer control for occupation). Workers who are nominally overeducated for their occupations are quite dissatisfied—implying that education can reduce job satisfaction if it does not lead to employment in an "educated" occupation.

The fact that aggregate satisfaction has only weakly increased despite rising education and improving occupational composition suggests many intriguing hypotheses. One is that satisfaction is "positional"—people draw satisfaction from being more successful than others, and since rank is a zero-sum game, aggregate improvements in job conditions do not lead to aggregate gains in satisfaction.[10] A second possibility is that respondents' answers to the "satisfaction" question are intrinsically comparative statements—that is, they are reporting whether or not they are satisfied relative to

---

[10] Robert H. Frank, 2007. *Falling Behind: How Rising Inequality Harms the Middle Class*. Berkeley and Los Angeles: University of California Press.

expectations, not relative to a static baseline level of job quality. In this case, the stability of aggregate job satisfaction may simply mean that the job "quality" has not risen faster than people would expect given changing circumstances. This would *not* imply that workers of today would in fact be equally happy in the labor market of decades earlier (in fact, it may imply the opposite). Still a third possibility is that aggregate cultural, political, economic, or global trends have worked to offset gains in satisfaction. Thus, although education levels and working conditions have both improved, a creeping psychic tax has clawed back the latent rise in satisfaction that should have occurred.

INTERPRETING THE DATA

The surveys we've reviewed belong to a tradition that distinguishes between two kinds of measures of welfare. On the one hand are so-called "objective" measures, such as income earned, goods and services consumed, wealth amassed, hours worked, health, and so forth.[11] These contrast with the "subjective" measures, scales set up to represent people's responses to particular aspects of their lives.

Reliance on either of these measures (or on a combination of them) can be problematic. Objective measures will prove misleading if they are unrelated to the features of people's lives that matter most to them. Subjective measures go astray when the responses the subjects make don't represent what they would most deeply want. Dewey's diagnosis of the capitalism he knew pinpoints both dangers. Focusing on economic returns to assess workers' welfare will go awry if Dewey's claims about what workers want are correct, if the profit motive is artificial and getting along, supporting the family, and so on are the truly important things. Similarly, questioning workers might elicit answers that reflect the distortions imposed by capitalism on conceptions of what is desirable, as illustrated in the fascination with the lives of the rich and famous.

Perhaps because the potential errors of objective measures are so much more obvious, the studies we've analyzed give priority to subjective measures (effectively using the objective measures simply as extra support for the conclusions drawn). Indeed, it's tempting to think that, if subjective measures are used, only the carelessness of the investigators would generate inaccurate estimates of welfare. For, in the end, aren't people authoritative about how well or how badly their lives—or aspects of their lives—are going? Isn't it arrogant to think that sincere answers to well-crafted questions could be misleading?

---

[11] It's important to note a difference between the ways in which economists and philosophers treat "objective" measures of well-being. The philosopher's "objective list" would be more likely to include autonomous choice and community with others (and similar features) rather than the economic variables. There would probably be agreement on health.

Dewey conjectures that the social system under which people live can modify their "natural"—or their "deep" or their "fundamental"—aspirations and values, so that they betray their "real selves" in answering the investigators' questions as they do. (Our use of quotation marks indicates the difficulties of providing a clear and compelling formulation of the point; we shall attempt to remedy this shortly.) His diagnosis raises the possibility of widespread false consciousness.

Notions of false consciousness have been asked to do serious work in Marxian thought and in feminist theory. Our concept inherits none of the special features of the Marxian and feminist versions, but it does try to bring out what they have in common. A claim of false consciousness rests on supposing that the attitudes expressed by a subject under current conditions are importantly different from those the subject would have endorsed in a different context, one more fully representative of who he or she is. Like the unsatisfactory phrases of the previous paragraph, the characterization of that special context needs to be made more precise. We suppose that the attribution of false consciousness rests on seeing the subject as *confined* by the present circumstances. So the contrast is between the attitudes affirmed in a confining context and those that would have been affirmed if the factors producing the confinement were to be removed. Just as the choices people manifest when assailants put guns to their heads don't express their long-standing desires, so too with the responses they make under subtler forms of coercion and constraint.

Hypotheses about false consciousness are cheap.[12] The interesting ones are those for which it's possible either to create situations in which the allegedly confining factors are suspended or else to find apparently similar subjects who are freed from the supposed confinement. To assess the impact of work on welfare, we suggest a variant of the first type. It's possible that current surveys of worker attitudes, while admirably conscientious in exemplifying the methodological standards of this line of inquiry, pose their questions in ways that don't attend to the confining context, thus eliciting responses expressing false consciousness. *Different* questions, however, might prompt subjects to reflect on broader possibilities for themselves, liberating them, temporarily, from the causes of confinement. More sophisticated surveys might absorb the results of consciousness-raising.

Consider the question posed in the GSS: "Taken all together, how would you say things are these days, would you say you are very happy, pretty happy, or not too happy?" The formulation has two unfortunate features. First, its vague temporal reference ("these days") invites respondents to think about a short (possibly very short) period of time. Rather than reflecting on their lives as a whole, and whether the current situation is undermining the long-term things they want, they're encouraged to think episodically, about their experiences and moods over recent days and weeks. Second, the terms in which the scale is set up ("very happy, pretty happy, not too happy"—note that "bloody miserable" isn't an option!) reinforce the focus on

---

[12] That emphatically does not mean that false consciousness is unimportant, or that we shouldn't explore the extent to which it occurs. We are grateful to Susan Neiman for pressing us on this point.

particular events and experiences, perhaps provoking an attempt by the subject to calculate the balance of "hedonic pluses and minuses." On the account of welfare we offer in the next section, this question appears badly designed to measure it.

The Pew survey on emerging markets does much better.[13] It measures life satisfaction by trying to free respondents' reflections from the constraining features of the actual circumstances.

> *Here is a ladder representing the "ladder of life." Let's suppose the top of the ladder represents the best possible life for you and the bottom the worst possible life for you. On which step of the ladder do you personally stand at the present time?*

We regard this formulation as superior because it treats the impact of circumstances on welfare in terms of the effects on the subject's entire life, thus downplaying the importance of the hedonic character of episodic experiences, and because it prompts people to reflect on the things they want in (or from) their lives. Yet the vaguely characterized top and bottom steps of the ladder allow quite radical departures from the current situation. We find it hard to tell how far from actuality we're allowed to go in thinking of the best and worst possible lives for ourselves: Does David receive the Nobel Prize in Economics and Philip the Nobel Prize in Literature (emulating Russell) at the top of the scale?[14] Do both of us live in abject slavery and conditions of periodic torture at the bottom? Do our loved ones attain similar highs and corresponding lows? A better question would focus on the subject's views about what matters most in her *actual* life and how the course of her life up to and including her current situation bears on her receiving or attaining the things that are of primary concern.

Another Pew survey, focused on the changing character of the family and evolving attitudes about the family, goes in the right direction, although it considers only a single candidate for what matters most.[15] Respondents were asked to answer the following question:

> *Which of the following statements best describes how important your family is to you at this time: the most important element of my life; one of the most important elements, but not the most important; not an important element of my life?*[16]

Of those surveyed, 76 percent saw the family as the most important element, a further 22 percent took it to be one of the most important but not the most important (we assume that these people either ranked something else as most important or saw the

---

[13] "People in Emerging Markets Catch Up to Advanced Economies in Life Satisfaction." Pew survey, released October 30, 2014.

[14] This is surely too modest to pick out our best *possible* lives. Think of the possibility that one of us utters words of such extraordinary wisdom as to bring about a condition of perpetual human peace.

[15] "The Decline of Marriage and the Rise of New Families." Pew survey, released November 18, 2010.

[16] We've amended the punctuation slightly, separating questions by semi-colons rather than commas, in the interests of clearer demarcation of alternatives.

family as on a par with at least one other element), leaving a mere 2 percent who either clearly identified family as unimportant or else didn't have a view on the issue.[17]

We suggest that surveys intending to probe worker satisfaction would make progress with respect to problems of false consciousness if they extended the approach of the marriage survey.[18] Our preference is for survey instructions that instantiate the following schema:[19]

> *Please reflect on the aspects of your life that matter most to you, on the domains in which achieving your goals is most important. Please identify each of these domains (e.g. family, participation in local community, making a contribution through work etc.) With respect to each of these domains, give a value, on a scale of 1–10 (with 10 being the highest value), that represents how well the course of your life so far, in that area, has gone. Then, for each of the following features of your circumstances of work [a list follows[20]], and for each important domain, assess whether that feature has an impact on that domain of your life; here you should use the following scale: −2 (strongly negative), −1 (negative), 0 (neutral), +1 (positive), +2 (strongly positive).*

After a preliminary survey to discover which aspects or domains were frequently cited by respondents, later investigations might provide a list of domains. Examples might include: family life, forming and deepening friendships, contributing to a community, achieving important goals through work, and, doubtless, a number of others. The list of properties of the circumstances of work might cover wages, work schedule, interactions with co-workers, attitudes of customers/clients, opportunities for independent decision, and so forth. We strongly suspect that experts on questionnaires would be able to streamline our formulation. Our claim is that some question along these lines stands a better chance of discovering how work relates to worker welfare.

The task of the next sections is to offer a philosophical perspective that justifies this claim, and to pose some preliminary questions, provoked by the results of the surveys already conducted.

---

[17] "The Decline of Marriage," 49.

[18] We don't claim that the style of question we recommend is guaranteed to avoid all problems of false consciousness, but rather that it overcomes some such problems afflicting the current approaches. Indeed, the very high fraction of respondents reporting that family is "the most important element" of their lives raises the concern that responses are skewed by social desirability bias.

[19] The approach we introduce here is akin to that pursued by Brian Little and his colleagues in a wide range of articles over three decades. See for example Brian Little, 1983. "Personal Projects: A Rationale and Method for Investigation." *Environment and Behavior* 15: 273–309, and many subsequent papers. Thanks to Valerie Tiberius for drawing our attention to Little's work.

[20] The list might include such things as: income, work hours, amount of autonomy, support from colleagues, and similar headings. For example, let's say a respondent's important domains include family life and making a contribution to knowledge. With respect to the circumstance *hours of work*, the impact on family life might be −2; with respect to contributions to knowledge, the contribution of *hours of work* might be +1. With respect to the circumstance *autonomy of decision making*, the contribution to both domains might be −2.

LIVES AND THEMES

Start with an idea common to thinkers as different as John Stuart Mill, John Rawls, and Bernard Williams:[21] people's lives are centered on a conception of themselves and what they want to be and do. Call this a "life theme." That needn't connote something grand. Ordinary people have life themes, some centered on nurturing a family, others on sustaining a small community. (Perhaps the data in the Pew marriage survey already indicate that 76 percent of contemporary Americans are focused on the family.) Your life theme might specify a single dominant role you play. Or it might assign you a number of roles, taken on successively or simultaneously. ("And one man in his time plays many parts.")

A life theme structures your wants and aspirations, picking out some of them as central. Much that we strive for could be missed or given up without serious loss. Other goals are crucial for our lives to go well. If, for example, someone's life theme is focused on the family, it is likely to be important that parents are cared for in their closing days, that a marriage remains strong and rewarding for both partners, and that children grow to happy and responsible maturity.

Mill emphasized the need for autonomous choice of life theme. A person's role should not be something thrust upon her, but freely chosen.

> The only freedom which deserves the name, is that of pursuing our own good in our own way, so long as we do not attempt to deprive others of theirs, or impede their efforts to obtain it.... Mankind are greater gainers by suffering each other to live as seems good to themselves, than by compelling each to live as seems good to the rest.[22]

Mill's fundamental freedom is very demanding. In its ideal form it can only be achieved if people have the opportunity to select from a wide menu of options for themselves, and to pick the one best suited to their talents and predilections. That opportunity requires becoming acquainted with a variety of patterns for human lives ("experiments of living") and enough exploratory trials to discover your skills and limitations—in short, an education that has been extremely rare in human history and that remains a privilege today.

The "life theme" approach suggests two ways to measure well-being. On the more demanding version, emphasizing the need for a special type of education to allow a genuinely autonomous choice, well-being is a function of the ability to choose a theme from a rich set of alternatives, and to pursue it successfully. Given the low chances of having the appropriate style of education, this measure is utopian for any purposes of examining the relation between work and life. So we propose relaxing the conditions on autonomy, supposing that the education and socialization available to many young

---

[21] Brian Little follows Williams in using the terminology of a personal "project."
[22] John Stuart Mill, 1859. *On Liberty.* London: John W. Parker and Son, West Strand.

people in the world's affluent democracies suffice for them to be able to "choose their own good"—we differentiate the choices of young Americans from those made by young women in many religious fundamentalist societies around the world. We'll measure the well-being of people in affluent societies by considering whether or not they are able to satisfy the central desires that flow from their life theme.[23]

To clarify: the mathematical form of this measure is two-dimensional. On the first—dominant—dimension, lives either go well or they do not. Given sufficient attainment of the goals that really matter, the life is a good one, even if there are any number of disappointments regarding peripheral aims. Conversely, no amount of minor successes or pleasures (victories for a favorite sports team, fabulous parties, or even luck in the lottery) can make up for the shipwreck of the central projects. Utilitarian addition breaks down. Discreteness is the better part of value.

(*Brief digression*. Abandoning a dominant *continuous* dimension is required to address a problem posed by Derek Parfit.[24] Assume that welfare is understood in terms of quality of life, that this can be measured on a continuous scale, and that (viewed in these terms) interpersonal comparisons of welfare are always available. How is welfare maximized when the size of the population is allowed to vary? Parfit argues cogently that treating the social welfare function as the sum of the welfare values over the population generates a conclusion we ought to reject (the "Repugnant Conclusion"): aggregate welfare increases when a world in which many people live very well is replaced by one in which an enormously larger number of people live lives that are barely worth living. He also shows that taking social welfare to be average welfare is problematic, and he poses the question of how to find an appropriate social welfare function. One of us (Kitcher) has offered an impossibility proof: no social welfare function can meet all Parfit's—well-motivated—conditions.[25] The root of the trouble seems to be the Archimedean axiom: for any two positive real numbers r_1 and r_2 there's a positive integer N such that $Nr_1 > r_2$. If the dominant dimension of welfare is continuous, the Archimedean axiom holds. Hence the dominant dimension must be discrete.)

You might want to complicate things a bit. Maybe the notion of a worthwhile life comes in several "passing grades." You might say of one person's life, "Well, she didn't have all that much choice about what to do, and several of her important goals weren't realized, but overall she achieved many things that were important to her"; and of another, "He was very fortunate to be given a wide range of choices about what he wanted to be and do, he reflected carefully and continued to endorse his early decisions, and virtually all his aspirations were satisfied." So there's the "overall successful life"

---

[23] In line with our earlier acceptance of the possibility of false consciousness, we don't suppose that this is the last word. A fully satisfactory approach to these questions should promote a system of education aimed at broadening the horizons within which human aspirations are currently confined. We'll start, however, with a simpler and more urgent problem.

[24] See part IV of Derek Parfit, 1983. *Reasons and Persons*. Oxford: Clarendon Press.

[25] Philip Kitcher, 2000. "Parfit's Puzzle." *Noûs* 345: 50–77.

and the "supremely successful life."[26] Nevertheless, we should resist the idea of some continuous measure of the worth of lives. You can't convert an unhappy life into a rewarding one by adding lots of little positive experiences.

There's plenty more to say about what kinds of factors make for worthwhile lives. We'll focus on just two things. First, like Dewey, we take the Anglo-Saxon emphasis on negative freedom (protection from interference) to need supplementing. Lives gain worth through their positive effects on other lives, so that a theme devoid of any form of personal interaction (either direct or through achievements to help others), however autonomously chosen, would not be a theme for a valuable life. It follows from this that certain forms of community are important for us. Second, there are very general features of people's situations whose lack makes it very difficult, even impossible, for their lives to go well. Rawls' emphasis on primary goods can be seen as directed toward ensuring that these features are in place. In our view, Amartya Sen's formulation in terms of capabilities is a clearer and more direct account of what worthwhile lives require, and his list of capabilities recognizes the most fundamental preconditions.[27] A significant number of workers in the affluent world are deprived, in that they lack some of Sen's basic capabilities. But we don't get a complete account of worker deprivation unless Sen's list is extended (we think—hope!—Sen would agree).

KINDS OF LIVES

Underlying the interpretation of issues about work and life begun in section three is a threefold distinction among the workers of the affluent world.

Themeless workers are those who have no overall sense of what their lives are about. Faced with the question of what they want to be or do, they can only respond with some vague answer—"Get rich" or "Have fun"—indicative of an unfocused consumerism or an unfocused hedonism.

Job-focused workers are those for whom the work they do contributes directly to some goals determined by their life theme. Some of them regard their job (or, more likely, their career or vocation) as the central element of their theme. Others pursue a mix of ends, among which are goals unrelated to their work.

Job-means workers are those for whom the work they do has no intrinsic significance. Their jobs are strictly a means to the pursuit of goals unrelated to work. For workers of this type, potential jobs are ranked according to the positive effects on realizing the work-unrelated goals.

---

[26] This would allow an analogue of the Repugnant Conclusion: an enormous number of "overall successful lives" would outrank a much smaller number of "supremely successful lives." It's not obvious, however, that this conclusion is still repugnant.

[27] See, for example, Amartya Sen, 1999. *Development as Freedom.* New York: Oxford University Press.

Questionnaires and surveys that restrict themselves to economic issues, or that ask vague questions about happiness, treat all workers as if they were themeless. Such workers are aptly treated within a utilitarian framework that measures utility in terms of money earned or hourly wage or units of pleasure (hedons). That framework already breaks down for job-means workers, for whom the appropriate questions concern whether or not enough of the central goals are being achieved. For similar reasons, it is entirely inadequate for job-focused workers.

One important (and, so far as we know, neglected) question about the relation of work to life is whether the conditions of contemporary employment (or the broader capitalist/consumerist framework in which they are embedded) contribute to a rise in the percentage of themeless workers. That might come about either because the demands of the economy undercut reflection on what course of life might suit a person best; the early phases of life are simply seen as preparation for making a living. Or it might be the product of a culture that views the positive aspects of life in terms of acquisition or transient pleasures or status competition (or some mixture of the three). Themelessness seems to us to be a sad human condition, and, if it is increasing, we ought to be concerned. But, for present purposes, we'll henceforth mostly ignore the themeless.

The line of thought in our epigraph from Dewey emerges from an important insight of Adam Smith, one taken up by the young Marx. Although Smith begins *Wealth of Nations* (WN) with a celebration of the benefits of the division of labor—including the spur the division of labor supposedly gives to the imagination and enterprise of the young worker—he eventually offers a very different picture. Book V of WN is devoted to reviewing the background conditions required for the proper functioning of the market, and, in this context, Smith takes up the question of worker education. His critique of the prevailing emphasis on classical languages and literature, and of the standard organization of university teaching, leads him to propose that all children, even the poorest, be taught to read and write, and to become acquainted with the rudiments of arithmetic and "mechanics." Presumably, he sees these skills as being valuable in the nascent industrial economy. Yet, as he addresses questions about what workers need to know, honesty compels him to acknowledge the pressures of a finer-grained division of labor. As industry splits tasks into smaller subroutines, the work assigned to individual workers comes to consist of repeating a small repertoire of movements. Hence the candid answer to what workers need to know *for the purposes of their work* is "very little." Gone is the conviction that the enterprising young worker—possibly aided by knowing the rudiments of arithmetic and "mechanics"—will make improvements to the production process. Instead, Smith paints a dismal picture of the worker's predicament:

> The man whose whole life is spent in performing a few simple operations, of which the effects too are, perhaps, always the same, or very nearly the same, has no occasion to exert his understanding, or to exercise his invention in finding out expedients for removing difficulties which never occur. He naturally loses, there-fore, the habit of such exertion, and generally becomes as stupid and ignorant as it is

possible for a human creature to become. The torpor of his mind renders him, not only incapable of relishing or bearing a part in any rational conversation, but of conceiving any generous, noble, or tender sentiment, and consequently of forming any just judgment concerning many even of the ordinary duties of private life.[28]

Smith does not ask whether a different—richer—education might provide resources for relieving this torpor. Nor does he see his verdict as requiring him to return to the opening chapters and introduce some revisions. He simply moves on to the next topic.[29]

Some six decades later, Marx set about learning political economy by reading the works of the British and French authors who had developed it (primarily Smith, Ricardo, and Eugene Say). The first three papers collected as the "Economic and Philosophic Manuscripts of 1844" are, in effect, the reading notes of an exceptionally gifted student. Then, apparently, Marx came to the passage just quoted. The fourth manuscript begins:

> We have started out from the premises of political economy. We have accepted its language and its laws. We presupposed private property; the separation of labor, capital, and land, and likewise of wages, profit, and capital; the division of labor; competition; the conception of exchange value, etc. From political economy itself, using its own words, we have shown that the worker sinks to the level of a commodity, and moreover the most wretched commodity of all; that the misery of the worker is in inverse proportion to the power and volume of his production.[30]

Unlike Smith, Marx pauses at this point, and explores the condition of *alienation* (or, in some translations, *estrangement*) that afflicts the worker.

He distinguishes four modes of alienation. The first two are straightforward: the worker is alienated both from the objects he produces and from the process of production. The third is more puzzling (and stems from Marx's immersion in German philosophy, particularly in Feuerbach): workers are alienated from their "species being." The fourth returns to relative clarity: workers are alienated from their fellows.

We gloss these diagnoses (possibly missing the complexity of some Marxian ideas) as follows:

1. The object the worker produces has no significance in relation to the goals that stem from the worker's life theme (assuming the worker has a theme).
2. The process of production has no significance in relation to the goals that stem from the worker's life theme (assuming the worker has a theme).

---

[28] Adam Smith, 2007 [1776]. *An Inquiry into the Nature and Causes of the Wealth of Nations*. Edited by S. M. Soares. MetaLibri Digital Library, May 29, pp. 602–3.

[29] In contrast to Smith, contemporary economic scholars argue that the endlessly greater division of labor is a necessary—or even a probable—consequence of technological progress. See, for example, Wouter Dessein and Tano Santos, 2006. "Adaptive Organizations." *Journal of Political Economy* 114(5): 956–95.

[30] Karl Marx, 2007 [1844]. "Estranged Labor." Translated and edited by Martin Milligan. *Economic and Philosophic Manuscripts of 1844*. Mineola, NY: Dover Publications, p. 67.

3. Human beings are social animals for whom productive work should be central to their life themes. Workers are forced to choose themes (to the extent that they do) that emphasize trivial, "animal," fulfillments. ("man (the worker) only feels himself freely active in his animal functions—eating, drinking, procreating, or at most in his dwelling and in dressing-up, etc.; and in his human functions he no longer feels himself to be anything but an animal. What is animal becomes human and what is human becomes animal."[31])

4. Human beings are *social* animals for whom work should create community with others. Capitalist production induces competition among workers and erodes solidarity.

It's not hard to understand points 1 and 2 within the context of the industrial capitalism Marx was beginning to recognize (largely through Engels' documentation of working-class life in Manchester). The division of labor removes any distinctive product in which a worker might take pride, and mass production generates goods that may lack any recognizable significance. Moreover, the worker is easily replaceable by almost anyone else, so that the final product bears no trace of an individual contribution. Finally, the process consists of mind-numbing repetitions of simple movements. (Here, Marx is simply reiterating Smith's prophetic description.)

Assuming that workers become focused on obtaining the bare necessities for continued existence (and their own "reproduction" through children who will eventually replace them), it's clear also that, in the absence of combined efforts that might resist factory-owners' attempts to decrease the costs of production, workers are likely to become engaged in a struggle to retain their employment. Others in the same situation become rivals with the potential to undercut current demands for compensation. But Marx is surely on shakier ground here, given the prior emergence of movements to increase worker solidarity (already defended by Smith).

Point 3 is, in our view, Marx's deepest. One way to read him is as recognizing *two* of the three categories introduced earlier. We might think of *alienation from species being* as *themelessness*. Essentially, Marx would be declaring that human beings are thinking animals for whom a life of pleasure and/or consumption is stripped of the conscious identification with what matters that ought to distinguish human existence. So far, the point seems entirely correct. But Marx adds to this the suggestion that the unalienated life ought to be job-focused: without productive work as a central part of your theme, you haven't conceived for yourself a properly human life. The addition appears dubious (not to us personally, but as a blanket prescription). Marx overlooks the possibility of job-means workers who live valuable lives.

Of course, the circumstances of work today in the affluent world aren't those Smith foretold, Engels (and even Orwell) described, and Marx tried to analyze. But we don't think that Marx's categories are merely of historical interest. It's worth asking whether

---

[31] Marx, "Estranged Labor," p. 67.

the kinds of alienation he hypothesized recur at different sites in the post-industrial economy, even if two of his assumptions—that worker solidarity is inevitably eroded and that work must be central to any satisfactory life theme—are rejected.[32] If you think about welfare in the ways we've recommended, introducing surveys designed to probe worker welfare and the features of work conditions that affect it (perhaps in the way recommended at the end of section three), it seems that you should want to know if the products and processes of the workplace seem trivial against the background of workers' life themes, if the circumstances of labor erode community and autonomy, and if they interfere with the central elements of themes. (And, as we have remarked, whether the framework within which work is conducted contributes to themelessness.)

Questions

We'll conclude with a sequence of further questions about the relationship between work and life in contemporary affluent democracies. The questions are accompanied with brief commentary.

1. Is the philosophical account developed in section four (and, in essence, presupposed in our epigraph from Dewey) borne out by investigations of workers' attitudes? This basic question needs to be posed. We can't assume in advance that the conceptual framework emerging from a long philosophical tradition, based primarily on introspection on the part of some exceptional thinkers (and, perhaps, conversations with their friends—"Think over the men and women you know . . ."), will necessarily prove valuable in classifying the responses people actually make. Categories need revision in the light of changing purposes and empirical findings: that, after all, is the heart of our concerns about the surveys that have actually been conducted. So this first question might lead to a more sympathetic view of the probative power of those actual surveys, or to the conclusion that the approach we have taken is justified, or to a way of investigating welfare entirely different from both of these alternatives. Our subsequent questions will assume that our approach is vindicated, i.e. that people respond to inquiries about the important aspects of their lives in illuminating ways (rather than simply finding the survey alien and baffling).

2. To what extent do employment opportunities today allow job-focused workers to obtain satisfaction? It's easy to suppose that the transition from a manufacturing economy to a service economy must exacerbate the dissatisfaction of contemporary workers. The obvious rationale for the supposition is the thought that

---

[32] The tendency of economists to suppose that everything Marx wrote is bunk is unfortunate. However erroneous many of his conclusions may be, some of the concepts he introduced are extremely valuable. *False consciousness* and *alienation* are two of them.

those who serve are inevitably treated as servants, members of a subordinate class to whom no respect is due. Plainly, many of those who serve in all sorts of capacities encounter considerable rudeness and some hostility. Is that an inevitable feature of their occupations? We're inclined to think that many service jobs connect the work done to goals the workers view as important—receptionists, flight attendants, gardeners, firefighters, and doctors can all view themselves as contributing to the flourishing of other people's lives. Similarly, service jobs can be sufficiently varied to escape the monotony Smith predicted and Marx saw in the processes of production. Hence, the move from manufacture to service can actually diminish the first two forms of alienation. The principal challenges for meaningful work in a service economy are the need to overcome the conception of service work as "menial" and the appreciation of the importance of contributing to others. That could be achieved if there were a clear, publicly acknowledged view of the dignity of service labor—if members of a society came to appreciate one another as equal participants in a community project through which the lives of all go better than they would otherwise have done. What economic and social changes would be needed to achieve that?

3. To what extent do job opportunities today interfere with the central goals of job-means workers? Following the striking finding of the marriage survey that family is the most important aspect of life to 76 percent of respondents—and notwithstanding the concern that this response is skewed by social desirability bias—we *conjecture* that there are many workers in the affluent world for whom work is primarily a means to the truly important things. Some of them may obtain satisfactions from aspects of the work they do, but they would conceive these as secondary. They hope for employment that is mildly pleasant and sometimes mildly rewarding, but their principal demand is for conditions of work that enable them to pursue the work-independent goals that matter to them. Obviously some such conditions are economic: a high enough wage to support the significant pursuits (maintaining the family and securing its future, for example). Others concern not only the length of the workday, but also its impact on other activities. Probably for most people (another empirical issue) an ability to plan is critical. You can't combine work with adequate nurturing of children unless you can determine, in advance, the times at which you'll be away from home. To what extent do the circumstances of work today set up conflicts with job-means workers' primary goals? What types of conflicts emerge? What economic and social changes are needed to resolve them?

4. *The work–life balance problem.* There are workers for whom the job (career, vocation) is intrinsically important, but who have central goals unrelated to their work. The classic case involves both a dedication to work and to the nurturing of children, but this is only one instance of a more general pattern. (It's worth asking what other forms are common.) With respect to which spheres of work do conflicts between career goals and independent goals typically arise? What economic and social changes might relieve these conflicts?

5. *Cross-generational feedback.* To what extent do the conditions of work create feedback cycles, in which certain forms of work are viewed as necessary for promoting non-work-related goals, in which the competition for those forms of work is severe, and the recognition of its severity undermines attempts to achieve the goals in question? Many parents today want their children to have opportunities for a successful life, including a successful family life. They see those opportunities as available only if the children are admitted to one of a small class of schools. To prepare them for admission they are then forced to work extra hours and to regiment early childhood in a fashion they see as antithetical to their family-related goals. Are affluent societies trapped in an increasingly intense competition that makes it ever harder to realize non-work-related values? Does the emphasis on preparing students for success prevent the educational system from fulfilling some of its most important functions? If so, what can be done to remedy the situation?

We hope that future surveys will be framed so that the questions posed here can be explored empirically.[33]

. . . .

COMMENTS AND DISCUSSION

Drawing on a range of survey data, Autor and Kitcher consider the extent to which different kinds of work generate job satisfaction. And they suggest that we might improve our approach to such surveys through questions that more deeply connect the experience of people at work to their broader set of life goals, i.e. to "themes" by which they organize their aims and activities.

> *How can we best measure and conceptualize satisfaction that people derive from the workplace?*

At the Society for Progress' second assembly, Tiberius observed the importance of the difference between assessments of happiness, understood as a function of episodic emotional states, and the broader notion of life satisfaction. How should we think about the relative priority of these notions in thinking about welfare? Is the latter something important in itself? Or is it merely correlated with other things that matter? In thinking about the relationship between work and satisfaction, Autor observed that it is a mistake to think of work solely as a disutility that requires compensation. For most people, work is itself a constitutive aspect of their identity, and losing work altogether is among the factors that are most destructive of happiness. But how much

[33] The approach developed by Brian Little (see n. 19) shows this to be more than a pipe dream. Little's framework could easily be elaborated to produce the kinds of surveys we have in mind.

does work really drive happiness levels as opposed to wealth or other factors? How malleable is individual happiness at all? As Autor observed, Easterlin's classic work[34] seems to suggest that people's happiness tends to revert to a strong baseline, though both Autor and Schmidtz pointed to more recent research (Easterlin and Stevenson/ Wolfers[35]) suggesting otherwise.

How do broader social and economic conditions affect the satisfaction that people derive from their work?

Autor and Kitcher's essay explicitly considers the role of "false consciousness" in assessments of satisfaction, and a number of commentators picked up on this theme. Neiman observed that our satisfaction with a given occupation depends significantly on "what we think is possible" and what goals we conceive to be valuable. Thus, desperately overworked employees in finance may experience satisfaction with their jobs because they have come to see that kind of life as part of the good life. And as Meyer observed, those who obtain high-status occupations may come to feel internal and external pressure to report satisfaction with those occupations because of that perceived status. On the other side of the economic spectrum, Sen noted that exploited laborers can often report some degree of life satisfaction simply because "there is no hope" for anything better. Structural features of the economic system also seem important in shaping satisfaction. Sen observed—following Adam Smith—that the division of labor is the key engine to the creation of wealth but, at the same time, tends to foster soulless, one-dimensional occupations. What does the future of capitalist economies look like in this regard? Kitcher expressed concern about the growth of a more freelance economy, in which platforms (like Uber) make working life considerably less certain and secure. On the other hand, Snabe suggested that technological advances might make it much easier for people to create their own jobs, thereby achieving a certain autonomy. Neiman noted an odd statistic she had seen: hairdressers are among the most satisfied workers, while architects are among the least. Perhaps this is because the former have control over what they do, while the latter are constantly having their vision frustrated? As Battilana noted, organizational structure and mission also seems crucial in this domain. What is the comparative job satisfaction of those who work at social enterprises, for example, compared to traditional for-profit organizations?[36]

---

[34] Richard A. Easterlin, 1974. "Does Economic Growth Improve the Human Lot? Some Empirical Evidence." In Paul A. David and Melvin W. Reder (eds.), *Nations and Households in Economic Growth: Essays in Honor of Moses Abramovitz.* New York: Academic Press, pp. 89–125.

[35] Betsey Stevenson and Justin Wolfers, 2008. "Economic Growth and Subjective Well-Being: Reassessing the Easterlin Paradox." *Brookings Papers on Economic Activity* (spring): 1–102.

[36] We are grateful to the participants of the Society for Progress' second assembly, held on November 6 and 7, 2015, for their questions and comments. As we have revised the original draft, the suggestions of Valerie Tiberius have been particularly valuable.

CHAPTER 9

PURPOSE-DRIVEN BUSINESS FOR SUSTAINABLE PERFORMANCE AND PROGRESS

EBBA ABDON HANSMEYER, RAMÓN MENDIOLA,
AND JIM HAGEMANN SNABE

Abstract

This chapter proposes and discusses how a "purpose-driven" approach can help business reinvent and sustain itself and serve society. It outlines and explains a "tesseract model" which has purpose at its core and four vertices corresponding to economic, human, social, and environmental values. To be effective, a company's purpose has to be authentic, ambitious, and achievable. A company's purpose can furnish meaning and status, and act as a matching/sorting device for attracting compatible employees, investors, and customers. Based on the authors' first-hand experience, this chapter describes two concrete instances of firms that adopted this purpose-driven approach. In an organization that adopts a societally oriented purpose, employees become emotionally engaged, energized, and differentiating in ways that can sustain performance and progress.

BACKGROUND: SUSTAINABLE PERFORMANCE?

The Swedish predecessor of the now Finnish company Stora Enso is reported to have issued shares in 1288, becoming a forerunner of joint ownership and limited liability. Stora began in copper mining prior to shifting into pulp and paper, and later merged with Enso. Today, it is a leading paper and pulp manufacturer.

Companies such as Stora Enso are exceptions. Few companies have such an extensive lifespan. The biggest and most stable companies that create significant value to society seem to survive for an average of only forty years. The trend has shown that this time frame has now become shorter. The average lifetime of a company on the S&P 500 has decreased from ninety years in 1935 to eighty years today.[1] Since the last decade, 50 percent of the companies on the S&P 500 have been replaced. The damage resulting from this trend is not just a matter of shifts in the S&P 500 list, but the significant repercussions it represents for jobs, livelihoods, communities, and economies.

These facts indicate that although many businesses are currently well managed for short-term profit-optimization goals, they fail in achieving sustainable long-term success. In addition, corporations have increasingly been viewed as a major cause of social, environmental, and economic unrest. Companies and shareholders are widely perceived to prosper at the expense of the broader community. Consequently, public trust in business and business leaders has fallen to unprecedented levels, leading policymakers to increase regulation and compliance requirements. This has resulted in a vicious cycle, making it more difficult to accelerate positive change in businesses.

It is our view that businesses tend to fail because they are mainly concerned about delivering short-term shareholder value. Managers continue to rely on the traditional way of thinking. Although capitalism has resulted in many economic and social benefits, it has also proven to have its shortcomings. In addition, as societal and environmental issues are growing the theoretical boundaries among sectors of society are disappearing. As Stephan Schmidheiny stated: "It's impossible to build successful companies in failed societies."[2]

It is evident that business requires a fundamental change in the role that it plays, and how we define success. Now that capitalism is under attack, more holistic approaches for business are being developed and implemented. Concepts such as "embedded sustainability," "shared value theory," and "triple bottom line theory" all conclude that the only sustainable path for a business to ensure its long-term success is to contribute actively to society at large and align business goals with long-term stakeholder goals.

How can we reinvent the fundamentals of business and capitalism to create long-term, sustainable success based on delivering value to all stakeholders and to society? How can we reinvent the definition of performance in business to include more than performance in terms of profit, and to also include the "balance sheet of the future" indicating the likelihood of performance in the future and the impact on society and the planet?

Many leading companies have embarked on this journey to prove that it is possible to do well in business by "doing good." *Fortune* magazine recently developed a "Change the World" list,[3] which highlights companies that have made significant progress in addressing major social problems as part of their core business strategy. These companies have proven that corporate social responsibility can be successful and

---

[1] Source: INNOSIGHT/Richard N. Foster/Standard & Poor's.
[2] INCAE Business School, 1996.
[3] *Fortune*, 2015. "The 'Change the World' List." September 1.

sustainable over time, if it is based on a genuine purpose and embedded in the core of its business strategy.

This chapter, developed by a diverse group of academic and business leaders, argues that companies managed on the basis of a meaningful higher purpose are able to create sustainable success for all stakeholders. Purpose-driven organizations have the capacity of rapidly reinventing themselves. A purpose-driven business is able to deliver sustainable performance and also drive progress for society—all at the same time.

In the chapter we first define the key elements of a purpose-driven organization. Case studies exemplify companies that have successfully implemented a genuine purpose and holistic management approach. These companies are from different sectors, geographical locations, and cultural contexts. Based on the case studies, recommendations are made on how to implement a purpose-driven organization and how business leaders, investors, and policymakers can redefine business performance to hasten the beginning of a new era of capitalism where performance and progress are reconciled.

THE PURPOSE-DRIVEN ORGANIZATION

A Restated Concept of the 1700s

The concept of a purpose-driven organization is not new. In the pre-industrialized world, business and society were closely interconnected. The rise and spread of the limited liability company, with open-ended gains and capped private losses, saw capitalism prosper and with it increased standards of living worldwide. Yet, increased standards of living could not mitigate a growing divide between the interests of business and the interests of society. Maximizing shareholder value soon became the first lesson taught by every self-respecting MBA program.

The Challenge Ahead: Sustainable Value for All Stakeholders

It can be argued that the traditional definition of capitalism, based on the Newtonian approach of maximizing profits for shareholders, was partially correct until modern times. The former, outdated notion of business was based on a one-dimensional analysis involving one kind of value—short-term economic success for shareholders (see Figure 9.1).

FIGURE **9.1.** A traditional business model

Today, the speed of light is analogous to the fast pace of globalization, technology, radical transparency, population growth, growing environmental and societal challenges, and the speed of business cycles. Holistic capitalism reflects Einstein's approach to the theory of capitalism—a holistic view that can analyze the dominant economic model of our era (capitalism) and take it to a greater level of effectiveness and relevance. Holistic capitalism considers itself an organic and dynamic system where all elements are interconnected and evolve simultaneously. Companies must, therefore, constantly reinvent themselves and experience a rebirth from its core (purpose), like the phoenix in Greek mythology. The end result is a more precise and sophisticated manner of doing business.

The Tesseract of Business: "A Holistic, Purpose-Driven Organization"

A tesseract, the four-dimensional analog of a cube, is to a square what holistic, purpose-driven business is to traditional shareholder-centered business. Holistic capitalism is an evolving paradigm that offers business leaders a more comprehensive and precise definition of what a business could be and should be.

This new business paradigm requires that executives embrace a comprehensive four-dimensional approach to business by establishing a deep connection to its core (purpose), deeper connections with their stakeholders (and not only their shareholders), create holistic value with positive economic, social, and environmental impact, and better connect with the essence of its business—its employees (see Figure 9.2).

A holistic, purpose-driven company is characterized by the following elements.

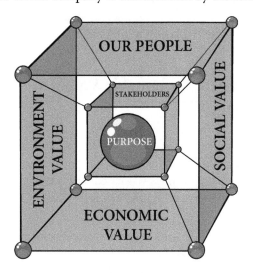

FIGURE **9.2.** The tesseract business model
Source: FIFCO.

A deeper connection with its core—the company purpose. A company's purpose is what makes it unique. It is the glue that holds the pieces of the organization together. Embracing a higher purpose inspires, helps, and strengthens the company. It establishes a common goal among its employees and serves to attract and engage the right stakeholders.

A deeper connection to its essence—its people. Employees are the heart and soul of a business; they are the foundation of its operations. A business cannot run unless its employees create value through their work. A *holistic business leader* must engage the minds and hearts of employees.

A deeper connection with its stakeholders. The best business leaders make decisions to satisfy the needs and desires of multiple stakeholders. They do not work as a silo but in partnership with society (including both government and civilians). A holistic, purpose-driven company expands its potential to create value beyond the company boundaries.

A commitment to creating holistic value. The business strives to create an equilibrium of economic, social, environmental, and human value. It does not believe in trade-offs among economic, social, human, and environmental prosperity but establishes synergies among the four.

How to Develop a Deeper Connection to the Business Core: Company Purpose

When is a Company Purpose a Genuine Purpose?

A company must discover its genuine purpose. It is not something that can be designed or manufactured. It must be based on introspective analysis of the business and its people, and compound insight from the entire organization. The company must ask itself: Why do we exist? How do we add value and for whom?

A company's higher purpose must meet three main criteria (3As):

1. It must be *authentic* and reflect the essence of the company and how it does business. It must remain true to the company's identity, commitments, and contribution to society.
2. It must be *ambitious* enough to inspire employees and stakeholders, allowing them to "dream big."
3. It must be *achievable* and realistic. While an attainable purpose may require a team "to go the extra mile" to achieve it, employees must not consider it to be unattainable.

How Can an Organization Bring Life to Its Purpose?

A company can achieve its full potential (beyond profit maximization) by embracing its higher purpose and sharing its uniqueness. The following aspects should be considered.

Understand the company purpose. Every company employee must understand what the company stands for. It is critical for company leaders to communicate the company purpose internally as well as externally to all stakeholders.

The need for two-way dialogue. To harmonize purpose and current business practices, company leaders must provide feedback to their employees. Employees must also be allowed to voice their concerns and future expectations about the company. Leaders must demonstrate consistency between the company purpose and its priorities.

Act on it. Employees must uphold the company's sense of purpose in their jobs and take concrete actions to implement it.

Set an example of leadership. Senior management must champion the company purpose and model congruent behaviors. Such institutional grounding is essential to develop stewards of leadership among company employees.

Finding the Connection among Purpose, People, and Long-Term Performance?

An organization's higher purpose serves the organization threefold (the three Ss):

1. *Sense of purpose.* A higher purpose establishes a profound connection with the minds and hearts of employees. Employees and stakeholders identify with the company purpose as being aligned with their own life purpose.
2. *Sorting.* A company purpose functions as a litmus test to measure how well employees are aligned with the company goals. Employees that are closely engaged with the company purpose will be more motivated and better prepared to help the company obtain long-term success. It can also help identify more resilient employees better suited to facing future challenges. This may also be replicated with the company's stakeholders. A sense of purpose can attract the right investors, clients, and customers for a company.
3. *Status (non-monetary).* A powerful company purpose instills employees with a sense of satisfaction and pride that is not based on monetary rewards. Employees consider that they occupy a unique status by fitting into the bigger company picture. It also builds stronger networks and partnerships.

A company can develop a highly motivated team, capable of tackling even the most difficult business and social challenges. Business leaders will, consequently, adopt a mindset of positive long-term performance, which translates into a unique competitive advantage for the business (see Figure 9.3).

FIGURE **9.3.** A deeper connection among purpose, people, and long-term performance

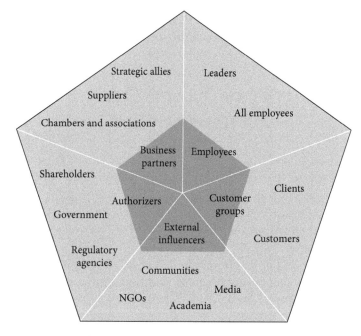

FIGURE **9.4.** Stakeholder mapping

Source: FIFCO, adapted from Dell stakeholder mapping model.

How to Develop a Deeper Connection with Stakeholders

In 1983, Edward Freeman and David Reed revisited the 1963 concept of a stakeholder—a person or group with a stake in the activities of a business. Every business should carry out its business activities considering the needs and expectations of its stakeholders. Traditional business models focus on trade-offs among stakeholders, whereas purpose-driven business models seek synergies and convergence. A company must, first, define its stakeholders or those individuals who impact and are impacted by the business—through *stakeholder mapping* (see Figure 9.4).

The Dell Stakeholder Mapping Model consists of four groups of key stakeholders: business partners, authorizers, customer groups, and external influencers. Employees were deliberately taken from business partners to create a fifth group. Employees must be analyzed separately since they reflect the spirit of a business and are the most important stakeholder of the organization.

As a second step, stakeholders are *prioritized* based on who can most influence the actions of the company, both positively and negatively. The third step is to encourage *open dialogue* with all key stakeholders to obtain their insight and perception about the company. What are the company's strengths and weaknesses? What are its major footprints (products or processes that could potentially destroy value)? What are stakeholder expectations? This dialogue will help to *gather insights* that can be used to *reinvent the organization*. The final step is to inform stakeholders about the progress of the organization (accountability). Stakeholder dialogue is a continuous process and must be done periodically to enrich the strategy.

ASSESSMENT OF TRADE-OFFS: REAL OR THEORETICAL?

Business leaders may seem to be constantly confronted with trade-offs where they must decide on balancing short-term performance against investing for the future. Many business leaders and investors assume that it will be detrimental to the shareholders if a company focuses its efforts on a higher purpose and delivers value to all stakeholders, at least in the short term.

However, an organization that is purpose-led and pursues value for all stakeholders will, ultimately, build up company trust and positively impact performance due to:

1. *More sophisticated consumer preference.* Consumers will select products and services that are more environmentally friendly or socially responsible when faced with choosing over similar price, quality, and availability. Consumers are now expecting more and better at the same price. They do not believe in trade-offs. "They want it all here and now."
2. *More engaged employees*, resulting in a higher productivity level.
3. *Better conditions from suppliers* and other value chain actors who are inspired by the purpose.

So, does purpose hurt financial performance? In one longitudinal analysis reported in *Firms of Endearment*, Sisodia, Wolfe, and Sheth find significantly superior financial performance for purpose-driven organizations.[4] As their estimates (reproduced in Table 9.1) show, these companies outperformed the S&P 500 index by a factor of ten over a fifteen-year period (1996–2011).

---

[4] Rajendra Sisodia, David Wolfe, and Jagdish Sheth, 2014. *Firms of Endearment: How World-Class Companies Profit from Passion and Purpose.* Upper Saddle River, NJ: Pearson.

Table 9.1. Financial performance of purpose-driven companies relative to the S&P 500

Return	Cumulative (%)	Annualized (%)
Purpose-driven companies	1,646.1	21.0
S&P 500	157.0	6.5

From Rajendra Sisodia, David Wolfe, and Jagdish Sheth, 2014. *Firms of Endearment: How World-Class Companies Profit from Passion and Purpose.* Upper Saddle River, NJ: Pearson.

Leaving aside the valid question of the direction of causality in such empirical studies, it is also our own experience that implementing a purpose-driven approach is a worthwhile pursuit. In the next section, drawing on this experience, we share two case studies of successfully implementing a purpose-driven approach and the organizational implications, including those for financial performance.

CASE STUDIES

Case Study I: SAP AG

In February 2010, SAP initiated a purpose-driven transformation aimed at increasing its strategic relevance and impact in the world, while at the same time doubling the revenue.

Background

SAP AG was founded in 1972 by five IBM software engineers who shared a vision of standardizing business software for real-time business processing. At the end of 2009 SAP had developed into a global leader in business software with more than 40,000 employees and more than 100,000 customers in 190 countries.

At the end of 2009 SAP delivered solid financial results despite the 2008–9 financial crisis, during which company revenue declined by 8 percent to 10.7 billion euros. However, the implementation of a cost-saving and restructuring program and the introduction of a price increase in 2008 helped the company increase its operational margin from 23.3 to 24.3 percent.

Although shareholders applauded the financial results, SAP's principal stakeholders voiced their dissatisfaction. Customers felt that the company had taken unfair advantage of the relationship through the price increase during 2009. At the same time employees were disappointed by the cost reductions and the restructuring program initiated in the fall of 2008. By February 2010, the rising dissatisfaction of SAP's two main stakeholders, its customers and employees, led the supervisory board to change the CEO and embark on a process to transform the company despite solid financial results.

The Strategy

With new management in place, the company initiated a strategic process to reinvent the company based on a growth strategy driven by innovation and a holistic management model focused on delivering value to all stakeholders. Although the company was the market leader in the traditional enterprise resource planning and business intelligence market, it was evident that the company needed to find new growth areas to stay relevant and create new opportunities for customers and employees.

The goal was to find a way to double the addressable market of the company and drive growth through increased value to customers instead of increasing prices. It was clear that the core business of the company was valuable for the future. However, it represented limited growth opportunities due to the high market share. As a result, the new management team decided to invest in adjacent market opportunities, which was characterized by high growth, strategic importance, and high relevance for the customers.

An ambitious long-term financial target was developed based on strategic options. The goal was to double company income over the course of five years. Financial goals were defined as a logical consequence of the strategy to increase customer value by delivering new strategic innovations at a higher speed, but at lower costs for the customer.

The Dream—Connecting to the Core: The Purpose

The strategy seemed logical and the financial goals were ambitious enough to excite shareholders. It was obvious, though, that to transform the company, management would need more than logical arguments in order to gain commitment from all its shareholders.

A holistic management model was developed to guide efforts and set priorities. The management model was based on an assumption that a deeper connection to all stakeholders, including society at large, would result in a better and more sustainable financial performance.

In order to inspire all stakeholders, management decided to revisit the purpose of the company. In its core the company had gained external recognition, particularly from a customer-oriented tagline it had used for many years: "The Best Run Companies Run SAP." Yet, the strategic importance of the company was not generally recognized.

In a growing world of nearly seven billion people and an increasing concern about the scarcity of resources, sustainability, and climate change, SAP was faced with a unique opportunity to increase its relevance and impact in the world. With thirty-eight years of experience in managing resources for enterprises in all industries, from mining and manufacturing to consumer services such as retail, SAP had an important role to play in managing and optimizing the scarce resources of the world, not just within a single enterprise but across entire value chains.

As a result, the company rediscovered itself and adopted a new sense of purpose, "helping the world run better and improving people's lives," which reflects a deep commitment to the core of the company by managing resources for enterprises with the ambition to make a difference for more people and society at large.

The Details—Implementing the Strategy

The new purpose was inspiring and provided an opportunity to improve the relevance and perception of the company both internally and externally. However, there was a risk that the new purpose would be perceived as a simple marketing tagline. Therefore, it was very important to support the new purpose with visible actions to increase its credibility. Management decided to pursue two sustainability strategies that involved: (a) making the company more sustainable, so that SAP could serve as a role model; and (b) creating business opportunities to develop IT solutions that enable customers to make their own businesses more sustainable.

SAP as Role Model

To boost the credibility of the company's new purpose, SAP concentrated on demonstrating leadership by improving its social, environmental, and financial performance. Efforts in the social dimension, for example, varied from attracting and developing employee talents to providing IT training to the unemployed in Europe and creating job opportunities for autistic individuals with special skills.

Regarding environmental activities, SAP committed to reducing its emissions. The goal was to achieve a 50 percent reduction compared to the peak in 2007 despite significant growth, as well as shift 100 percent to renewable energy sources.

The key to building credibility around the new purpose was demonstrating that SAP's social and environment undertakings would lead to better financial performance instead of the traditionally assumed trade-off between shareholder value and value for society.

SAP as Enabler—Connecting to the Stakeholders: Customers

While SAP's internal efforts toward becoming a role model were paramount in creating credibility for the new purpose, its external focus in enabling customers to combine social, environmental, and financial concerns proved to be crucial for the purpose. SAP's customer base included most of the largest companies throughout the world. It was estimated that more than half of greenhouse gas emissions from business came from SAP customers. Helping customers manage their resources more efficiently would, thus, contribute significantly to the purpose—and at the same time create new business opportunities for SAP.

By 2013, SAP had developed a number of sustainability-related solutions, including energy management and product safety stewardship. Sustainability had also been embedded in SAP's main products, providing current customers with a broader and more holistic view of resources management. By implementing these solutions, SAP was able to increase its relevance and generate revenue at the same time.

The Results

In order to track progress and verify the referenced case, SAP implemented an integrated report to track financial and social performance, employee engagement, environmental performance, and customer satisfaction. The data were made available online and showed performance in all dimensions as well as the relationship among the different dimensions.[5] The results were assessed quarterly and made publicly available as part of the normal financial reporting.

Environmental Results

Environmental metrics are mainly focused on the company's greenhouse gas emissions, total energy consumption, and data center energy consumption as well as percentage of renewable energy used.

The report (see Figure 9.5) shows the early gross emissions as the sum of offset emissions (bars above the zero axis) plus net emissions (bars below the zero axis). From 2010 to 2014, net emissions were reduced by almost 300 kilotons of CO_2 or almost 50 percent from the peak in 2007. This was achieved despite three significant acquisitions,

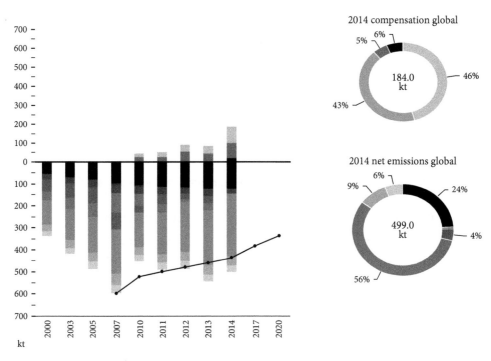

FIGURE **9.5.** SAP greenhouse gas emissions, 2010–14

Source: SAP Integrated Report, 2014. <http://sapintegratedreport.com/2014/en/performance/performance-summaries/chart-generator/category/environment/subcategory/greenhouse_gas_emissions.html>.

---

[5] Retrieved from SAP Integrated Report 2014. <http://sapintegratedreport.com/2014/en/performance/social-performance/employees-and-social-investment.html>.

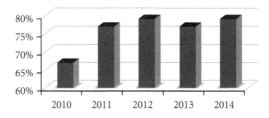

FIGURE **9.6.** SAP employee engagement index, 2010–14

Source: Company reports.

and adding significant data center infrastructure and more than 15,000 individuals to the employee base. The negative effects of the acquisitions were more than offset by investments in renewable energy for buildings and data centers.

Social Impact

In the SAP integrated report, social metrics focuses on employee engagement, turnover, percentage of women in top management positions, and employee health. In a knowledge-based organization like SAP, one of the most important long-term success factors is employee engagement. In 2010, employee engagement was at an all-time low at 68 percent (see Figure 9.6). A purpose-driven strategy led to new opportunities and fostered a sense of pride among employees. Employee engagement then grew rapidly to 77 percent in 2011, reaching 79 percent in 2014.

In addition to a focus on social and human aspects within the organization, SAP also engaged in a number of external social activities, particularly in the areas of education and entrepreneurship. SAP contributed cash and, most importantly, donated technology to non-governmental and non-profit organizations. In 2014 alone, 11,000 non-profit organizations received technology donations, including comprehensive technology implementation at Specialisterne, an organization that secures employment for people affected by autism, and Emprego Ligado, a social organization that offers online job market placement to Brazil's working class. SAP also spearheaded an effort in Europe to train 100,000 unemployed individuals in IT, thereby increasing the skill base for technology companies, such as SAP and its partners. SAP employees have volunteered approximately 188,000 hours in their communities in forty-seven countries, with more than 40 percent of their time devoted to sharing their unique talents and abilities.

Financial Results

Aside from regular financial reporting, as is the case with publicly listed companies, the report also addressed financial metrics that analyze revenue, operating income margin, and return on equity. From 2010 to 2014, SAP experienced four years of double digit growth.

During that same period, profit after taxes almost doubled from 1,813 billion euros to 3,280. These strong financial results were achieved despite a dramatic shift in the business model from upfront revenue recognition to subscription-based cloud services.

Links Between Financial, Social, and Environmental Performance

A key aspect of the integrated analysis and reporting was that it allowed SAP management to see the links between social, environmental, and financial performance. As an example, the integrated report shows estimates of the relationship between employee engagement and operating profit (see Figure 9.7). For each percentage point increase in employee engagement, operating profit was estimated to rise by 35 million to 45 million euros.

An analysis is also shown correlating greenhouse emissions and operating profit (see Figure 9.8). A reduction in greenhouse gas emissions of 1 percent is estimated to have a positive impact of 4 million euros on the operating profit.

The integrated report demonstrated that the holistic management approach targeting social, environmental, and financial aspects of the business in a parallel manner delivered value to all key stakeholders without trade-offs and enabled a more sustainable business model. Consistency among the company purpose, and social, environmental, and financial actions, enabled SAP to transform its size and historic success at high speed.

The transparency and progress attained by SAP was duly recognized. The company was awarded with external recognitions for its transformation and sustainability efforts resulting from its purpose. In 2012 and 2013, SAP led the Dow Jones Sustainability

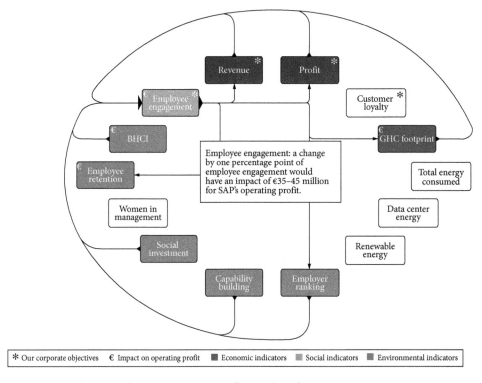

FIGURE **9.7.** Linking employee engagement to financial performance at SAP

Source: SAP Integrated Report 2014. <http://sapintegratedreport.com/2014/en/
strategy/integrated-performance-analysis.html>.

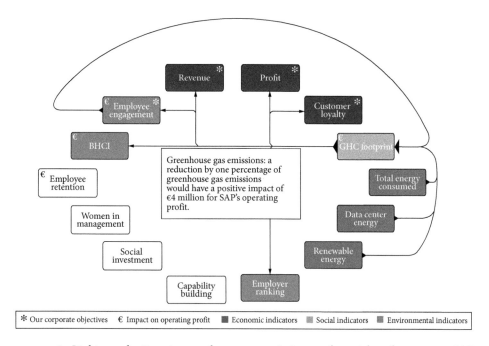

FIGURE **9.8.** Linking reductions in greenhouse gas emissions to financial performance at SAP

Source: SAP Integrated Report 2014. <http://sapintegratedreport.com/2014/en/strategy/integrated-performance-analysis.html>.

Index, a key benchmark for sustainability investment performance. The company also held top-ten spots on other indexes, including the Carbon Disclosure Leadership Index, Carbon Performance Leadership Index, and the NASDAQ QMX CRD Global Sustainability 50 Index, in addition to other recognitions for its sustainability efforts.

The SAP case study is a clear and measurable illustration that a large multinational company from the developed world can change and grow as a result of adopting a higher sense of purpose. It shows that it is possible to integrate performance and progress by strengthening relationships with all stakeholders, embracing consistency, and keeping a holistic approach (economic, social, and environmental) to create a long-term competitive advantage.

The case study that we outline next is that of a relatively smaller company in the developing world. This case study suggests that the underlying principles of the holistic purpose-driven organization are likely applicable to other firms despite differences in geography, cultural context, industry, and firm size.

Case Study II: Florida Ice & Farm Co.

Costa Rica-based Florida Ice & Farm Co. (FIFCO) has been undergoing transformational change for over a decade. Initially focused on maximizing profit, FIFCO's transformation was to become a source of value for all its stakeholders. This journey

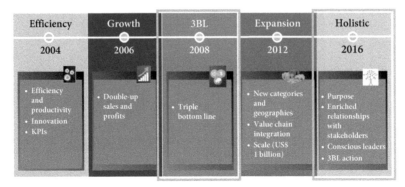

FIGURE **9.9.** FIFCO's five stages of evolution to a holistic way of doing business

Source: FIFCO.

consisted of five major phases (see Figure 9.9). The first two (in 2004 and 2006) focused on creating economic value. The latter stages (2008 and beyond) expanded FIFCO's scope of action and included a deeper connection with its stakeholders, a three-pronged approach (addressing economic, social, and environmental concerns), and a conscientious effort to nurture its people, particularly company leaders, to position the future evolution of the company.

Background

Founded by the Linda Morales brothers in 1908 in the Costa Rican town of La Florida of Siquirres, FIFCO grew from a small brewery into a Central American holding company and a leading beverage and food company, including a promising beverages endeavor in the United States and potentially successful ventures in the hotel industry and retail business in Costa Rica.

The last twelve years have been the most critical for FIFCO, in terms of transformational change. The company grew its sales from US$100 million to US$1.2 billion with a compound annual growth of 32.3 percent, thereby driving its profitability at a compound rate of 28.7 percent. At the same time, FIFCO expanded its operations to the rest of Central America and the United States, exporting its beverages and food products to twenty-two countries in America, Asia, Europe, and Oceania.

FIFCO then became a "comprehensive beverage company" with over 2,700 products in both alcoholic and non-alcoholic categories. It also partnered with such world-class players as Heineken, PepsiCo, and Diageo. The company entered the retail business in 2012, and pursued investments in real estate including the hotel business, partnering with Marriott, a hospitality world leader. Yet, FIFCO's most significant transformation occurred in 2008 when it became a triple bottom line company.

Signals from Society and the 3BL Journey (2008)

In 2008, FIFCO posted its best financial results ever with sales climbing from US$239 to US$534 million. The company, however, faced the challenge of more stringent regulatory requirements and higher tax obligations. Customers became more demanding and the 2008 global financial crisis wreaked havoc. Though Costa Ricans considered FIFCO to be at the economic forefront, it did not enjoy that same recognition with regard to its social and environmental sustainability. To address these concerns FIFCO implemented a triple bottom line (3BL) business model.

The company embarked on its journey by promoting *open and continuous dialogue with all stakeholders* (employees, customers, consumers, suppliers, shareholders, government officials, NGOs, media, and academia) to better understand how they perceived the company's economic, social, and environmental strengths, footprints, and expectations. Excessive alcohol consumption, solid waste disposal, water and energy use, and CO_2 emissions emerged as their main concerns.

After listening to its stakeholders, FIFCO was ready to "triple the business" through a 3BL approach that would include profit, people, and planet as part of its business strategy.

Ambitious and Specific 3BL Strategic Goals

The heart of the 3BL social agenda was turning FIFCO into the best company to work at. This goal would be attained by improving the lives of FIFCO employees and their families, being leaders in safety, and creating a work environment that fostered employees' personal and professional development. In addition, FIFCO defined three main goals for its external social component: improving alcohol consumption patterns in Costa Rica, becoming a strategic social investment leader, and being accountable and transparent to stakeholders. Economic and financial goals included scaling up business to sales of US$1 billion, becoming first or second in all categories/segments in which FIFCO competed, diversifying risk (reduce dependency on beer in Costa Rica), and maximizing profits. Regarding its environmental goals, FIFCO committed to becoming a zero solid waste company by 2011, water neutral by 2012, and carbon neutral by 2017.

FIFCO became a worldwide 3BL pioneer by monitoring and measuring 3BL performance. This was accomplished by linking strategic goals to employees' variable compensation—60 percent of variable compensation for executives is based on economic indicators and 40 percent on social and environmental key performance indicators (KPIs).

With regard to accountability, FIFCO used the Global Reporting Initiatives (GRI) standard to analyze and communicate improvements in all three 3BL dimensions starting in 2009. In 2016, FIFCO was the first company in the world to present its integrated report (a groundbreaking innovation that merged the results of the sustainability report with the annual financial report) with GRI standards.

Harvesting 3BL Results and Creating Holistic Value

As part of the new business model, FIFCO executives developed 3BL plans for their specific business units, and launched numerous key initiatives. The new business strategy had enormous positive impact and instilled a sense of pride in employees. Results were assessed monthly and all business units made progress in all three areas.

Creating Environmental Value

Environmental results were based on FIFCO's three main goals: (a) zero solid waste, (b) water neutrality, and (c) carbon neutrality. The goal of becoming a zero solid waste company was accomplished by 2011, and 99.8 percent of FIFCO's total solid waste is currently reused, recycled, or used as a renewable energy source. FIFCO offsets non-recoverable solid waste (0.2 percent) through voluntary solid waste collection efforts in local communities. The company increased post-consumption recycling from 25 percent in 2008 to 65 percent in 2017, with the goal of 100 percent recycling of all its packaging materials (PET plastic bottles, aluminum and tin cans, Tetra cartons, and glass bottles) by 2020.

In 2012, FIFCO's beverage business became water neutral by embracing three steps: measuring its water footprint, water-use reduction, and compensation. The input consumption of water used for production was reduced from 11 to 4 liters (60 percent reduction) per liter of final output. Water offset projects include aqueducts, rainwater harvesting, and conservation of watersheds. In 2015, FIFCO became one of the first companies worldwide to certify its water footprint by becoming ISO 14046 certified for the production of one of its main products—*Cristal* bottled water; and in 2017 its main beer brand, Imperial, became the first water-positive beer in the world.

Despite its impressive growth in the last seven years, FIFCO's total carbon footprint has decreased from 55,000 tons of CO_2 to 40,000 in 2017. Its total carbon footprint has been certified through ISO 14064 and has been totally compensated, allowing FIFCO to become carbon neutral.

Creation of Social Value

FIFCO's main social footprint is related to harmful alcohol consumption. To address this issue, the company conducted a baseline study in 2010 to determine alcohol consumption patterns in Costa Rica. The company resolved to track improvements every five years and benchmark with other Latin American countries and Canada, one of the world's best examples of responsible alcohol use. Based on Canadian best practices, FIFCO developed a 360° strategy involving all critical stakeholders (employees, clients, consumers, decision makers, and opinion leaders). The company started with its own employees and then approached clients at the point of sale to promote moderation. FIFCO launched a major campaign partnering with the Costa Rican Ministry of Health and cancelled all marketing activities that stood against moderation. In the years that followed, the strategy evolved into a concept of "smart drinking," that is, moderate drinking in healthy adults and no consumption by minors and other sensitive populations. Five years after, in 2015, the Latin American Faculty of Social Sciences in Costa Rica concluded that people were beginning to understand the concept of smart drinking and the importance of moderation as part of a healthy lifestyle.

Prior to the implementation of the 3BL strategy, FIFCO invested approximately 1 percent of its profits in philanthropy. From 2008 to 2017 that percentage grew to

7.5 percent. In addition, FIFCO decided to spend 10 percent of its profits on philanthropic initiatives and invest 90 percent of profits on initiatives related to core businesses, thereby minimizing and offsetting FIFCO's social and environmental footprints. According to a study by Boston Consulting Group, only 1 percent of companies worldwide invest more than 6 percent of their profits in social initiatives. Over the last seven years, FIFCO has invested in water, recycling initiatives, smart drinking projects, and recently in Nutrivida, a social business with the mission to eradicate undernutrition in Central America and Haiti through a strategic partnership with Nobel Peace Prize laureate, Muhammad Yunus.

In 2009, FIFCO launched a volunteer initiative for employees called "You can choose to help." Since then, FIFCO's employees have volunteered 470,000 hours on social and environmental projects during paid workdays. In 2017, 95 percent of FIFCO's employees (in all localities) did volunteering.

Leveraging Partnerships and Engaging the Ecosystem

FIFCO's 3BL approach also entailed forming partnerships intended to create small-scale ecosystems. Partners included Educ'alcool, GRI, the Yunus Global Social Business, the Costa Rican Health Ministry, and the Latin American Brewers Association.

In 2015, FIFCO began to extend its 3BL initiatives to its value chain. Starting with a "Responsible Suppliers" program, the company developed and communicated a 3BL protocol adopted by all suppliers (more than 2,200 companies in varying industries and geographies). Since then, FIFCO evaluates and selects its suppliers based not only on economic criteria, but also on social and environmental footprints. A similar initiative with clients was launched in 2014 ("Sustainable Clients").

A 2011 study conducted by the Boston Consulting Group, in collaboration with the World Economic Forum, identified FIFCO as one of sixteen "new sustainability champions" from several hundred leading enterprises worldwide. In the last few years, FIFCO's proactive and systematic approach to sustainability has been featured in various journals, including the *Harvard Business Review* and case studies by the BCG, INCAE, and INSEAD business schools.

Signs from Within and a Quest for Purpose (2013)

From 2009 to 2013, FIFCO significantly expanded its scope to include new categories (wines, spirits, and retail) and locations (particularly the United States). Such rapid growth and diversification created new challenges, fatigue, and lack of cohesion among business units. In 2012, FIFCO employees began to voice their unrest and concerns. It was time to reconnect and re-energize FIFCO. A higher purpose was needed, a reason to exist that connected the company deeply to its core values and rallied all employees and stakeholders around a common goal. Something was missing, and it was something more powerful than a strategy; it was a purpose.

FIFCO's CEO realized that this was not a marketing exercise that could be delegated. In July 2014, a small group of the company's upper management which represented the diversity of FIFCO's team (different geographic areas, business units, gender, age, and professional background) started searching for FIFCO's purpose. Embarked on this introspective analysis of FIFCO and its people, executives started individually, and then collectively, reviewing insights from all over the organization and asking questions such as: Why does FIFCO exist? Why does it need to exist? What triggers employees to keep growing and learning? What makes FIFCO, a small Costa Rican company, truly unique? Why is the world better because of FIFCO?

After a few days, they came up with the breakthrough that it was how it did business that constituted FIFCO's uniqueness: by becoming genuinely interested in all of its stakeholders and creating holistic value (economic, social, and environmental). "We bring a better way of living to the world." This purpose should remain unchanged through time and circumstances. It should unite the organization, uphold continuous improvement throughout FIFCO, and resonate in the hearts of its employees.

FIFCO's leadership team in Costa Rica decided to shut down the entire company for the first time in a hundred years to share the company purpose with all of its employees. This was later replicated in Guatemala and the United States so that every single employee would learn about FIFCO's purpose, first hand. From that point on, every decision made at FIFCO had to meet the following criteria: Will this help make the world a better place?'

Bringing Purpose to Life (the Ten Commandments)

These communication exercises were not one-sided. FIFCO's leaders participated in feedback exercises where employees expressed their concerns and future expectations. During these gatherings, top executives proposed a list of initiatives (referred to as the "Ten Commandments") to act upon and demonstrate consistency between the company's purpose and priorities.

One of the most powerful requests from employees was helping them escape poverty. Though FIFCO paid competitive wages, some employees lived below the poverty line (this is a reality in many companies throughout the world). FIFCO committed itself to eradicating poverty internally among its employees in less than three years (estimating that it takes seven to ten years to lift an individual from poverty).

Another key initiative arising from the purpose was building a culture of entrepreneurship where any employee could innovate and contribute ideas and solutions to help solve FIFCO's commercial, social, and environmental challenges. Today, more than 500 employees have contributed their ideas to this program.

Results of the Purpose

FIFCO's focus on its purpose has deeply energized and transformed its people. After the purpose was disseminated throughout the company, it triggered enthusiasm and expectation.

A year and a half after the purpose rollout, FIFCO began to see positive results. A study was conducted to better understand the impact of the purpose on employee engagement. Based on the "Strong Sense of Purpose Key Driver of Business Investment" study published in 2014 by Deloitte, FIFCO's executive team defined four premises. First, that a sense of purpose contributes positively to business by creating a greater sense of confidence among employees regarding the future of the company. Specifically, an organization with a genuine purpose: (a) acquires a long-term business perspective, and (b) invests in its long-term growth. The findings of the study reveal that managers were more attuned to company 3BL goals and invested more in nurturing talent and innovation, thereby aligning themselves to the strategic pillar of *innovating with purpose*.

The second premise was that "having a sense of purpose provides companies with an increased capacity to build confidence among its employees." Results confirm that, overall, 89 percent of the employees are optimistic regarding the company's future, while 80 percent of the employees surveyed reported that they now enjoy their work more. They have a better sense of balancing work and life, and have found more growth opportunities at work.

At FIFCO, trust is the key to building this new culture and leadership model. The study shows that 90 percent of the surveyed staff considered that collaborators' engagement with the organization had grown with the purpose. Employees stated that purpose was the main reason why they are happy at FIFCO and desire to continue working there. In addition, 94 percent of the employees stated that FIFCO was truly committed to attaining its purpose. They saw an explicit connection between purpose and the 3BL approach. When asked about the reasons for identifying with the purpose, their answers included that they "needed to transcend," and that they wanted to "set an example for their families" or "give back to their communities."

The third aspect that management wanted to understand was if a high level of employee commitment to the company's purpose strengthened employee satisfaction. Employee satisfaction increased at a higher annual rate than in any previous year.

Employees also reported that their opinions were being heard more, and that they were more confident in proposing, experimenting, and asking for help. They added that the organization showed more acceptance and openness as a result of the new entrepreneurial culture.

In 2014, the company issued its new set of core values along with the purpose. Research has shown that the staff saw clear changes in their daily work after embracing the new values. Emphasis was given to celebrating and acknowledging the value of all collaborators. FIFCO also endeavored to modify its leadership style, introducing a more people-focused corporate environment. This serves as the basis for the fourth premise—that a defined purpose will help leaders come to own it.

A majority of the people surveyed (75 percent) acknowledged that leadership had changed for the better, with a closer relationship between supervisors and their employees, more willingness from leaders to consider the opinions of others, and a more proactive attitude. Leaders were also more willing to acknowledge a job well done. Specifically, 77 percent considered that their superiors had taken the initiative to become mentors, and a similar percentage of employees (75 percent) stated that their bosses had adopted the role of a coach. Leaders have stated that they identify with the purpose, consider it possible and attainable, and are taking action to put it into practice.

They also perceive an influence of the company's purpose on their personal lives. They state wanting to be an "example for their family, colleagues and teams."

A year after the discovery and communication of its "purpose," FIFCO noticed positive changes in their employees. They had a better attitude and an optimistic outlook toward the future. They also showed increased commitment to the organization through finding special meaning in what they do. Employee satisfaction improved, fostering mutual trust and strengthening interpersonal relationships. The positive impact of the purpose was especially visible in 2016, when FIFCO was recognized as the number one company in Central America and the Caribbean in the prestigious "Great Place to Work" ranking.

A transformation in leadership styles is FIFCO's next step. What leaders say and do will set the foundation for a culture that is open and develops the talent of its people.

FIFCO understands that this journey is just beginning. For 2020, FIFCO has defined new, very ambitious 3BL goals. It aims to double its size in terms of revenues and profit, at the same time as making these seven commitments to society a reality:

1. Complete one million hours of volunteering work.
2. Be recognized as one of the best companies to work for in the world.
3. Promote the smart consumption of all its beverages and food.
4. Eradicate poverty within FIFCO.
5. Become a water, carbon, and solid waste *positive* company through its brands.
6. Achieve 100 percent recycling of its bottles.
7. Lead through brands that make the world a better place (FIFCO Air Brands).

With these seven commitments, FIFCO aims to accelerate its path to innovation and action toward making a positive impact on the lives of everyone they touch and, consequently, "bringing a better way of living to the world."

RECOMMENDATIONS FOR BUSINESS LEADERS AND KEY ACTORS

There is a big opportunity to improve businesses and work toward building a better society where companies can extend their positive impact beyond profit maximization. The key lies in convincing business leaders that working with a holistic business approach is a viable solution.

For that reason, we offer recommendations for business leaders on how to implement this model based on key lessons learned from the SAP and FIFCO case studies. In order to adopt this new business model, policymakers and investors must support the model as key actors in the economic and social system.

Recommendations for Business Leaders

Business leaders may consider the following recommendations as they strive toward a purpose-driven organization and adopting a holistic management approach:

- *Business context is irrelevant.* This approach may apply to any organization, despite its size, revenue, profit, number of employees, industry sector, geographic location, cultural differences, and stage of development, and whether it is located in an emerging or developed economy.
- *There is no specific order when implementing the components of the tesseract model.* This novel approach to business is based on a four-dimensional paradigm where executives must: (1) strengthen their connection with the purpose of the company; (2) intensify their connection with all stakeholders; (3) deploy a holistic model that produces positive economic, social, and environmental value; and (4) build strong relationships with their employees. The aforementioned case studies describe how SAP started with the purpose and then developed a holistic model that encompassed financial, social, and environmental approaches. FIFCO, on the other hand, discovered its "purpose" after adopting a 3BL approach, thereby proving that the order in which a company implements its "purpose" is inconsequential. Business leaders must decide what dimension is most important to address first, depending on their organizational culture, business cycle, and development stages.
- *Listen carefully to your stakeholders and understand their expectations.* Open communication channels with all stakeholders (not only shareholders). This is key for long-term business success. Companies must create a deep connection with all stakeholders. Every business should carry out its business activities considering the needs and expectations of all its stakeholders. Traditional business models focus on trade-offs, whereas purpose-driven business models seek synergies and convergence.
- *Your company purpose must be genuine*: A company's purpose must be a sincere and true reflection of its essence and how it does business. It must be ambitious enough to drive the interest of stakeholders yet grounded enough to compel employees to deliver results.
- *A company's higher sense of purpose resonates if it is clearly aligned to its core business.* Employees must understand how their business activities interact with the company's purpose. The stronger the connection between the core business and the purpose, the easier employees will identify with the purpose and start acting upon it.
- *Employees' hearts (and not only their minds) must connect with the company's higher purpose.* When employees identify with their company's greater sense of purpose, they improve their engagement, motivation, and commitment to the company. FIFCO CEO, Ramón Mendiola, states: "If you win the hearts of your employees, you will have their minds forever."
- *Use your sense of purpose to attract the right stakeholders.* Having a company purpose can help identify more resilient employees. This may also be replicated

with current company stakeholders. Having a higher sense of purpose can help attract the right investors, clients, and customers for your company.

- *Embrace a holistic business approach.* Endeavor holistically to create value. Demonstrate leadership in improving social, environmental, and financial performance simultaneously.
- *A systematic model for faster results.* The holistic tesseract model provides business leaders with a comprehensive, accurate, and sophisticated method for reconciling a company's performance and progress.
- *Social and environmental goals should be aligned to core business and company footprints.* If the social and the environmental dimensions are closely aligned to core business segments and footprints, the success of the company in the long term will depend on tangible progress made in these areas. This will lead employees to accept social and environmental responsibility as an intrinsic part of their strategies.
- *A public commitment by the company.* FIFCO's decision to make its social and environmental commitments public has fostered a sense of pride and enthusiasm among its employees and stakeholders. Their acceptance in carrying out these commitments is a vital part of FIFCO's success criteria.
- *Importance of financial, social, and environmental metrics to the overall picture.* Most social and environmental goals can be linked to KPIs. Defining concrete and quantitative goals is critical for measuring progress. SAP attributes its success to the development of integrated reporting methods. In this manner, management was able to understand the correlation among the social, environmental, and financial performance. By linking financial and non-financial performance, SAP employees, stakeholders, and consumers were able to understand that company success was all-encompassing. Financial success could not be attained independently if it was not accompanied by social and environmental success.
- *Employee compensation aligned to holistic success.* Financial performance should not be the sole determining factor used to measure success. Executive and employee compensation should be based on social, environmental, and economic indicators, which comprise a more holistic method of measuring success.
- *Purpose allows the company to maintain its North Star.* Strategy will always change and markets will be transformed. Business leaders have to look within for inspiration from its core—its purpose, which will endure through time. Organizations with a purpose have a long-term perspective. They become stronger and more resourceful and employees become more assertive and capable of facing even the most difficult challenges.
- *Purpose as a source of positive energy and direction for employees.* A purpose creates a powerful connection among employees, allowing them to stay focused when faced with changing business environments. It also disciplines in balancing short-term and long-term perspectives.

- *No proven trade-off between progress and performance.* The idea of success based solely on short-term economic success for company shareholders is an outdated concept. Upholding the notion of trade-off between economic performance and its positive impact on society has also become obsolete. A purpose-driven organization no longer compromises economic, social, or environmental prosperity, but establishes synergies among them. It does not believe in trade-offs between shareholders and other stakeholders and supports the premise that it is the responsibility and opportunity of a company to create sustainable value for all stakeholders.

Recommendations for Investors and Policymakers

A purpose-driven business model requires the support of both investors and policymakers. Investors are the most efficient stakeholders to act upon since they own capital. Policymakers and government officials are critical stakeholders since they create the policies and incentives that will promote the model throughout the world. To develop the model systematically with the support of these key actors, a three-pillar process is helpful. It involves *better knowing*, *better choosing*, and *better acting*. These three steps will help further this new paradigm for businesses, where companies embrace the creation of social, environmental, and economic value.

Better Knowing

Our current approaches to measuring business performance are limited. To "know better" we need a more holistic measure of business performance and its contribution to progress.

At the national level, traditional measures of economic progress are limited to GDP, GDP growth, and productivity indicators based on GDP per capita. The concept of GDP was developed in the aftermath of the Great Depression and World War II, becoming the single most important measure of economic well-being. Yet evident shortcomings arose, such as identifying growth as development and the blind pursuit of economic growth per se. This led to the 1990 launch of the Human Development Index (HDI) and later the Social Progress Index, which measures how well economic growth translates into social progress.[6] The World Economic Forum also recently launched *The Inclusive Growth and Development Report 2015*.[7]

---

[6] Human needs = health, hygiene, shelter, safety. Foundations of well-being = access to basic knowledge, information, wellness, ecosystem sustainability. Opportunity = personal rights, freedom, tolerance, advanced education.

[7] <http://www.weforum.org/reports/inclusive-growth-and-development-report-2015>.

Parallel to the development of the GDP measure, standard reporting of business performance needs to be developed. Current reporting standards for business (IFRS—International Financial Reporting Standards; and GAAP—generally accepted accounting principles) focus on measuring historic financial performance and are limited to activities within the company.

To measure the overall performance of a company and better align it to social progress, a more comprehensive approach is required to determine corporate success and value. This type of approach measures success beyond the financial data and incorporates other dimensions that address likelihood of future performance, and benefits to all critical stakeholders and society at large.

In order to measure the true value and sustainable performance of a company, we recommend a "balance sheet of the future." Unlike the pure financial balance sheet, which shows the actual financial position and risk, a "balance sheet of the future" would include investments made to improve the future performance and reputation of a company.

The "balance sheet of the future" should, besides the financial balance sheet, include elements like:

- *Human resources balance sheet*: investments in human resources in order to strengthen the human capital of the company in the future.
- *Innovation balance sheet*: investments in research to increase innovation capabilities in the future.
- *Environmental balance sheet*: investments in environment-related areas to improve the environmental impact of the company in the future.
- *Social balance sheet*: investments in relevant social initiatives that foster social progress in the future.

For each of the elements in the "balance sheet of the future" the company should report investments done within the company, as well as investments done in the ecosystem and/or value chain of the company for indirect impact and societal value.

Through the implementation of the "balance sheet of the future" investors would be in a better position to evaluate the long-term performance of a company, and business leaders would be able to focus beyond the short-term performance and ensure that the required investments are made for sustainable success.

An example of a more holistic performance measurement is the GRI guidelines, which has pioneered sustainable reporting since the late 1990s. GRI works with a global multi-stakeholder network with over 600 organizations from all over the world.

Our recommendation for investors is to demand more holistic performance reporting from companies, in order to better estimate the future success and real value of a company.

Our recommendation for policymakers is to help enhance business reporting standards to include the "balance sheet of the future" and the impact a company has on society. This would enable business leaders to report the company's success—balancing short- and long-term priorities. In addition, all stakeholders including shareholders would be able to assess not just the short-term performance of a company, but its long-term potential and risks, and thus be better informed in their decision making.

Better Choosing

There is a paradigm that business leaders must sort trade-offs between short-term and long-term performance or between different expectations from shareholders and other stakeholders. The same is expected from investors who must guide business leaders on how to choose between these theoretical trade-offs. In practice these trade-offs need not be so sharp or constraining. Implementing a holistic approach to measuring progress and performance will help create the required knowledge and transparency for business leaders, policymakers, and stakeholders at large. In addition, an active role by policymakers to increase alignment between objectives for business and society through incentives and regulatory frameworks will reduce the trade-offs expected by business leaders.

Encouraging, sustaining, and enhancing growth and sustainability in a country requires decisive action by business leaders to complement governmental investments as well as a clear government intervention to foster this new way of doing business. Specifically, three types of policy intervention are desirable:

1. *Raising awareness.* Instruments represent an important tool for governments in disseminating the idea of purpose-driven organizations and providing incentives for business to adopt it.
2. *Partnering.* Partnering instruments lie at the heart of the purpose-driven business model. It is important to understand that governments do not have all the necessary resources to solve every social, environmental, and economic problem in a country. Partnerships and strategic alliances combine the expertise, competencies, and resources of the public sector with those of business and other societal actors to address action areas within the national agenda, thus creating benefit for all stakeholders.
3. *Proactive soft interventions.* Non-regulatory interventions (i.e. sustainability guidelines, tax incentives, national action plans, etc.) can provide a fertile ground for companies to put their innovative capacities to good use, enabling them to be better than the law requires.

The same applies to investors who have a tremendous opportunity to create social and environmental value while continuing to profit economically. One can argue that fear could be used to convince them. Fear of additional regulation and restrictions, fear of losing their license to operate in a particular community, fear of higher taxes that may reduce profits, fear of losing consumers (who are now more sophisticated and demand more from companies).

However, there is a better alternative to convincing investors to redirect their business practices so that they may continue to create economic value and simultaneously create positive social and environmental value. They need to understand that trade-offs among these three dimensions of value creation are not real.

Investors must feel compelled to follow their moral compasses and realize that, today, companies must have a higher purpose in order to ensure long-term success.

Better Acting

Visible actions by business leaders supported by policymakers and investors are critical to setting new standards for business in society and building a critical mass of purpose-driven companies.

The case studies in this chapter will hopefully inspire more leaders to adopt new business standards toward more sustainable performance and progress in society based on a purpose-driven holistic approach.

As many world leaders have argued, it is time to take action. It is time for business leaders to reinvent themselves and experience a rebirth of their companies from its core—purpose.

However, when considering the starting point, not all companies are created equal. According to an article in the October 2011 issue of *Forbes* magazine, "Global corporate control has a bow-tie shape, with a dominant core of 147 firms radiating out from the middle. Each of these 147 own interlocking stakes of one another ('super connected companies') and together they control 40 percent of the wealth in the network. A total of 737 companies control 80 percent of it all."

The time has come for these "super connected companies" to take action. Business leaders worldwide must draw from this new sense of higher purpose to reinvent their business. This change must start from the core, from the hearts of the employees by instilling in them a higher sense of purpose. Strategies will always change and markets will continue to be transformed. The real challenge, however, lies in convincing boards of directors and CEOs at top global companies that holistic capitalism is the next phase of evolution for the economy. Holistic capitalism will infuse their companies with a renewed sense of purpose, allowing them to create sustainable value for all stakeholders.

Epilog

It may be tempting to believe that changing legal arrangements (such as limited liability) and increasing regulation are the best ways to check the downsides of enterprise capitalism. We propose in this chapter, however, that it should be a question of leadership and stewardship rather than ownership, per se. We can all influence our leadership—and we should not have to lean, yet again, on the reach of the law to lead in the right way. It is a choice that business leaders need to make on their own.

Fortunately, this change toward societal progress is already starting. In January 2017 at the annual meeting in Davos, the World Economic Forum recommended business leaders to commit themselves to "The Compact for Responsive and Responsible Leadership." The Compact was initiated by business leaders who felt an increasing need for businesses to take an active leadership role in ensuring societal progress. The Compact was signed by more than one hundred of the largest and most influential companies in the world and is an endorsement of the need for businesses to be driven by a stronger purpose serving all stakeholders.[8]

· ·

COMMENTS AND DISCUSSION

Hansmeyer, Mendiola, and Snabe draw on case studies from their own experience in business to identify a "purpose-driven" organizational model that can address the dual objectives of addressing economic and societal interests.

In what ways does the traditional shareholder model of investing support or undermine the dual pursuit of profit and social good?

In weighing Hansmeyer, Mendiola, and Snabe's proposal for business that is more thoroughly attuned to the social good, a number of participants at the Society for Progress' second assembly pointed to problems with the present system of shareholder governance. Collomb noted that business leaders are generally prepared to accept a more long-term, "purpose-driven" model, but that there is considerable resistance to this among shareholders. Pettit noted that this problem is particularly acute in the US system, where the pressures of the short-term earnings cycle are especially strong among both managers and investors. He suggested that the purpose-driven model might fit better with the German variety of capitalism, in which corporate governance is much more oriented toward the broader community of stakeholders. On the other hand, Davis observed, the recent case of Volkswagen's diesel emissions scandal suggests that the German model of "communitarian capitalism" is susceptible to the same problems as the US alternative. Are shareholders really the problem?

How might we improve accountability to stakeholders in a way that serves social ends?

Barney pointed out that the stakeholders of any company constitute an enormously heterogeneous group with often deeply conflicting interests. A viable stakeholder model of business, he suggested, depends on a good theory of how to sort out such

[8] We would like to thank Subramanian Rangan for his guidance and inspiration, as well as Gisela Sánchez Maroto, Scarlet Pietri, and Prothit Sen for their invaluable assistance.

interests. A further problem in fostering accountability to such diverse interests is that, as Davis observed, modern capitalism is defined by "highly dispersed supply chains," which makes it extremely difficult to assign responsibility for particular harms to an individual firm. Instead, we should be thinking about responsibility in terms of business "ecosystems" (collections of interrelated firms) for creating things. One crucial means of fostering better accountability to stakeholders, Anderson argued, is democratic representation: we need a genuine empowerment of stakeholders in corporate governance.

Accountability to social goods is also dependent on the way in which investment products are structured. Hong suggested that, in this respect, bond investing might be a better model than equity insofar as bonds allow investors to focus on very specific, definable goals (e.g. prison reform, or carbon impact) and agree to give up a specific amount of their yield based on progress toward those goals. Meyer noted that the extent to which financial and social goals are in tension depends in part on the way in which a social ethos is institutionalized. As social impact comes to be seen as part of a rational case for business, more and more investors will take that into account in their appraisal of the firm.

How does the mission and internal management structure of firms shape their service of social goods alongside financial objectives?

Hong noted the recent development of B corporations and benefit corporations, in which the firm's mission is explicitly cast in terms of the pursuit of some social good. One way to negotiate that joint social/financial pursuit is, as Hansmeyer, Mendiola, and Snabe suggest, to look for synergies across these dimensions. Alternatively, Battilana observed, some firms very successfully navigate this divide by maintaining a "creative tension" within their internal management structure.

CHAPTER 10

BEHIND EVERY GREAT FORTUNE IS AN EQUALLY GREAT CRIME

JAY B. BARNEY AND DAVID SCHMIDTZ

Abstract

This chapter examines the accuracy of the quote "behind every great fortune is an equally great crime," attributed to Balzac. In our times great individual fortunes are generally generated via the instrument of the business firm. The question then becomes when are firm profits a crime? Firm profits are, in general, explained by one or more of three factors: luck, efficiency, and collusion. While it is difficult to regard luck as a crime, luck does not reflect merit. Profits due to efficiency seem like the least problematic case, and collusion seems the clearest case of when fortune coincides with crime. A variety of cases lie, at least in a dynamic sense, at the intersection of the three conditions. Unfortunately, history suggests that big business and big government can collude to keep profits flowing to the former and contributions flowing to the latter. While luck and efficiency may help initiate wealth, the system tolerates connivance, making Balzac's statement more plausible than it ought to be.

The title of this essay is a quotation attributed to Balzac. If, as the quotation suggests, the only way to accumulate wealth is by criminal and presumably unethical means, then the accumulation of wealth is lamentable. It may also be preventable, which suggests a rationale for egalitarian policies aimed at putting a stop to the accumulating of great fortunes. To some economists (Krugman 2007) and many in the public at large (Newport 2015), this basic idea is compelling, or at the very least highly plausible.

There is, of course, another point of view. In this view, outsized wealth accumulation, far from signaling unethical and/or illegal activities on the part of individuals, signals outsized ability to identify and then satisfy market needs.[1] In this view, wealth

---

[1] "*Homo sapiens* became the wisest of primates around forty thousand years ago, when we learned to make deals with strangers. Many steps we've made in our social evolution involved expanding the

accumulation is a logical consequence of a particular type of competitive process, and provides incentives for individuals to innovate in ways that improve the lives of many (Jaffe and Lerner 2007).

One reason for these different interpretations is that wealth accumulation is not a homogeneous phenomenon. Sometimes, after all, wealth accumulation does reflect great crimes; sometimes it instead reflects a great innovation (and lest we trivialize the notion of crime, we cannot regard being innovative as an instance). Indeed, some fortunes may combine aspects of both.

The purpose of this essay is to specify conditions under which wealth accumulation is likely to be bad for society, when it is likely to be good, and how the social consequences of wealth accumulation evolve over time. Note that economic wealth can be defined in various ways. Accountants typically define wealth as the difference between the market value of all the tangible and intangible assets owned by an economic entity and the liabilities of that entity, essentially, its debt. This concept is also known as "net worth."

The accumulated wealth or net worth of a variety of economic entities can be calculated, including the wealth of individuals, families, and, in some circumstances, countries. This essay focuses on wealth accumulation by individuals and families. However, in a modern economy, much of the wealth accumulated by individuals and families was originally created by firms they founded and/or owned (Piketty 2014)—either as entrepreneurs or as an inheritance. This essay will focus on how firms generate wealth that can be accumulated by individual and family owners.

In general, a firm that generates profits—that is, revenues exceeding costs (Barney 2013)—will generate more wealth that can be accumulated by their individual and family owners than firms that do not generate these economic profits. In this sense, understanding whether wealth accumulation involves a "great crime" becomes equivalent to understanding whether the economic profits generated by firms are derived from such a crime.

Sources of Economic Profits

Firms have numerous ways of generating an economic profit (Mahoney and Qian 2013). This essay will focus on three of the most important: a firm (and its owners) can be lucky (Frank 2016), firms can collude to restrict output, or a firm can address market needs more efficiently than others (Demsetz 1973). And as will be discussed later in this essay, many ways of generating profit—including lobbying the government for special favors (Schmidtz 2015)—can be understood as special cases of these three.

---

spheres of mutually advantageous commerce. Paradoxically, we are inclined, perhaps even biologically programmed, to see commerce as a zero-sum game: that is, we see people who profit by selling us food or tools as getting rich at our expense. Eons ago, though, brave souls began to imagine what human beings could do, and saw that the key to a better life was trade. Thus began our liberation from the brutality of life as cave-dwellers" (Schmidtz and Brennan 2010: chapter 1).

Luck and Firm Economic Profits

We can credit economic profits to luck when a firm has no special insights into the market value of the assets it is assembling, and that value turns out to be much higher than what anyone—including those selling these assets—had in mind (Barney 1986). For example, a person who buys a piece of land from a farmer for the purpose of farming pays a price that reflects the land's expected value as a farm. Suppose, however, that this land turns out to be located on a huge gold deposit that no one knew about, *ex ante*. Once this gold deposit is discovered, the market value of this land rises significantly, but the cost of acquiring this land—originally priced as a farm—has not changed. Thus, the difference between the market value of the assets controlled by this entity—in this case, the farmer—and the total cost of assembling these assets is positive, and an economic profit has been created. The farmer can accumulate the wealth created by this economic profit either by selling her interest in the land (now repriced as a gold mine) or by mining the gold and selling it on the market. We take the profit to the buyer as a fairly clear example of pure luck. Since this farmer thought she was acquiring a farm, and only became aware of the potential of this land as a gold mine much later, the economic profits she created must be attributed to her good luck, rather than to her skill as a land appraiser, farmer, or anything else.

Note also that those who sell this land to our farmer must be equally ignorant of the land's true value, or they would not sell it at the farm price. In this sense, they were unlucky. Clearly the seller will have regret about the sale, and the buyer will experience the windfall value as manna from heaven, more or less. Yet, there is nothing in the case that makes the transaction a crime, or that makes it bad for society. It is simply luck.

Collusion and Firm Economic Profits

A second way that firms can create economic profits has to do with collusion and the exercise of monopoly power (Schmidtz 2016). This process is well documented in the economics literature, and will only be briefly summarized here.

In a competitive market, supply of a product or service tends to rise (or fall) to equal demand for this product or service. Supply rises when prices are driven higher by excess demand. Suppliers cut back when excess supply drives prices lower. Competitive markets thus tend toward an equilibrium price at which the quantity supplied equals the quantity demanded.

Firms pursuing similar product market strategies *collude* when they cooperate to reduce supply below the competitive level. When firms successfully collude, they prevent supply from rising to meet demand, prices do not fall, and thus remain above the competitive level. High prices would normally encourage new entry which, in turn, would increase competition and lower prices and lead to zero economic profits for firms in the long run. So, to collude successfully and thus keep prices high, it is not enough for colluding firms to cooperate in limiting their own supply; they must also erect barriers to entry that effectively prevent new suppliers from entering the market. Such barriers can exist because of the nature of the product or services being exchanged—through economies of scale or product differentiation acting as barriers to entry (Porter 1980)—or they can be created by the actions of firms or governments, independent of the nature of these products or services. An example of this latter approach—called "contrived deterrence"—is when a firm builds excess manufacturing capacity waiting to come on line should new firms enter the market. Such capacity has the potential to deter entry insofar as bringing it online would reduce profits, both for incumbent and new entrant firms (Barney 2013).

Thus, collusion to reduce supply below its competitive level, linked with barriers to entry to keep supply low, can, together, sustain high prices. If the cost of creating collusion and erecting barriers to entry is less than the revenue generated by high prices, collusion can create economic profits for colluding firms which, in turn, can lead to the accumulation of wealth by the individuals or families that own this firm.

Efficiency and Firm Economic Profits

A final way that firms can create economic profits builds neither on luck nor collusion, but on the ability of some firms to address market needs. Prices can remain above a dominant firm's production cost insofar as capabilities are not uniformly distributed among firms and do not diffuse rapidly (Barney 1991).

In this setting, some firms will be more efficient at addressing consumer preferences than others, and firms without the requisite capabilities may have difficulty imitating them (Demsetz 1973; Barney 1991). Those that have been able to develop these special capabilities will be able to accumulate wealth for their owners while those without these capabilities will not.

In this context, an important question becomes: Why don't those without these capabilities simply develop them, increasing the competitiveness of the market, and reducing the ability of any firm to generate economic profits? There are at least three reasons.

First, some capabilities are costly to imitate because they are path dependent and reflect a firm's unique path through history (and history is costly to imitate) (Arthur 1989). For example, Caterpillar Corporation was able to develop a worldwide supply and distribution network in the heavy construction industry at extremely low cost because it was the primary supplier of heavy construction equipment to the allies during World War II (Rukstad and Horn 1989). Firms seeking to imitate this supply and distribution network at this same low cost would simply have to recreate conditions that existed in the war—a challenging task indeed.

Second, some capabilities are costly to imitate because they are socially complex, reflecting deep-seated values in a firm's culture, its way of doing business, and relationships between a firm and it customers and suppliers. Those without these socially complex capabilities will find it costly to develop them (Barney 1991).

Finally, it is not always clear what capability, or complex set of capabilities, is generating an advantage. This is the condition of causal ambiguity (Lippman and Rumelt 1982). Such ambiguity exists whenever there are multiple explanations about why a firm is as capable as it is, and testing alternative explanations is costly. In these settings, competitors may not know what to imitate.

Note that when consumers have heterogeneous preferences, and firm capabilities are heterogeneously distributed in stable ways, some firms may gain a larger share in a particular market than others. However, in this context, larger market share is not a prerequisite for collusive actions that reduce supply below competitive levels, but rather is an indicator that some firms are more successful at addressing market needs than others.

Are All Economic Profits Created by a Great Crime? The Pure Cases

While described separately, it will often be the case that a firm's profits reflect multiple sources of these profits all at once. A firm may be both lucky and efficient, and the combination may generate great wealth for a firm's owners. These combinations will be discussed later in the essay. To ground these more complex discussions, it is first convenient to discuss whether each of the sources of economic profits identified here necessarily imply some sort of "great crime."

Great Crimes and Economic Profits Attributable to Luck

At one level, it is difficult to think of economic profits generated through luck as criminal or unethical. After all, in this luck setting, a firm that assembles the resources needed to engage in business, and firms supplying these resources, are equally ignorant about the true future value of these resources. There is no duplicity, no misrepresentation, no insider trading. Accordingly, there is no great crime here. There may or may not be an exploiting of information asymmetry to the disadvantage of one party to an exchange, but if there is, it would not be a crime and (especially if the better informed party makes no attempt to hide the information) need not be unethical either. The key issue is simply the lack of information.

Decision makers in real-world economies do not know everything, and some know more than others. Generally speaking, society has no interest in preventing the movement of resources from agents who do not know how to put them to their best use to agents who do.

However, there might be some ethical issues associated with individual or family wealth being accumulated because a firm was lucky. For example, many have argued that superior performance attributable to superior effort or superior effectiveness is not problematic (Schmidtz 2002). After all, these superior performers, in a sense, "get what they deserve."

This is not the case if the only reason a firm is generating economic profits is because it was lucky. In this setting, superior performance is not a reward for superior effort or superior capabilities, but rather a reward for simply being in the right place at the right time. It would not be surprising if many countries developed policies that had the effect of redistributing the wealth of individuals or families that was generated primarily through luck (Piketty 2014).

Indeed, this is one logic that underlies inheritance laws (Saez and Piketty 2013). While it is usually difficult to attribute the wealth created by an initial investor/ inventor/entrepreneur entirely or even mostly to luck, the wealth accumulated by this person's descendants, from the point of view of these descendants, at least, results almost entirely from luck. In particular, these children and grandchildren are lucky to have been born into a family with great wealth. Do such "lucky" children, in some sense, "deserve" the great wealth they control, wealth that was created by someone else? And if not, is it appropriate for the government (or some other entity) to enact policies that effectively reduce the size of this accumulated wealth?

Should every gift be looked at in this skeptical way? Should those whose innovations, efforts, and capabilities generate well-deserved fortunes be regarded as having no right to give their money to their children, to charities, and so on?[2]

Great Crimes and Economic Profits Attributable to Collusion

The idea that profits attributable to luck constitute a "great crime" is dubious, and threatens to trivialize the idea of a great crime. Not so with collusion. It is not for no reason that collusion is illegal in most countries. The deleterious effects of collusion on the welfare of individuals in the economy are well documented. Economic profits generated by successful collusion, in this sense, often rise to the status of a "great crime."

This does not imply that collusion is by definition a great crime. Neither does it imply that consumers never benefit from firms engaging in explicit collusion. Consumers who have strong preference for a monopolist's products may purchase these products, despite their high price. Indeed, as long as consumers retain the right to not consume a monopolistic firm's product offerings at the stated price, non-consumption can create some discipline for a monopolist.

---

[2] Needless to say, this sort of skepticism leads quickly to the conclusion that no one deserves anything and it becomes a tautology that no one deserves anything, but see the chapter on "How to Deserve" in Schmidtz 2008 for observations about how common-sense conceptions systematically differ from academic conceptions and how common-sense conceptions allow for the possibility that people can deserve an opportunity on the basis of what they do with that opportunity after the fact. Someone who by luck is given an opportunity can still do justice to that opportunity.

Great Crimes and Economic Profits Attributable to Efficiency

There are no obvious legal or ethical issues associated with economic profits generated by a firm's ability to more efficiently and effectively address the preferences of its consumers (Demsetz 1973). Firms with special skills in these markets are likely to generate higher economic profits than firms without these skills, but these higher profits are attributable to these firms' special skills, and not to anti-competitive actions.

Prices for products or services purchased from these special firms may be higher (if demand for these products is greater than supply—think of Apple iPhones) or lower (if special firms are able to obtain cost advantages not available to other firms—think of Walmart). In the former case, consumers will be willing to pay higher than "competitive market prices" for the products in question because they are able to gain value from these products that they would not be able to gain otherwise. In the latter case, consumers will be able to pay less for a product than would otherwise be the case. In both settings, customers will be satisfied.

Note also that, in this setting, firms with valuable, rare, and costly-to-imitate capabilities may not only be more profitable than firms without these skills, they may also become larger—in terms of market share—than these other firms. Again, that market share is not necessarily an indicator that a firm's profits are due to its ability to reduce supply below the competitive level. It can instead indicate a firm's ability to meet customer needs more efficiently and effectively.

ARE ALL ECONOMIC PROFITS CREATED BY GREAT CRIMES? MIXED CASES

To this point, it has been suggested that firm economic profit (and great fortunes to which it can give rise) is sometimes based on great crimes (e.g. when profits are generated through supply reducing monopoly practices), is sometimes not (e.g. when profits are generated through efficiently meeting customer needs), and sometimes has an ambiguous ethical status (e.g. wealth inherited from those who generated economic profits by more efficiently meeting customer needs). However, only pure cases—only luck, only collusion, or only efficiency—have been considered so far. Rarely will the economic profits of a firm be attributable exclusively to one of these factors. The implications of mixed cases are examined in what follows.

Economic Profits Attributable to Luck and Collusion

Consider the great fortune accumulated by Cecil Rhodes (Rotberg 1988). Rhodes left England in his later teenage years to become a cotton farmer in South Africa. After a few years, he left his farm to work in the diamond fields at Kimberly. For a couple of years, Rhodes was a reasonably successful diamond miner—purchasing claims, developing new claims, buying and selling diamonds. His own evaluation was that he was earning an income from diamond mining that would have qualified him to live in the upper middle classes of Victorian England.

Then, at age 19, Rhodes had a heart attack. Forced to cease his mining operations, Rhodes went on an eighteen-month trek across Africa to recover. Rhodes returned to the mines to discover that the diamond output in the mines at Kimberly had fallen, and that many people were willing to sell their claims at highly discounted prices. Despite the fact that the only evidence available suggested that diamond production had reached its peak, Rhodes believed that below the first level of diamonds in the mine he would be able to find a second level of diamonds.

Based on this belief, Rhodes purchased all the Kimberly mine claims that he could. At one point, Rhodes owned over 90 percent of the Kimberly claims. Rhodes organized the De Beers Company to manage these claims.

And then, a second layer of diamonds was discovered, Rhodes became one of the richest people in the world, and De Beers had a virtual monopoly on mining and selling diamonds throughout the world. This monopoly continued for almost a century, well after Cecil Rhodes died of a second heart attack at age 48.

While not discounting Rhodes' personal determination and stamina, the ability of Rhodes to purchase over 90 percent of the mining claims at significant discounts, and then to generate massive economic profits from doing so must be largely attributed to luck. Rhodes had no better information about the true value of these claims than those who sold them. It turns out that Rhodes' expectations were correct, but they just as easily could have been incorrect.

But Rhodes' decision to organize De Beers and to create a monopoly on the diamond trade is not luck—it is a classic example of using collusion/monopoly to generate economic profits, or more precisely, to protect the economic profits that Rhodes' luck was generating. Some of the great wealth that Rhodes accumulated must be attributed, then, to these monopolistic actions.

Was there a great crime behind Cecil Rhodes' great fortune? In one sense, no—Rhodes simply made a lucky bet. But, in another sense, yes—since he chose to leverage his lucky advantage by creating a monopoly. Moreover, Rhodes used the great fortune that he "lucked into" and created to engage in a variety of expansionist activities that most modern observers label as "great crimes."

Economic Profits Attributable to Luck and Efficiency

Consider the remarkable success of Bill Gates and Microsoft (Isaacson 2014). In its early days, Microsoft was a provider of programming languages for Apple Computers. It originally had no operating system products. The dominant operating system for PCs during the early 1970s to the early 1980s was CPM, a product built by Digital Research, Inc.

In the early 1980s, IBM decided to enter the personal computer market. To reduce competition on the basis of hardware or software and, instead, to focus competition on sales and support—areas where IBM was particularly strong—IBM decided to purchase its hardware and software components from outside suppliers.

In the process of developing its PC, IBM realized it needed an operating system. IBM managers approached Bill Gates, then president and CEO of Microsoft, about buying an operating system from Microsoft for IBM's machine. Bill Gates answered honestly—Microsoft did not, at that time, have a PC operating system, and that the best operating system for PCs was built by Digital Research, namely CPM.

Armed with this insight, IBM approached Digital Research to ask about licensing their software for the IBM PC. Wary of this huge mainframe computer company, Digital Research was reluctant to meet with IBM. CPM was thus not going to be IBM's operating system.

IBM managers returned to Seattle, to once again meet with Bill Gates. Gates quickly recognized the potential for licensing an operating system to IBM and contacted a colleague who had developed such a system for his own use. This operating system was known as QDOS—which stood for "Quick and Dirty Operating System." Gates purchased this operating system for $50,000, renamed it MSDOS—which stood for "Micro Soft Disc Operating System"—and then turned around and licensed it to IBM. The license specified that Microsoft would be paid a royalty for every IBM PC that was sold with a Microsoft operating system.

Within a few months of being introduced, IBM PCs came to dominate the PC market, and Microsoft generated enormous economic profits which led to huge wealth accumulation by Bill Gates and many of the early employees of Microsoft. IBM's bet that their ability to sell and service PCs would give them an advantage in the marketplace—a very reasonable bet at the time—turned out to be incorrect, and much of the economic profit created by IBM's entry into the PC market ended up being appropriated by critical suppliers, including Microsoft and Intel.

So, was Bill Gates lucky or good? Probably both. He was lucky in the sense that IBM asked his company, Microsoft, to supply an operating system, even though everyone in the industry knew that Microsoft did not have an operating system to license. Gates was also lucky in that Digital Research was unwilling to license CPM to IBM.

However, he was skilled in recognizing that IBM needed an operating system and in moving quickly to position Microsoft to supply one. Using the language developed previously, Gates was more effective and efficient than the competition in addressing the needs of a customer—IBM. This differential ability generated huge wealth for Bill Gates and members of his management team.

Economic Profits Attributable to Efficiency and Collusion

Fast forward the Microsoft story some ten years (Gavil and First 2014; Liebowitz and Margolis 2001). Microsoft has become the leading provider of operating systems for all personal computers through its MSDOS software. Building off product developments created by its former partner, Apple Computers, Microsoft also introduced Windows— initially a much friendlier shell which facilitated a user interface with MSDOS, but later a PC operating system in its own right. Microsoft has also developed and implemented the Office Suite—a set of programs that take full advantage of the Windows operating system and employ the same easy-to-use interface that Microsoft used in its Windows products. By linking its operating system (Windows) and its applications products (Office), Microsoft has become the dominant software provider in the PC industry.

The rise of the Internet then created a new challenge and opportunity for Microsoft—namely, how could Microsoft extend its dominance of the standalone PC software market into the Internet space? It developed its own web browser— Explorer—and bundled this software with its other PC products.

Other web browser providers, including Netscape (with its product Navigator) objected to Microsoft's bundling strategy, arguing that Microsoft was "exporting" its dominant position in PC operating systems and office software into the web browser market. In the end, the court agreed.

Was Microsoft being efficient in addressing its customer preferences, or was it acting as a monopolist? Again, the answer is probably both. Indeed, one of the ironies in conducting these kinds of analyses is that whether a firm is able to generate substantial economic wealth because it was lucky or because it was efficient, once it has generated this wealth, it often has strong incentives to act as a monopolist.

DISCUSSION

Adam Smith on Organized Crime

In at least one respect, Balzac's poetic protest may hold more than a grain of truth. First, we labor under a political infrastructure that is always threatening to decay into crony capitalism: that is, always subject to capture by mercantilists who lobby for subsidies for exporters, protectionists who lobby for tariffs and other trade barriers, monopolists who pay kings for a license to be free from competition altogether, and so on. Partnerships between big business and big government lead to big subsidies, monopolistic licensing practices, and tariffs. These ways of compromising freedom have been and always will be touted as protecting the middle class, but their true purpose is (and almost always will be) to transfer wealth and power from ordinary citizens to well-connected elites.

As a result, an ordinary citizen's pivotal relationships are not with free and equal trading partners but with bureaucratic rulers: people whose grip on our community is so pervasive that we cannot walk away from such terms of engagement as they unilaterally propose. Thus, to Adam Smith, we are always in the business of reinventing feudalism, and figuring out how once again to put ourselves at the mercy of lords:

To widen the market and to narrow the competition is always the interest of the dealers. To widen the market may frequently be agreeable enough to the interest of the public; but to narrow the competition must always be against it, and can serve only to enable the dealers, by raising their profits above what they naturally would be, to levy, for their own benefit, an absurd tax upon the rest of their fellow-citizens. The proposal of any new law or regulation of commerce which comes from this order, ought always to be listened to with great precaution, and ought never to be adopted till after having been long and carefully examined, not only with the most scrupulous, but with the most suspicious attention. It comes from an order of men, whose interest is never exactly the same with that of the public, who have generally an interest to deceive and even to oppress the public, and who accordingly have, upon many occasions, both deceived and oppressed it.   (Smith 1776: I.xi.p.10)

Resistance to such oppression requires eternal vigilance, with no hope of final victory:

People of the same trade seldom meet together, even for merriment and diversion, but the conversation ends in a conspiracy against the public, or in some contrivance to raise prices. It is impossible indeed to prevent such meetings, by any law which either could be executed, or would be consistent with liberty and justice. But though the law cannot hinder people of the same trade from sometimes assembling together, it ought to do nothing to facilitate such assemblies; much less to render them necessary.   (Smith 1776: I.x.c.27)

Unfortunately, kings wanting to fight wars employing expensive mercenaries have always been driven to sell monopoly licenses to generate revenue. This market for political power has a singularly unhappy logic. Namely, kings adopt policies systematically favoring merchants who have lost their economic edge, because inferior competitors are the ones most willing to pay for the imposition of tariffs and other legal barriers to competition. As David Hume saw, the easy transfer of external goods was both an enormous opportunity and an enormous problem, a foundation of both the promise and the downfall of capitalism. It makes piracy possible, and enables crony capitalists to enlist the help of kings to bureaucratize piracy and make it routine.

Second, we labor under a related and equally ubiquitous threat of being shackled by "men of system." As Samuel Fleischacker (2004: 235) says, "the limitations Smith describes on what anyone can know about their society should give pause to those who are confident that governments can carry out even the task of protecting freedom successfully. Taken together with his skepticism about the judiciousness, decency, and impartiality of those who go into politics, this is what gives punch to the libertarian reading of Smith." As Smith saw it, the "man of system"

is apt to be very wise in his own conceit. . . . He seems to imagine that he can arrange the different members of a great society with as much ease as the hand arranges the different pieces upon a chess-board. He does not consider that the pieces upon the chess-board have no other principle of motion besides that which the hand impresses upon them; but that, in the great chess-board of human society, every single piece has a principle of motion of its own, altogether different from that which the legislature might cause to impress upon it.   (Smith 1759: VI.ii.2.17)

A "man of system" moves pawns in pursuit of his goals, but pawns tend to respond in an irritatingly contrarian way. First, they have interests of their own. Second, their interests are not always narrow but may be bound up in a constellation of loyalties, habits, and mutual expectations that make communities what they are; moreover, part of what communities are is resistant to change. So, Smith says, public spirit leads people both to respect their traditions but also to want to see their institutions perfected.

In peaceful times the potential conflict between these two impulses is not a problem, but in times of strife the two impulses of public spirit can come apart, and a "man of system" gripped by a vision of perfection can do great damage. A man of system moves the pieces, but the pieces respond as if they have minds of their own, which, after all, they do. Pieces respond with a view to their own hopes and dreams, but also with their own sense of what their society is about and where it needs to go from here (Smith 1759: VI.ii.2.17). Incensed by the pawn's contrarian response, men of system make adjustments, now seeking more to dominate "pawns" than to help them, and any virtue these would-be public servants initially brought to public office is corroded.

Compounding the problem, the reins of power come at a price. Anyone acquiring the reins will be a person to whom such power is worth the price. Moreover, the more power there is to acquire, the more it will be worth, the more people must invest to acquire it, and thus the more that such power gets concentrated in the hands of people intent on using it for all that it is worth. So, the process by which people gain political appointment will systematically tend, and increasingly tend, to select the wrong person for the job.

Consequently, there is a predictable even if not inevitable disconnect between what truly benevolent people seek and what men of system deliver. Such tension is driven by the logic of offices that align bureaucratic interests with that of "dealers" in particular rather than of the public in general. As Smith sees it, the law cannot circumvent this logic, but at least it can avoid requiring dealers and bureaucratic men of system alike to be driven by it. Thus there is a presumption of liberty, allowing ordinary merchants a measure of freedom from regulation by dealers and such men of system as the dealers co-opt.

Crime as Ideology

If we suppose that there is nothing wrong with the history of a great fortune, there are still ideologies according to which the mere possession of a great fortune comes to represent a great crime unless it is shared in the right way. This sort of argument starts with the obvious grain of truth that we all immediately recognize when politicians say, as politician Elizabeth Warren said in 2012, "Nobody in this country got rich on his own" (Frank 2016).

Clearly, it would be a great crime if teams of workers contracted to build roads and bridges for a firm, and then the firm used such infrastructure but refused to pay what it had promised to pay. There are ideologies, however, according to which anyone who produces a great fortune should pay vastly more than that, simply on the assumption that they would not be collecting a great fortune for the services they render unless they were in some sense paying too little for services rendered to them. To people in the grip of this argument, it feels logically inescapable.

But from the outside, we can acknowledge that large numbers of people cooperate to do the work that produces any great fortune, and no one has any claim to the total product of the cooperative effort. The only claim that anyone has is to their own marginal product—that is, the value of what they brought to the table and contributed to the cooperative effort. By definition, of course, no one's contribution would have a given *marginal* value except for the efforts of the other members of the team. That's a reason why everyone should be paid their marginal value, although on some egalitarian ideologies this is recast as a reason why outsize contributors should not be paid the marginal product of their effort.

Even to those not in the grip of an egalitarian ideology, then, there is still a real implication. Namely, no one is asking to be paid society's total revenue, and no one deserves to get paid that either. People should ask no more, and perhaps no less, than that they be paid the value of their own marginal contribution to the wealth of the nation. That is when they are asking for no more than what they deserve. That one person did a lot and therefore deserves to be paid a lot is perfectly compatible with the sentiment, expressed by politicians such as Elizabeth Warren, that many other people also contributed a lot, and also deserve to be paid accordingly. But there is no *desert* argument leading to the conclusion that anyone deserves less than the worth of their marginal contribution to the making of a wealthy nation.

CONCLUSIONS

So, is it the case that behind every great fortune is an equally great crime? Not really, unless we work with an extremely sloppy rendering of "great crime." Some great fortunes are a result of firms being more efficient and effective in addressing customer needs than any of their competitors. Some are a result of sheer luck. But, with great success frequently comes great temptation to extend and protect this success through the implementation of monopoly or collusive strategies. And this becomes a great crime.

COMMENTS AND DISCUSSION

Barney and Schmidtz consider the conditions under which wealth accumulation is likely to be good and bad for society. They argue that societies benefit when wealth accumulation results from the ability to identify and serve market needs, though the exploitation of monopoly power provides an important exception to this generalization. Government interventions in the market promise social benefit in principle but in practice tend to foster harmful monopoly power.

> *What kinds of needs in the marketplace is it morally legitimate for commercial actors to serve, and what are the moral obligations of commercial actors in shaping those needs? What institutional conditions best promote service to morally valid market needs?*

At the Society for Progress' second assembly, a variety of discussants observed the various ways in which firms may profit by serving market needs that are morally problematic, or by manipulating consumer preferences in problematic ways. How should a theory of legitimate market wealth accommodate these kinds of cases? Kitcher observed the way in which pharmaceutical companies have tipped the research agenda toward lifestyle drugs through heavy marketing campaigns. Similarly, Davis noted the use of chemical ingredients in foods which promote unhealthy dietary habits (Cheetos), and websites like mugshots.com, which profit by receiving payments to remove mugshots which they themselves publish on the Internet. Frank and Pettit separately observed the way in which the financial industry has profited from behaviors that perform a function in the market without creating real social value (e.g. by leveraging miniscule advantages in trading speed).

> *What are the obligations of market actors to direct their behavior to social goods independently of profit? What institutional conditions are most conducive to this?*

Even when wealth is acquired through the legitimate service of market needs, there might still be moral duties to pursue less profitable ends. Considering the case of pharmaceutical companies, Neiman asked why such firms require a profit incentive to address vital human needs. Why assume that only the profit motive does or should suffice? On that point, Tiberius observed that the profit motive serves as a kind of "lowest common denominator" but that we might also situate commercial activity within the broader conception of a morally good life. Anderson noted John Dewey's observation that the significance of the profit incentive ought to diminish with the volume of wealth one has accumulated (given the diminishing returns to wealth and, likewise, the non-financial returns associated with doing social good). And Risse observed that the legitimate entitlement of a producer to profits is itself a matter of social convention to be regulated through the tax regime.

What are the implications of technological change for our model of morally legitimate commerce?

Barney noted that the growing economy of digital platforms creates a tendency toward "natural monopolies," in which companies like Facebook and eBay effectively maximize their service to consumers by becoming dominant providers. That model creates enormous market power for those who win this competition. How should we think about the morality of monopolies in such cases, and how can the downside of monopoly be combated while retaining the value of such services? At the same time, Snabe observed, technological tools are also increasingly enabling low-cost, individualized production. How will such tools affect the creation of value in the market? Can they be sustained through private initiative alone?

References

Arthur, W. B. 1989. "Competing Technologies, Increasing Returns, and Lock-In by Historical Events." *Economic Journal* 99: 116–31.

Barney, J. 1986. "Strategic Factor Markets: Expectations, Luck, and the Theory of Strategy." *Management Science* 32(10): 1231–41.

Barney, J. 1991. "Firm Resources and Sustained Competitive Advantage." *Journal of Management* 17: 99–120.

Barney, J. 2013. *Gaining and Sustaining Competitive Advantage*, 4th edition. Upper Saddle River, NJ: Pearson.

Demsetz, H. 1973. "Industry Structure, Market Rivalry, and Public Policy." *Journal of Law and Economics*, 16: 1–9.

Fleischacker, S. 2004. *On Adam Smith's Wealth of Nations*. Princeton: Princeton University Press.

Frank, R. 2016. *Success and Luck*. Princeton: Princeton University Press.

Gavil, A. and First, H. 2014. *The Microsoft Antitrust Cases*. Cambridge, MA: MIT Press.

Isaacson, W. 2014. *The Innovators*. New York: Simon and Schuster.

Jaffe, A. and Lerner, J. 2007. *Innovation and its Discontents*. Princeton: Princeton University Press.

Krugman, P. 2007. *The Conscience of a Liberal*. New York: Norton.

Liebowitz, S. and Margolis, S. 2001. *Winners, Losers, and Microsoft*. Oakland, CA: The Independent Institute.

Lippman, S. and Rumelt, R. 1982. "Uncertain Imitability." *Bell Journal of Economics* 13: 418–38.

Mahoney, J. and Qian, L. 2013. "Market Frictions as Building Blocks of an Organizational Economics Approach to Strategic Management." *Strategic Management Journal* 34(9): 1019–41.

Newport, F. 2015. "Americans Continue to Say U.S. Wealth Distribution is Unfair." <http://www.gallup.com/poll/182987>, accessed January 2016.

Piketty, T. 2014. *Capital in the 21st Century*. Cambridge, MA: Harvard University Press.

Porter, M. 1980. *Competitive Strategy*. New York: Free Press.

Rotberg, R. 1988. *The Founder*. New York: Oxford University Press.

Rukstad, M. G. and Horn, J. 1989. "Caterpillar and the Construction Equipment Industry in 1988." Harvard Business School Case No. 9: 389–697.

Saez, E. and Piketty, T. 2013. "A Theory of Optimal Inheritance Taxation." *Econometrica* 81(5): 1851–86.

Schmidtz, D. 2002. "How to Deserve." *Political Theory* 30: 774–99.

Schmidtz, D. 2008. *Person, Polis, Planet*. New York: Oxford University Press.

Schmidtz, D. 2015. *Corruption in Performance and Progress: Essays on Capitalism, Business, and Society*. Edited by S. Rangan. Oxford: Oxford University Press, 49–64.

Schmidtz, D. 2016. "Adam Smith on Freedom." In R. P. Hanley (ed.), *Adam Smith: His Life, Thought, and Legacy*. Princeton: Princeton University Press, 208–27.

Schmidtz, D. and Brennan, J. 2010. *A Brief History of Liberty*. New York: Blackwell.

Smith, A. 1759. *Theory of Moral Sentiments*. London: printed for A. Millar, and A. Kincaid and J. Bell.

Smith, A. 1776. *The Wealth of Nations*. Indianapolis: Liberty Fund.

CHAPTER 11

TAMING PLATFORM CAPITALISM TO MEET HUMAN NEEDS

GERALD F. DAVIS AND S.D. SHIBULAL

Abstract

We are witnessing the emergence of an information and communication technology (ICT)-enabled platform capitalism in which traditional corporations are being displaced. Railing against traditional firms to rescue capitalism would, under these circumstances, seem like misdirected effort. The "working anarchies" (e.g. Uber, Wikipedia) and "pop-up firms" (e.g. Vizio) of this new world use "labor on demand." Here too there is risk that platform owners exploit their power and become rapacious. Yet, ICT can enable platform capitalism to create community-based, locally controlled alternatives to corporations and states. Cooperatives and democratic software platforms (e.g. Linux) must be important business forms in the future.

SINCE the turn of the twentieth century, governments and corporations have been the dominant institutions for meeting human needs through the provision of goods, services, employment, and social welfare support for their constituents. Yet we are now witnessing the emergence of a third alternative, enabled by information and communication technologies (ICTs): platform capitalism. Platform capitalism is what happens when the costs of transacting and collaborating are radically reduced by ICTs and pervasive connectivity. One result is that in many domains, social institutions such as the traditional corporation are no longer economical. Early glimpses of alternatives are emerging in several areas, from transportation (Zipcar, Uber) and shelter (CouchSurfing, Airbnb) to financing (Prosper and other peer-to-peer lending platforms) to education (Sarojini Damodaran Foundation) and even food (Germany's Foodsharing.de). Some platforms are strictly for-profit businesses, yet they provide proof-of-concept for locally based alternatives to the state and the corporation, namely the community-owned cooperative platform (cf. Scholz 2016).

ICTs are changing what a firm can look like, and therefore how their activities might be channeled to serve human needs. In economics, firms are "the economy's basic units of production" that buy inputs and transform them into goods and services that they aim to sell for a profit (Putterman and Kroszner 2009). We generally imagine that firms have employees whose actions are directed by a manager or an entrepreneur. But what about Linux or Wikipedia, where labor is voluntary and self-directed? The World Wide Web runs largely on non-proprietary open-source software created without traditional "employees" or "managers" (e.g. Apache, Drupal, WordPress; see Benkler 2013). Many essential "units of production" today do not look like firms. It is increasingly feasible and cost-effective for impromptu enterprises to be snapped together from parts available on the web, or as "off-the-rack" software solutions. Even highly complex enterprises are susceptible. Twenty years ago John Reed, then CEO of Citibank, noted that the banking industry (that is, banks with marble lobbies and vaults and tellers and illustrious boards of directors) was ultimately doomed, as banking would be reduced to "a little bit of application code in a smart network" (quoted in Mayer 1997: 34). Reed's dream has come true. Today, Infosys sells Finacle, a universal banking product that enables anyone with a banking license to set up shop. As of this writing Finacle serves 450 million customers around the world, or nearly one in five adults with a bank account. The giant banks that we fear may be paper tigers.[1]

Our "enterprise ontology" needs updating. We imagine that corporations run our world, and that corporations consist of employees and bosses that ultimately report to a responsible agency such as a CEO and a board of directors. We imagine that getting corporations to behave themselves will create a more civilized world. But traditional corporations are an increasingly outdated hypothesis about how economic activity is organized. Railing against corporations may come to seem like French writers who continued to rail against the superstition and oppression of the Catholic Church, long after its influence had faded away.

At different times and in different places, governments and corporations have played leading roles in the provision of social goods such as jobs and economic security. In India after independence, the government was a predominant source for social order. Those seeking stable employment and economic security often found the civil service to be the best choice. Business grew up under the shadow of the License Raj, which limited the growth of the private sector and added a layer of risk to a corporate career. Since the reforms of the mid-1990s, however, corporate growth has been explosive, and the greatest economic opportunities have been in business. India has seen an explosion of entrepreneurship, particularly in cities like Bangalore.

In the US, corporate growth preceded the growth of the government. US Steel's revenues in 1910 were nearly twice those of the federal government, and business employment far outpaced government employment (Davis 2016). The corporate

---

[1] Recall that the Big Five US investment banks in early 2008 included Bear Stearns, Lehman Brothers, Merrill Lynch, Goldman Sachs, and Morgan Stanley. Within a year, only the last two were left, propped up by public assistance.

economy had already reached its adolescence at a point when there was no income tax, no Federal Reserve, no Department of Labor, and very little business regulation: in contrast to India, government adapted to business rather than the other way around. Thus, the corporate sector has long been the source of jobs and economic mobility. Health insurance, wage security, and retirement pensions all fell to corporate employers.

Recent times have seen an intriguing reversal. The number of exchange-listed corporations in the US has declined by more than half since 1997 due to the relatively higher transaction costs of organizing business as a corporation. Private alternatives have proven more nimble and more economical than large corporations, due in part to their low overheads. By 2010 Vizio, with 400 employees, sold far more televisions in the US than Sony. Non-corporate forms of enterprise such as Linux and Wikipedia are also proving robust, while corporations are surprisingly fragile in the US. On the other hand, by 2009 India had surpassed the US (as well as the rest of the world) in its number of public corporations. The new companies often took on roles traditionally taken by the state (through, for instance, company towns as in Tata Steel's Jamshedpur). Whether this is sustainable is an open question.

Like American corporations, governments around the world are increasingly embattled, from the failed states of central Africa and the Middle East to the overstretched state and municipal governments of the US, whose pension obligations far outstretch their budgets. We are likely to witness a cascade of government bankruptcies in years to come as governments are simply unable to meet their fiscal obligations. Like American corporations, many governmental units may have commitments that cannot be met without substantial reforms. It is not coincidental that General Motors (GM) and the city of Detroit both ended up in bankruptcy in recent years.

In this situation, the emergence of online platforms for connecting individuals in real time creates opportunities for non-governmental, non-corporate, self-organized alternative institutions for meeting human needs. The various applications in the so-called "sharing economy" provide early examples. These platforms lower the costs for creating markets between individual buyers and sellers; "sharing" is a misnomer for ICT-enabled market transactions. But under the right circumstances these platforms demonstrate the possibility of horizontal communities that are neither corporate nor governmental.

Platform capitalism is in its early Wild West stage right now, much as corporate capitalism was in the early twentieth century. Many models are emerging and competing, and it is not obvious which will be survivable. But it is not too early to consider how the development of platform capitalism might be guided to balance progress and profit. At the moment, in the wake of thirty years of shareholder value *über alles*, there is little reason to expect balance. New business enterprises are typically created and funded with the expectation that they will ultimately become shareholder-owned corporations, and under current (misguided) understandings of the purpose of the corporation, the balance will tilt decisively toward profit. But just as corporate capitalism was tamed by the Progressive movement, which helped channel the new forces of mass production and mass distribution in the US in the early part of the twentieth century, we believe that platform capitalism can also be civilized if guided by the right principles.

Platform capitalism need not be rapacious: it has the raw materials to create community-based, locally controlled alternatives to corporations and states. Whereas mass production was most compatible with the corporate form, platform capitalism opens up a range of alternatives.

In this chapter we first examine the diversity of business enterprises around the world and provide an account to explain why businesses look so different at different times and places. Corporations represent only one of many possible ways to organize enterprise, and they are not the inevitable way to do business. We then briefly contrast the recent histories of corporations in two former British colonies, India and the US, to illustrate how technology and politics influence the use of the corporate form. Next we describe the advent of platform capitalism and argue that it is analogous to the mass production revolution of the early twentieth century. The significance of platforms like Uber is not simply that it is a cheap and convenient alternative to taxis, but what it implies for the organization and compensation of labor and other human activities. Much of the world of work may come to look like a virtual version of a Home Depot parking lot at 7.00 a.m., a continuous spot market for labor summoned via app. This will delight consumers who still have incomes, who may soon be using diaper-changing apps to hail debt-burdened liberal arts grads in the middle of the night ("Duber"?). But it will leave a large gap in the social safety net that will need to be filled as corporate employers continue to disappear. We close with suggestions for Progressivism 2.0, a set of principles for taming this new system to balance progress and profit.

The Diversity of Enterprise Around the World

Business enterprises take on vastly different forms around the world, from how big they are to how they are legally organized and financed. Take size. Denmark's biggest domestic corporation is ISS Group, with over 500,000 global employees. Relatively small nations from Scandinavia are home to large multinationals in retail (Ikea), pharmaceuticals (Novo Nordisk), shipbuilding (Maersk), oil (Statoil), electronics (Ericsson), autos (Volvo), beer (Carlsberg), and small plastic bricks (Lego). Colombia is ten times the size of Denmark, yet its biggest domestic corporation in 2006 was Bancolombia, with only 7,000 employees. Unlike Scandinavia, or Switzerland, or the Netherlands, Latin America has few giant corporations, and small family-owned businesses predominate.

Corporations are not the only way to organize an economy, and countries vary widely on how "corporatized" their economies are and how reliant they are on financial markets for funding business. China's stock markets were closed from the revolution in 1949 until 1990; by 2014 it had over 2,600 listed corporations, and its stock markets had some of the world's largest valuations. Meanwhile, Germany—another export-oriented powerhouse—has only 600 public corporations, about the same as twenty years ago, and much of the business sector consists of medium-sized family enterprises that draw on banks for financing. Even Volkswagen, Germany's largest business, is effectively family-controlled.

There are a lot of ways to organize the economy, and although Americans think of the exchange-listed corporation as the default form of doing business, it is not. The range of possibilities is vast, and it is sensible to focus not on formal organizations, with heads and members and goals and boundaries, but enterprise. "Enterprise" describes the various ways that transactions can be organized to deliver goods and services, whether within firms or among more emergent forms.

Political scientists explain the diversity of enterprise around the world in terms of national institutions. In the US and the UK, the exchange-listed corporation is often seen as the default form of business, but only half the world's economies have stock markets, and financial markets tend to be more consequential in English-speaking countries and former British colonies (LaPorta et al. 1999). The "varieties of capitalism" program of research describes how national institutions shape the raw materials for firms (Amable 2003). The most critical institutions include *labor markets* and their regulation; *financial markets* and other ways of channeling capital to business; *product markets* and how competition among firms is regulated; *educational systems*; and the nature of the *social safety net*, including the provision of healthcare, unemployment, and retirement income. The basic premise of varieties of capitalism is that the kinds of firms that are possible and survivable depend on the configuration of these institutions in a national economy. This helps explain why different kinds of firms and industries thrive in different settings. For instance, Germany's precision manufacturing firms rely on a labor force with strong technical education, product market regulation that favors exporters, banks with the wherewithal to fund family-owned businesses, and a safety net that allows firms (and their workers) to weather economic downturns. America's high-tech firms rely on venture capitalists and vast financial markets, lightly regulated labor markets, and well-funded research universities.

But while national institutions are like the terrain and climate that host an ecosystem, we need more to make sense of how enterprises change over time. Evolution in the form of enterprises can be explained in terms of technological, legal, and social factors. Major shifts in technology ("industrial revolutions") are often seen as some combination of Cambrian explosion and mass extinction. The invention of the steam engine created a source of power that allowed factories to operate anywhere and enabled continent-spanning forms of transportation, while cottage industries became unsustainable. Mass production and distribution technologies created economies of scale that made larger firms more efficient, while killing off small-scale local businesses in many industries. Information technologies and the web allow collaboration to take place across geographical and organizational boundaries and enable efficient small-scale and customized production, often at the expense of large corporations. Each of these shifts changes the scale and form of enterprise.

Political changes also shape the evolution of enterprises, such as how they are financed. British colonies generally inherited common law legal systems, while French colonies inherited systems of code law. Common law property rights are more amenable to financial markets and the protection of small shareholders than code law; thus, nearly all former British colonies have had stock markets for decades, while former French colonies rarely had them until fairly recently (Weber et al. 2009). Sometimes these transitions are abrupt: when the Soviet Union collapsed and Yugoslavia split apart, programs of mass privatization distributed shares of state-owned enterprises in countries that had no experience with stock markets in living memory. At one point Romania had thousands of exchange-listed corporations, comparable to the US (and more than Western Europe).

Social factors also influence what enterprises look like. In the US after World War II, the provision of health insurance and retirement income for employees and their families became the responsibility of corporate employers, whereas in most of Europe and Canada these were provided by the welfare state. These obligations change the cost profile of organizing as a corporation rather than using other forms.

We tend to become aware of only those forms of enterprise that become prevalent and successful, and particularly those in countries with scholars to document them. The dominance of the public corporation in the US, the world's largest economy, gave it prominence in the eyes of scholars and the public as the default form of enterprise, while other forms got short shrift. Industrial districts, as in northern Italy (and now Silicon Valley), were largely ignored until Piore and Sabel (1984) pointed out their long-term durability. Cooperatives are evidently uninteresting to Americans, even though they are prevalent throughout much of the rest of the world. It is as if scholars treated American football as the default sport while the rest of the world plays soccer.

Transaction cost economics gives a good starting point for considering what forms of enterprise survive under different circumstances. In his 1937 article on "the nature of the firm," Ronald Coase wrote, "The main reason why it is profitable to establish a firm would seem to be that there is a cost of using the price system. The most obvious cost of 'organizing' production through the price mechanism is that of discovering what the relevant prices are." There were costs to organizing transactions: using the market wasn't free, and factors that influence the cost of using markets would shape how firms are organized. Oliver Williamson (1985) expanded on Coase's original argument and laid out the case for seeing transaction costs as a central reason why some exchanges happened inside organizations and some occurred in markets (the "make or buy" decision). At the end of the day, the forms of organizing that survived were those that could cover their costs.

Ontologically, transaction cost economics is indifferent between different formats and does not regard formal organizations as the inevitable winners. The cheapest way to organize, say, the production of TV sets is likely to win. Sony traditionally designed and manufactured its LCD televisions in factories that it owned, and carefully managed their distribution through approved retailers. Vizio, based in Irvine, California, contracted out the production of its LCD televisions to a Taiwanese-owned generic manufacturer and distributed through warehouse stores like Costco. Sony, founded in 1946, had 150,000 employees; Vizio, born in 2002, only 200. By 2007 Vizio had surpassed Sony in sales in the US with its low-cost products, and Sony ended up spinning off its television division. A dispersed supply chain organized by a few dozen people in a strip mall in Orange County is substantially cheaper than a vertically integrated corporation run from lavish headquarters in Tokyo. Corporations are not the inevitable victors in this battle.

Forms of enterprise are survivable if they can cover their costs, but costs depend on background conditions that change over time. As Coase pointed out, the telephone enabled businesses to grow much larger because the cost of coordination went down when headquarters could communicate instantaneously with local offices. But the telephone did not make companies big everywhere in the world (e.g. in Colombia). Without supportive institutions, technology alone will not create enterprises; put another way, enterprises emerge from a combination of technology and institutions.

The period since the turn of the twenty-first century has witnessed a proliferation of different kinds of enterprises, from apps to pop-up businesses to platforms. At the moment it is uncertain which forms will prevail. (Recall that in 2000 it appeared that AOL and Yahoo would rule the Internet through their superior "portals," and Microsoft seemed like an unstoppable monopoly.) Big corporations in the early twentieth century did not win just on cost: they also had to win politically. Consider the reception of Uber in different locales. In many cities in the US, Uber is pervasive. By September 2015 there were over 327,000 regular Uber drivers in the US—far more than the number of GM employees—and many millions of customers who had the app. In France, in contrast, Uber continues to be politically contentious, and many of its "driver-partners" are operating illegally, sparking massive protests from the taxi industry. And in Germany, Uber has withdrawn from Frankfurt, Hamburg, and Dusseldorf because it has been unable to recruit enough drivers with the proper licensing and health tests; meanwhile, local ride-hailing apps created with the collaboration of drivers and unions thrive.

We are at an inflection point where what comes next is open to conscious shaping. History suggests that politics and not just economics will decide what forms survive.

INDIAN AND AMERICAN ENTERPRISES

A comparison of two former British colonies provides an illustration of alternative trajectories that enterprise can take under different political conditions (see Figure 11.1). India and the United States have a number of institutional and historical features in common. Both inherited a system of common law and its approach to property rights. Both have had domestic stock exchanges for generations. Both are huge countries with ethnic and religious diversity. And both threw off their hated British oppressors in order to chart a bold and independent path. Unsurprisingly, both were fertile soil for public corporations. Compare the prevalence of listed corporations over the past twenty years. Both saw a surge of net listings in the 1990s. Yet while the US subsequently experienced a long-term decline, India has not, and today it is the world's largest domicile for public corporations. Why?

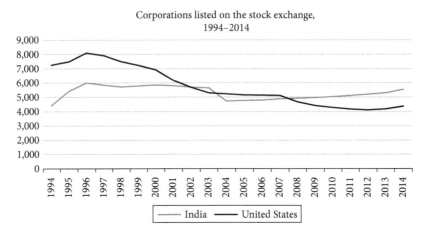

FIGURE 11.1. US and Indian corporations listed on the stock exchange, 1994–2014

Source: World Bank, *World Development Indicators*.

The history of corporations in the two countries illustrates a very different trajectory. In the US, corporations grew very large long before the federal government did. In 1910 the US already had billion dollar corporations like US Steel, AT&T, and General Electric at a point when there was no income tax, no Federal Reserve, and no Department of Labor (Davis 2016). Big corporations far outweighed the national government in the early years of the twentieth century, when norms around corporate behavior were being settled. The federal government thus grew up fitfully in the shadow of business. Indeed, a more robust and centralized state was the major project of the Progressive movement, aimed at reining in powerful businesses and channeling their activities for public benefit (Davis 2015). After World War II, when European governments were building their welfare states, American corporations ended up becoming the primary providers of social welfare services such as health insurance, retirement income, and wage stability, a tradition ratified by the so-called Treaty of Detroit, a labor agreement between GM and the United Auto Workers union in 1950 (Levy and Temin 2007).

This ultimately proved costly, as GM and other corporations ended up saddled with vast financial obligations when their workers began to retire en masse. According to Theresa Ghilarducci, "The cost of retiree health care [at GM] in 1993 was less than $400 per retiree per year; by 2007, it was $15,000 per year" (Ghilarducci 2007: 17). Even before its bankruptcy, GM's CEO rued the company's former generosity: "Most of the companies we compete with... have a different benefits structure. A significantly greater portion of their retirement [cost] is funded by a national system. We're now subject to global competition. We're running against people who do not have these costs, because they are funded by the government" (quoted in *Wall Street Journal* 2006). As Davis has written at length elsewhere, American firms today seek to avoid taking on the various institutional responsibilities that come with being a public corporation, and particularly the cost of being an employer (Davis 2016).

In India, by contrast, the state was economically dominant for generations before large-scale private enterprises appeared in large numbers. When India became independent in 1947, it inherited a fractured economy from the British. The policymakers had a Herculean task of building the national economy. India had many problems: lack of infrastructure, lack of capital, unemployment, and high poverty, to name a few. Having been a victim of colonialism, and having seen the flip side of capitalism during the Great Depression, the first prime minister of independent India, Pandit Jawaharlal Nehru, was convinced of the merits of socialism. Therefore, the policymakers made a decision to adopt mixed socialism or democratic socialism, where both government and private sectors coexisted and competed with each other. Private sector enterprises were issued licenses to produce and sell their products in the country. All aspects of the economy would be controlled by the government, allowing them to fix targets and to address inequities across classes and regions. Trade restrictions and tariffs were put in place to ensure that nascent domestic industries remained protected from foreign competition.

This trade policy is also called *import substitution industrialization* (ISI), as it advocates replacing foreign imports with domestic production, with the aim of promoting local production by reducing foreign and private competition. As building public infrastructure was the need of the hour, public sector government-run industries were able to generate employment, and the wages earned by people would be spent on goods being manufactured in India, thus giving a fillip to the economy. Though this may have been a prudent decision at that point of time, as benefits of national resources reached the masses, the system of controls became too restrictive. The stifling ecosystem discouraged entrepreneurship. The licenses were controlled by government officials and politicians and handed over to a select few who found favor with the government. The private sector largely consisted of family-owned conglomerates. To set up a private business one needed the approval of many government agencies which was time- and resource-consuming, hence curbing the enthusiasm of aspiring venture capitalists.

Even after the approval of required agencies, the producer did not have the independence of determining the scale of operations. The quantity of goods produced, the capital, and the price were under the scanner of the government and regulated at its discretion. The option of exit and reduction in workforce also did not rest with the producer. Furthermore, high import tariffs and requirement of licenses deterred sale of foreign products in the Indian subcontinent. The License Raj was effective in the 1950s but it eventually led to slow growth rates and investment in the 1980s. The liberalization of the economy in 1991 sounded the death knell for the License Raj.

With the disintegration of the USSR and the Gulf War, India faced a balance of payments problem which made reforms inevitable. This was also necessary under a recovery pact with the International Monetary Fund. Government made a systemic shift to a more open economy with greater reliance upon market forces and a larger role for the private sector, including foreign investment. The industrial sector was deregulated to bring in the element of competition and increase efficiency. The government now controls only very few strategic and defense sectors, rendering most of the sectors free from licensing. An import substituting inward-looking development policy was discarded in the modern globalizing world. Import licensing was abolished for capital goods and intermediates in 1993, simultaneously with the switch to a flexible exchange rate regime. Quantitative restrictions on imports of consumer goods and agricultural products were gradually removed. Financial sector reforms have ensured that the Indian financial structure is inherently strong, functionally diverse, efficient, and globally competitive.

Liberalization has far-reaching impacts on all spheres of life in India and made it a huge consumer market. Today, most of the economic changes in the country are based on the demand–supply cycle and other economic factors. It has also made a favorable impact on various important economic segments. Today, the service sectors, industrial sectors, and the agriculture sector have grown. Around 54 percent of the annual GDP of India comes from the service industry while the industrial and agriculture sectors contribute around 29 percent and 17 percent respectively. With the improvement of the market, new sectors have reaped profits such as IT services, chemicals, textiles, and the cement industry. The strongest revolution of the new century has been one of information technology because it made possible the transfer of real-time human labor across nations, without transferring humans themselves. The increase in the supply level also improved the rate of employment. Over the years, India has become one of the fastest growing economies in the world. It has become the fourth largest economy in the world in terms of the purchasing power parity. The average yearly economic growth which was stagnating at 4 percent in the 1980s improved to a range between 6 percent and 7 percent.

The divergent trajectories of India and the US illustrate the variety of influences on how enterprises are structured, and in particular how political changes influence the prevalence of different forms. American corporations grew into social institutions with a wide range of obligations to various "stakeholders," particularly their employees. As the costs of these obligations rose, corporations increasingly sought to limit their employment growth. Today, given the high cost of being a social institution and the wide availability of inputs that can be rented rather than owned, American corporations are in long-term decline, displaced by alternative forms. Indian corporations continue to thrive, in part because their obligations to employees are clearly delimited (to provide a job) and their markets increasingly global. Yet this too is unlikely to be an end state.

The Coming of Platform Capitalism

ICT, and most recently the spread of ubiquitous smartphones, are creating a regime shift in the costs of organizing similar in scope to the mass production revolution. Consequently, we expect to see a large shift in the form of enterprise comparable to the rise of the large corporation in the early twentieth century that coincided with the mass production revolution.

In 1949 Peter Drucker published a series of essays about the corporation in the post-war era, based largely on his experience with GM. He said:

The world revolution of our time is not communism, fascism, the new nationalisms of the non-Western peoples, or any of the other "isms" that appear in the headlines... The true world revolution is "made in USA," and its principle is the mass production principle. Nothing ever before recorded in the history of man equals in speed, universality, and impact the transformation that modern industrial organization has wrought in the foundations of society in the 40 years since Henry Ford developed the mass production principle to turn out the Model T.

And:

The war showed that the basic principle which underlay Henry Ford's first plant 40 years ago was completely independent of specific tools or techniques and could be applied to the organization of all manufacturing activities. *Today it has become abundantly clear that the mass-production principle is not confined to manufacturing but is a general principle of human organization for joint work.*

(Drucker 1949, emphasis added)

Drucker was right. Mass production principles were applied to services (e.g. insurance and banking; fast food), agriculture (the green revolution), education (K-12 teaching), healthcare (the teaching hospital), research (e.g. pharmaceutical R&D), family life (*Cheaper by the Dozen*), and war (the D-Day invasion).

Mass production was, according to Drucker, a new operating system that had spread across all industries and around the globe. It was relatively cheap and efficient and could be applied quite broadly. Anything that needed to be accomplished at a grand scale would benefit from adopting this operating system.

The corporation as an organizational form was perfectly suited to the "mass production principle," enabling investments in long-lived specialized assets and creating a structure for protecting long-term employment relations. Indeed, one contemporary definition of a "firm" (of which the corporation is one type) states that firms usually entail "(a) long-term contracts between at least some input providers and (b) an assignment of control rights in which some agents hire others and direct them in the activities of production. Rather than being momentary assemblages of cooperating factor suppliers, then, *firms are ongoing organizations that manage and coordinate the activities of participating actors*" (Putterman and Kroszner 2009: 8, emphasis added).

But "the firm" is only one hypothesis about how the economy is organized. It is not true by definition that production of goods and services must be accomplished by firms. Linux, Apache, Drupal, Wikipedia, and indeed most of the software underpinning the World Wide Web are not provided by corporations or governments, but are products of "working anarchies," in Yochai Benkler's terms. They are created by voluntary labor without contracts under property regimes without residual claimants. As Benkler (2013: 214) puts it, "Over the course of the first decade of the twenty-first century, commons-based peer production has moved from being ignored, through being mocked, feared, and regarded as an exception or intellectual quirk, to finally becoming a normal and indispensable part of life." It is only a slight exaggeration to say that the web could operate without corporations and their proprietary wares, but it would collapse tomorrow without open-source software.

We speculate that smartphones and the prior developments they build on are accomplishing something similar to what mass production did, by creating a regime shift in the cost of organizing human activity. It may seem premature for such a claim, but the past few years have seen many signs of such a shift, from the Arab Spring to the rapid spread of Uber and other platforms for spot-contracting. Instant, cheap global communication is enabling a new "general principle of human organization for joint work." Unlike mass production, it does not require formal organization, but can be accomplished more or less spontaneously, and at lower cost than formal organizations.

Uber is perhaps the best known of the new platforms that rely on smartphones. To use Uber as a consumer, you download an app to your phone and enter payment information (your credit card). Uber uses your phone's GPS to sense where you are, and if you want to call for a ride, you tell the app where you want to go. Your request is then posted to nearby drivers, and when one has agreed to transport you, the app tells you who the driver is and when they will arrive. When the ride is complete, payment is transferred to the driver (with a cut for Uber), and both passenger and driver have an opportunity to rate each other's performance on a 1–5 scale. Drivers for the most popular version of the service simply use their own cars, and have their own version of the app that they can turn on when they are willing to provide rides. Drivers are not required to provide any ride, and many of them contract with competing on-demand services (e.g. Lyft).

Uber creates a market for mobility that is only possible using GPS-enabled smartphones. (You can't order a ride from your laptop.) Uber is not a taxi service, with open-ended pricing, but a platform or marketplace in which prices are known in advance to both drivers and riders. Drivers are explicitly *not* employees of Uber but driver-partners or "micro-entrepreneurs." Indeed, Uber is fighting on many fronts to make sure that they are not considered an employer, but simply an enabler of exchanges, like the stock market.

One of the most significant effects of platforms is to undermine the rationale for corporations. Recall Coase's claim that firms exist in part because it is costly to use the price system. If it was costless to price inputs, firms would look rather different. Consider Vizio, or other similar pop-up firms: all the parts for creating such firms are available off the shelf and can be snapped together to create an instantaneous enterprise, just as a website can call on resources distributed in databases to create a webpage. Thirty years ago John Meyer wrote that "the building blocks for organizations come to be littered around the societal landscape; it takes only a little entrepreneurial energy to assemble them into a structure" (Meyer and Rowan 1977: 345). This poetic vision is now literally true: you don't need to leave your chair to create a firm today, because all the relevant inputs are available via the web.

The one piece of the puzzle that was not so readily available online was in-person labor. For many kinds of tasks, it was just not possible to contract for on-demand labor inputs. There are places where such spot markets for labor operate: when Californians have discrete manual tasks to be accomplished (e.g. picking grapes, yardwork), they often head to the Home Depot parking lot to assemble a crew for the day, to be paid a negotiated rate in cash at the end. (The group riding in the back of a pickup truck to a worksite is in some sense an "enterprise," but it does not really have a name because of its ontological fluidity.) But this was peripheral; employment by firms was the norm.

Why do firms hire employees rather than going to the Home Depot parking lot every morning? According to Coase, hiring employees and showing them the ropes is costly, and it's impractical to do it every morning. On average it's cheaper to just keep workers around all day with the understanding that they will adjust what they do according to circumstances.

But what if technology made it cheap to contract for the performance of specific tasks, without the trouble of hiring employees? This is the true significance of Uber and other platforms: to drastically reduce the cost of using the price system for labor inputs. By allowing individuals to contract for discrete performances, Uber, Upwork, TaskRabbit, and other platforms make the world a Home Depot parking lot. Denizens of San Francisco today can download apps for almost any conceivable human activity, from on-street valet parking and sex to jet chartering and physician house calls. If you can specify the performance you want to pay for, it can be (and probably is) an app (a process we might call "Uberization").

Williamson (1985) pointed out that high levels of skill are not enough to warrant hiring someone as an employee rather than a contractor. Only skills that are *uniquely valuable to a particular enterprise* ("firm-specific human assets") merit creating an employment relation. Uber drivers and surgeons are both generic in this sense; both could in principle be rented via apps.

On-demand contracting for labor is one of the most potentially consequential implications of the ICT revolution. It is now cost-effective to create markets for things that would have been hard to imagine before, like the fanciful diaper-changing app. And the demography of the people creating these apps tilts toward the 20-something denizen of the Bay Area, not toward moral philosophers, which may explain why so many apps involve hooking up (Tinder, Grindr), food delivery (DoorDash, Grubhub), and weed (Eaze).

SOFTWARE PLATFORMS AND BUSINESS PLATFORMS

Before going into more detail, it is worth making some distinctions that will help clarify the different possibilities. We distinguish between *business platforms* and *software platforms*. In a *business platform*, the infrastructure provider and the business entity are the same. The infrastructure is being used by a single business entity. The value created on a business platform is consumed by the end users and the profits earned are with one business entity, e.g. Uber or Airbnb. In a *software platform*, on the other hand, an external entity builds the business or creates value. It can be provided to different consumers/end users. These consumers will consume this value. The profit generated by the business entity belongs to the business entity. A small portion of the profit is given to the infrastructure provider on a monthly/yearly basis or in the form of a license fee. The infrastructure provider creates profits from the fees it receives from software users. Think of a software platform as being like a mall that rents space to a particular store (e.g. Salesforce.com).

One can use the following parameters to draw the distinction between business platforms and software platforms:

1. *Ownership.* A typical business platform is owned by an entity and uses it for its own customers or network whereas a software platform is something that is owned by a service/platform provider which enables multiple parties to transact among each other.
2. *Nature of interactions.* A software platform typically solves a wide range of problems, e.g. Eduflex is a software platform that allows schools to use its resources, providing value to teachers, students, and parents. A business platform, on the other hand, is quite narrow in context, e.g. Uber allows people who want a ride to connect with drivers who are available to offer the ride to a particular destination. Airbnb produces availability of accommodation on top of a platform.
3. *Degree of openness.* Typically software platforms are open for others to contribute and build something that can be made available on the platform. For example, much of the business of Salesforce.com is a software platform, an enterprise cloud ecosystem where industries and companies of all sizes can connect to their customers using the latest innovations in mobile, social, and cloud technology. Business platforms resemble closed systems. While software platforms can be configured externally, business platforms are totally internal.
4. *Monetization.* A typical business platform requires a producer (the business entity) and buyers of the producer's products/services whereas in a software platform there are only transactions on the platform which the business platform user monetizes.

The evolution of the platform economy is taking place at two levels: the platforms themselves are enterprises, and they enable alternative forms of enterprise. Platforms often have few employees or assets. They rely heavily on contractors and typically rent rather than build server space. Uber has perhaps 4,000 actual employees, but hundreds of thousands of "driver-partners," each of whom is a "micro-entrepreneur" (and absolutely NOT an employee of Uber). Airbnb has 1,600 actual employees, and over one million rooms for rent around the world. Similar figures hold for other "platform" firms: they are typically light on tangible assets (preferring to rent rather than to own) and hire very few employees, because few are needed to create and manage a platform. Amazon has far more employees than do pure platforms like Uber or Airbnb (roughly 231,000), but it also follows a pattern of relying heavily on temporary staffing and "employment aversion." It added 120,000 temp workers just for the 2016 holiday season (*USA Today* 2016).

In addition to being extremely lightweight enterprises in their own right, platforms make possible other new forms. Uberization of the labor force will inevitably shape organization design going forward, as firms aim to create formats that allow them to rent labor rather than hiring employees. As Davis (2016) describes it:

> The rapid global expansion of Uber, in spite of vehement opposition from taxi drivers and governments, shows the potential of platform capitalism to re-shape both industries and the nature of the employment relation...The platform-capitalism model seems certain to spread widely, given its cost advantages. And it is not hard to imagine this model encroaching on retail and other employment. Might Walmart decide to offer certifications for various tasks and open them up to platforms on an as-needed basis? Why not dispense with set wage rates and allow pay to vary with demand each day? Why not create competitions for day-work that go to the lowest bidder, like MTurk? This might not be compatible with current employment law, but of course laws are not set in stone. As should be obvious, the possibilities for upward mobility in a world of tasks looks different from that in a world of jobs or careers...
>
> If you were an efficiency-minded IT consultant designing a new concept in retail management, given the tools available today, you might consider being the Uber of retail. Associates (as minimum-wage retail employees are inevitably called) hate being scheduled by algorithms. They hate having to work until close, open the store the next day, close again, open again, and then have five days off when they really, really need the hours to pay their rent. The new rules about health insurance, and what counts as part-time or full-time, are a pain in the neck. But customers have not responded well to self-checkout, making it difficult to do without human labor entirely. So, the concept: stores staffed entirely by app-based contractors, who will be referred to as "Self-employed micro-entrepreneurs." Choose your own hours! Work at different stores, for as many or as few shifts as you like! (Note: subject to availability.) Take vacations whenever you want! Surge pricing! Enjoy fun gamefied competitions to see who gets to take a shift!

The models are not yet settled, but we can make some initial sense of the emerging platform capitalism. Juliet Schor (2014: 2) describes a typology for new forms in the "sharing economy": "recirculation of goods [e.g. eBay and Craigslist], increased utilization of durable assets [Airbnb and Uber], exchange of services [TaskRabbit, time-sharing banks], and sharing of productive assets [makerspaces, co-working spaces]." Some of these are simply online versions of old ideas (e.g. tool libraries, classified ads), but the "labor on demand" apps are something different, and these are the likely source of the greatest future social change.

What do we know so far about platforms? By any accounting, platforms seem to be a boon for consumers. Ride-hailing apps like Uber are an instant success almost anywhere they are tried, and consumers have been known to protest when governments seek to regulate them. They are convenient and cheap, and in some respects safer than cabs. For workers, they have also been a success on some dimensions: Uber has experienced exponential growth in the number of driver-partners in the US, and on some accounts the compensation beats that of traditional cab drivers (who, due to the cash they often carry, are frequent targets of robbery). The longer-term consequences for employment are unknown; Uber has made it clear that it will be replacing driver-partners with self-driving cars when they become technologically feasible.

But there are also noted violations of privacy. Uber gathers detailed metadata about those who use its app, and its 20-something brogrammers have been known to use these data (e.g. the starting and stopping points of different consumers) to uncover, for instance, the incidence of one-night-stands (CNN 2014). How many of us know whether the end-user licensing agreement permits Uber to track our movements even when we have not requested a ride? There are also violations of citizens' autonomy. As private businesses, these new marketplaces are not subject to democratic control. Finally, there are violations of dignity.

Social scientists, philosophers, and businesspeople can provide some guidance for the future development of these forms so that they can better serve human ends within local contexts.

Proposal for the Platform Economy

In prior generations, people built their careers with one company, often spanning twenty to thirty years. However, over the past three decades careers have increasingly shifted to jobs. Rather than staying with a single employer, people were more likely to shift to jobs with better prospects and salaries, or more stimulation. Conversely, firms may be reluctant to hire long-term employees. More recently, jobs are being transformed into tasks, where people are paid for the amount of work done.

Task-oriented employment has some advantages. It provides flexibility to both the employer and employee as to how the task should be executed in terms of time/venue/remuneration. The disadvantages of a task-oriented system is that the employees have little or no benefits such as medical insurance, retirement savings, or wage security. The employer employs the skill, not the person. If the skill becomes outdated, the employer does not invest in the employee through upgrading.

Business platforms (the way we define them) are forcing people to be task-oriented. A large chunk of the profits are going to the business entity. But what does the platform contribute? Linux does not get a cut of all economic transactions that take place on the millions of servers it enables. (If it did, the web-based economy might collapse.) Farmers' markets typically take a flat fee to rent a stall; they do not expect to take a 30 percent cut of all the tomatoes and cauliflowers that their vendors sell. Why should platforms reap such large benefits from the transactions they enable but do not actually perform?

In the past, when the producers of value have been marginalized, producers have formed cooperatives. They are rooted in the community and subject to democratic control. In an economy dominated by mass production, coops were often out-competed by traditional corporations. But in platform capitalism, when transactions are often personal and local, we see room for a revival of cooperatives.

Our proposal is to create a non-proprietary, open-source software platform that can be used to support local cooperatives. We are inspired by the examples of Linux, Apache, MySQL, PHP, Drupal, and countless other open-source software projects, which are typically created by volunteer labor and offered for free to users, with no person or entity owning the copyright or collecting royalties.

All enterprises need a handful of functions to be accomplished. They need to connect with suppliers and consumers. They need to keep track of the money coming in and going out. They need to make decisions. They need to sequence and schedule work. There are already platforms that ease the creation of businesses by offering online "stores" for rent and automating transactions (e.g. collecting payments). But these are often operated remotely, and are most compatible with virtual businesses. We envision a platform that enables locally based enterprises (say, a cab company) to benefit from the manifest advantages of platforms while also encouraging local economic development and the accumulation of wealth by those providing the goods and services rather than the platform provider. That is, baked into the platform would be affordances that encouraged local and democratic enterprise that would enable participants to build up community wealth. Rather than paying a "tax" to Uber in San Francisco, local cab coops (or grocery coops, or delivery coops, or healthcare coops) would offer the same conveniences while keeping business local.

The affordances of software create a surprisingly powerful inertia in users. Consider how Facebook shapes the way humans interact online (or their notions of what categories relationships might take, or what counts as a "friend"). Suppose that the default settings of your accounting app favored transparency (also known as "open book management"), allowing participants to see where the money came from and where it went. Or the decision-making app favored democratic deliberation, along the lines of Loomio.org. Creation of a suite of enterprise apps available for free, in an open-source format, could greatly encourage the creation of locally based, democratic, and accountable enterprises.

CONCLUSION

Businesspeople and business academics often begin with the premise that the most important question to address is: "How can we create a profitable enterprise?" In a period where the basic form of enterprise can be taken for granted (e.g. the public corporation in the twentieth century), this might make sense. Theorists can attempt to figure out why some firms perform better than others, and derive "best practices." But in unsettled times, where the very form of enterprise itself is up for grabs, it is more useful to start with first principles about what it is we want enterprises to accomplish.

Our aim here is not to give advice to businesses or entrepreneurs, but to contemplate what policies might channel enterprise toward enhancing human well-being. Business is a means, not an end in itself, and we want to make sure the conversation revolves around the ends, which are to serve human needs. If Uber is likely to create a *lumpenproletariat* that lives in their cars, then we might want to consider changing the laws to encourage enterprises that will enhance economic stability for families. This was the goal of the Progressive movement in the early twentieth century: to tame the new forces of commerce to better serve human needs.

Given the characteristics of platforms—light in assets and employees, with modest needs for capital—it is not obvious why they should be organized as large-scale private businesses. In the early days of the personal computer, IBM was a well-known brand, but entrepreneurs like Michael Dell found that building a PC with off-the-shelf technology was not that difficult. Many others had the same insight: there was no particular reason IBM should be dominant. Many towns had their own local PC companies, just as many towns have microbrewers today. In Singapore there are a half-dozen Uber alternatives, and platforms are proliferating around the globe. It is not self-evident that a few brands will or should win in the platform economy.

Shareholder-owned corporations were particularly suited to the mass production technologies of the twentieth century and the institutional milieu of particular national economies. Their animal spirits were tamed by political pressures such as the Progressive movement, and they became central social institutions. In the US, corporations provided not just products for consumers, profits for investors, and jobs for employees, but essential social welfare services that governments provided in other countries: health insurance for families, wage stability, retirement income. The high overheads for being a corporation, coupled with shareholder demands, has made the traditional corporation increasingly unsustainable. We have lost the social contract that the Progressive movement and its heirs created.

The rise of platform capitalism is enabling a new set of alternative forms of enterprise. In the absence of guiding social principles to balance progress and profit, these new enterprises are unlikely to fill the gap in social needs left by the collapse of corporations. "Creative destruction" thus far has been great on the destruction, but not so much on the creation, at least as far as jobs and social welfare go. Here we propose one idea that might guide future development so as to balance progress and profit.

. . . .

COMMENTS AND DISCUSSION

Davis and Shibulal survey a cluster of important changes in the capitalist economy, as business increasingly moves away from the traditional corporate organizational form toward a highly decentralized "platform" model. They note the potential for platform capitalism to threaten worker welfare and social values in important ways, and propose a set of principles—privacy, autonomy, and dignity—to help alleviate that threat.

Is platform capitalism compatible with healthy economic competition?

At the Society for Progress' second assembly, a number of commentators observed the danger that platform capitalism will tend to facilitate the greater consolidation of economic power in the form of monopolies. In principle, Snabe noted, platforms create shared standardization and infrastructure that will promote opportunity for everyone. In practice, Barney and Frank noted, platform capitalism has important features of winner-take-all markets, in which successful enterprises tend to gain insuperable advantages over their competitors. Battilana observed that the principles articulated by Davis and Shibulal—privacy, autonomy, and dignity—apply to the treatment of individuals but are nonetheless compatible with monopoly at the level of the firm. Perhaps we need normative principles that speak to this organizational scale: a commitment to social purpose or value creation? Power consolidation is one problem. Another, Fuerstein noted, is that platforms tend to "smear around" responsibility across their decentralized network of contracting participants. Can the economy of esteem work effectively under such circumstances to incentivize socially responsible behavior? Snabe suggested that the rise of spontaneous, individualized feedback—star ratings and the like—might offer a solution to this problem.

How will workers fare in the platform model, and what organizational structures are best suited to it?

In spite of the great hype surrounding platform enterprises like Uber, Autor pointed out that workers in general do not show much enthusiasm for it: self-employment rises and falls inversely with general economic trends. We may fantasize that "everyone will be an artisan, creating their own baby socks on Etsy." But the platform economy only tends to work well, Autor suggested, for high-skilled workers with differentiated skills. Most of the "free agent" economy is constituted by people driving rickshaws and the like. In general, people want to know how much they will make and where they will work. Likewise, Anderson observed, they want a reliable place to make retirement investments (what will that look like if the corporate model dissolves?). The group considered a variety of potential solutions. One crucial fact noted in the essay is that the vulnerability of workers declines significantly when there is a robust social safety net to protect them between "gigs." Thus, Autor suggested, the Affordable Care Act is a meaningful step in that direction in the US. Another possibility, Pettit noted, is a legal mechanism that guarantees workers the right to work for multiple platforms. While a highly decentralized economy seems to undermine collective bargaining structures like unions, legal protections such as this could offer workers a measure of important leverage. Another possibility, Barney proposed, would be cooperative ownership structures. On a more existential level, Neiman noted, working in the gig economy seems to deny us a sense of participating in something bigger than ourselves. Is there some equivalent to that to be found in a platform future? What would it look like?

REFERENCES

Amable, B. 2003. *The Diversity of Modern Capitalism*. New York: Oxford University Press.

Benkler, Y. 2013. "Practical Anarchism: Peer Mutualism, Market Power, and the Fallible State." *Politics & Society* 41: 213–51.

CNN 2014. "Uber Removes Racy Blog Posts on Prostitution, One-Night Stands." November 25. <http://money.cnn.com/2014/11/25/technology/uber-prostitutes/>.

Coase, R. 1937. "The Nature of the Firm." *Economica* 4: 386–405.

Davis, G. F. 2015. "Corporate Power in the 21st Century." In S. Rangan (ed.), *Performance and Progress: Essays on Capitalism, Business and Society*. Oxford: Oxford University Press.

Davis, G. F. 2016. *The Vanishing American Corporation: Navigating the Hazards of a New Economy*. Oakland, CA: Berrett-Koehler.

Drucker, P. F. 1949. "The New Society I: Revolution by Mass Production." *Harper's Magazine*, September: 21–30.

Ghilarducci, T. 2007. "The New Treaty of Detroit: Are Voluntary Employee Benefits Associations Organized Labor's Way Forward, or the Remnants of a Once Glorious Past?" Institute for Research on Labor and Employment. Berkeley, CA. <http://irle.berkeley.edu/conference/symposium-ulman/ghilarducci.pdf>.

LaPorta, R., Lopez-de-Silanes, F., and Shleifer, A. 1999. "Corporate Ownership Around the World." *Journal of Finance* 54(2): 471–517.

Levy, F. and Temin, P. 2007. "Inequality and Institutions in 20th Century America." NBER Working Paper No. 13106, Massachusetts Institute of Technology.

Mayer, M. 1997. *The Bankers: The Next Generation*. New York: Truman Talley.

Meyer, J. W. and Rowan, B. 1977. "Institutionalized Organizations: Formal Structure as Myth and Ceremony." *American Journal of Sociology* 83: 340–63.

Piore, M. J. and Sabel, C. F. 1984. *The Second Industrial Divide: Possibilities for Prosperity*. New York: Basic.

Putterman, L. and Kroszner, R. 2009. *Reintroducing The Economic Nature of the Firm*. Cambridge: Cambridge University Press.

Scholz, T. 2016. "Platform Cooperativism: Challenging the Corporate Sharing Economy." Rosa Luxemburg Stiftung (New York Office).

Schor, J. 2014. *Debating the Sharing Economy*. Boston: Great Transition Initiative.

USA Today 2016. "Looking For a job? Amazon's Hiring 120,000 Holiday Workers." October 13. <https://www.usatoday.com/story/money/2016/10/13/looking-job-amazons-hiring-120000-holiday-workers/91992248/>.

Wall Street Journal 2006. "GM's Decision to Cut Pensions Accelerates Broad Corporate Shift," 8 February. <https://www.wsj.com/articles/SB113936666969167992>.

Weber, K., Davis, G. F., and Lounsbury, M. 2009. "Policy as Myth and Ceremony? The Global Spread of Stock Exchanges, 1980–2005." *Academy of Management Journal* 52: 1319–47.

Williamson, O. E. 1985. *The Economic Institutions of Capitalism*. New York: Free Press.

PART III

THE EFFECTIVENESS PROBLEM

CHAPTER **12**

....

CORPORATIONS IN THE
ECONOMY OF ESTEEM

....

ROBERT FRANK AND PHILIP PETTIT

Abstract

Even in a regulated and competitive market economy the behavior of firms leaves much to be desired. Beyond the invisible hand of the market and the iron hand of the law, this chapter outlines arguments for an intangible hand of civil society. The central mechanisms in the model rely on social esteem and self-esteem. These depend on assessments of true intentions and dispositions for costly pro-social actions. Instrumental pro-social actions matter little in the economy of esteem. What is required is a common belief that conformity to certain costly standards benefits all; and that conformity is observable and elicits social approval (and vice versa). Challenges are considerable for the intangible hand model. Moralizing the firm's agents, inducting the voice of affected parties in the deliberation of firms, delayed disclosure of internal deliberations, and public commitments by leaders all offer promise.

Two powerful influences on human behavior are routinely recognized in the social sciences, and indeed in common sense. One is the influence of material reward, the other the influence of material penalty. The first is invoked in the invisible hand model, under which a collective benefit comes from people's acting for their own material gain, as in seeking to sell high and buy low. The other is invoked in the iron hand model, under which the state ensures a collective benefit by coercing people to conform to its dictates, under threat of material or behavioral loss.

In this essay we explore a third powerful influence on the behavior of individuals—the desire for esteem, both in the eyes of others and of the self. We explore how far this desire might also be used to support collective benefits, focusing on its potential as a motive for corporations. The essay is in two sections. In the first, we give an account of this force as it operates among individuals; in the second, we look at the possibility of using it to mobilize corporate bodies in general and corporations in particular.

The reason for our interest in the potential influence of esteem derives in part from skepticism about the potential of the invisible hand of the market and a sense that on its own the iron hand of the law is also likely to be unable to get corporations to abide by appealing standards. The invisible hand does not reach very far in the standards it can support, as we shall see later. And while the iron hand of the law is certainly necessary in setting standards for corporations, including standards relevant for esteem, it can often elicit resistance among those bodies, presenting itself as a foe to be foiled rather than an authority to follow.

The Economy of Esteem Among Individuals

The Esteem Motive

We have separately subscribed in previous writings to the existence of a force in social life that is distinct from the material incentives invoked under the invisible hand of the market and the iron hand of the law. This consists in the first place of an attraction to scoring high in the eyes of others and an aversion to scoring low.[1] Scoring high means winning social esteem for being a reliable or robust source of good: in effect, for doing good out of a virtuous disposition, not just because it's in your narrow material interest to act that way. But individuals can enjoy a second form of esteem not only when others give them esteem, but also when they themselves know that they merit that esteem, whether or not others actually deliver it. In this case they score high in their own eyes, if not in the eyes of others; they enjoy self-esteem rather than social esteem. As scoring high in the eyes of the self or of others is attractive for most of us, scoring low is aversive. This means suffering disesteem for not being a reliable source of good or, in the extreme, for being a reliable source of evil: in effect, for doing bad out of the lack of a virtuous disposition or out of a disposition that is positively vicious.

Under the esteem hypothesis you are esteemed or disesteemed, not for doing good or bad, no matter what the motives, but for doing good robustly or failing to do good robustly or, the extreme case, for doing bad robustly. How others esteem you, and how you esteem yourself, is a function of the dispositions out of which you act, not just of the deeds that you perform; it is driven by the sort of person you show yourself to be in your actions, not by the particular actions that circumstances happen to trigger.[2]

The metrics of good and bad required for the esteem incentive may vary in some degree between societies or within a society between subcultures; honor among thieves

---

[1] For Frank's work see, among others, Frank (1985, 1988, 2004). For Pettit's the primary source is Brennan and Pettit (2004) but see also Pettit (1990, 1995a, 2008). For a recent study in which the economy of esteem plays a major part see Appiah (2010).

[2] There is an asymmetry between good and bad, as registered here, insofar as doing bad may mean failing to target the good or actually targeting the bad. For background on this asymmetry see Pettit (2015: chapter 6).

is not the same as honor among regular folk. But in all communities the dispositions for whose presence you can score high or low in our sense are matters over which you as an agent exercise some control: they are not as fixed by nature or background as your looks or girth or hair color. You may win or lose admirers depending on your looks but you can only win or lose esteem, in our sense—and at the limit suffer disesteem—for dispositions that speak for you as an agent.

The Attraction of Esteem

What makes it attractive to enjoy esteem, and aversive to suffer disesteem? The sanctions in the case of social esteem consist in the fact of being more or less saliently held in high or low regard by others. The sanctions in the case of self-esteem consist in the fact of being able to hold yourself in high regard or being forced to hold yourself in low regard. Three sources of data argue for thinking that self-esteem and social esteem are both attractive for human beings and, by implication, that corresponding forms of disesteem are aversive or repellent. These sources are: common sense, social science, and long tradition.

Taking self-esteem first, common sense testifies to its attraction insofar as we all associate having high self-esteem with satisfaction, and having low self-esteem with frustration or depression. And data from social science support the intuition. Most people, for example, tip at the customary rate even when dining in restaurants they will never visit again (Bodvarsson and Gibson 1994). And in one experiment, more than half of those who'd found wallets on a sidewalk in New York City returned them by mail to their ostensible owners with the cash intact (Hornstein et al. 1968). Such behavior might just be due to inherent, unthinking virtue but it is plausibly associated, at least in part, with the desire that we all recognize to be able to think well of ourselves.

The importance of self-esteem in people's psychology is also emphasized within the long tradition of moral and social thought. Adam Smith (1982) made it a centerpiece of his moral psychology, for example, when he argued in *The Theory of Moral Sentiments*, published in 1759, that the desire to please an imagined "impartial spectator" often motivates people to subordinate their own interests to the common good, even when no others are looking.

What is so attractive about social esteem as distinct from self-esteem? We acknowledge that it may often be attractive for its material or behavioral consequences. If I think well of you, and if I think that you are generally well thought of, I will be disposed thereby to treat you as a reliable, attractive partner in different arenas of cooperation. But should either condition fail, I am likely to be very cautious in my dealings with you. I will see you as someone with whom it makes little sense to cooperate, or at least as someone with whom I cannot cooperate without sending a questionable message to others about my own judgment or disposition.

While the social sanctions of esteem and disesteem do have motivating consequences of these material kinds, however, we assume that human beings care about those sanctions, even in cases where associated material consequences are unlikely to materialize. In other words, they care about the social sanctions, as they care about the sanctions in self-esteem, for their psychological attractions. There is evidence for this claim on the three fronts invoked earlier: common sense, social science, and historical testimony.

That the claim answers to common sense shows up in widely shared experiences and expectations. Thus we all expect people in public office to worry about their posthumous standing, even when they do not now stand to benefit materially from it. And equally we expect people to shrink with embarrassment from being judged negatively by observers they are unlikely ever to meet again: think of how you would feel if you realized that the stranger in the car beside you in stalled traffic is observing you as you pick your nose.

This commonsense belief in people's inherent attraction to esteem, and aversion to disesteem, is borne out in social scientific studies. Think of the result of a study of New York public washrooms showing that whereas only about 35 percent of women washed their hands after using the toilet when there was no one else present in the public area of the washroom, nearly 80 percent did so when there was someone else there (Munger and Harris 1989). Or consider a review of studies of people who are induced to do things they themselves consider wrong, which suggests that people may generally act "out of fear of embarrassment, or of threat to their own or another's face" (Sabini et al. 2001: 13). The claim that the sanctions of social esteem matter independently of their material consequences is also borne out in long tradition (Lovejoy 1961). From classical writers like Polybius and Cicero, through medieval and Renaissance authors as diverse as Aquinas and Machiavelli, down to the European Enlightenment, it was a routine and recurrently emphasized assumption that people care deeply about what others think of them, independently of how this leads others to act.

John Locke (1975: chapter 28, §12) put the assumption forcefully in his *Essay Concerning Human Understanding* of 1689: "he who imagines commendation and disgrace not to be strong motives to men to accommodate themselves to the opinions and rules of those with whom they converse, seems little skilled in the nature or history of mankind: the greatest part whereof we shall find to govern themselves chiefly, if not solely, by this law." Adam Smith (1982: 116) echoes the theme in *The Theory of Moral Sentiments*: "Nature, when she formed man for society, endowed him with an original desire to please, and an original aversion to offend his brethren. She taught him to feel pleasure in their favourable, and pain in their unfavourable regard. She rendered their approbation most flattering and most agreeable to him for its own sake; and their disapprobation most mortifying and most offensive."

Toward an Economy of Esteem

Given the existence of an attraction to esteem, and an aversion to disesteem, we should expect this to play a part in driving people's actions, in shaping their adjustments to the actions of others, and of course in determining their responses to the aggregate effects of such actions and adjustments overall. The esteem motive in its full socially and self-oriented forms should come into operation in any context, to mention two salient but plausible conditions, where people share certain standards for assessing behavior, and are generally exposed to the assessment of others as well as to their own.

The esteem-based rewards and costs of different actions—in effect, their prices—are likely to vary, depending on how far the actions priced are prevalent in the culture and depending, consequently, on the standards assumed in common by the parties. Among monks, honesty may be taken for granted, not particularly prized, and dishonesty may be treated as a matter of deep disgrace. Among politicians, honesty may merit honor and praise, dishonesty may be so run-of-the-mill as to go unremarked. You may gain little for displaying honesty among monks, whether in your own eyes or in the eyes of others, and you may lose a lot by proving dishonest. You may gain a lot for displaying honesty among politicians, again in your own eyes or the eyes of others, and you may lose little by proving dishonest. There is a market in the dispositions you display, as there is a market in the goods and services you provide, and that market is going to determine the relative prices your actions command.

This is to suggest that we should expect an economy of esteem to arise in almost any context of shared standards and mutual exposure. But there is a problem that may seem to block its emergence, and it is important that we address this and show that it is not a fatal obstacle.

Suppose that people recognize the social gains they can make by proving to have dispositions for good—say, honesty or trustworthiness or kindness—and the losses they must face by failing to do so or by proving to have dispositions for bad. And now imagine that, desirous of doing well in the social esteem stakes, they act virtuously with a view to achieving such rewards and avoiding penalties; and this, as a matter presumably manifest to all. Doesn't that mean, paradoxically, that they are bound to fail, since their acting that way will display only an opportunistic rather than a reliable desire for the esteem of others, not any more admirable virtue—not even a desire for self-esteem—or indeed any more despicable vice? Jon Elster (1983: 66) raises the problem nicely, with a focus on the virtue side. "The general axiom in this domain," he says, "is that nothing is so unimpressive as behavior designed to impress."

There are three points to make in response to the Elster problem. They each invoke a plausible psychological effect, and we describe these as the attribution effect, the backgrounding effect, and the habituation effect. While any one of those effects might not completely resolve the problem and explain how an economy of esteem emerges, they serve together to make such an economy seem highly plausible. The effects are liable to materialize, as we shall argue, even on the assumption that people care only about social esteem. But they are bound to be reinforced under the assumption that they care also about the self-esteem they can muster.

The Attribution Effect

The first response is that even if you act honestly or trustworthily out of a desire for esteem, not out of the virtue of honesty or trustworthiness, still you are likely to be taken, as a matter of common attribution, to display the virtue. This is because of the fundamental attribution bias that, by widespread consent, is taken to shape our observations of one another. This bias is the tendency with any form of behavior to explain it by a closely related, more or less low-level disposition—one like honesty or trustworthiness—rather than by a high-level disposition to adapt suitably to circumstance: say, by the disposition to take whatever means the situation provides for achieving esteem.[3]

In support of this suggestion, consider this remark by E. E. Jones (1990: 138): "I have a candidate for the most robust and repeatable finding in social psychology: the tendency to see behavior as caused by a stable personal disposition of the actor when it can be just as easily explained as a natural response to more than adequate situational pressure." The finding that people are deeply prone to the fundamental attribution bias supports the idea that, even when they are conscious of their own sensitivity to a force like the desire for esteem (Miller and Prentice 1996: 804)—even when they are lacking to that extent in self-esteem—people will be loath to trace the behavior of others to such a situational pressure. They will be much more likely to see honest behavior as a sign of honesty, trustworthy behavior as a sign of trustworthiness, and so on.

This response to the Elster problem may be less than satisfactory because it supposes that an economy of social esteem will materialize only to the extent that you consciously mislead others, acting out of a desire for social esteem while seeking to be taken to act out of one or another virtue. According to this response, you will dupe others in leading them to think you have virtues that you simulate but do not truly possess or, at the other extreme, to think that you do not have vices you do actually harbor but are masking for strategic reasons.

The Backgrounding Effect

A second response to Elster's objection is that if you simulate virtue out of a rational desire for social esteem, then it should quickly be clear that it makes no sense to continue to deliberate, case after case, in support of the conclusion that the esteem you seek argues for simulating virtue. Assuming that it will be good policy in the general run of cases to act as virtue would require—it will pay for itself in esteem dividends—it would be a waste of effort to continue with such strategic thinking. It would be more efficient for you in those cases to have a policy of acting virtuously without a second thought, and to allow yourself to reflect explicitly on your strategic ends only when the red lights go on: only when there are strong indications that acting virtuously would impose costs sufficient to eclipse the benefits of esteem.[4] And not only would this be a

---

[3] For a defense of this way of casting the fundamental attribution bias, see Sabini et al. (2001).

[4] It is plausible that the costs involved—say, the costs of risking your life—will eclipse the benefits of esteem only where taking account of them and so failing to act virtuously does not attract a high degree of disesteem: in effect, only where the costs count in common perception as reasonable excuses for such a failure.

more efficient use of your time. It would also be a more effective strategy for winning esteem, since others are likely to see that you are only simulating virtue if you make a habit of case-by-case strategic deliberation.

This second response suggests that a rational policy for anyone seeking social esteem may be to background the end of esteem—to put it out of your mind—and to act on automatic pilot in meeting the requirements of virtue. This means that the distinction between strategically simulating virtue and actually possessing and displaying it may not make for any real, behaviorally significant difference.

The observation is important because it suggests that unlike other strategic rewards and penalties, the attraction to social esteem and the aversion to social disesteem are unlikely to crowd out virtue. There is a good deal of evidence that as people are induced to focus on a strategic end as a reason to act virtuously, this may drive out virtue or block its development: pay people for doing overtime, for example, and they are unlikely to preserve or develop an independent inclination to work beyond normal hours (Frey and Jegen 2001). But the crowding-out effect materializes, plausibly, only when the strategic end is salient and palpable. And given that a desire for social esteem argues for backgrounding strategic thinking and acting virtuously without a second thought, there is little reason to think that it will crowd out virtue in the same way.

Our second response to the Elster problem is, in short, that the clear gains from economizing on cognitive effort may indeed support a general policy of doing the right thing, of not bothering to calculate whether each new situation constitutes a profitable opportunity to cheat. But, as the first response is less than fully satisfactory, so the same is true of the second. For if saving cognitive effort were people's only motive for behaving well, they would see little reason not to cheat if someone else were to point out that the odds of being punished for cheating were sufficiently low in a specific instance.

Consider a man who drives for forty-five minutes through heavy traffic to return a gallon of unneeded pesticide to an approved disposal facility. If he does this merely because it didn't pay to calculate the odds of being caught disposing of it improperly, we would expect him to change his behavior if someone pointed out that the government had no practical means of detecting when someone pours unwanted pesticides down his basement drain at midnight. Some might indeed respond in this way, but many others would be offended at the mere thought.

The Habituation Effect

A third response to the Elster problem is the observation that if tradition is to be believed—in particular, a tradition of Aristotelian provenance—then simulating virtue in the way social esteem requires is likely to bring virtue into existence, making it a matter of second nature. In our terminology it is likely to habituate agents in the exercise of virtue. Generating a more or less autonomous disposition for virtuous behavior, it is likely to turn the virtue they simulate into a reality: to make the *philotomos*, the lover of honor, into a *philagathos*, a lover of good.[5]

How likely is it that the Aristotelian effect will materialize and that many people, under the influence of an economy of social esteem, can be brought to conform reliably to socially endorsed standards? There is no saying in the abstract; the question is essentially empirical. But the likelihood of people's behaving in a reliably virtuous way—virtuous, by local standards—is certainly going to be increased if they are moved, not just by a desire for social esteem, but also by a desire for self-esteem. After all, there is little or no difference between someone's acting virtuously as a matter of habit and their acting in that way out of a wish to be able to think well of themselves: that is, to be able to regard themselves as virtuous in the relevant manner.

If the Aristotelian effect materializes in you, then you will no longer operate under a desire for social esteem, whether foregrounded or backgrounded; you will presumably let that motive disappear entirely from consciousness. But does this mean that the motive will then play no role in shaping your behavior and that the economy of esteem—or at least the economy of social esteem—will no longer operate in your life? No, it does not. For it may well be that if you did not enjoy esteem for displaying the dispositions you possess—or, worse, if you suffered disesteem for displaying them—that would have a corrosive or corrupting impact on their presence; it would tend to change you, although perhaps only over time, into a different sort of character.

Is it plausible to postulate such sensitivity? Yes, if as received lore suggests, the presence of the ring of Gyges would be likely over time to corrupt even the best of people, undermining their virtue and their wish for self-esteem (Pettit 2015). This ring would make wrongdoing—all sorts of wrongdoing, we may suppose—undetectable and would shield wrongdoers from the disesteem of their fellows. Hence it would raise the opportunity costs of virtue enormously—or, equivalently, remove entirely the social disesteem costs of vice—and lead in all likelihood to a great decline in virtue. If this is right, then people's virtue, no matter how Aristotelian in character, is contingent on the relative attraction of the social esteem it wins.

Even if you become fully virtuous on one or another front, then, your behavior may still be deeply shaped by your attraction to social esteem and your aversion to social disesteem. Think about how the cowboy in traditional movies rides herd on his cattle, controlling them in a standby fashion: he generally lets them follow their head but is ready to intervene if any animal wanders off the track he wants them to follow. The social esteem motive may ride herd on your actions, and the dispositions manifested and reinforced by your actions, in roughly the same way (Pettit 1995b). It may not be there as an active driver of what you do but may nevertheless control your actions in a standby fashion, being ready to be activated in any case where, as we put it earlier, the red lights go on. It may let you behave under the impact of other forces—your

---

[5] These Greek terms do not appear in Aristotle, to our knowledge, but they are used by Polybius (1954), who was a great enthusiast for the economy of esteem, and embedded in the republican tradition of thought which he did much to create and shape.

virtuous disposition—only insofar as the presumptive benefits of social esteem make this sensible.

The Feasibility of the Economy of Esteem

What we have observed so far is that there are good grounds for thinking that no matter what their other motives—say, their interests in material gain—people are likely to be shaped in some part by the impact of a desire for social esteem and a reinforcing desire for self-esteem: in short, by the attraction of the psychological benefits that either form of esteem promises.[6] But presumably people differ in the degree to which they become virtuous agents—or behavioral simulacra of virtuous agents. And the economy of esteem can work well in shaping people's behavior toward one another only to the extent that they can detect whether those with whom they are dealing really do have the dispositions—or the simulacra of the dispositions—that the economy of esteem promises to elicit. So a crucial question is how far they can reliably discern such praiseworthy dispositions in others.

There is a body of empirical literature that bears on this issue. It is often focused on how reliable people are in identifying those who are likely to cooperate in interactions that have the character of a prisoner's dilemma. These are interactions where it is in the interest of each to defect on the other, regardless of whether the other defects or cooperates; and this, despite the fact that each does better if they both cooperate than if they both defect.

In an earlier experimental study, Frank et al. (1993) found that subjects were surprisingly accurate at predicting who would cooperate and who would defect in one-shot prisoner's dilemmas played with near strangers. In that study, the base rate of cooperation was 73.7 percent, the base rate of defection only 26.3 percent. A random prediction of cooperation would thus have been accurate 73.7 percent of the time, a random prediction of defection accurate only 26.3 percent of the time. The actual accuracy rates for these two kinds of prediction were 80.7 percent and 56.8 percent, respectively. The likelihood of such high accuracy rates occurring by chance is less than one in one thousand.

Subjects in this experiment were strangers at the outset and were able to interact with one another for only thirty minutes before making their predictions. It is plausible to suppose that predictions would be considerably more accurate for people who have known one another for a long time.

In general, we may expect that scrutinizing the character of potential trading partners entails at least some cost. It takes time to get to know someone, after all,

---

[6] And this is all the more likely, of course, given that people who earn the esteem of others, and their own self-esteem, are generally going to do better than material self-seekers in the prisoner's dilemma and other interactions where reliable cooperators normally do better than opportunistic defectors.

and even after substantial periods of contact, observable symptoms of emotional predispositions to behave honestly are likely to be noisy. Just as it would not pay to incur the expense of installing a burglar alarm in a neighborhood where burglaries never happen, it would not pay to incur the cost of scrutinizing potential trading partners if everyone were honest. You'd do better just to trust everyone indiscriminately.

Does this mean that there is likely to be no need for the monitoring of others and no value in the capacity to monitor accurately? No. For cheaters could easily invade any social environment of the kind imagined. And over time, their numbers would multiply until the cost of vigilance came into balance with the corresponding benefits of being victimized less frequently. The expectation, then, is that any equilibrium population will contain at least some dishonest individuals. So while the economy of esteem may enable honest individuals to hold their own in competition with their dishonest counterparts, we cannot reasonably expect it to eliminate the need for vigorous monitoring and enforcement of pro-social regulations.

Illustrating the Economy of Esteem

There are many examples where the economy of esteem can help us explain the vagaries of social life (Appiah 2010). But we conclude with a somewhat speculative case that illustrates nicely the interaction possible between the attraction to esteem, on the one side, and the aversion to disesteem on the other (McAdams 1997; Brennan and Pettit 2004: part 2).

The example bears on the rise of recycling in many countries over the past quarter century or more. At the start of this development, standards began to emerge that made recycling look desirable and, those standards being widely shared, this meant that the relatively few individuals who went to the trouble of recycling would have earned great esteem for their efforts, in the eyes of others and in their own eyes. This being so, we can imagine that forces of imitation, buttressed by the returns in positive esteem, may have helped to increase the numbers and to persuade governments to take steps that made recycling ever easier. But with the increase in numbers and the rise in the ease of recycling, the motive of positive esteem would presumably have grown weaker in its impact, raising the possibility that the recycling movement would stall, decline, or oscillate.

The movement did not stall or decline or oscillate, however, and one possible explanation for why it didn't is readily available within the economy of esteem. For at the point where it ceased to be positively estimable for someone to recycle—at the point where it would have taken pure virtue or sheer habit to assume or maintain the activity—it would likely have begun to be decidedly disestimable not to recycle. At that point recycling would have been a pattern, individually burdensome but collectively beneficial, sustained by a large number of people in society. And in such a scenario, plausibly, it would have been a matter of shame, before others and before yourself, not to play your part. Thus, as the pressure of positive esteem that had supported the rise of recycling tapered off, the pressure of negative esteem—disesteem—would have appeared to provide a second boost to the pattern and to establish recycling as an accepted norm.

The Intangible Hand

The economy of esteem is of interest to any of us who think about how societies and polities might be better organized: that is, organized so that, despite the individual burdens involved in doing so, people act so as to promote collective benefits that count as attractive on more or less all sides or to avoid collective costs that count as aversive on more or less all sides. The economy of esteem holds out the prospect that there may be a third source of beneficial social ordering apart from the invisible hand of the market and the iron hand of the law; this we might describe as the intangible hand of civil society (Brennan and Pettit 2004: part 3).

The various social thinkers of the past who invoked people's desire for social esteem as a potential source of benefit, casting it as "a saving vice" (Lovejoy 1961), saw it in precisely this light as a force to be harnessed for the promotion of the common good (Hirschman 1977). Thus John Locke (1975: chapter 28, §10) argues that, no matter the circumstances of a society, people "retain still the power of thinking well or ill; approving or disapproving of the actions of those whom they live amongst, and converse with: and by this approbation and dislike they establish amongst themselves, what they will call virtue and vice." The Baron de Montesquieu (1989: book 3, chapter 6) takes up the theme in 1748 in his *Spirit of the Laws*, when he argues that "honor . . . is capable of inspiring the most glorious actions, and, joined with the force of laws, may lead us to the end of government as well as virtue itself."

As we noted earlier, there are two plausible social conditions that would seem to foster the full use of the intangible hand to promote certain aggregate benefits—results that are collectively beneficial by almost everyone's lights—despite requiring individually burdensome behavior. One, it becomes a matter of common belief that the good of others, indeed the good of all, requires each to conform to certain standards. And two, it becomes a matter of common belief that no one can be suitably sure that they may breach those standards without being detected and disesteemed by others; and/or it becomes a matter of common belief that each can be suitably sure that if they conform to those standards, others will recognize this and positively esteem them for their conformity.[7]

---

[7] Being suitably sure in each case means being sure in a measure sufficient to make the expected cost of non-conformity or the expected benefit of conformity high enough to outweigh the temptation to free ride: that is, to share in the benefit procured by those who conform without bearing the burden required of conformers.

The fulfillment of these two conditions facilitates the operation of the intangible hand in the dimension of social esteem. But self-esteem is going to be relevant too. The first condition ensures that you will enjoy self-esteem to the extent that by relevant standards you merit self-esteem. And the attraction of self-esteem, the appeal of being able to think well of yourself, means that even as the second condition fails—even as you escape the eyes of others—the behavior may still remain in place. The greater the attraction of self-esteem, the higher the degree of certainty of non-detection that is required to make cheating attractive. Cheating is bound to cause a loss in self-esteem and that loss will have to weigh against the expected satisfaction of cheating without being detected.

The intangible hand may operate to the benefit only of a subgroup in any community, of course, and to the detriment of society as a whole; honor among thieves may make theft a more rewarding and more common occurrence. But when honor or esteem attaches only to behavior that benefits almost everyone, then it should be clear that it can operate for the good of society overall. We think it operates in this way among teachers who can get away with not doing their best but make every effort to advance the education of their students; with doctors for whom a professional code, associated with the Hippocratic oath, keeps them fastened on the interest of their patients, even at a cost in hours at the surgery or in remuneration earned; and with workers in any area who avoid the temptation to shirk and, recognizing that they receive a good day's pay, seek to provide a good day's service in return.

The intangible hand can operate to the same effect with businesspeople who abide by codes of fair dealing, even when there are powerful temptations to exploit a customer. One of us has had the following experience, now some years ago, in buying a house directly from the builder of a small housing estate. The price was verbally agreed in April of that year for a house due to be ready in June, at the same time as the other houses. But in May the builder managed, to his surprise, to sell the other, identical houses at much higher prices. When he suggested to the purchaser that he would therefore have to raise the April price, he was reminded of the verbal agreement and declared in response: "I've always boasted that I never renege on a deal on which I have shaken hands and I'm not going to start now. Let's shake on it again: the house is yours at the price we agreed."

THE ECONOMY OF ESTEEM AMONG CORPORATE BODIES

We are happy for current purposes to think of corporations and other corporate bodies as agents (List and Pettit 2011). They qualify as agents insofar as they are systems that are representable as reliably pursuing determinate purposes according to reliably formed representations of the opportunities and means available. And not only are they representable in that way. Like individual human beings—and unlike mute animals—they represent themselves to others in such terms, inviting others to rely on their having the purposes and representations they avow and on their performing the actions that they pledge. It is in virtue of those capacities that they can establish ongoing relationships with different sorts of stakeholders, whether those be other corporations or individual human beings.

Assuming that corporate bodies are agents, the question we want to consider is whether the economy of esteem can operate among them, in particular among corporations, to the same effect as among individuals. Assume, as is plausible, that in any society there will often be shared standards that we think corporate bodies should satisfy; and that it will be more or less obvious to all of us, both within and without those bodies, whether or not they abide by those standards. The question then is whether the intangible hand can push them, as it can push individuals, toward the robust provision of collective benefits. Can it ensure their robust conformity with standards that serve the common good, according to common perceptions?

Beyond the Economics of Corporate Reputation

There is no problem in organizing corporations for the robust provision of at least one form of collective benefit in this way. This is the benefit of providing commodities and services of high quality at competitive cost: that is, at a cost such that were it any lower the suppliers would likely go out of business. It is a common, and we assume plausible, claim that in a competitive market corporations are bound to try to attract customers by looking for an attractive balance in quality and cost and, as a result, are bound to want to foster a reputation for being providers that can be relied upon to do so: that is, for being reliable or robust performers in regard to these standards. The invocation of market reputation, which is commonplace in economics, looks like an appeal to the economy of esteem. And the argument that a concern for reputation will drive corporations to try to keep quality up and cost down appears to be an argument within the economics of esteem.

Appearances in this case, however, are quite misleading. The reputation that corporations and other economic producers seek in a competitive market is not necessarily a reputation for being concerned as such with the social benefit of providing high-quality, low-cost goods—for being virtuously focused on serving the community in that way. If a strategically sensible corporation operates in a competitive economy, seeking to increase its market share and its market return, then that will be enough in itself to mobilize an appropriate effort to keep quality up and cost down. And so the only reputation corporations need seek in such a market is the reputation for being canny and prudent enough to respond to the challenges of the market in an appropriate way. They need not have any interest in being taken to promote a good cost–quality mix for the social return it promises and no interest in being regarded as virtuous agents: good corporate citizens, as it is sometimes put.

It is common in economics to invoke the importance of reputation, as in the example cited. But there is a clear distinction between the economics of reputation in that sense and what we think of as the economics of esteem. To be concerned about reputation on a certain action front—say, in producing high-quality, low-cost goods—is to have a primary interest in behaving after that fashion and a derived interest in being reputed to behave in that way. To be concerned about esteem on any front—say, in sticking to promises, as in the example of the builder—is to have a primary interest in enjoying esteem as someone who reliably keeps their promises and a derived interest in actually keeping them: failing to keep them is a sure way, in the absence of excuse, of losing esteem as a promise-keeper. In the first case producing high-quality, low-cost goods appeals to the agent, presumably for the material advantage it promises, and the attraction of a good reputation is simply that it will create more opportunities for benefiting from the performance. In the second case it is being esteemed as a promise-keeper that primarily appeals—this may be in the eyes of the self as well as in the eyes of others—and the attraction of the behavior is that it is a means or precondition for enjoying such esteem.

It is not the intangible hand, then, that leads corporations within a competitive economy to produce high-quality, low-cost goods. Rather it is the invisible hand. By each seeking their own market advantage in the production of suitable goods, and a reputation for reliably producing them, they combine to generate as by an invisible hand—as a not necessarily foreseen or desired consequence—the collective benefit that consists in the availability of such goods. There is no suggestion that they produce that benefit out of a wish to be esteemed for their attachment to community welfare—for their virtue as corporate citizens—as the intangible hand would require.

Toward an Economics of Corporate Esteem

These observations show that we may hope to mobilize the economics of reputation—and more generally, the invisible hand—in getting a corporation to achieve a collective benefit, if that benefit has a particular character: like the quality–cost ratio, it correlates directly with the interests of the individual consumers that the corporation is seeking to satisfy. Because consumers are individually interested in buying products that score well on the scale of quality and cost, corporations are bound to respond to that interest and to help ensure, as by an invisible hand, that the collective interest in having access to high-quality, low-cost products is satisfied. But the observations also suggest, alas, that collective benefits that are not so closely tied to the properties of a corporation's products cannot be generated on the same basis. And the collective benefits we as a society might want corporations to promote are mostly of this kind.

Consider the benefits that lead many of us to think that corporations—and, where relevant, corporate bodies more generally—should abide by the following standards:[8]

---

[8] If you do not endorse these particular standards, there are many similar examples you might put in their place.

- As taxpayers, corporate bodies should be ready to pay the full tax expected and levied under the laws of the relevant jurisdiction.
- As employers, they should be willing to make every effort to look after employee safety, to remove the threat of summary dismissal, and to respond to complaints.
- As producers, they should guard against any risks to consumers, even risks that can be kept hidden or be countered more cheaply by paying court-imposed damages.
- As members of the local community, they should guard against environmental risks associated with company activity, cooperating fully with government.
- As political agents, they should make arguments publicly, avoiding the temptation to win government favors by buying off or threatening politicians privately.

We as a society—we as a body of citizens—may wish that corporations reliably abide by standards like these. But that civic interest, as we may describe it, does not connect with an individual or consumer interest in the manner illustrated in the case of the low-cost/high-quality standard. The products or services we purchase from corporations appeal to us primarily, so at least standard economic wisdom suggests, for inherent properties like cost and quality that are there to be observed or inferred at the moment of purchase, and not for properties to do with their origin: for example, their being produced by reliably abiding with the standards illustrated, thereby displaying a form of corporate virtue or responsibility. And since corporations are in a position to be aware of this, there will be no incentive to conform to those standards; there will be nothing like the incentive they have to produce goods and services with a good cost–quality profile.

This means that if we are looking for a form of social ordering—a discipline of penalty and incentive—to get corporations to display or simulate virtue or responsibility, then we can only rely on the economics of esteem. We have to hope that it is possible to induce an interest among corporations in being esteemed for a disposition to abide by suitable standards and to be led by that interest into actually abiding by them. We have to look for reasons why they should seek to be considered virtuous by consumers and other stakeholders in the corporate world; and perhaps also for reasons why they should want to be able to sustain a degree of self-esteem: a self-conception under which they are indeed virtuous or responsible bodies.

We look at this issue in the discussion that follows, beginning from a model of corporate esteem-seeking in the non-commercial sector. We shall see that there are grounds for concern about how far corporations can be incorporated in the economy of esteem. But before coming to that, it is worth noting that the prospect that they can be mobilized by a desire for esteem, however utopian it may be, is not entirely groundless. There are some empirical observations that suggest, contrary to standard economic doctrine, that corporations may be capable of being incorporated and mobilized within this discipline.

Standard economic models suggest, for example, that buyers will be unwilling to pay a premium for products produced by socially responsible firms. Thus consumers may not like the fact that Acme Tire Corporation pollutes the air, but it is supposed in those models that they will realize that their own purchase of Acme tires will have a virtually unmeasurable effect on air quality. And so it is predicted that if Acme tires sell for even a little less than those produced by a rival with a cleaner technology, consumers will buy from Acme.

There is evidence, however, that people with an interest in virtuous corporate behavior will prefer dealing with socially responsible firms even when they realize that their own purchases are too small to affect the outcomes they care about. Conventional economic theory predicted that consumers would not support Patagonia's strategy of charging higher prices to cover the added cost of producing only environmentally friendly products. In the event, however, Patagonia has enjoyed consistently robust profits. Any consumer who stopped to ponder the matter would know that a single household's jacket purchase decision would have no discernible impact on the fate of the planet. Even so, it appears that many consumers have been willing to pay higher prices in the name of a cause they care about (Reinhardt 1999).

Nor does this example stand alone. Chipotle Mexican Grill, the restaurant chain, openly touts its willingness to incur higher costs by buying meats only from suppliers who do not treat their animals with hormones and antibiotics. Chipotle's consumers are in no position to verify that claim, but the chain's robust growth suggests that many view it as credible (Edwards 2015). Although no individual consumer would have an incentive to have Chipotle's ingredients tested, investigative reporters have powerful incentives to do so. And Chipotle executives are undoubtedly aware of the dangers they would be courting if their claims about their healthful ingredients were discovered to be false.

These observations suggest that people may be prepared to pay a cost for dealing with socially responsible corporations and that corporations, seeking the esteem of such customers, may be ready to abide by certain demanding standards, regardless of the market risk involved. But there is also some evidence that corporations may have a concern that they should be able to think of themselves—in effect, that their employees should be able to think of them—as responsible bodies, and in that sense that they should enjoy a corresponding level of self-esteem.

One reason that corporations may be expected to have this sort of concern consists in the fact that socially responsible firms appear to enjoy a relative advantage in recruiting employees. Jobs differ in countless dimensions, one of which is the degree to which workers are part of a socially responsible enterprise: one, broadly, that contributes to overall well-being. If job applicants have an interest in being part of such an organization—a body where members are capable of thinking well of what they do together—then that will presumably motivate corporations to be of a kind that supports such self-esteem. It means, for one thing, that they may find it easier to recruit those they want. And it also means that employees may be willing to accept lower salaries than they would otherwise demand.

We see evidence of this effect in the fact that there is a correlation between the social virtue or responsibility of organizations and the fact that employees are willing to accept relatively lower remuneration for the work they do there; they are willing to trade off lower individual salaries for greater corporate virtue, thereby offsetting the costs the organization may have to bear as a result of its responsibility. The competitive advantage this gives socially responsible bodies may be quite significant. In a large sample of recent college graduates, for example, those occupying the most desirable jobs on this dimension earned less than half as much as those occupying the least desirable jobs (Frank 2004: chapter 5).

This pattern in the data is predicted by the theory of compensating wage differentials, which dates back as far as Adam Smith. It holds that, all other factors held equal, competition will force employers to offer higher wages in order to fill jobs that potential applicants consider unattractive and that the jobs that prove more attractive—in our case, more attractive for being posts with a responsible or virtuous firm—need not be paid at the same rate. But is it reasonable to take wage patterns to be shaped in this way by competitive forces in the labor market? Since the economy operates at full employment most of the time, and since most workers have at least some latitude in their choice of jobs, we believe that it is.

Non-economists often object to this claim by pointing out that the jobs with the highest salaries also tend to have the most attractive working conditions. CEOs, for example, get both high pay and nice conditions. But that objection ignores the other-things-equal assumption of the argument. Because people bring vastly different amounts of human capital to the labor market, they have vastly different endowments with which to bargain for both higher salaries and more pleasant working conditions. Those with high human capital typically use some of it to buy pleasant conditions and the rest to buy higher pay. In contrast, those with low human capital tend to fill jobs with both low pay and unpleasant conditions. In a heterogeneous cross section of individuals, we should thus expect a positive correlation between wages and desirable conditions.

But if we confine our attention to workers with a fixed amount of human capital, our observation is supported: we see a negative relationship between desirable conditions and pay. Evidence suggests that compensating salary differences for what we'll call "the moral high ground" is the most important way in which socially responsible firms are able to overcome what might otherwise be a fatal cost disadvantage.

Corporate Esteem in the Non-Commercial Sector

Are there practical means by which we might implement the intangible hand in the corporate arena? The intangible hand operates successfully with individual agents in virtue of one or more of three effects mentioned earlier: the attribution effect, the backgrounding effect, and the habituation effect. And so the issue is whether those effects can materialize with corporate bodies and encourage the development of suitable forms of corporate virtue. Are corporate bodies capable of being fastened on collective benefits in a manner that robustly disposes them to provide the benefits more or less automatically in appropriate contexts? And are they susceptible to the force of esteem in keeping them locked on to collective benefits in that way?

Corporate bodies are a large category, of which corporations are but one species. Looking at corporate bodies generally, it is possible to imagine a variety of organizations that can display a counterpart to individual virtue. This would be a disposition, written into its mode of corporate organization, that more or less peremptorily and robustly requires individuals who act in its name—that is, authorized under its rules—to provide one or another sort of benefit.

Thus consider those monastic communities of the middle ages that operated under the Rule of St. Benedict, a set of precepts dating from the sixth century. While the rule could be altered by the autonomous communities that submitted to it, and while it was altered under various reforms through the centuries—this, we may presume, in the face of what were perceived to be red lights—it had a powerfully unchallengeable status in most monasteries and nunneries. The policy makers in those communities would have embraced the rule as expressive of their goals. And the policy takers—the ordinary monks and nuns—would have been virtuously motivated to conform, at least if they joined up voluntarily. Even if their individual virtue failed, indeed, the intangible hand would have been there to nudge them into simulating virtue.

Among other things, the rule required communities to display the virtue of hospitality in quite a high and demanding degree with travelers who came to their doors. Can we say that such a community was hospitable in a manner that characterizes the organization as such, not necessarily its members individually? Yes, we surely can. It is quite plausible to imagine a community that is hospitable at the organizational level, even while the individual monks or nuns may fail in virtue and do so with ill grace, perhaps resenting the demands on community resources. If hospitality requires a more or less robust or reliable response to the needs of a traveler as such, regardless of the various costs involved, then it is surely plausible to say that the organization imagined is designed to satisfy the standard of hospitality, displaying the required virtue.

If an organization is capable of displaying a virtue in the relevant sense—a disposition to provide a collective benefit robustly—then it is surely going to be the case that it can be mobilized under the economy of social esteem to do so. As we can imagine a monastic community displaying the virtue of hospitality, so we can imagine its being moved, if only in a standby fashion, by the desire for esteem. Suppose, then, that this counterfactual is true of the community: that if its hospitality made it a sucker for free-riders, and a laughing-stock in the community at large, then it would revise the rule under which it operates. In that case, it is true as things actually are that its display of hospitality is contingent on its earning esteem benefits in the surrounding society for that hospitality. And this is so, even if the issue of its standing in that society never arises in its internal deliberations.

The role of social esteem in shaping the behavior of a body like our monastic community is likely to be buttressed at the same time by the appeal of self-esteem. We can imagine that individuals associated with the body derive personal self-esteem from the fact of working for an admirable organization. And we can perhaps think of the organization itself taking pride in what it exemplifies and what it does. This will be true to the extent that its members are proud, not of how they perform themselves in their individual agency, but of how they perform as a body.

The fact that a genuinely hospitable organization may operate under the control of the intangible hand means that other possibilities are also open. In principle an organization might not actually be hospitable but act hospitably for the sake of the esteem this earns, relying on something like the attribution effect to hide the strategy it is following. And in principle the organization might simulate hospitality, backgrounding the pursuit of esteem on the grounds that this promises to do best in making the pursuit successful.

The lesson taught by our recherché example applies in contemporary cases too. We can readily imagine a voluntary organization relying on the attribution effect, the backgrounding effect, and perhaps even the habituation effect to present itself as virtuous on one or another front—say, in the provision of welfare or healthcare or education for a local community—and to win thereby a high level of esteem and standing. Consider the church that moves into a new territory, the NGO that needs to gain acceptance in an alien culture, the political party that hopes to increase its electoral salience in a constituency, or indeed the revolutionary or terrorist group that depends on local acceptance for its survival. In any such case, it is entirely plausible that the organization should adopt a rule governing the behavior of its members that effectively invites esteem for the organization as such.

Corporate Esteem in the Commercial Sector

But while the lesson of our recherché example may apply in a range of contemporary cases, the question we must face now is whether it is likely to apply to corporations or companies or firms: corporate bodies organized to do business in a relatively competitive market. It should be clear from the earlier example that the lesson applies only under quite strict policy-maker and policy-taker conditions. In order for an organization to be able to operat in the economy of esteem, it must be in the overall interest of policy makers to establish relatively inflexible rules. And equally it must be in the overall interest of policy takers to conform, in the absence of plausible red lights, to those rules. The question we face, then, is whether there is any hope of those conditions being fulfilled in the case of corporations. And the first set of observations we make is that the situation poses significant challenges.

Some Negative Observations

Taking the policy-maker condition, is there a good prospect of finding relatively inflexible rules such that it is likely to be in the interest of those who ultimately determine the policy of a commercial corporation—presumably, the board of directors—to impose them? Not in all cases, certainly, for the simple reason that maximizing shareholder value under the constraint of law, which is normally taken to be the goal of corporations, is unlikely to argue in the deliberation of directors for abiding more or less automatically by any rule or standard of the kind illustrated in our earlier list of examples. The law might seek to set such standards and even try to impose them, as by an iron hand, with coercive penalties. But the inevitability of loopholes means that the law will be very ineffective unless the directors internalize the standards and actively impose them from within; if they do not internalize them, indeed, they may see the law as an intruder and actively resist its efforts.

Take the five benefits mentioned in our examples. It is easy to envision cases in which boards might view it as contrary to the interests of shareholders to abide more or less robustly and inflexibly by the corresponding rules. The law will always allow loopholes for avoiding certain tax payments or will always be imperfect enough to leave scope for evading them. And something similar will be true of other cases like reducing costs in providing for employees, taking a softer line in guarding against consumer risk, playing fast and loose with environmental standards, and looking for favors from government. If a corporate board believed that survival required doing no more than required by law—on the minimal interpretation of those requirements—it would be reluctant to commit to any of our five standards in a binding, robust fashion.

But even if the policy makers on the board of a company were willing to commit to a rule in any of these areas, it would still be necessary to induce the policy takers among the executives of the company to background deliberation reliably, letting the rule govern their decision making in a relatively mechanical fashion. Anybody like a corporation is going to have one or a number of committees whose members are responsible for what is done, now over this domain, now over that, in the company name. And that means that if the corporation is to abide by a rule—in particular, a rule with a red lights exception built in—then it must be in the interests of such committee members to abjure deliberation about the merits or demerits of following the rule and not to overuse the red lights exception to argue that the organization can benefit by neglecting the rule in this or that case.

There is no problem with the idea that an individual might adopt the policy, and get into the habit of not deliberating case by case about whether the esteem benefits continue to argue for following a certain rule. That individual can outsource the signal that activates deliberation, letting indications from the environment determine whether or not the red lights are on. But the executive members of any committee may be tempted to argue that there are enough red lights present in any case for the corporation to think again about a rule in place.

There are two aspects to challenging a rule that are bound to make it attractive to executives. The first is that challenging a rule, even challenging a rule supported powerfully by a law or norm—say, a rule governing the payment of taxes or the treatment of the environment—may not bring much disesteem down on the challengers. They can present themselves to fellow members, and even to the world at large, not as seeking personal benefit, but as caring for the benefit of their principal: the corporate person. When you act for yourself in a self-regarding way you run the risk of being shamed for your egoism—for the extent to which you are relatively indifferent to the welfare of the community at large. When you act for another entity like a corporation you do not run a similar risk, for you can present such vicariously self-regarding behavior as motivated by an other-regarding concern. You are not an egoist, so it will seem; you are just doing your duty by the principal you serve.

The second aspect that is likely to make it attractive for executives in a company to challenge a rule of the kind envisaged is that by doing so, they can show their identification with the organization, looking for esteem in the currency of organizational welfare. All members must acknowledge the relevance of that currency, on pain of putting their own commitment to the body in doubt. The currency is well grounded in the only common ground that they may share: their interest in the corporation that they each serve. This consideration was registered very clearly by David Hume, although he had a political rather than a corporate context in mind. "Honour is a great check upon mankind," he wrote. "But where a considerable body of men act together, this check is, in a great measure, removed; since a man is sure to be approved of by his own party, for what promotes the common interest [of the party]; and he soon learns to despise the clamours of his adversaries" (Hume 1994: 24).

The considerations so far suggest that there are serious difficulties in the way of getting corporations to respond to the economy of esteem and to be guided by the intangible hand. They make it hard to see how to suppress the effects that would render corporations incapable of being robustly bound to standards in the same virtuous manner as individuals. Yet these difficulties may sometimes be surmounted, and we close with some more positive observations.

Some Positive Observations

The policy-maker condition that must be satisfied if the intangible hand is to operate in the corporate world certainly poses a challenge. But it is not by any means impossible to satisfy. Thus a majority of shareholders might demand that the board follow some relatively inflexible rules, reflecting accepted laws or norms; this might happen under pressure from public opinion, for example, in particular from various social movements and NGOs. Alternatively a CEO might command enough confidence among shareholders to be sure of winning a majority to his or her side in responding to such pressure and announcing a strict and demanding policy.

Let us suppose that corporations can satisfy the policy-maker condition, as we have described it, and embrace relatively inflexible standards. They will be capable of robustly conforming to such standards, however—and of being motivated by the esteem that such conformity will presumably earn—only if they can meet the policy-taker condition as well. They must be able to shut down deliberation about conformity other than in cases where it is plausible, by anyone's perception, that the red lights are on. Are there means whereby this result might be secured? Are there ways in which we might induce corporate executives to abide by standards like those governing tax payment, consumer protection, environmental provision, and the like?

There are four possibilities to register in answer to this query, which might be individually realized or realized in a mutually reinforcing way. The first would seek to moralize executives, while the other three would try to inhibit them: one, by introducing outsiders into decision-making committees; a second, by exposing such committees to outside publicity; and a third, by inducing corporations to make pre-commitments that it would be catastrophic not to honor.

The idea in the first approach would be to get the executives responsible for the most important forms of corporate decision making to endorse cultural standards of the sort we have in mind, making it a matter of shame for them to support a breach, or even to countenance the possibility of a breach.

Consider the way we expect our judges to be resistant to taking bribes, given the depth of their professional commitment to impartiality. Or consider the way we expect our auditors to be resistant to cooking the books, given the depth of their professional commitment to independence from the organizations they audit. Judges and auditors know that it means professional death to be caught out breaching their professional standards, this being evident from the cases where breaches are detected. And so we expect them to invest in impartiality and independence, however demanding those standards may be, because they represent minimal prerequisites for standing and acceptance in their professional and even larger communities. Is it a matter of professional ethics that judges and auditors respect those standards? Yes, in a sense. But it is not a matter of an ethics that only the saintly could expect to realize. More importantly, it is a matter of professional ethos: a habit of professional behavior that it would be deeply shameful for anyone not to display.

One way in which corporations may be brought under the economy of esteem would be by inducting corporate professionals into a corresponding economy at the individual level. This individual economy would make it a matter of professional shame, even ostracism, for a business professional to propose or support—even perhaps not to blow the whistle on—a corporate decision to skimp on taxes, put consumers at serious risk, allow environmental damage, or anything of that kind. It would establish a professional ethos that made it unthinkable for executives or directors to countenance a neglect of relevant standards for the sake of organizational advantage.

The other three ways in which corporations might be brought under the economy of esteem would not strictly require this moralization of professionals, as we might call it, although they would certainly be reinforced by such a development. They would work by inhibiting executives rather than by moralizing them.

The first would consist in bringing outside observers or even contributors into the committee rooms where crucial corporate decisions are made. Those outsiders might come from the workforce, from the local community, or from bodies representative of consumers. Their presence might be expected to inhibit the rule-challenging temptations to which executives would otherwise be exposed.

This possibility is supported by a study of how far judges on federal appeals courts are affected by the diversity of appointments on a three-member court. The presence of a democratic appointee on a court with two republican judges or of a republican appointee on a court with two democratic judges has an enormous influence on how the court tends to rule on issues of an ideological kind. The evidence is that such mixed courts are considerably less partisan than completely republican or completely democratic courts; and, remarkably, that in many cases they rule on much the same pattern as one another: which party appointees are in the majority does not make a significant difference (Sunstein et al. 2004).

If the ideological leanings of judges can be inhibited by the presence of just one judge from the other side, that is likely to be because of an esteem effect. Plausibly, judges are much more inclined to be careful about ruling impartially in the presence of someone whose assessment of their performance is unlikely to be affected by belonging to the same party. But that suggests that the presence of outsiders on corporate committees is likely to have a similar effect in inhibiting the executive temptation to challenge any relatively inflexible rules. It would take a degree of shamelessness for an executive to support avoiding taxes in the presence of individual taxpayers or to support loosening safety standards in the presence of employee representatives.

The second way in which the challenging of rules might be inhibited, and the possibility of corporate virtue facilitated, is really a variant on the second and is supported on the same basis. It would involve opening up committee-room deliberation and decision making to public scrutiny although perhaps, for reasons of commercial confidentiality, only after an interim period of five to ten years. Presumably the prospect of such exposure, however far into the future, might be enough to inhibit executives from challenging rules that would force a corporation to pay its taxes, guard against consumer risk, respect the environment, and so on. That prospect ought to have the same chilling effect—and ultimately the same moralizing effect—as forcing executives to issue challenges to the rules they question in the presence of people who stand to benefit from such rules.

But there is also a third way to inhibit the tendency of executives to challenge inflexible rules. This would come about through the corporation as a whole making such a public, even heroic commitment to following certain rules on the environmental, workplace, or fiscal fronts that it would be a disastrous publicity event for them to be found out breaking or bending those rules. The recent Volkswagen scandal shows that even in the presence of such a commitment, the executives of a corporation may well be tempted to act inconsistently with its pledges. But it is only in recent decades that corporations have begun making commitments of the kind undertaken by Volkswagen. And if the fallout from the car maker's failure is serious enough, that may establish a common acceptance in the corporate world that no executives should run the sort of risk that Volkswagen executives proved themselves willing to take. Thus we might hope that the executives of Chipotle will be motivated by the environmental commitments of their company to stick to the relevant rules. After all, such executives could hardly hope to win the approval of their colleagues for proposing a course of action that would put the corporation at risk of catastrophically bad publicity.

We began this discussion by assuming that the policy-maker condition can be readily satisfied, concentrating then on the ways in which we might try to ensure that the policy-taker condition can be satisfied as well. But it is worth observing that if the policy-maker condition is satisfied as a result of a passionate commitment by the leader of a company—a commitment that shareholders might readily endorse in the case of a successful company—then that could serve to make the fulfillment of the policy-taker condition rather easier to achieve. It might serve to inhibit any backsliding among the executives who have to apply the policy and might even prompt them to internalize it strongly.

At Apple's 2014 annual shareholders' meeting, for example, a representative of the National Center for Public Policy Research, a conservative shareholder activist group, demanded that the company abandon any social responsibility efforts that entailed a penalty to the company's bottom line. In response, a visibly angry Apple CEO Tim Cook responded, "When we work on making our devices accessible by the blind, I don't consider the bloody ROI [return on investment]." He added that the company also made substantial investments in environmental issues, worker safety, and other areas beyond what could be justified on narrow profitability grounds. "We want to leave the world better than we found it," he said (Denning 2014). Apple, of course, has long been the most profitable corporation on the planet.[9]

This sort of CEO commitment is likely to catch on among other executives of the company, whether out of pure or mixed motives. And it is likely, of course, to prove important in the recruitment of personnel. In *True North*, Bill George, former CEO of Medtronic, and his co-author Peter Sims, trace the personal histories of more than a hundred CEOs of successful companies (George and Sims 2007). They argue persuasively that much of the success of these companies is down to their ability to communicate a commitment to broader goals than profit maximization. People with these values often have the capacity to identify and recruit immediate subordinates who share those values, who in turn can recruit like-minded people to work under them, and so on. The corporate conduct that emerges under such leadership is likely to be valued by both customers and employees in ways that reinforce a company's reputation. And since companies with better reputations can hire on more favorable terms and sell at higher margins, the idea that some companies could remain competitive despite serving the broader goals on our list is hardly far-fetched.

However inconclusive they are, this must bring our reflections to a close. It is of the first importance that we should be able to identify a discipline under which corporations can be brought to abide by our civic norms. The iron hand of the law, operating on its own, is unlikely to be able to impose such a discipline successfully, for the familiar reason that it casts the corporation relative to the state in the role of hare versus

---

[9] Apple has been criticized, however, for its energetic efforts to minimize its tax bills.

hound, thereby encouraging corporate evasion. And the invisible hand of the market is unlikely to be able to get corporations to abide by any civic norms other than those related to product quality and cost. We have sketched the considerations in this essay out of a hope, however faint, that the intangible hand of esteem may prove better suited to the task. We do not suppose that they establish any firm conclusion and offer them only as a starting point for further discussion.[10]

. . . .

COMMENTS AND DISCUSSION

Frank and Pettit's essay asks a basic question about the motivational psychology of firms and those who work within them: How is it that the motivations of such agents can be properly aligned with the social good? They suggest that the desire to be seen as morally virtuous by others, and the desire to deserve that perception, supports an "economy of esteem" that, under the right conditions, can sustain non-monetary incentives for virtue.

What are the conditions under which esteem effectively attaches to moral virtue?

At the Society for Progress' second assembly a number of comments focused on various factors by which the economy of esteem can become either detached from or coupled to moral virtue. Anderson noted the observation of thinkers like Hobbes, Rousseau, and Smith, that people too easily tend to admire those who are wealthy and powerful, rather than those who actually do good things. On a related note, Fuerstein pointed to the power of a parallel "sham" economy of esteem, in which large companies spin false narratives according to which their behaviors are good for society. What mechanisms are available for undercutting that kind of dynamic? Meyer observed that esteem often attaches to the performance of specific institutional roles rather than the identity of individuals considered as a whole. This suggests the need for more research exploring the kinds of organizational structures by which the economy of esteem might best be nourished as a vehicle to social good. Lingering in the background are questions about generational and cultural differences: How is technology and social media changing the way people seek and earn moral esteem? How do cultures of esteem vary across cultures and occupations?

How should we think about esteem in relation to moral motivation?

Collomb observed that the motivational psychology of esteem seems to reinforce an economic paradigm according to which moral motivations are merely instrumental: we

---

[10] This essay has been much improved as a result of the excellent discussion of an earlier draft at the meeting of the Society of Progress in London, November 2015. We are most grateful for all the comments we received.

do good only if we expect some kind of selfish reward in return. What about doing good for its own sake? On a similar note, Sen observed that the attraction that people feel to socially beneficial work is often connected to their broader life story and self-conception—"what kind of life do I want?" and "who am I?"—more than the pursuit of some kind of compensation or reward (whether in the form of esteem or money). Likewise, whether or not individuals are willing to cross moral lines for selfish gain often depends on their acceptance of moral rules that constrain or override maximizing behavior. To what extent do "economic" models of human motivation suffice for thinking about the moral tendencies of business? How might these kinds of non-economic models of moral behavior be used to supplement sociological work in institutional design?

REFERENCES

Appiah, K. A. 2010. *The Honor Code: How Moral Revolutions Happen*. New York: W.W. Norton.

Bodvarsson, O. B. and Gibson, W. A. 1994. "Gratuities and Customer Appraisal of Service: Evidence from Minnesota Restaurants." *Journal of Socioeconomics* 3: 287–302.

Brennan, G. and Pettit, P. 2004. *The Economy of Esteem: An Essay on Civil and Political Society*. Oxford: Oxford University Press.

Denning, S. 2014. "Why Tim Cook Doesn't Care about 'the Bloody ROI.'" *Forbes*, March 7.

Edwards, J. 2015. "Understanding Chipotle's Recent and Exponential Growth." *Investopedia*. <http://www.investopedia.com/articles/markets/092315/understanding-chipotles-recent-and-exponential-growth.asp>.

Elster, J. 1983. *Sour Grapes*. Cambridge: Cambridge University Press.

Frank, R. 1985. *Choosing the Right Pond*. New York: Oxford University Press.

Frank, R. 1988. *Passions within Reason: The Strategic Role of the Emotions*. New York: W.W. Norton.

Frank, R. 2004. *What Price the Moral High Ground?* Princeton: Princeton University Press.

Frank, R., Gilovich, T., and Regan, D. 1993. "The Evolution of One-Shot Cooperation." *Ethology and Sociobiology* 14: 247–56.

Frey, B. and Jegen, R. 2001. "Motivation Crowding Theory: A Survey." *Journal of Economic Surveys* 15: 589–611.

George, W. and Sims, P. 2007. *True North: Discover Your Authentic Leadership*. New York: Jossey-Bass.

Hirschman, A. O. 1977. *The Passions and the Interests: Political Arguments for Capitalism before its Triumph*. Princeton: Princeton University Press.

Hornstein, H. A., Elisa, F., and Homes, M. 1968. "Influence of a Model's Feeling about His Behavior and His Relevance as a Comparison Other on Observers' Helping Behavior." *Journal of Personality and Social Psychology* 10: 222–6.

Hume, D. 1994. *Political Essays*. Edited by K. Haakonssen. Cambridge: Cambridge University Press.

Jones, E. E. 1990. *Interpersonal Perception*. New York: Freeman.

List, C. and Pettit, P. 2011. *Group Agency: The Possibility, Design and Status of Corporate Agents*. Oxford: Oxford University Press.

Locke, J. 1975. *An Essay Concerning Human Understanding*. Oxford: Oxford University Press.

Lovejoy, A. O. 1961. *Reflections on Human Nature*. Baltimore: Johns Hopkins University Press.

McAdams, R. H. 1997. "The Origin, Development and Regulation of Norms." *Michigan Law Review* 96(2): 338–433.

Miller, D. T. and Prentice, D. A. 1996. "The Construction of Social Norms and Standards." In E. T. Higgins and A. W. Kruglanski (eds.), *Social Psychology: Handbook of Basic Principles*. New York: Guilford Press, 799–829.

Montesquieu, C. d. S. 1989. *The Spirit of the Laws*. Cambridge: Cambridge University Press.

Munger, K. and Harris, S. J. 1989. "Effects of an Observer on Handwashing in a Public Restroom." *Perceptual and Motor Skills* 69(3): 733–4.

Pettit, P. 1990. "*Virtus Normativa*: Rational Choice Perspectives." *Ethics* 100: 725–55; reprinted in P. Pettit. 2002. *Rules, Reasons, and Norms*. Oxford: Oxford University Press.

Pettit, P. 1995a. "The Cunning of Trust." *Philosophy and Public Affairs* 24: 202–25; reprinted in P. Pettit. 2002. *Rules, Reasons, and Norms*. Oxford: Oxford University Press.

Pettit, P. 1995b. "The Virtual Reality of Homo Economicus." *Monist* 78: 308–29. Expanded version in U. Maki (ed.) 2000. *The World of Economics*. Cambridge: Cambridge University Press; reprinted in P. Pettit. 2002. *Rules, Reasons, and Norms*. Oxford: Oxford University Press.

Pettit, P. 2008. "Value-Mistaken and Virtue-Mistaken Norms." In J. Kuehnelt (ed.), *Political Legitimization without Morality?* New York: Springer, 139–56.

Pettit, P. 2015. *The Robust Demands of the Good: Ethics with Attachment, Virtue and Respect*. Oxford: Oxford University Press.

Polybius. 1954. *The Histories*. Cambridge, MA: Harvard University Press.

Reinhardt, F. L. 1999. "Bringing the Environment Down to Earth." *Harvard Business Review* 17: 149–57.

Sabini, J., Siepmann, M., and Stein, J. 2001. "The Really Fundamental Attribution Error in Social Psychological Research." *Psychological Inquiry* 12: 1–15.

Smith, A. 1982. *The Theory of the Moral Sentiments*. Indianapolis, Liberty Classics.

Sunstein, C., David, S., and Ellman, L. M. 2004. "Ideological Voting on Federal Courts of Appeals: A Preliminary Investigation." *Virginia Law Review* 90: 301–54.

CHAPTER 13

....

NEW PROSPECTS FOR ORGANIZATIONAL DEMOCRACY?

How the Joint Pursuit of Social and Financial Goals Challenges Traditional Organizational Designs

....

JULIE BATTILANA, MICHAEL FUERSTEIN,
AND MIKE LEE

Abstract

The joint pursuit of commercial and societal objectives will likely require non-traditional (non-hierarchical) ways of organizing. This chapter discusses the prospects for one promising alternative: "organizational democracy." This is a flatter form characterized by distributed decision rights, a deliberative culture, and employee ownership. Other alternatives to hierarchy have emphasized individualistic values of autonomy and empowerment. In contrast, organizational democracy emphasizes the collective. Relevant work in political philosophy underlines analogous dimensions including representation, deliberation, and a collective point of view. The last point makes it different from work on solidarity and class or group interest. In multi-objective organizational democracy there are trade-offs and these are negotiated. Representation and deliberation come to the foreground. Unlike in traditional organizations, however, negotiations are not regarded as transaction costs to be minimized; rather they are brought to the foreground and cultivated. The chapter illustrates these ideas and discusses challenges and avenues for future research.

INTRODUCTION

....

FOR an extended period during the first half of the twentieth century, industrial democracy was a vibrant movement, with ideological and organizational ties to a thriving unionism. In 2015, however, things look different. While there are instances of democracy in the business landscape, hierarchical forms of organization remain dominant and organizational democracy commands only scant attention in organizational theory. The precise reasons for this trend are undoubtedly complex and bridge economic, sociological, and psychological concerns. Nonetheless, a key indicator of this trend is the dominance of the view of organizational economists that hierarchy outperforms non-hierarchical alternatives (including democracy) on grounds of economic efficiency across a wide range of contexts (Coase 1937; Williamson 1981; Ouchi 1980). The underrepresentation of democratic models compared to hierarchy would thus seem to reflect, in part, a triumph of this economic logic (e.g. Hansmann 1996).

What does the balance of arguments look like, however, when values besides efficient revenue production are brought into the picture? The question is not hypothetical. In recent years, an ever increasing number of corporations have developed and adopted socially responsible behaviors, thereby hybridizing aspects of corporate businesses and social organizations (Margolis and Walsh 2003; Kanter 2009; Porter and Kramer 2011). Particularly striking is the marked growth of social enterprises, which adopt a social mission as their principal objective but sustain themselves through commercial activities (Battilana and Lee 2014; Battilana 2015). This deliberate integration of social concerns into the value proposition of businesses—be they corporate businesses or social enterprises—is notable in its own right as a challenge to conventional conceptions of what the very practice of business is about. It is also notable, from an organizational point of view, insofar as it raises questions about what model is best suited to the integration of non-financial concerns. Does the joint pursuit of commercial and social objectives require new ways of organizing?

In this essay we argue that it does. Or at least—to put our thesis in more measured terms—we argue that the joint pursuit of financial and social objectives warrants significant rethinking of organizational democracy's merits compared both to hierarchy and to non-democratic alternatives to hierarchy. In making this argument, we draw on some parallels with political democracy: the success of political democracy as a model for integrating diverse values offers some grounds for thinking about parallel virtues in the business case. Our goal is not to offer any general prescription for organizational democracy at this stage but, instead, to argue that the merits of more democratic models of organizing deserve significant reevaluation in the context of organizations pursuing multiple objectives.

We proceed, first, by drawing on an extensive literature review to assess the way in which organizational democracy has been conceptualized in recent decades, and to document the relative lack of substantive discussion about it in comparison with some other alternatives to hierarchy. We then characterize the recent surge of socially engaged models of enterprise and press the case that this turning point warrants reconsideration of the merits of organizational democracy. We close with some reflections on the future prospects of the democratic model and the limitations of our argument.

THE NOTION OF DEMOCRACY
IN ORGANIZATION THEORY

Any exploration of democratic models of organization must begin with the understanding that hierarchy has been and remains the dominant form of organizing (Gruenfeld and Tiedens 2010; Pfeffer 2013). Organizational hierarchies are organized around two main principles: first, vertical differentiation of responsibilities and second, authority that is vested in one's hierarchical position and gives one the authority to direct, manage, reward, and punish those who hold roles below one's position in the organizational hierarchy (Jaques 1996; Weber 1947). In contrast, as we detail in what follows, organizational democracy is a flatter organizational form that is characterized by greater decision rights for employees, a special kind of organizational culture, and the possibility of employee ownership.

The Dominance of Organizational Hierarchies

The classic statement of hierarchy's rise came from Weber (1947), who saw hierarchy as a distinctly rational organizational form that enabled efficiency and operational scale. In further exploring why organizational hierarchies have become dominant, scholars across economic, sociological, and psychological disciplines have advanced a number of distinct arguments. First, economists in the transaction cost tradition have famously argued that in the presence of human-bounded rationality and opportunism, hierarchies enable firms to minimize transaction costs and maximize efficiency (Coase 1937; Williamson 1981; Jaques 1996; Simon 1947; Ouchi 1980; Pfeffer 2013; Martin et al. 2013; Zeitoun et al. 2014).

Relatedly, a second line of argument posits that hierarchies align with basic psychological drives toward status orderings (Gruenfeld and Tiedens 2010; Pfeffer 2013). Such arguments build on research showing that status orderings emerge spontaneously in groups and that such orderings are functional and even evolutionarily adaptive (Báles et al. 1951; Slater 1955; Gould 2003).

A third line of reasoning, which is rooted in organizational sociology, argues that organizations adopt hierarchy not so much out of concerns for efficiency but rather to be regarded as legitimate in their field of activity (Meyer and Rowan 1977; DiMaggio and Powell 1983). According to this line of thinking, organizational hierarchies are socially shared structures that have become so ingrained in the daily life of organizations that they are taken for granted. This makes it difficult to change them even when there is a desire and a reason to do so.

Still, despite the dominance of organizational hierarchy, organization scholars have long documented its limitations, and argued for alternatives (e.g. McGregor 1960; Ouchi and Jaeger 1978). In particular, there has been a growing call for "flatter" organizational designs that are intended to create a more flexible organization built on individual autonomy (Malone 2004; Hamel 2007). Yet surprisingly—as we will discuss—most of the discourse on alternative ways of organizing does not substantially invoke notions of democracy.

Democracy in Organization Theory: A Dormant Topic

In an effort to better understand the role of democracy in organizations, we conducted a systematic literature review of articles from peer-reviewed journals as well as a few of the leading practitioner journals.[1] We began by conducting a broad search of the following twenty-six search terms to capture alternatives to hierarchical models of organizing: democracy, corporate democracy, democratic, worker democracy, workplace democracy, worker ownership, economic democracy, industrial democracy, self-management, democratic management, democratic decision making, democratic governance, democratic organizations, non-hierarchical management, post-bureaucratic, self-managed teams, self-directed work teams, self-manage, distributed authority, decentralized authority, participatory management, worker participation, empowerment, heterarchy, network organization, flat organization. The search results from three databases produced a preliminary list of 3,661 articles. After reading through the abstracts of these articles, we selected 213 of them that dealt with alternatives to typical organizational hierarchies. We also consulted with expert scholars who specialize in the study of alternatives to typical organizational hierarchies and, following their suggestions, we included twenty-seven additional articles that are relevant to our topic, resulting in a final list of 240 articles published between 1960 and 2014.

Our systematic review of these articles revealed that while calls for less hierarchical forms of organizing have been frequent, only a small minority explicitly invoke democratic notions of organization. Of the 240 articles in our comprehensive literature review, forty-seven invoke the term "democracy" or "democratic" in the abstract or title. However, upon closer inspection, of these only twenty-seven tackle democratic

---

[1] Literature review methodology. In our effort to explain how research in organizational studies has accounted for alternatives to typical organizational hierarchies, we began by conducting a broad search in the following article databases: ABI/ProQuest, Business Source Complete, and Web of Science. We limited the search to the following thirty-seven peer-reviewed journals: *Academy of Management Journal, Academy of Management Review, Academy of Management Annals, Academy of Management Perspectives, Administrative Science Quarterly, Organization Science, Management Science, Strategic Management Journal, Organization Studies, American Sociological Review, American Journal of Sociology, Annual Review of Sociology, Social Forces, Harvard Business Review, MIT Sloan Management Review, Stanford Social Innovation Review, California Management Review, Nonprofit and Voluntary Sector Quarterly, Voluntas, World Development, Development, Global Governance, International Studies Quarterly, American Journal of Political Science, Journal of Business Ethics, Business Ethics Quarterly, Philosophy and Public Affairs, Ethics, Journal of Applied Ethics, Episteme, Business History Review, Business History, Enterprise and Society, Human Relations, Entrepreneurship Theory and Practice, Journal of Business Venturing, Strategic Entrepreneurship Journal, Journal of Social Entrepreneurship.*

forms of organizing.[2] Discourse on democracy in organizational theory has thus been relatively dormant in recent decades.

Democracy in Organizations in Recent Decades: A Multidimensional Concept

We analyzed how democracy was discussed in the twenty-seven articles in our review that invoke the term and induced three primary dimensions of organizational democracy: greater decision rights, democratic culture, and employee ownership. While the first two dimensions are discussed in the majority of the articles that tackle organizational democracy, the third one is discussed in only a small minority. Organizations may adopt more or less democratic arrangements on each of these dimensions, as we now explain.

Decision Rights

Nearly all of the twenty-seven articles in our literature review invoke the term democracy as meaning, in part, the right of employees to participate in the making of decisions that affect them. More specifically, decisions rights are the legitimate entitlement to participate in and exert influence on an organization's ongoing management (Brenkert 1992). Whereas the centralization of decision-making power characterizes hierarchies, the diffusion of decision-making power characterizes more democratic organizations (Brown 1985; Harrison and Freeman 2004).

The specific descriptions of the contours of decision rights in organizations vary in the literature based on several dimensions, including formality—spoken or unspoken (Cafferata 1982); scope—within the parameters of an individual's work or beyond (Petit 1959; Ackoff 1994); and holder—imbued to employees only or also to other stakeholders, such as suppliers and community members (Moriarty 2010; Sankowski 1981). While some organizations may formally grant authority to their employees to participate in decisions beyond their individual work, such as deciding on a new strategic orientation or helping select a new leader (Kerr 2004), other organizations only give decision-making authority to their employees within the realm of their individual work. Hsieh (2005: 116) also differentiates between "the right to contest decisions" and "a right to govern economic enterprises." Grounded in Rawls' conception of justice, he argues for the right to protection from "arbitrary interference" in the workplace (Hsieh 2008: 91). Giving some decision rights to outside stakeholders is yet another step, suggesting a process in which all affected parties are given a say in a deliberative process (Moriarty 2010; Moog et al. 2015).

---

[2] Other articles address democracy in unions, shareholder democracy, and even democracy in interorganizational alliances. While these are all valuable topics, our focus is on alternatives to the hierarchical structure that organizes employees and managers, that is, conceptions of workplace democracy, industrial democracy, or corporate democracy.

Organizational Culture

About half of the twenty-seven articles in our literature review that invoke the term democracy explicitly discuss the importance of norms or values that support democracy in organizations. These articles emphasize the importance of organizational culture in enabling democratic processes and systems. A democratic organizational culture creates space for discourse, deliberation, and negotiation (Slater and Bennis 1990). Creating and maintaining such a democratic culture is particularly important for organizations as it sustains participation through an ethos that values employees as more than cogs in a machine (Cochran 1956). Democratic cultures address the tension between individualist and community values through the idea that participation in the community is itself an important way of realizing individual potential (Manville and Ober 2003).

In democratic organizations, organizational members thus have both the right and the obligation to participate in deliberations. Interestingly, in its historical (early twentieth-century) form, industrial democracy arose from the need to protect the shared interests of manufacturing laborers, and thus was closely allied with collective bargaining powers and a conception of class identity (Derber 1970). The idea thus entailed a significant cultural emphasis on group identity and, likewise, a need to negotiate individual concerns with other members of the group. While contemporary notions of organizational democracy are no longer centered in the same way around class solidarity, many invoke a notion of citizenship that involves both rights and responsibilities to the collective (Forcadell 2005; Manville and Ober 2003).

Ownership Stakes

A minority of the twenty-seven articles that invoke the notion of organizational democracy emphasize the conception of employee ownership (for examples, see Sankowski 1981; Collins 1995; Forcadell 2005). While ownership may be concentrated in shareholders, it is not always the case. When ownership is not concentrated in shareholders but also includes employees, they have greater grounds for legitimate participation in organizational decisions, as well as a greater scope of interest beyond their narrowly defined roles (Sauser 2009). When ownership stakes exist, they can facilitate and complement a broad diffusion of decision rights and a democratic organizational culture.

Mondragón, like most cooperatives all over the world, is a well-known and well-documented modern example of an organization in which employees are also "joint owners" (Forcadell 2005: 257). As cooperative members, Mondragón workers have ownership stakes in the firm. Sharing not only in the decision making of the organization, codified in the corporate management model (Flecha and Ngai 2014), but also in profits helps Mondragón overcome "the capital-labor confrontation" (Forcadell 2005: 257; for discussion of broader-scale evidence of performance benefits of shared ownership, see Blasi et al. 2013). Shared ownership inflects an organization's ethos and the channels of decision making and conflict resolution. For example, in studying Nir taxi station in Tel Aviv, Darr (1999) describes the worker cooperative as "democratic" as all workers (also owners) elect managers for limited terms. In unpacking conflict resolution mechanisms in this cooperative, he suggests that the organization's egalitarian ethos regarding ride distribution stemmed from the founders' aim "to attribute meaning to their shared ownership of the station" (Darr 1999: 297). Accordingly, the shared ownership structure imbued legitimacy for equity claims in the cooperative, as well as for the informal and formal manifestations of conflict and resolution.

In short, notions of organizational democracy converge significantly around an organizational model involving (a) a broad diffusion of decision rights; (b) an organizational culture that entails some form of commitment to integrate individual perspectives with that of the broader organization; and finally (c), in some cases, a broad diffusion of ownership rights. Still, conceptions of organizational democracy were a relative rarity in our literature review on alternatives to hierarchy. In contrast, as we will discuss, other alternatives to hierarchy have received more attention.

THE RISE OF ALTERNATIVES TO HIERARCHIES

While hierarchy has been and continues to be the dominant form of organizing, its limitations have become increasingly acute over time, which has led to the rise of alternative forms of organizing. Three historical trends have made hierarchy's limitations particularly acute, thereby opening the door to alternatives. First, organizations today face a more dynamic, turbulent, and competitive environment than in the past, and this requires more rapidly adaptable forms of organization than hierarchies (Manz and Sims 1984; Holland and Lockett 1997; Ahuja and Carley 1999; de Leede et al. 1999; Starkey et al. 2000; Ancona et al. 2002; Martin et al. 2013) that tend to create delays in the decision-making process, and limit employee morale and incentives (Kirsch et al. 2010; Hamel 2011; Fjeldstad et al. 2012). Second, in order to adapt to today's knowledge-based economy, managers need to rely on employees to be more proactive and creative, and to solve increasingly complex, non-routine problems (Simons 1995; Adler et al. 2008; Tangirala and Ramanujam 2008; Kirsch et al. 2010; Bresman and Zellmer-Bruhn 2013). Many scholars have argued that hierarchies are not suited for this set of challenges (e.g. Adler 2001; Fjeldstad et al. 2012). Finally, the increasingly networked nature of the world has made the limits of hierarchies more acute. Characterized by well-delineated boundaries, hierarchies may no longer be a viable option for organizations as the boundaries of organizations are increasingly challenged and blurred (Davis 2010).

Given these limitations, authors have set forth various alternatives to organizational hierarchies. Building on our in-depth literature review of these alternatives, in this section we analyze the conceptions of less hierarchical forms of organization that are prevalent in the organizational literature and highlight the relative scarcity of democratic forms of organizing. Indeed, as we explain, recent conceptions of alternatives to hierarchy have tended to privilege psychological empowerment over structural empowerment and market-based designs over democratic designs. These recent trends stand in stark contrast to the relative vibrancy of the debate about workplace democracy during the industrial democracy movement of the early twentieth century. As corroborated by a Google Ngram search, the concept of industrial democracy, which enjoyed popularity in the 1910s and 1920s, has dramatically waned since. At the same time, over the last half-century, alternative conceptions of less hierarchical organizations, particularly notions of self-management, have become predominant (with a particular spike of interest in such ideas occurring in the 1980s and waning significantly thereafter).

From Structural to Psychological Empowerment

Our literature review highlights two important trends in the recent discourse on less hierarchical organizations. First, recent discourses on empowerment and employee voice have privileged notions of psychological empowerment or making employees feel more powerful rather than formal or structural empowerment. Management literature on empowerment up until the 1980s emphasized "participative management" techniques such as quality circles, management by objectives, and goal-setting by subordinates that aimed to shift formal decision-making authority within the organization (Conger and Kanungo 1988; Bennis and Nanus 1985; Kanter 1979).

However, beginning in the late 1980s, more psychological or interpretive concepts of empowerment entered the discourse. These authors argued that empowerment is not so much a matter of formal authority within an organization but is instead primarily a feature of individuals' experience or interpretation of their environment that affects their sense of self-efficacy or motivation within the organization (Conger and Kanungo 1988; Thomas and Velthouse 1990; Spreitzer 1996). In this sense, to be empowered is ultimately determined by how powerful one feels rather than simply a matter of whether one has decision-making authority. For this reason, critics or skeptics of such approaches argue that psychological empowerment is but a watered-down or softer notion of empowerment that fails to change the formal "hard" power within organizations. These critics further argue that organizational efforts to empower employees without giving them more formal power creates an illusion that employees have greater control over their circumstances when, in fact, ultimate control remains in the hands of the same people within the organization (Covaleski et al. 1998; Ezzamel and Willmott 1998; Ciulla 1998).

The Rise of Market-Oriented Notions of Organizational Design

A second noticeable feature of the discourse on alternatives to traditional organizational hierarchies evidenced in our literature review is the emphasis on market-like approaches to organizational design. Drawing on the pioneering work of Coase and Williamson, scholars have explored organizational models that combine elements of hierarchical control with elements of market control. These hybrid market-based designs are attractive in principle because they combine the benefits of hierarchical organization with the basic advantages of markets, namely, superior flexibility with respect to autonomous adaptation (Williamson 1996; Foss 2003; Zenger 2002).

Market-based approaches seek efficiencies by granting individual workers and worker-teams substantial freedom from managerial oversight within a given domain, and employing structures of internal competition among individuals to guide decision making. In one example, organizations primarily comprise project teams. Individuals have the freedom to pitch and choose which projects to work on, and projects are selected not by managers but rather by the internal market mechanism of supply and demand (Foss 2003; Wingfield 2012).

Self-managed teams, perhaps the most popular alternative to the traditional hierarchical form, represent another example of infusing a hierarchical organization with elements of market control. Such teams—which are given full autonomy over a given task, function, or project, but are measured and incentivized on the delivery of specific outputs—function under market control akin to external subcontractors (Zenger 2002).

Beyond specific design choices that mimic the market, a wide swath of the broader discourse on less hierarchical organization aligns with the ethos of markets and market-oriented notions of individual freedom. Conceptions of flexible, loosely coupled, modular, or network-based organizations comprising autonomous individuals and teams, which are frequently offered as alternatives to the traditional hierarchy (Fjeldstad et al. 2012; Bahrami 1992; Volberda 1996; Liebeskind et al. 1996), mirror the prevailing images of the market as dynamically evolving based on the decisions of independent actors.

Comparing the recent conceptions of less hierarchical organizations with the conception of organizational democracy discussed earlier, a clear distinction emerges. The recent discourse, filled with concepts such as self-management and empowerment (Kokkinidis 2015), emphasizes individualistic values of autonomy and independence, and individual psychological experience ("empowerment"). In contrast, organizational democracy seeks to grant workers substantial control over their work environment through participation in, and cultural identification with, a social collective within the organization. This collective orientation is strongest in historical models of industrial democracy (Sorge 1976), but is also evident in the emphasis of contemporary theorists on democracy's cultural elements of equality and deliberative engagement.

Is Now a Turning Point? Changes in the Objectives of Organizations

The distinctive advantage of democracy over both hierarchical and non-hierarchical alternatives, we propose, lies in its capacity to integrate diverse values in decision processes. By "integrate" we mean the process of balancing, accommodating and, in some cases, reconciling diverse values to achieve coherent and effective decision making within an organization. Given the growing need for businesses to perform this kind of value integration, we believe that more democratic approaches to organizing deserve a re-examination. We acknowledge the continuing relevance of long-standing arguments for organizational democracy that emphasize the significance of decision rights for protecting workers' interests, and likewise the intrinsic value of procedural fairness in decision making (Dahl 1985; McMahon 1994). Nonetheless, as these arguments appear more or less unaffected by the changes we discuss here, we will set them aside for the purposes of this essay in spite of their continuing importance.

There are new currents in the business world that suggest a more multifaceted value proposition for enterprise. Over the last decades, some corporations have developed and adopted socially responsible behaviors, thereby hybridizing aspects of corporate businesses and social organizations (Margolis and Walsh 2003; Kanter 2009; Porter and Kramer 2011). While historically the commercial and social sectors have evolved on fairly separate tracks, over the last thirty years we have witnessed a blurring of the boundaries between these two sectors. As noted at the beginning of this essay, the epitome of this trend is the increase in social enterprises pursuing a social mission as their primary goal, but engaging in commercial activities to sustain operations. By "social mission," we refer to an explicit, non-financial objective that plays a sustained role in guiding a firm's activities, and that is constituted by some significant aspect of human welfare. Prime examples of those kinds of objectives include access to healthcare and education, the reduction of poverty, and the promotion of social and political capabilities. The pursuit of a dual mission by an increasing number of organizations is reflected in a growing range of novel legal statuses that such organizations have adopted, such as the low-profit limited liability company (L3C) and the benefit corporation in the United States, as well as the community interest company in the United Kingdom.

Beyond these observations about the changing value-orientation of many businesses, there are the underlying concerns that have driven this change in the first place. While some businesses have been driven toward social concerns through consumer pressures, many in the social enterprise movement are driven by a moral concern for significant social failures: environmental degradation, poverty, inadequate healthcare, and other profound yet unmet social needs. In the face of such problems, there is a growing sense in the business world that enterprise can and ought to play a role in addressing such concerns more directly (Margolis and Walsh 2003). The recent financial crisis has intensified skepticism toward the model of shareholder value maximization (Battilana 2015) and made calls for an increased emphasis on the social and environmental features of business firms that have been made for some time (Courpasson and Dany 2003; Forcadell 2005; Brickson 2007) more prevalent. From this point of view, the need for businesses to integrate social, environmental, and financial values is a moral need as much as anything else.

As an increasing number of organizations aim not only to maximize shareholder value creation, but also to achieve a social mission, they face a new governance challenge: they need to pursue commercial goals while not losing sight of their social ones (Ebrahim et al. 2014). At the same time, they need to make sure that their social goals do not prevent them from generating commercial revenues. According to long-standing and more recent research in organizations, the odds are low that corporations will succeed in maintaining this delicate balance. Indeed, a long tradition of scholarship highlights the risk for organizations that follow a typical hierarchical model and their workforces of losing sight of their purpose and values in the quest for organizational survival and efficiency (Selznick 1949; Weber 1946). Further supporting this claim, recent research on social enterprises, such as commercial microfinance organizations (Battilana and Dorado 2010) and work integration social enterprises (Battilana et al. 2015), that aim at pursuing social and financial objectives, shows that the risk of mission drift (i.e. straying from their social missions in the pursuit of profit) is one of the main challenges that these organizations face, as they also have to set up and maintain effective commercial operations. Does this context create a renewed case for more democratic ways of organizing? This is the question that we tackle in the next section.

A Renewed Case for Organizational Democracy

The idea that there is a growing need for business to integrate fundamentally different types of values suggests a significant parallel with one of the core motivations for democracy in the political case. Below, we first build on the political philosophy literature to discuss the success of political democracies in integrating diverse values. We then discuss the application of lessons from the deliberative political model in business.

The Success of Political Democracies in Integrating Diverse Values

Historically, some of the most significant arguments for political democracy have revolved around the fact that just and competent governance requires managing the competing values of a diverse citizenry. We suggest that there are three core, inter-related features of political democracies by which they tend to succeed, better than alternative forms of political organization, in integrating diverse types of values. We do not hold that all of these features are fully or adequately realized in all political democracies. Nor do we hold that these features are conceptually necessary to the idea of democracy. Our suggestion is (a) that democracies have tended better than alternative political systems to integrate diverse values in decision making, and (b) that these three features play a crucial role in explaining that success where it exists. The following model loosely corresponds to the idea of "deliberative democracy" as it has been explored in political theory, and we will adopt that terminology ourselves.

Structural Representation of Diverse Values

First, political democracies allocate decision-making powers equally across members of diverse value constituencies. This best ensures the adequate representation and the fair negotiation of competing values in the process of decision making. Democracies achieve this through equal voting rights, guarantees of basic civil liberties, and representative legislative bodies. They also achieve this—to the extent that they do—through the better distribution of meaningful capabilities to participate in social and political life across diverse social groups. Examples of such capabilities include the ability to persuasively present one's views in public, access to important venues of speech, access to social influence, and access to basic economic and material conditions that enable such participation (Anderson 1999).[3]

Democracies' legally mandated decision-making powers—especially inclusive, egalitarian voting procedures—provide a mechanism through which citizens are able to represent the bearing of their values on legislative representatives and, in some cases, specific policies. Voting processes manage conflicts of value both through the substance of their outputs (as reflections of majority or plurality sentiment), and through the procedural fairness by which inputs are weighed.

But on its own voting is inadequate as an expression of diverse values. This is partly because of some well-known problems with voting procedures, such as cycling and strategic behavior (Riker 1982). More fundamentally, however, the aggregation of judgments or preferences through voting does not in itself speak to the quality of the judgments or preferences that are inputs to the system. When citizens vote on the basis of ethnic hatred, rank ignorance, or selfishness, for example, the outcome simply amplifies those pre-existing flaws in citizens' outlook (Fuerstein 2008). A crucial part of the case for democracy thus derives from the fact that the ethos and institutions of democracy facilitate due reflection on the full spectrum of moral considerations that properly bear on public decision making (Dewey 1927; Anderson 2006).

Deliberative Culture

Given the crucial role of deliberation in good decision making, political democracies depend on a culture of reasons and justification that fosters some measure of accountability in one's beliefs and uses of power. This idea is perhaps the singular dominant theme in recent democratic theory (Cohen 2002; Habermas 1996).[4]

---

[3] We are not arguing that democracies in fact succeed in all these dimensions. We are arguing that where democracies do succeed in better representing diverse value constituencies, it is in significant part because of their superiority in these dimensions.

[4] There are of course important dissenters to the deliberative democratic approach (e.g. Mouffe 2000; Sanders 1997), in spite of its general dominance. Space constraints nonetheless prevent us from exploring the main lines of objection and the most plausible responses to them. Translating these concerns from the political to the business context would of course add yet another layer of complexity.

Ongoing social deliberation is crucial to good decision making because it continually exposes citizens to the concerns of others. But the success of any deliberative process depends on the acceptance of norms of rational accountability that compel the reasoned adaptation of one's own views to others' articulated concerns. Successful deliberative cultures are domains in which rational consistency is valued, in which naked appeals to power or selfish interest are regarded as illegitimate, and in which there are significant social sanctions attached to hypocrisy in action (in other words, one's arguments are taken to provide viable constraints on one's actions) (Fuerstein 2013; Elster 1997).

The deliberative polling experiments of James Fishkin and others offer significant evidence of the potential benefits of social deliberation in improving democratic decision making (Fishkin 2009).[5] Fishkin's experiments also show the importance of background conditions that improve the significance of arguments and information over power dynamics, social tensions, and pre-existing biases (Sunstein 2003).

Public Point of View

Third, political democracies depend on the cultivation of a "public" point of view, i.e. a conception of collective identity that shapes individual behavior so as to fairly promote the good of all constituents. Thus, as much as deliberative processes depend on fidelity to rational norms, they depend more fundamentally on the extent to which citizens attach moral worth to one another and regard one another's claims as worthy of fair consideration. Likewise, the adequate cultivation of capacities to participate in deliberative exchanges depends on more general norms of inclusiveness in domains of education, employment, and social organizations more generally (Anderson 1999). In this respect, democracy depends on cultural institutions and norms that foster attitudes of respect, social trust, and mutual concern across social groups. Such attitudes are not only rational; they also involve emotional sensibilities of empathy and sympathy that enable individuals to adequately represent the proper weight of others' concerns in tempering their own political positions (Krause 2008; Morrell 2010).

This third ingredient of political democracies' success offers a particularly compelling link to more democratic models of organizing. Whereas market-based alternatives to hierarchy involve the promotion of individual autonomy and the diffusion of decision making across an organization, more democratic models of organizing seek to empower workers primarily through their participation in the exercise of collective power, and require of workers a substantial commitment to negotiating their values and preferences in light of the concerns of others. Likewise, in the political case, the idea of a "public point of view" involves the requirements of modifying individual preferences and judgments in light of concerns expressed by others. In contrast with

---

[5] Fishkin's "deliberative polling" model involves highly structured public meetings that precede electoral decisions. The meetings are governed by various rules designed to insure that all parties get an equal say, to promote respectful engagement, and to facilitate the presentation and assimilation of authoritative, relevant factual information.

economic models of political behavior (Downs 1957), deliberative models of democracy conceptualize citizens' freedom in terms of participation in the construction and negotiation of joint action (Richardson 2002).

The value of all three conditions is tightly interdependent and mutually reinforcing. A good deliberative culture requires the wide adoption of a public point of view because it requires the ability to constrain the pursuit of self-interest by a respect for others, and by a fidelity to rational norms that benefit everyone. A public point of view likewise requires a deliberative culture because individuals are inherently limited in their capacity to identify and accommodate the public good without deliberative engagement. A structural representation of competing values creates a diffusion of social power that enables diverse parties to be heard, provides aggrieved groups with real leverage in pursuing their claims, and backs norms of discourse with a legally enshrined public recognition of equal status. In this way it helps to sustain attitudes of respect and mutual regard that constitute a public point of view, and provides the basis for a deliberative culture in which all valid perspectives are taken seriously. A public point of view and a deliberative culture, at the same time, are instrumental in insuring that legally enshrined powers, such as voting rights, are matched with cultural mechanisms of social influence (the ability to persuade others, to gain access to positions of power, to develop social capital, etc.). Deliberative democracy leverages these three features in tandem.

Pursuing Lessons from the Deliberative Political Model in Business

In general form, the political model of deliberative democracy closely resembles organizational democracy as it has been understood by organizational theorists. Organizational democracy, we noted, has generally been conceptualized in terms of (a) a broad diffusion of decision rights, (b) an organizational culture that emphasizes communal or organizational values, and in some cases (c) employee ownership stakes. The deliberative and voting procedures that one finds in deliberative democracy provide a reasonable analog of (a), while the importance of a public point of view and a deliberative culture in the political model of democracy roughly correspond to (b). The most straightforward analog to (c) is the sense in which all citizens of political democracies have a clear stake in the outcomes of political decision making. They are "owners" of their society in at least that sense.

In its orientation toward the representation and integration of competing values, political democracy is nonetheless distinct from organizational democracy as it has traditionally been conceived. That is because, following the conventional logic of business organization, financial values are presumed to be dominant. On that premise, the pursuit of substantial questions of value, and the resolution of substantially competing values, are not central organizational functions. Hence they do not animate principles of institutional design in a significant way. Our suggestion is that, once we see the project of representing and integrating diverse and potentially competing values as central to business, the political analogy presents some novel advantages of democracy in the workplace.

Given limited evidence at this stage, these advantages can only be presented in a speculative, exploratory spirit. Without offering definitive conclusions or prescriptions, we make some suggestions which are grounded in evidence from one of the authors' previous work on social enterprise, combined with observations drawn from contemporary organizational theory and case studies.

Work integration social enterprises (WISEs) provide a particularly appropriate setting to examine this issue. WISEs are organizations devoted to helping the long-term unemployed move successfully back into the workforce. WISEs hire the individuals whom they are trying to help, who then produce goods that are commercially sold, with the revenues going to support the continuing operation of the organization. WISEs employ social workers who work with their beneficiaries to provide employment and training, and also employ a managerial staff that keeps its eye on the bottom line and brings goods into the commercial marketplace. Fulfilling the social mission in this case requires diverting resources toward beneficiaries' training and support, while commercial profitability requires achieving competitive quality and cost control. In this respect, WISEs present a paradigm case of organizations that depend on the integration of financial and social values, which are often in tension.

In their study of WISEs in France, Battilana et al. (2015) highlight the paradox that WISEs face: they need to have a social orientation from their inception in order to avoid losing sight of their social mission; yet this orientation risks undermining success in their commercial operations. In order to understand how WISEs can overcome this paradox, the authors pursue a comparison between two different WISEs, one of which attained notably superior measures of both social performance and economic productivity. They observe two crucial features of the successful WISE that they followed. First, the successful WISE was defined by a clear structural differentiation of responsibilities and decision-making powers across the social and commercial divisions of the organization. Social workers in this organization were responsible for the recruitment, training, and performance appraisal of employees. At the same time, professional managers with a business background were responsible for handling the sales and production of goods.

Second, in order to manage constant tensions between the two branches of the organization, the successful WISE relied on a combination of mandatory meetings and formal coordination processes to negotiate concerns from both sides. Meetings were organized around the articulation of concerns from business and social constituencies with the goal of enabling them to voice their respective concerns and of finding a mutually agreeable resolution. Likewise, formal coordination processes were used to foster successful joint planning on such matters as worker scheduling, where questions of worker productivity and performance had to be traded off against the desire to distribute opportunities for the purposes of employee growth. Such a polyarchic system

(Courpasson and Clegg 2012), in which power is invested in both business and social constituencies, contributes to the creation and maintenance of spaces of negotiation, defined as arenas of interaction that allow members of each constituency to discuss the trade-offs that they face (Battilana et al. 2015).

The two conditions that we highlighted earlier nicely mirror two of the three features of political democracy that we argued are crucial to success in the integration of diverse values. In the political case, there is a structural representation of competing values that is built into the distribution of formal and informal sources of power. In the successful WISE described earlier, there is an organizational division of labor into the firm's social and financial aspects and a corresponding equal representation of these distinct points of view in the processes by which the firm makes decisions. In the political case, decision making proceeds significantly through the deliberative negotiation of tensions among the various values at stake. Likewise, in the successful WISE, conflicts between business and social constituencies are confronted and negotiated on an ongoing basis through deliberative interactions in which concerns from both sides are addressed through reason-giving and the pooling of information.

In the political case, we suggested that deliberative democracy combines these first two elements with the wide social adoption of a public point of view. Likewise, in the social enterprise example under consideration, deliberative and formal interactions between the business and social sides are governed by a shared desire to modify the distinct objectives of each branch in light of the overall good of the organization. Much as political communities draw on historical and cultural narratives to sustain this kind of public ethos, the WISE under consideration was able to facilitate an orientation to common objectives through an array of socialization mechanisms such as company retreats, training programs, internal communications, and job shadowing. In the political case, we argued, a public ethos plays a crucial role in political democracies in enabling the benefits of a deliberative culture and the structural representation of competing values. We hypothesize that, likewise, an orientation to the overarching good and mission of a firm plays a parallel role in the success of negotiating competing types of value.

One particularly rich data point in support of this hypothesis is Ashforth and Reingen's (2014) in-depth study of the organizational tensions within a natural food cooperative. The cooperative's mission displayed the paradigm characteristics of a hybrid organization. It was devoted to advancing the social values of justice, peace, environmental sustainability, and democratic governance. And yet, at the same time, the cooperative depended on profits as a successful commercial enterprise, and a majority of its customers were non-coop members. As Ashforth and Reingen detail in depth, the conflict between these two aims was a constant source of tension among the membership, and manifested itself in the clustering of members into "idealist" and "pragmatist" groups which, roughly speaking, placed greater priority on social and commercial values respectively. The coop was nonetheless able to weather—and even benefit from—these tensions as a consequence of a shared commitment to the over-arching mission of the organization: a commercially self-sustaining grocery business that nonetheless remained faithful to considerations of justice and sustainability. That mission was ingrained in members through substantial socialization processes, and was regularly invoked in governance meetings as a way of ameliorating conflict.

Interestingly, unlike the WISE case, the coop was not defined by a strict differentiation of roles across the social/financial divide. Members nonetheless self-sorted into groups that placed a higher priority on these distinct dimensions, and regular, intensive deliberative meetings were the means through which these self-selecting groups worked to integrate their different perspectives toward a common purpose. Another notable feature of the coop case for our purposes is that, on Ashforth and Reingen's analysis, one of the crucial means by which the organization preserved its operational unity was through the regular cycling of power between the pragmatist and idealist camps. In this respect, the coop reveals a structural differentiation of power that forced both groups to accommodate the other's concerns through the exercise of equal decision-making authority.

Both of these cases broadly conform to core ideas of organizational democracy as traditionally conceived. They employ a broad diffusion of decision rights and leverage a deliberative culture that emphasizes some form of communal identity. What they draw from the political analogy, however, is a distinctive model of implementing these conditions that is calibrated to the representation and negotiation of values. Thus, a "broad diffusion of decision rights" amounts to distributing decision rights in such a way that meaningful decision power is spread across individuals whose work is animated by different value schemes. In the WISE case, this value division mapped very neatly on to role differentiation within the organization, and thus the organization's crucial feature is a division of decision power across social and financial roles. In the coop case, however, the relevant value-divisions were spread much more dynamically across various roles within the organization, and thus effective value representation involved a more generic form of egalitarian voting rights for individuals.

The WISE example illustrates particularly nicely why a wide diffusion of powers and participation is important in the business context. In that case, tensions between social and financial values play out in a highly localized way, at the level of individuals doing their daily work. Thus, in working with employees/clients, the firm's social workers must be responsive to their particular skill set, the particular difficulties of scheduling and evaluating them, and their specific path to development in the labor market. Likewise, on the financial side, managers must be responsive to a constantly changing commercial marketplace, new technologies, new competitors, etc. In this context, success in the firm's overall mission is dependent on understanding how the tension among its values plays out in its daily work. And that, in turn, requires at least the need for substantial, ongoing consultation with employees doing this work. Structurally empowering them—through formal and informal powers of participation—is, in effect, a way of ensuring that decision making is genuinely responsive to the full spectrum of relevant concerns.

With respect to culture, both the WISE and the coop very deliberately created an environment in which difficult confrontations between value orientations were central to organizational life. At the same time, they worked from a strongly cultivated ethos of shared organizational mission to negotiate these differences. Whereas historical models of organizational democracy were largely oriented toward communal ideals of class solidarity, the examples discussed here involve a fidelity to a more abstract notion of the organization and its objectives. "Community" in this context is grounded, not in some model of fraternity (as in politics), nor in interests (as in an identity of economic class); it is grounded in a shared sense of a common purpose that is believed to be worthwhile.

Our suggestion is thus not that a broad diffusion of powers is strictly necessary in this context; rather, our suggestion is that hybrid organizing—whether in social enterprises or in corporations that engage in corporate social responsibility—tends to foster a certain kind of dynamic complexity in decision-making challenges, and that managing this kind of complexity, in turn, requires a responsiveness to the diverse information and experience of employees in pursuing a firm's mission. In this respect, our argument for organizational democracy connects nicely with some of the more general arguments against hierarchy canvassed earlier. Hierarchies, we observed, are best suited to static, routinized work environments, but confront distinct challenges in contexts that require employees to adapt quickly and dynamically to changing conditions. If we are correct that the integration of financial and social values tends to create dynamic complexity in the work environment for individual workers, then that would provide a clear rationale against hierarchy.

The deliberative model of organizational democracy can also be helpfully contrasted with market-based approaches which, as we discussed earlier, prioritize the individual autonomy of workers in the sense of minimizing interference with their workplace activities. Market-based approaches seek to benefit from the initiative and creativity of workers who are free to make decisions about how best to pursue the objectives defined by their workplace role. On this approach, the ongoing attempt to negotiate one's activities by reference to the concerns and practices of others is a transaction cost that undermines efficiency, even if it is not entirely avoidable. On a market approach, thus, the deliberative negotiation of workplace aims is minimized and, likewise, the dominant ethos is one of individual initiative and "self-management" rather than participation in joint action.

Oticon, a European manufacturer of hearing devices, and Valve, a leading developer of computer games, provide a case in point. In the 1990s, Oticon became famous for adopting a market-based organizational design that it called the "spaghetti organization." Valve has earned recognition for adopting a similar approach. The basic premise of both designs is that the organizational hierarchy was drastically reduced and employees could now self-organize into projects of their own choosing rather than being assigned to projects by managers (Foss 2003; Wingfield 2012). At Oticon and Valve, the actions and preferences of individuals were coordinated not by the authority of managers, nor a deliberative process of negotiation and integration, but by the mechanism of supply and demand. The ideas that attracted the greatest demand won out. By contrast, organizational democracy emphasizes that coordinated actions be shaped by a process of deliberation about the shared objectives and activities of the firm. Such an approach enables organizations to simultaneously pursue social and financial objectives, while not losing sight of one of them.

It is worth observing that, in principle, the logic that we have advanced in favor of democracy is not limited to hybrid organizing. Even within a traditional for-profit framework, businesses must juggle a variety of local objectives that are often in tension, at least in the short term. Should an organization invest more in research and development, or should it push those resources toward marketing its existing products? Should it prioritize cost reduction or employee development? There is significant research suggesting that diversifying deliberative input is, in general, a vital route to answering well-defined questions like these (Page 2007).

While we do not deny the promise of such arguments, we wish to underscore what is distinctive about the challenge that hybrid organizing presents. In the kinds of dilemmas just described, a firm can pursue the reconciliation of competing local objectives by reference to an overarching aim: the maximization of profit. Such dilemmas thus become questions of instrumental rationality, i.e. the most efficient means to a predetermined end. In contrast, hybrid organizations must negotiate competing goals in a context where there is no predetermined aim or standard available to govern their resolution. The question of how to integrate social and financial objectives is thus a question principally about the ends which ought to be adopted.

Democracy, in this context, is a process through which diverse perspectives are recruited for the continual interpretation and reinterpretation of such "ultimate" or overarching ends. And the distinctive value of democracy here is not only that diverse sources of information are, in general, useful. It is that the expressions of tensions between social and financial objectives are sufficiently diverse that it requires ongoing consultation with individuals occupying the full plurality of organizational roles.

CHALLENGES FOR THE MODEL AND FUTURE RESEARCH DIRECTIONS

So far we have tried to do two things: first, to establish the dominance of non-democratic approaches (both hierarchical and market-based) to business organization in recent decades; and, second, to argue that recent trends in the business world give us reason to reconsider the merits of organizational democracy against non-democratic alternatives. Drawing on some salient merits of political democracy, we argued that a deliberative democratic approach plausibly captures those merits in the case of the workplace, and provides a viable framework for pursuing the merits of more democratic models of organizing.

Ultimately, this argument must be put to an empirical test, to examine whether more democratic designs better enable hybrid organizations to balance multiple objectives than traditional hierarchical designs or even non-democratic alternatives to hierarchy. As more organizations search for alternatives to traditional hierarchical designs, we believe that such empirical research will become both possible and incredibly important.

We close by first articulating what we see as the most significant challenges associated with organizational democracy. Each of these challenges raises a series of puzzles and questions that call for further research on more democratic ways of organizing and their implications for enterprises that pursue multiple objectives. Second, we highlight the potential role of new technologies in addressing these challenges. Last but not least, we discuss how well more democratic models of organizing may generalize to the full spectrum of business models across various industries and institutional contexts.

Challenges

Can Organizations that Adopt a Deliberative Democratic Approach Achieve Sufficient Efficiency to Compete in the Marketplace?

The answer to this question depends in part on what value proposition structures the relevant marketplace competition. Nothing we have said so far is directly responsive to the concern that democracy entails transaction costs that undermine financial efficiency relative to alternatives. Deliberative democracy is nothing if not costly by way of transactions. However, we have argued for the merits of the deliberative approach in a context where the value proposition is fundamentally different. Hybrid organizing requires responsiveness to the value of financial efficiency alongside social concerns. Our argument is that, given such a value proposition, more democratic models of organizing may have significant advantages relative to alternatives. Whether or not those advantages are decisive remains an open question. It might very well turn out that, in general, the costs to financial efficiency are typically so significant as to outweigh those advantages. Nonetheless, that question cannot be decided by appealing to arguments from a non-hybrid context. We need more research across industries and countries to properly address this question.

Can Democratic Cultures be Created and Maintained in Organizations?

Deliberative democratic cultures are difficult to create. First, they require an egalitarian ethos that involves the challenge of changing power structures. Argyris, in studying many organizational efforts to empower employees, notes that most efforts to change power structures fail because neither managers nor employees are sure they want empowerment. Often efforts to reduce hierarchy serve to highlight the persistence of hierarchy either through the emergence of a new hierarchy or the re-emergence of the previous hierarchy (Courpasson and Clegg 2006; Barker 1993; Argyris 1998). For example, paying particular attention to the interplay of formal and informal dynamics, Diefenbach and Sillince (2011) find that hierarchies persist and thrive even in seemingly alternative forms of organization—representative democratic, postmodern, and network organizational forms. Several keen observers argue that successfully achieving an egalitarian ethos within organizations requires special personal qualities such as wisdom, maturity, or higher orders of consciousness (Hackman 2002; Argyris 1999; Kegan 1998) that are rare. Together, these writings convey the point that organizational hierarchy is a deeply rooted social tendency that resists easy change. Further research is needed on how hierarchical power relations in organizations can be changed sustainably (Diefenbach and Sillince 2011; Nelson 2001).

Second, a deliberative approach to democratic organizing requires fostering a shared identity that necessitates overcoming well-documented tendencies for social groups to cleave apart. Classic research in social identity theory highlights how even minimal and trivial distinctions between randomly assigned subgroups reliably lead to competitive or discriminatory responses toward members randomly assigned to the outgroup (Tajfel and Turner 2007). From a psychodynamic perspective—as exhibited in the Ashforth and Reingen (2014) food coop study which we discussed earlier—groups facing internal tensions often split or disown parts of themselves that are troublesome. They then project these negative feelings or attributes on to a subgroup that is held responsible for the relevant problems. These different studies suggest how easily social divisions and conflicts emerge that pose challenges to adopting the sense of common concern critical for democratic forms of organizing. Future research will thus need to examine whether, and if so how, more democratic models of organizing can be implemented and sustained.

Third, research suggests that the ideal of rational deliberative discourse in which deliberation leads to the tempering of viewpoints and the integration of new knowledge is an ideal that is difficult (though hardly impossible) to achieve in practice. This is well documented in the political context (Carpini et al. 2004; Sunstein 2003), and one only needs to look at the current state of political discourse in the United States for evidence that a deliberative culture is not guaranteed, even in a society with a strongly democratic culture. Furthermore, research on voice and psychological safety highlights the struggle that organizations and teams encounter in seeking to learn from and integrate multiple viewpoints, because individuals often fail to speak up with critical information or defer to those with higher power or status (Edmondson 1999; Milliken and Morrison 2003). From an information processing perspective, research in confirmation bias highlights how individuals filter information to support their pre-existing beliefs, enabling individuals to cling stubbornly to beliefs even in the face of contradictory evidence (Mercier and Sperber 2011; Nickerson 1998).

Furthermore, research in groupthink and premature closure suggests that the act of integrating and negotiating conflicting viewpoints or values is a stressful and aversive experience that can lead groups to adopt a dominant viewpoint prematurely as a way of satisfying a need for closure or certainty (Esser 1998; Kruglanski et al. 2006). Finally, as they engage in these negotiations, employees may not act in the organization's best interest during deliberative decision-making processes due to political considerations that are inherent to organizational life (Pfeffer 1981). Even if they are willing to act in the organization's best interest, they may lack the exposure, training, or experience to understand "the big picture" (Harrison and Freeman 2004). Future research will thus need to explore whether, and if so how, socialization processes and systems, including training and incentive systems, can enhance employees' willingness and ability to participate in productive deliberations that are a critical component of democratic models.

Is Democratic Organizing Scalable?

Our analysis has drawn heavily on a few select examples of relatively small organizations. But what would it mean for a very large organization to implement the deliberative democratic model? How would it determine which employees should be part of which conversations? And how, ultimately, would decisions get made?

One possible model is offered by a recent organizational design innovation called Holacracy (Robertson 2015). Holacracy is a management system that democratizes the decisions of how workgroups are organized. Individuals in this system are able to propose changes to their workgroup's structure, such as creating, amending, or deleting roles, work accountabilities, and policies relevant for their workgroup(s). Authority for these types of design decisions are typically held by only the most senior executives in most organizations. But in Holacracy, the ability to participate in these decisions is distributed to the entire organization.

Holacracy has been adopted in both small and larger organizations (the largest of which employs 1,500 employees). One of the authors has intensively studied the adoption of Holacracy in an organization and found that three unique features of Holacracy may enable such democratized decisions to occur at scale. The first feature of Holacracy critical to its scalability is a highly structured discussion and deliberation process. Within Holacracy, formal "governance meetings" are called where changes to a workgroup's structure are proposed and discussed.

The structured process is designed to ensure that relevant information and input is offered on each proposal and that proposals that may cause harm will not pass. However, the highly structured nature of the discussion process helps to ensure that everyone participates and that these discussions do not take up too much time. In addition, the operative decision-rule does not require consensus; instead, it merely requires the absence of objections. This shifts the default presumption from inertia to change, making such changes easier, and yet still provides a way for the group to stop proposals that might cause harm.

A second feature that is critical to enabling democratized decisions to occur at scale in Holacracy is a clear delineation of the domains in which individuals can effect change. In Holacracy, individuals are able to propose changes only in the workgroup to which they belong. In cases requiring exceptions, representatives from a workgroup can be granted a formal decision role in another workgroup, thus enabling individuals' influence in other matters that are relevant to them while limiting the membership in each workgroup's deliberation process.

A third important factor enabling the scaling of democratized decisions in Holacracy is the existence of an organizational constitution. The process by which structural decisions are discussed and made are codified in a document called the "Constitution." This document explicitly lays out the rules by which such changes are discussed and decided upon, which increases the likelihood that such rules are consistently understood and applied throughout a large organization.

Holacracy offers one possible model for how a deliberative approach could be implemented at scale. However, further research is required on such models of organizing, and more specifically on the tools, processes, and systems that could enable democratic decision making at scale to be sustained in organizational contexts.

The Role of Technology

Does new ICT have the potential to help organizations overcome obstacles to the implementation of deliberative democratic models that we have already discussed? ICT has undeniably changed the way people work together. Some argue that ICT even makes the traditional, hierarchical way of organizing obsolete (Hedlund 1994). Indeed, observers have remarked that new digital technologies are leading to new organizational forms with fewer boundaries and less hierarchy (Fulk and DeSanctis 1995; Davis 2016a; Davis 2016b). The intraorganizational dimensions that Fulk and DeSanctis (1995) identify that are changing in response to electronic communication technologies include horizontal coordination, communication cultures, and ownership, which our three dimensions of organizational democracy echo (namely, decision rights, organizational culture, and ownership stakes). While such views do not necessarily imply the emergence of democratic forms of organization, it is not a stretch to presume that the emergence of new technologies could enable a deliberative approach, especially when we are considering scaling such designs. Scholars have made parallel suggestions in the political case (Sunstein 2001).

ICT has been shown to facilitate lateral communication, support coordination and collaboration across space and time, and lead to more decentralized decision making within firms (Fulk et al. 1995; Ahuja and Carley 1999; Argyres 1999; Kirkman et al. 2004; Hamel 2011; Briscoe 2007; Fjeldstad et al. 2012). In facilitating information sharing, ICT can also enable organizations to tap into the collective intelligence within and outside organizations (Pinsonneault and Kraemer 1997; Bonabeau 2009). Studying the case of IBM's "Innovation Ham," Bjelland and Wood (2008) describe how digital tools can enable employees to take ownership of their projects and think outside the box. By making decentralized decision making easier and helping to leverage collective intelligence, ICT can contribute to setting some of the conditions that are necessary for more democratic ways of organizing to be developed and sustained.

Yet it would be naïve to believe that technology will automatically dislodge underlying power structures in organizations. For example, in studying how a major Scandinavian automotive company implemented an electronic business system, Eriksson-Zetterquist et al. (2009) find that the new electronic system actually increased hierarchy in the company. Echoing this set of findings, Pfeffer (2013) argues that the proliferation of technologies may mask the persistent reality of organizational hierarchy. The question that arises is thus to know whether, and if so under what conditions, ICT can help develop and sustain more democratic ways of organizing. Such research will no doubt have critical implications for organizations, as ICT is becoming increasingly pervasive in most aspects of organizational life.

Generalizability

Having discussed the challenges that more democratic models of organizing face, as well as the extent to which new technologies may help address these challenges, we now need to consider the extent to which our argument extends beyond the hybrid case to the full spectrum of business models across institutional contexts. While this is an open question, we suggest that rather than think of organizations in terms of a binary of traditional versus hybrid models, we should think in terms of *degrees* of hybrid organizing. At one end of the spectrum are firms that pursue financial objectives as their dominant, exclusive goal, and pursue social values only to the extent that such values serve financial objectives (this might be the case for companies that have corporate social responsibility divisions which function primarily as a public relations arm). At the other end of that spectrum are firms that give a fundamental, primary role to social values alongside financial concerns, and that are explicitly attuned to the tension between these values. In-between is a wide range of possible configurations.

In the present business climate, as an increasing number of firms claim that they pursue a double or triple bottom line (financial, social, and environmental), hybrid organizing may be becoming the norm rather than the exception. This trend, we argue, raises new questions about the organizational forms needed to foster and sustain these multiple objectives. We expect that in cases where the social/financial tension is deepest, the relevance of the democratic model will be greatest.

Similarly, we suggest that the three elements that characterize the deliberative approach lend themselves to degrees of implementation. Rather than thinking of organizational democracy as a binary, we suggest that an ideal of democratization would be more analytically fruitful.

It is important to note that in addressing all the research questions that we have highlighted in this section, future studies will need to account not only for organizational characteristics but also for characteristics of the institutional environment in which organizations are embedded. It may be that some institutional environments have characteristics that enable the creation and maintenance of more democratic models of organizing. Legal rights for workers to participate in corporate management vary greatly across the globe, with some being anti-democratic and others facilitating workers' participation. A well-known example of a participative system is co-determination in Germany, where all corporations with more than 500 workers and all stock corporations are subject to laws that mandate the appointment of workers to firms' supervisory boards (Gorton and Schmid 2000). Another key component of the German system is works councils, required in establishments exceeding five employees, which are elected by the labor force and have formal rights to information, consultation, and negotiation (Addison et al. 2001). Future research will need to examine the role that such institutional arrangements play in the development and sustainability of democratic models of organizing.

CONCLUSION

While more democratic models of organizing might not have been effective at a time when corporations were merely aiming at maximizing shareholder value creation (i.e. maximizing on one dimension), we argue that we might have reached a turning point. As an ever increasing number of organizations—be they social enterprises or corporations—engage in hybrid organizing and pursue a triple bottom line, we propose that more democratic models of organizing may become a better fit. This is because they have the capacity to better represent and integrate diverse and competing values in decision-making processes than hierarchical and market-oriented models.

This provocative proposition needs to be empirically tested. We hope that our essay will convince organization scholars of the necessity to do so. We must not assume that everything we have learned from organization and management research about how firms can maximize shareholder value creation applies to the joint pursuit of commercial, social, and environmental objectives. Instead, we need to question these assumptions and understand the factors that enable organizations to pursue double or triple bottom lines successfully.[6]

COMMENTS AND DISCUSSION

Battilana, Fuerstein, and Lee argue that the growth of businesses that treat social objectives as primary aims warrants rethinking some traditional arguments against democratic organization. Drawing on parallels from the political case, they argue that democratic organization offers significant promise as a means of integrating financial and social objectives in decision making.

[6] We are grateful to David Courpasson, Jean-Claude Thoenig, and Jeffrey Moriarty for their thoughtful comments on earlier drafts of this essay. We would also like to thank participants from the third meeting of the Society for Progress for valuable discussion. Finally, we owe a significant debt to Shiya Wang and Marissa Kimsey, for their assistance in preparing the manuscript and conducting background research.

Can the democratic model work across diverse organizations, and how effectively does it scale to large organizations? What organizational structures and technologies offer promise in seeking a scalable democratic model?

Battilana, Fuerstein, and Lee's model of democratic organization draws on the deliberative model of political democracy, emphasizing deliberation across diverse groups organized around a shared conception of organizational aims. Much of the discussion focuses specifically on the scalability of that particular kind of model given—as Snabe and others noted at the Society for Progress' second assembly—the immense size of many corporations. One possibility, suggested by Barney, is to focus the democratic model principally within the diverse, small subgroups that pursue the daily business of most corporations. Indeed, thinking along those lines, one might want to push beyond the narrow confines of democracy itself: Risse pointed to recent work by Daniel Bell and Joseph Chan articulating a Confucian alternative to democracy that combines inclusive deliberative participation at the local level with a more hierarchical meritocracy as one moves up to positions of greater power. Pettit suggested that we might think about a "five capitals" model of businesses, where employee democracy is targeted specifically to those aspects where it is most effective/relevant: human and social capital, for example.

Another possibility is to harness the potential of technology. Is there a "platform" model, Snabe asked, that might enable large organizations to coordinate the activities of many small deliberative groups? Davis pointed to recent technological developments that enable individuals to share ideas much more rapidly in a deliberative vein and, likewise, technology that makes it easy to aggregate judgments and preferences quickly within large groups (through smartphones, for example). One particularly salient problem, Collomb noted, is that corporations must often act rapidly in response to crises or important developments. In such cases, democracy is simply too inefficient. Might technology change this fact?

Can organizational democracy work in contexts defined by friction among heterogeneous interests?

Kitcher observed that the deliberative, town hall-style models of discussion admired by Tocqueville tended to rely on the relative homogeneity and equality within the agrarian nineteenth-century United States. By contrast, businesses often seem to be characterized by a plurality of constituencies with very different kinds of interests and concerns. Is there a viable conception of shared organizational aims that is sufficiently unifying in such a context? Barney observed that firms tend to produce mission statements which are hopelessly bland and uninformative. Are there alternatives to this that would in fact serve effectively in unifying employees, non-cynically, around a sense of common mission? Walsh noted that an individual employee may often simultaneously occupy distinct stakeholder roles: he/she might be a customer, an investor, and a particular kind of employee, all at the same time. Recommending deliberation is one thing; but what kind of logic might enable such tensions to be negotiated, both for an individual and among diverse individuals within the organization? Rangan observed that, unlike political organizations, businesses seeking to satisfy social objectives must also compete within the marketplace. Does that create an inevitable pressure toward the dominance of financial objectives? Or is a genuinely integrative model possible?

REFERENCES

Ackoff, R. 1994. *The Democratic Corporation: A Radical Prescription for Recreating Corporate America and Rediscovering Success*. New York: Oxford University Press.

Addison, J. T., Schnabel, C., and Wagner, J. 2001. "Works Councils in Germany: Their Effects on Establishment Performance." *Oxford Economic Papers* 53(4): 659–94.

Adler, P. S. 2001. "Market, Hierarchy, and Trust: The Knowledge Economy and the Future of Capitalism." *Organization Science* 12(2): 215–34.

Adler, P. S., Kwon, S.-W., and Heckscher, C. 2008. "Professional Work: The Emergence of Collaborative Community." *Organization Science* 19(2): 359–76.

Ahuja, M. K. and Carley, K. M. 1999. "Network Structure in Virtual Organizations." *Organization Science* 10(6): 741–57.

Ancona, D., Bresman, H., and Kaeufer, K. 2002. "The Comparative Advantage of X-Teams." *MIT Sloan Management Review* 43(3): 33–9.

Anderson, E. 1999. "What Is the Point of Equality?" *Ethics* 109(2): 287–337.

Anderson, E. 2006. "The Epistemology of Democracy." *Episteme* 3(1–2): 8–22.

Argyres, N. S. 1999. "The Impact of Information Technology on Coordination: Evidence from the B-2 'Stealth' Bomber." *Organization Science* 10(2): 162–80.

Argyris, C. 1998. "Empowerment: The Emperor's New Clothes." *Harvard Business Review* 76(3): 98–105.

Argyris, C. 1999. *On Organizational Learning*, 2nd edition. Malden, MA: Blackwell Publishers.

Ashforth, B. E. and Reingen, P. H. 2014. "Functions of Dysfunction: Managing the Dynamics of an Organizational Duality in a Natural Food Cooperative." *Administrative Science Quarterly* 59(3): 474–516.

Bahrami, H. 1992. "The Emerging Flexible Organization: Perspectives from Silicon Valley." *California Management Review* 34(4): 33–52.

Báles, R. F., Strodtbeck, F. L., Mills, T. M., and Roseborough, M. E. 1951. "Channels of Communication in Small Groups." *American Sociological Review* 16(4): 461–8.

Barker, J. R. 1993. "Tightening the Iron Cage: Concertive Control in Self-Managing Teams." *Administrative Science Quarterly* 38(3): 408–37.

Battilana, J. 2015. "Recasting the Corporate Model: What Can Be Learned from Social Enterprises?" In S. Rangan (ed.), *Performance and Progress: Essays on Capitalism, Business, and Society*. Oxford: Oxford University Press.

Battilana, J. and Dorado, S. 2010. "Building Sustainable Hybrid Organizations: The Case of Commercial Microfinance Organizations." *Academy of Management Journal* 53(6): 1419–40.

Battilana, J. and Lee, M. 2014. "Social Enterprises As Hybrid Organization: A Review and Roadmap for Organization Studies." *Academy of Management Annals* 8(1): 397–441.

Battilana, J., Sengul, M., Pache, A.-C., and Model, J. 2015. "Harnessing Productive Tensions in Hybrid Organizations: The Case of Work Integration Social Enterprises." *Academy of Management Journal* 58(6): 1658–85.

Bennis, W. G. and Nanus, B. 1985. *Leaders: The Strategies for Taking Charge*. New York: Harper and Row.

Bjelland, O. M. and Wood, R. C. 2008. "An Inside View of IBM's 'Innovation Jam'." *MIT Sloan Management Review* 50(1): 32–40.

Blasi, J. R., Freeman, R. B., and Krus, D. L. 2013. *The Citizen's Share: Reducing Inequality in the 21st Century*. New Haven: Yale University Press.

Bonabeau, E. 2009. "Decisions 2.0: The Power of Collective Intelligence." *MIT Sloan Management Review* 50(2): 45–52.

Brenkert, G. G. 1992. "Freedom, Participation and Corporations: The Issue of Corporate (Economic) Democracy." *Business Ethics Quarterly* 2(3): 251–69.

Bresman, H. and Zellmer-Bruhn, M. 2013. "The Structural Context of Team Learning: Effects of Organizational and Team Structure on Internal and External Learning." *Organization Science* 24(4): 1120–39.

Brickson, S. L. 2007. "Organizational Identity Orientation: The Genesis of the Role of the Firm and Distinct Forms of Social Value." *Academy of Management Review* 32(3): 864–88.

Briscoe, F. 2007. "From Iron Cage to Iron Shield? How Bureaucracy Enables Temporal Flexibility for Professional Service Workers." *Organization Science* 18(2): 297–314.

Brown, L. H. 1985. "Democracy in Organizations: Membership Participation and Organizational Characteristics in U.S. Retail Food Co-operatives." *Organization Studies* 6(4): 313–34.

Cafferata, G. L. 1982. "The Building of Democratic Organizations: An Embryological Metaphor." *Administrative Science Quarterly* 27(2): 280–303.

Carpini, M. X. D., Cook, F. L., and Jacobs, L. R. 2004. "Public Deliberations, Discursive Participation and Citizen Engagement: A Review of the Empirical Literature." *Annual Review of Political Science* 7: 315–44.

Ciulla, J. B. 1998. "Leadership and the Problem of Bogus Empowerment." In J. B. Ciulla (ed.), *Ethics: The Heart of Leadership*. Westport, CT: Quorum Books.

Coase, R. H. 1937. "The Nature of the Firm." *Economica* 4(16): 386–405.

Cochran, T. C. 1956. "Business and the Democratic Tradition." *Harvard Business Review* 34(2): 39–48.

Cohen, J. 2002. "Deliberation and Democratic Legitimacy." In D. Estlund (ed.), *Democracy*. Malden, MA: Blackwell Publishers.

Collins, D. 1995. "A Socio-Political Theory of Workplace Democracy: Class Conflict, Constituent Reactions and Organizational Outcomes at a Gainsharing Facility." *Organization Science* 6(6): 628–44.

Conger, J. A. and Kanungo, R. N. 1988. "The Empowerment Process: Integrating Theory and Practice." *Academy of Management Review* 13(3): 471–82.

Courpasson, D. and Clegg, S. 2006. "Dissolving the Iron Cages? Tocqueville, Michels, Bureaucracy and the Perpetuation of Elite Power." *Organization Studies* 13(3): 319–43.

Courpasson, D. and Clegg, S. 2012. "The Polyarchic Bureaucracy: Cooperative Resistance in the Workplace and the Construction of a New Political Structure of Organizations." In D. Courpasson, D. Golsorkhi, and J. J. Sallaz (eds.), *Rethinking Power in Organizations, Institutions, and Markets: Research in the Sociology of Organizations*, 34. Bingley: Emerald Group Publishing.

Courpasson, D. and Dany, F. 2003. "Indifference or Obedience? Business Firms as Democratic Hybrids." *Organization Studies* 24(8): 1231–60.

Covaleski, M. A., Dirsmith, M. W., Heian, J. B., and Samuel, S. 1998. "The Calculated and the Avowed: Techniques of Discipline and Struggles over Identity in Big Six Public Accounting Firms." *Administrative Science Quarterly* 43(2): 293–327.

Dahl, R. A. 1985. *A Preface to Economic Democracy*. Berkeley: University of California Press.

Darr, A. 1999. "Conflict and Conflict Resolution in a Cooperative: The Case of the Nir Taxi Station." *Human Relations* 52(3): 279–301.

Davis, G. F. 2010. "After the Ownership Society: Another World is Possible." In M. Lounsbury and P. M. Hirsch (eds.), *Markets on Trial: The Economic Sociology of the U.S. Financial Crisis: Research in the Sociology of Organizations*, 30B. Bingley: Emerald Group Publishing.

Davis, G. F. 2016a. *The Vanishing American Corporation: Navigating the Hazards of a New Economy*. San Francisco: Berrett-Koehler Publishers.

Davis, G. F. 2016b. "Can an Economy Survive Without Corporations? Technology and Robust Organizational Alternatives." *Academy of Management Perspectives* 30(2): 129–40.

de Leede, J., Nijhof, A. H. J., and Fisscher, O. A. M. 1999. "The Myth of Self-Managing Teams: A Reflection on the Allocation of Responsibilities between Individuals, Teams and the Organisation." *Journal of Business Ethics* 21(2): 203–15.

Derber, M. 1970. *The American Idea of Industrial Democracy*. Urbana, IL: University of Illinois Press.

Dewey, J. 1927. *The Public and Its Problems*. New York: H. Holt and Company.

Diefenbach, T. and Sillince, J. A. A. 2011. "Formal and Informal Hierarchy in Different Types of Organization." *Organization Studies* 32(11): 1515–37.

DiMaggio, P. J. and Powell, W. W. 1983. "The Iron Cage Revisited: Institutional Isomorphism and Collective Rationality in Organizational Fields." *American Sociological Review* 48(2): 147–60.

Downs, A. 1957. "An Economic Theory of Political Action in a Democracy." *Journal of Political Economy* 65(2): 135–50.

Ebrahim, A., Battilana, J., and Mair, J. 2014. "The Governance of Social Enterprises: Mission Drift and Accountability Challenges in Hybrid Organizations." *Research in Organizational Behavior* 34: 81–100.

Edmondson, A. C. 1999. "Psychological Safety and Learning Behavior in Work Teams." *Administrative Science Quarterly* 44(2): 350–83.

Elster, J. 1997. "The Market and the Forum: Three Varieties of Political Theory." In R. E. Goodin and P. Pettit (eds.), *Contemporary Political Philosophy: An Anthology*. Oxford and Cambridge, MA: Blackwell Publishers.

Eriksson-Zetterquist, U., Lindberg, K., and Styhre, A. 2009. "When the Good Times are Over: Professionals Encountering New Technology." *Human Relations* 62(8): 1145–70.

Esser, J. K. 1998. "Alive and Well after 25 Years: A Review of Groupthink Research." *Organizational Behavior and Human Decision Processes* 73(2): 116–41.

Ezzamel, M. and Willmott, H. 1998. "Accounting for Teamwork: A Critical Study of Group-Based Systems of Organizational Control." *Administrative Science Quarterly* 43(2): 358–96.

Fishkin, J. S. 2009. *When the People Speak: Deliberative Democracy and Public Consultation*. Oxford; New York: Oxford University Press.

Fjeldstad, O. D., Snow, C. C., Miles, R. E., and Lettl, C. 2012. "The Architecture of Collaboration." *Strategic Management Journal* 33(6): 734–50.

Flecha, R. and Ngai, P. 2014. "The Challenge for Mondragón: Searching for the Cooperative Values in times of Internationalization." *Organization* 21(5): 666–82.

Forcadell, F. J. 2005. "Democracy, Cooperation and Business Success: The Case of Mondragón Corporación Cooperativa." *Journal of Business Ethics* 56(3): 255–74.

Foss, N. J. 2003. "Selective Intervention and Internal Hybrids: Interpreting and Learning from the Rise and Decline of the Oticon Spaghetti Organization." *Organization Science* 14(3): 331–49.

Fuerstein, M. 2008. "Epistemic Democracy and the Social Character of Knowledge." *Episteme* 5(1): 74–93.

Fuerstein, M. 2013. "Epistemic Trust and Liberal Justification." *Journal of Political Philosophy* 21(2): 179–99.

Fulk, J. and DeSanctis, G. 1995. "Electronic Communication and Changing Organizational Forms." *Organization Science* 6(4): 337–49.

Fulk, J., Schmitz, J., and Ryu, D. 1995. "Cognitive Elements in the Social Construction of Technology." *Management Communication Quarterly* 8(3): 259–88.

Gorton, G. and Schmid, F. 2000. "Class Struggle inside the Firm." National Bureau of Economic Research Working Paper No. 7945.

Gould, R. V. 2003. *Collision of Wills: How Ambiguity about Social Rank Breeds Conflict.* Chicago: University of Chicago Press.

Gruenfeld, D. H. and Tiedens, L. Z. 2010. "Organizational Preferences and their Consequences." In S. T. Fiske, D. T. Gilbert, and G. Lindzey (eds.), *Handbook of Social Psychology.* Hoboken, NJ: John Wiley and Sons.

Habermas, J. 1996. *Between Facts and Norms: Contributions to a Discourse Theory of Law and Democracy.* Cambridge, MA: MIT Press.

Hackman, J. R. 2002. *Leading Teams: Setting the Stage for Great Performances.* Boston: Harvard Business School Press.

Hamel, G. 2007. *The Future of Management.* Boston: Harvard Business Review Press.

Hamel, G. 2011. "First, Let's Fire All the Managers." *Harvard Business Review* 89(12): 48–60.

Hansmann, H. 1996. *The Ownership of Enterprise.* Cambridge, MA: Harvard University Press.

Harrison, J. S. and Freeman, R. E. 2004. "Is Organizational Democracy Worth the Effort?" *Academy of Management Executive* 18(3): 49–53.

Hedlund, G. 1994. "A Model of Knowledge Management and the N-Form Corporation." *Strategic Management Journal* 15(S2): 73–90.

Holland, C. P. and Lockett, A. G. 1997. "Mixed Mode Network Structures: The Strategic Use of Electronic Communication by Organizations." *Organization Science* 8(5): 475–88.

Hsieh, N.-H. 2005. "Rawlsian Justice and Workplace Republicanism." *Social Theory and Practice* 31(1): 115–42.

Hsieh, N.-H. 2008. "Survey Article: Justice in Production." *Journal of Political Philosophy* 16(1): 72–100.

Jaques, E. 1996. *Requisite Organization: A Total System for Effective Managerial Organization and Managerial Leadership for the 21st Century.* Rockville, MD: Cason Hall and Co. Publishers.

Kanter, R. M. 1979. "Power Failure in Management Circuits." *Harvard Business Review* 57(4): 65–75.

Kanter, R. M. 2009. "Mergers that Stick." *Harvard Business Review* 87(10): 121–5.

Kegan, R. 1998. *In Over Our Heads: The Mental Demands of Modern Life.* Cambridge, MA: Harvard University Press.

Kerr, J. L. 2004. "The Limits of Organizational Democracy." *Academy of Management Executive* 18(3): 81–95.

Kirkman, B. L., Rosen, B., Tesluk, P. E., and Gibson, C. B. 2004. "The Impact of Team Empowerment on Virtual Team Performance: The Moderating Role of Face-to-Face Interaction." *Academy of Management Journal* 47(2): 175–92.

Kirsch, L. J., Ko, D.-G., and Haney, M. H. 2010. "Investigating the Antecedents of Team-Based Clan Control: Adding Social Capital as a Predictor." *Organization Science* 21(2): 469–89.

Kokkinidis, G. 2015. "Spaces of Possibilities: Workers' Self-Management in Greece." *Organization* 22(6): 847–71.

Krause, S. R. 2008. *Civil Passions: Moral Sentiment and Democratic Deliberation*. Princeton: Princeton University Press.

Kruglanski, A. W., Pierro, A., Mannetti, L., and De Grada, E. 2006. "Groups as Epistemic Providers: Need for Closure and the Unfolding of Group-Centrism." *Psychological Review* 113(1): 84–100.

Liebeskind, J. P., Oliver, A. L., Zucker, L., and Brewer, M. 1996. "Social Networks, Learning, and Flexibility: Sourcing Scientific Knowledge in New Biotechnology Firms." *Organization Science* 7(4): 428–43.

Malone, T. W. 2004. *The Future of Work: How the New Order of Business Will Shape Your Organization, Your Management Style, and Your Life*. Boston: Harvard Business School Press.

Manville, B. and Ober, J. 2003. "Beyond Empowerment: Building a Company of Citizens." *Harvard Business Review* 81(1): 48–53.

Manz, C. C. and Sims, H. P. 1984. "Searching for the Unleader: Organizational Member Views on Leading Self-Managed Groups." *Human Relations* 37(5): 409–24.

Margolis, J. D. and Walsh, J. P. 2003. "Misery Loves Companies: Rethinking Social Initiatives by Business." *Administrative Science Quarterly* 48(2): 268–305.

Martin, S. L., Liao, H., and Campbell, E. M. 2013. "Directive Versus Empowering Leadership: A Field Experiment Comparing Impacts on Task Proficiency and Proactivity." *Academy of Management Journal* 56(5): 1372–95.

McGregor, D. 1960. *The Human Side of Enterprise*. New York: McGraw-Hill.

McMahon, C. 1994. *Authority and Democracy: A General Theory of Government and Management*. Princeton: Princeton University Press.

Mercier, H. and Sperber, D. 2011. "Why Do Humans Reason? Arguments for an Argumentative Theory." *Behavioral and Brain Sciences* 34(2): 57–74.

Meyer, J. W. and Rowan, B. 1977. "Institutionalized Organizations: Formal Structure as Myth and Ceremony." *American Journal of Sociology* 83(2): 340–63.

Milliken, F. J. and Morrison, E. W. 2003. "Shades of Silence: Emerging Themes and Future Directions for Research on Silence in Organizations." *Journal of Management Studies* 40(6): 1563–8.

Moog, S., Spicer, A., and Bohm, S. 2015. "The Politics of Multi-Stakeholder Initiatives: The Crisis of the Forest Stewardship Council." *Journal of Business Ethics* 128(3): 469–93.

Moriarty, J. 2010. "Participation in the Workplace: Are Employees Special?" *Journal of Business Ethics* 92(3): 373–84.

Morrell, M. E. 2010. *Empathy and Democracy: Feeling, Thinking, and Deliberation*. University Park, PA: Pennsylvania State University Press.

Mouffe, C. 2000. *The Democratic Paradox*. New York: Verso.

Nelson, R. E. 2001. "On the Shape of Verbal Networks in Organizations." *Organization Studies* 22(5): 797–823.

Nickerson, R. S. 1998. "Confirmation Bias: A Ubiquitous Phenomenon in Many Guises." *Review of General Psychology* 2(2): 175–220.

Ouchi, W. G. 1980. "Markets, Bureaucracies, and Clans." *Administrative Science Quarterly* 25(1): 129–41.

Ouchi, W. G. and Jaeger, A. M. 1978. "Type Z Organization: Stability in the Midst of Mobility." *Academy of Management Review* 3(2): 305–14.

Page, S. E. 2007. *The Difference: How the Power of Diversity Creates Better Groups, Firms, Schools, and Societies*. Princeton: Princeton University Press.

Petit, T. A. 1959. "Industrial Democracy, Worker Status, and Economic-Efficiency." *California Management Review* 1(2): 66–75.

Pfeffer, J. 1981. *Power in Organizations*. Marshfield, MA: Pitman.

Pfeffer, J. 2013. "You're Still the Same: Why Theories of Power Hold over Time and across Contexts." *Academy of Management Perspectives* 27(4): 269–80.

Pinsonneault, A. and Kraemer, K. L. 1997. "Middle Management Downsizing: An Empirical Investigation of the Impact of Information Technology." *Management Science* 43(5): 659–79.

Porter, M. E. and Kramer, M. R. 2011. "Creating Shared Value." *Harvard Business Review* 89(1): 62–77.

Richardson, H. S. 2002. *Democratic Autonomy: Public Reasoning about the Ends of Policy*. Oxford and New York: Oxford University Press.

Riker, W. H. 1982. *Liberalism against Populism: A Confrontation between the Theory of Democracy and the Theory of Social Choice*. San Francisco: W. H. Freeman.

Robertson, B. J. 2015. *Holacracy: The New Management System for a Rapidly Changing World*. New York: Henry Holt and Company.

Sanders, L. M. 1997. "Against Deliberation." *Political Theory* 25(3): 347–76.

Sankowski, E. 1981. "Freedom, Work, and the Scope of Democracy." *Ethics* 91(2): 228–42.

Sauser, W. I. 2009. "Sustaining Employee Owned Companies: Seven Recommendations." *Journal of Business Ethics* 84(2): 151–64.

Selznick, P. 1949. *TVA and the Grass Roots: A Study in the Sociology of Formal Organization*. Berkeley; Los Angeles: University of California Press.

Simon, H. A. 1947. *Administrative Behavior: A Study of Decision-Making Processes in Administrative Organization*. New York: Macmillan Co.

Simons, R. 1995. "Control in an Age of Empowerment." *Harvard Business Review* 73(2): 80–8.

Slater, P. E. 1955. "Role Differentiation in Small Groups." *American Sociological Review* 20(3): 300–10.

Slater, P. E. and Bennis, W. G. 1990. "Democracy Is Inevitable." *Harvard Business Review* 68(5): 167–76.

Sorge, A. 1976. "The Evolution of Industrial Democracy in the Countries of the European Community." *British Journal of Industrial Relations* 14(1): 274–94.

Spreitzer, G. M. 1996. "Social Structural Characteristics of Psychological Empowerment." *Academy of Management Journal* 39(2): 483–504.

Starkey, K., Barnatt, C., and Tempest, S. 2000. "Beyond Networks and Hierarchies: Latent Organizations in the UK Television Industry." *Organization Science* 11(3): 299–305.

Sunstein, C. R. 2001. *Republic.com*. Princeton: Princeton University Press.

Sunstein, C. R. 2003. *Why Societies Need Dissent*. Cambridge, MA: Harvard University Press.

Tajfel, H. and Turner, J. C. 2007. "The Social Identity Theory of Intergroup Behavior." In W. B. Gudykunst and Y. Y. Kim (eds.), *Readings on Communicating with Strangers*. Boston: McGraw-Hill.

Tangirala, S. and Ramanujam, R. 2008. "Exploring Nonlinearity in Employee Voice: The Effects of Personal Control and Organizational Identification." *Academy of Management Journal* 51(6): 1189–203.

Thomas, K. W. and Velthouse, B. A. 1990. "Cognitive Elements of Empowerment: An Interpretive Model of Intrinsic Task Motivation." *Academy of Management Review* 15(4): 666–81.

Volberda, H. W. 1996. "Toward the Flexible Form: How to Remain Vital in Hypercompetitive Environments." *Organization Science* 7(4): 359–74.

Weber, M. 1946. *Essays in Sociology*. New York: Oxford University Press.

Weber, M. 1947. *The Theory of Social and Economic Organization*. New York: Oxford University Press.

Williamson, O. E. 1981. "The Economics of Organization: The Transaction Cost Approach." *American Journal of Sociology* 87(3): 548–77.

Williamson, O. E. 1996. "Transaction Cost Economics and the Carnegie Connection." *Journal of Economic Behavior and Organization* 31(2): 149–55.

Wingfield, N. 2012. "Valve, a Video Game Maker with Few Rules." *New York Times*, September 8.

Zeitoun, H., Osterloh, M., and Frey, B. S. 2014. "Learning from Ancient Athens: Demarchy and Corporate Governance." *Academy of Management Perspectives* 28(1): 1–14.

Zenger, T. R. 2002. "Crafting Internal Hybrids: Complementarities, Common Change Initiatives, and the Team-Based Organization." *International Journal of the Economics of Business* 9(1): 79–95.

CHAPTER 14

PHILANTHROPY AND INCOME INEQUALITY

ELIZABETH ANDERSON, ING-HAW CHENG,
AND HARRISON HONG

Abstract

Bill Gates recently argued that philanthropy by households at the top of the income distribution might help ameliorate income inequality, and that tax policies should take this into account. Much of the research in economics on giving has been focused on middle-income households, so very little is known about the motives for giving by the very rich. The chapter provides some initial evidence on what drives the giving of the richest Americans. First, it extrapolates anthropological evidence on how status concerns might influence philanthropy. Second, since the richest own a significant amount of equity, the Jobs and Growth Tax Relief Act of 2003 is used to see how their giving responded to unanticipated tax cuts, particularly for dividends. Third, the chapter considers the welfare implications of philanthropy as opposed to alternative models for redistributing the wealth of the extremely rich.

INTRODUCTION

In response to rising concerns about income inequality and proposals for higher capital gains taxes to address these inequities (Piketty 2014), Bill Gates, the world's second richest man and biggest philanthropist, points out the need to distinguish between wealthy households that merely consume their wealth versus those that give it back in the form of philanthropy (Gates 2014). His argument is that capital gains or other forms of wealth taxes are potentially inefficient to the extent that they impede incentives for households to accumulate wealth, which ultimately will be redistributed in the form of philanthropy.

Gates (2014) argues:

> Philanthropy also can be an important part of the solution set. It's too bad that Piketty (2014) devotes so little space to it. A century and a quarter ago, Andrew Carnegie was a lonely voice encouraging his wealthy peers to give back substantial

portions of their wealth. Today, a growing number of very wealthy people are pledging to do just that. Philanthropy done well not only produces direct benefits for society, it also reduces dynastic wealth.

His argument is not easily dismissed for a few reasons. First, his own philanthropic efforts in giving away the vast majority of his $50 billion dollar fortune through the Gates Foundation has dramatically increased funding in areas of high need, particularly global health. A *Lancet* (2009) editorial writes:

> The massive boost to global health funding that the Bill & Melinda Gates Foundation has given since its inception in 1994 is astonishing. The Foundation's current expenditure of around US$3 billion annually has challenged the world to think big and to be more ambitious about what can be done to save lives in low-income settings. The Gates Foundation has added renewed dynamism, credibility, and attractiveness to global health.

Second, his efforts with Warren Buffet in getting their fellow billionaires to pledge to give away their wealth has also been moderately successful. To date, 20 percent of the Forbes 400 billionaires have signed on to the Gates–Buffet pledge to give away most of their wealth to philanthropy. Third, aggregate numbers indicate, as we will show, that giving on the part of the top 5 percent of the income distribution accounts for nearly 40 percent of total individual giving each year.

Hence, understanding what drives giving by households at the top of the income distribution is important in the debate over income inequality. Yet, most work within economics has focused on giving by middle-income households (List 2011; Andreoni 1990). The main conclusion, obtained predominantly via laboratory experiments, is that individual giving is mostly driven by the "warm-glow benefits" derived from the provision of public goods. Similar to the paradox of voting, given how small an effect an individual has in terms of his voting on outcomes or giving small amounts in affecting public goods outcomes, the literature has concluded that individual giving is puzzling unless individuals derive intrinsic utility, labeled warm-glow benefits, from their altruism.

For the top income households, two other factors beyond warm-glow benefits are likely to be important determinants of their giving. First, giving by the top 1 percent is more visible and so generates prestige or status effects. For instance, universities name new buildings after the donors who fund them. Each time a new billionaire follows the Gates–Buffet pledge to give away their wealth, it is followed by some media coverage. Databases, such as the Million Dollar List of publicly announced philanthropic donations of at least that amount, testify to the ubiquity of publicity for large gifts (U.S. Trust and Lilly Family School of Philanthropy at Indiana University 2014).

Second, taxes are expected to affect giving. There is plentiful evidence that the top 1 percent are much more strategic in tax planning, as evidenced by the wide use of off-shore tax havens (Zucman 2013). Importantly, philanthropy is tax-deductible and hence the relative prices of consumption and giving are different for rich households than middle-income households.

In this essay, we provide some preliminary evidence on both of these motivations. We start by providing some summary statistics and aggregate trends in giving broken down by household giving, bequests, foundations, and corporations. Household giving constitutes the bulk of philanthropy each year—around 75 percent—in the United States. Our analysis here also shows, using the Survey of Consumer Finances (SCF) data on household net worth and giving, that the top 5 percent of households in the income distribution provide the bulk of household giving each year.

We then argue that another important household motive for giving beyond altruism is competition for status or prestige. Much earlier work in the domain of status and positional goods (see Heffetz and Frank 2008 for a review of this large literature) has made a similar argument for middle-income households. This literature has explained, for instance, why volunteering, which is more visible, might be a more high-status way of giving, since household giving tends to involve small sums. Of course, giving by the top 5 percent of households is very different in that the sums involved are often extremely large. For instance, the typical donation each year by households in the top 1 percent is nearly $500,000. We argue that anthropological evidence on "Big Man" societies offers compelling additional evidence for status competition as a key motive for giving by the richest households.

We then utilize the Jobs and Growth Tax Relief Act of 2003 (commonly known as the 2003 Dividend Tax Cut or the Bush Tax Cuts), which raised the effective ownership stakes of shareholders by cutting the highest statutory dividend tax rate from 35 percent to 15 percent. This tax cut is likely to affect the richest households who own stocks, and had a particularly strong effect on the after-tax ownership of top executives because they are exposed to the maximum statutory tax rate, unlike other large shareholders who can filter ownership through tax-advantaged accounts. These top executives are also likely to be among households in the top of the income distribution.

Chetty and Saez (2004) argue that the tax cut was unanticipated and led to a surge in dividend payouts. These dividend payouts were unlikely to have come from reductions in productive investment, because most corporate investment models predict that productive investment should weakly increase following the tax cut. Instead, Cheng et al. (2013) show that the tax cut led managers to substitute away from perk projects toward dividends after their effective ownership stakes increased. Consistent with their agency perspective, evidence from Poterba (2004), Auerbach and Hassett (2005), and Cheng et al. (2013) point to higher equity prices as a result of the tax cut.

By examining how the tax cut affected the giving of very rich households, we shed light on the potential influence of taxes on their giving. We expect the richest to give more after the 2003 Dividend Tax Cut for a few reasons. First, there is an income effect associated with the tax cuts, though such an income effect is unlikely to be important for the richest households, since they still give a relatively small fraction of their wealth or income each year. Second, there is the altruism or warm-glow effect, which would also suggest that the richest households should give more with the tax cut if they thought that the rest of society was now poorer and could not afford as much in the way of public goods. Third, status competition would also tend to amplify these underlying effects.

On the other hand, there are two substitution effects with tax cuts that would lead to less giving. First, a tax cut also lowers the income tax burden. To the extent that households are giving as a means to alleviate tax burdens, a tax cut can lead to less giving because the relative price of giving versus consumption has changed. Second, along with the dividend tax cut, there was also a temporary abatement of estate taxes, which might have confounding effects. The effect of estate taxes is less clear and created uncertainty for estates and their tax planning which might have impeded any decisions on giving (see, e.g., Harrison 2007). Additionally, temporary relief from estate taxes might have also led households to make more intergenerational bequests rather than philanthropy.

Using the SCF data, which samples households, including those at the top of the income distribution, every three years, we examine how giving by the richest households in 2003 and 2006 compared to giving in 2000. The 2003 Bush Tax Cuts, which were passed by Congress in the middle of 2003, applied to tax returns filed in 2003. We are observing the net of income effects, altruism, status effects, and substitution effects associated with the tax cuts. We find that there is little change in giving across these two cohorts. If anything, we find that the richest households that are stockholders—the ones most likely to get the 2003 Dividend Tax Cut windfall—decreased their giving. Our findings suggest that substitution effects dominate income effects associated with these tax cuts, even in the presence of strong motives for giving associated with altruism and status.

One worry is that we are only observing cross sections of households over time, as opposed to a panel of households where we can track changes in individual giving. Nonetheless, we think that it is not obvious why there would be sampling bias, and the fact that aggregates do not go up is nonetheless important. In short, Gates is right that tax policies matter for philanthropy. But his narrative implicitly assumes that income effects dominate substitution effects, when in fact the substitution effects associated with tax policies are first order when philanthropy is already subsidized in the tax code.

Our essay proceeds as follows. In the next section, we provide key summary statistics on individual giving and giving among the richest households. In section three, we provide anthropological evidence on the importance of prestige in giving by the richest households. In section four, we discuss the results associated with the 2003 Bush Tax Cuts. In section five, we consider the welfare effects of philanthropy, how they could be improved by changing the economy of esteem among the rich, and how philanthropy stands in relation to other means of redistributing the wealth of the rich.

AGGREGATE NUMBERS AND TRENDS OF INDIVIDUAL GIVING

We start with summary statistics from Giving USA Foundation on the relative importance of individual giving compared to other sources of giving, including corporations, foundations, and bequests (Giving USA Foundation 2015). Giving USA separates out Bequests from Individual Giving, but both sources together better approximates total individual giving. It is clear from Figure 14.1 that individuals constitute the bulk of individual annual giving. In real 2014 dollars, individual giving rises from $220 billion in 1999 to $264 billion in 2006, and is far greater than any other source of giving. Corporate giving fluctuates between $15 and $18 billion a year. Foundation giving ranges from

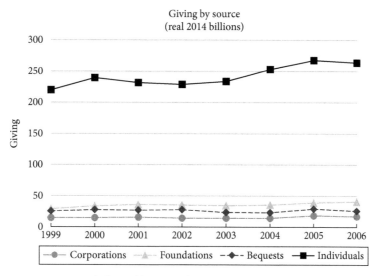

FIGURE 14.1. Annual charitable giving by source (real 2014 dollars in billions)

Source: Data tables of the Giving USA 2015 annual report.

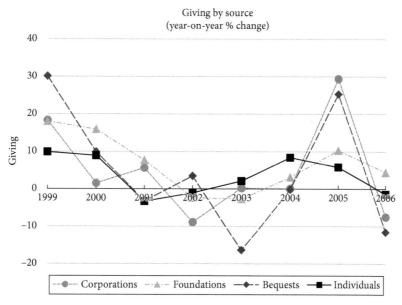

FIGURE 14.2. Year-on-year change in annual giving, by source (1999–2006, %)

Source: Data tables of the Giving USA 2015 annual report.

$30 to $40 billion each year. Bequests range from $20 to $30 billion each year. Of the total annual giving in 2006, individual giving comprises 75 percent of this total.

Over our eight-year period, total individual giving across all the years sums to around $2 trillion. In Figure 14.2, we show annual growth rates using the same Giving USA data. Over our sample period, growth rates fluctuate for all four sources of giving. The average annual growth rate for individual giving is 3.6 percent during this period.

Table 14.1. Charitable giving by high net worth households

Panel A: Giving in 2000 from 2001 SCF

Top %, SCF	Top %, population	Minimum net worth ($ million)	Total giving ($ billion)	% of all giving	% households that give	Average gift ($ thousand)
0–5	0.00–0.04	58.00	16.3	6.7	96.8	423.7
5–10	0.04–0.28	21.80	31.6	13.1	95.3	123.7
10–15	0.28–1.06	10.00	20.7	8.6	94.6	25.0
15–20	1.06–2.47	4.53	34.8	14.4	90.5	23.1
20–25	2.47–4.52	2.52	15.0	6.2	85.6	6.9
25–30	4.52–8.21	1.54	12.8	5.3	78.3	3.2
0–30	0.00–8.21		131.2	54.3	84.3	15.0
All SCF			241.6		39.1	2.3

Panel B: Giving in 2003 from 2004 SCF

Top %, SCF	Top %, population	Minimum net worth ($ million)	Total giving ($ billion)	% of all giving	% households that give	Average gift ($ thousand)
0–5	0.00–0.04	73.90	16.5	7.4	96.8	418.6
5–10	0.04–0.21	25.70	16.5	7.4	96.3	83.0
10–15	0.21–0.85	11.20	24.3	11.0	97.4	34.1
15–20	0.85–2.18	4.79	23.0	10.3	90.0	15.4
20–25	2.18–4.56	2.46	18.0	8.1	85.8	6.8
25–30	4.56–8.58	1.47	13.6	6.1	69.3	3.0
0–30	0.00–8.58		111.9	50.4	79.9	11.6
All SCF			222.1		38.6	2.0

Panel C: Giving in 2006 from 2007 SCF

Top %, SCF	Top %, population	Minimum net worth ($ million)	Total giving ($ billion)	% of all giving	% households that give	Average gift ($ thousand)
0–5	0.00–0.04	73.30	20.4	8.6	99.0	453.7
5–10	0.04–0.21	25.60	16.9	7.1	95.1	86.6
10–15	0.21–0.92	11.40	29.9	12.6	95.9	36.4
15–20	0.92–2.09	5.61	23.4	9.8	94.8	17.1
20–25	2.09–3.99	3.06	19.8	8.3	84.2	9.0
25–30	3.99–6.59	1.66	15.0	6.3	83.8	5.0
0–30			125.4	52.7	87.6	16.4
All SCF			237.8		40.7	2.0

Notes: This table reports weighted summary statistics for household charitable giving, by top percentiles of net worth, in the 2001, 2004, and 2007 SCF. Dollar amounts are reported in real 2014 dollars adjusted using the Consumer Price Index All Items series. For each household, the SCF contains five implicate records that contain imputed values for several fields. We compute totals and averages using all five implicates for each household, dividing the weight for each implicate by five.

Of this individual giving, we next show that most of it is accounted for by households in the top 5 percent of net worth. We begin in Panel A of Table 14.1 by examining how much the richest households give in 2000. Note that the households surveyed need not be the same across the years. This is not a panel. Rather, we take these snapshots to be proxies for aggregate giving at various income percentiles in the distribution.

For brevity, we take only the top 30 percent of the SCF sample in terms of net worth. The SCF oversamples households in the top of the income distribution, and delivers a set of survey weights that tell us how many households in the population each survey household theoretically represents. The top 30 percent cut-off in the SCF corresponds to the top 8.21 percent of the total population in 2001, the top 8.58 percent in 2004, and the top 6.59 percent in 2007. Similarly, the top 5 percent in the SCF corresponds to the top 0.04 percent in the top population. The top 15 percent of the SCF sample roughly represent the infamous top 1 percent in the population.

In 2001, the minimum net worth for the top 8 percent of the population distribution is $1.5 million, while the minimum net worth for the top 1 percent of the population distribution is $10 million. To count among the top 0.28 percent requires a minimum net worth of $21.8 million, and to count among the top 0.04 percent requires $58 million. We report and discuss amounts in terms of real 2014 dollars, adjusted using the Consumer Price Index published by the Bureau of Labor Statistics.

We next report the total giving of households in each 5 percent bracket of net worth in the SCF. Total giving in any bracket equals the survey-weighted sum of charitable giving. In 2001, households sampled in the top 0.04 percent gave $16.3 billion and accounted for 6.7 percent of the total giving. The average gift per household was $424,000. Households between the top 0.04 percent and the top 0.28 percent gave $31.6 billion. The top 8.2 percent of households in 2001 gave a total of $131.2 billion and accounted for 54 percent of giving in the SCF. In 2004, the top 8.6 percent of households gave $111.9 billion and accounted for 50.4 percent of total giving. Notice that the total giving from the SCF sample is close to the figure reported by the Giving USA Foundation.

We draw similar conclusions from Panel B for the 2004 SCF and Panel C for the 2007 SCF. The richest Americans account for most of the philanthropy by individuals, and hence understanding their motivations in contrast to middle-income households is important.

Some Anthropological Evidence on Status or Prestige Motives for Giving

One of the ways in which giving by the richest households differs from middle-income households is that giving by the rich is frequently accompanied by publicity. This suggests that status-seeking motivates giving, above and beyond altruism. The logic connecting esteem with giving goes back to the origins of humanity. All humans originally lived in small, egalitarian hunter-gatherer bands. In these bands, powerful norms of generalized reciprocity evolved as a kind of social insurance system. Because hunter-gatherers live at subsistence level, are vulnerable to large day-to-day variations in hunting success, and lack the ability to preserve and store meat for future consumption, there is nothing to be gained from hoarding a big kill for oneself. Whoever brings a large carcass to camp must share it with everyone else, on the understanding that they will be entitled to feast on others' kills when they are more successful. Nomadic hunter-gatherers enforce norms of equality by ridiculing anyone who boasts or acts superior to others. All observed nomadic hunter-gatherer societies observe such norms. Human capacities for generalized reciprocity, and dispositions to praise generosity, are likely the products of evolutionary selection among our prehistoric ancestors, who lived under similar conditions, and could have survived only by following the same norms (Boehm 1999: Kindle loc. 2458–87, 2577–83).

The advent of domestication in tribal societies made it possible for individuals to accumulate surpluses. Accumulation is accompanied by a subtle change in the underlying logic of reciprocity. While tribal societies continue to regard generosity as a praiseworthy virtue, and greed as a despised vice, they lift the ban on boasting that is critical to maintaining the status egalitarianism of hunter-gatherer societies (Boehm 1999: Kindle loc. 1604–5). This opens up opportunities for materially successful individuals to compete for superior prestige by giving away more than anyone else. Now, instead of being ridiculed for trying to act superior to others, "Big Men" who give away more than others can reciprocate gain status for their superior generosity. An economy of esteem emerges in which the rich can effectively buy prestige by giving away their wealth.

Prestige in such "Big Man" societies is a positional good. Although the original logic attaching prestige to gift-giving is derived from norms of reciprocity, which praise generosity and despise selfishness, the objective of a Big Man is "to humiliate his rivals by giving them more than they could repay." Big Men accumulate huge surpluses through successful farming, sharp trading, and borrowing from members of their clan, and then give it away in great feasts to which their rivals are invited. Competitive feasting can get so intense that a Big Man borrows more from his clan than he can repay, and falls into debt servitude (Flannery and Marcus 2012: 99). The logic of esteem competition based on giving away wealth is so compelling that Big Man societies have independently evolved multiple times across the globe (Fried 1967: 131, 134, 146–7; Flannery and Marcus 2012: 99–104, 117–20, 552–4).

It might be thought that matters are different in modern societies. Adam Smith argued that in pre-modern times, the rich—mostly landlords—had little choice but to give away most of their income, because their consumption possibilities were so limited. Hence, they spent most of it on "hospitality"—maintaining retainers and dependents, who were obliged to offer obedience to their lords in return. The rise of manufacturing and commerce enabled the rich to spend all their income on themselves. Once that opportunity arose, they substituted "diamond buckles" and other "vanities" for hospitality (Smith 1776: III.4.10). The logic of conspicuous consumption thereby replaced that of competitive generosity. The rich man "glories in his riches, because he feels that they naturally draw upon him the attention of the world" (Smith 1759: 99).

Yet it would be too quick to conclude that Big Man reasoning has left the scene. Notwithstanding the vast increase in consumption possibilities made available by advanced economies, time imposes limits to what the rich can *personally* consume. There are only so many homes, jets, cars, and vacation resorts one has time to use. At some point, acquiring more for private personal consumption is more trouble than it is worth (Buffett 2015; Linder 1970; Smith 1759: 99–100, 200–2).

There seem to be only two remaining welfare-enhancing ways to spend (as opposed to invest) great wealth. First is altruism—spending it on goods that benefit others. Second is spending for prestige. Giving wealth to heirs might seem to be a third possibility, but this is either a form of altruism, or, to the extent that it is devoted to building a dynasty, another way to pursue prestige.

Consumption for prestige may overcome the wealthy individual's personal time constraint. The rich can gain utility from knowing that others esteem them for owning a fancy mansion in Malibu, even if they can't spare a day to stay there. However, time constraints still apply, since prestige is obtained by drawing others' attention, and others have limited time to pay attention. In our society no less than in Big Man societies, prestige is a positional good, and competition for it is fierce. Since gaining prestige involves competition for the scarce attention of others, the wealthy must judge the costs of gaining attention by conspicuous giving, compared to conspicuous consumption.

Four cost considerations may give an advantage to philanthropy. First, conspicuous consumption gains prestige only by opening one's private life to the prying eyes of others. Celebrities may relish such attention; but many other wealthy people experience the loss of privacy as a cost. By contrast, it is easier to separate one's public acts as a philanthropist from one's private life. Second, generosity is viewed as an unalloyed virtue, whereas many, even among the wealthy, disparage extreme ostentation as in bad taste. Again, while narcissists enjoy even negative attention, most people much prefer the favorable kind. Third, it is often easier to gain the attention of others through great gifts than from flashy consumption. Great philanthropic gifts generally get greater publicity than great consumption. In addition, consumption lasts only until one's death, but one's name on a building or charitable foundation lasts for generations. Finally, the prestige obtained from others' praise, obtained when philanthropic organizations publicly thank their donors, generally enhances one's status more than tooting one's own horn, which is what conspicuous consumption amounts to.

No wonder, then, that philanthropy is a ubiquitous practice among the wealthy. Table 14.1 reports the amount of giving among high net worth US households. A similar pattern holds for the richest in other countries. Worldwide, ultra-high net worth (UHNW) individuals—those with a net worth of at least $30 million—are expected to give an average of $25 million over their lifetime, more than 10 percent of their average net worth of $240 million (Wealth-X and Arton Capital 2014: 7).

Qualitative interviews provide further insight into the important role of esteem competition in promoting philanthropy among the very wealthy. Francie Ostrower (1995: Kindle loc. 324–5, 2075–7, 415–16) interviewed ninety-nine wealthy donors in the New York City area, obtaining an 80 percent response rate from a sampling base that included 82 percent of New Yorkers listed by *Forbes* as among the richest Americans at that time. Besides donating their own money, 75 percent of her sample sat on the board of a philanthropic organization, 60 percent on multiple boards, and 78 percent raised money from other wealthy donors for their favorite organizations.

Ostrower (1995: Kindle loc. 465–8, 540–51, 584–90) finds that in fundraising, the wealthy observe norms of reciprocity: they give to others' causes to induce reciprocal giving to their own. They gain prestige by outdoing others not merely in personal giving, but in raising funds from others. Just as in Big Man societies, they do not compete solely by giving from their own personal wealth, but obtain donations from family members and associates to attain the highest esteem.

The prize for outdoing others in donating and fundraising for a given organization is a seat on its board. New York City's wealthiest recognize a prestige hierarchy of organizations, and use board seats for lesser organizations as stepping stones to more highly esteemed boards. All of this service might seem to be a pure cost. However, having a seat on the board is not only a prestigious post in itself. It also gives control over fundraising events such as balls, receptions, and dinners, including some control over invitation lists. The power to include and exclude others functions similarly, although more subtly, to the power to humiliate that Big Men exercise over their rivals. In addition, much of the social life of New York City's wealthiest revolves around giving and attending these functions, just as the social life of Big Men revolves around giving and attending feasts (Ostrower 1995: 590–603, 615–18, 636–50, 563–6).

While the wealthy gain some prestige from the admiration of the general public, they are most attuned to the attitudes of their peers (Ostrower 1995: 190–1). The wealthiest and most prestigious among them may therefore attempt to alter the economy of esteem in order to change philanthropic practices. This is the objective of the Giving Pledge, launched by Bill Gates and Warren Buffett in 2010 (Buffett 2015; Giving Pledge 2015). After proving their seriousness by donating the vast majority of their wealth to the Bill & Melinda Gates Foundation, they challenged the world's billionaires to pledge to give away the majority of their wealth, too. This is Big Man competition at the highest level the world has ever witnessed, and it appears to be gaining momentum: to date, 137 billionaires from fourteen countries, including ten in June 2015 alone, have signed the pledge (CNN Money 2015).

Thus, while in advanced economies conspicuous consumption competes with conspicuous giving as a way to attain status, the underlying logic of Big Man societies has retained considerable influence. We have offered several reasons for thinking that, at the highest levels of wealth, conspicuous giving may yield even more prestige than conspicuous consumption, and at lower cost. We also have evidence that the very wealthiest can raise the stakes in conspicuous giving contests among their peers, and thereby increase total giving. In the concluding section of this essay, we will consider some welfare implications of this phenomenon.

2003 DIVIDEND TAX CUT AND GIVING
BY THE RICHEST HOUSEHOLDS

We have suggested that two factors besides altruism might influence giving by the wealthy: prestige and taxes. We now test for the importance of taxes by examining the 2003 tax cuts. To see their net effect on household giving, we can compare the summary statistics for the 2001 SCF (surveying giving in 2000) to the summary statistics for the 2004 SCF (surveying giving in 2003) and the 2007 SCF (surveying giving in 2006) in Table 14.1. Notice that total giving in the SCF falls from 2001 to 2004, both among all SCF households (in real terms, $241.6 billion to $222.1 billion) and within the top 30 percent of SCF households ranked by net worth (from $131.2 billion to $111.9 billion). The percentage of giving represented by the top 30 percent of the SCF also falls from 54 percent in 2001 to 50 percent in 2004. We might worry that the rich may have slowly ramped up their giving, and so we can also consider 2006 giving in the SCF. In either case, we do not see an increase but actually see a decrease.

One worry with this simple comparison is if 2000 was a good year and 2003 a bad year for economic growth, giving might naturally be down in 2003 compared to 2000 due to business cycle considerations. However, the opposite is the case. The broad US stock market returned −11.3 percent in 2000 as the Internet bubble burst, as measured using data from the Center for Research in Securities Prices. The stock market return in 2003 was 33.1 percent, one of the biggest years in history, as markets rallied following the recession of 2000–2. Hence, our finding that aggregate giving fell between 2000 and 2003 is not plausibly attributable to recession.

Nonetheless, we might still worry that there are other unobservable aggregate trends, which might bias us toward finding a decrease in giving in 2003 compared to 2000. To address this concern, in Table 14.2 we split the richest households into those who own stocks (and hence are most likely to benefit from the dividend tax cut) and those who do not. We expect that, if anything, the poor year 2000 and the good year 2003 ought to imply that the richest households owning stock would give more in 2003 if our findings are mechanically linked to the stock market cycle.

Rather, we see that the richest stock-owning households gave less, consistent with substitution effects associated with the Bush Tax Cuts. Panel A of Table 14.2 provides a breakdown of giving by households who own stocks and households who do not within each of the net worth cut-offs for the 2001 cohort. Panels B and C provide similar statistics for the 2004 and 2007 cohorts. Panel D runs a difference-in-differences estimate comparing the 2001 and 2004 cohorts (giving in 2000 compared to 2003). We examine the amount given by each household, whether or not a household participated in giving,

Table 14.2. Differences in differences of giving by stock ownership

Panel A: Giving in 2000 from 2001 SCF

Top %, SCF	Top %, population	Fraction owning stock	Average gift, stock ($ thousand)	Average gift, no stock ($ thousand)
0–5	0.00–0.04	0.93	448.6	75.6
5–10	0.04–0.28	0.98	125.6	28.2
10–15	0.28–1.06	0.94	26.1	8.8
15–20	1.06–2.47	0.89	24.7	10.4
20–25	2.47–4.52	0.93	7.0	5.6
25–30	4.52–8.21	0.90	3.3	2.5

Panel B: Giving in 2003 from 2004 SCF

Top %, SCF	Top %, population	Fraction owning stock	Average gift, stock ($ thousand)	Average gift, no stock ($ thousand)
0–5	0.00–0.04	0.92	386.1	798.1
5–10	0.04–0.21	0.93	70.0	266.0
10–15	0.21–0.85	0.90	35.0	25.4
15–20	0.85–2.18	0.94	14.9	23.0
20–25	2.18–4.56	0.91	7.0	4.2
25–30	4.56–8.58	0.84	3.2	2.2

Panel C: Giving in 2006 from 2007 SCF

Top %, SCF	Top %, population	Fraction owning stock	Average gift, stock ($ thousand)	Average gift, no stock ($ thousand)
0–5	0.00–0.04	0.95	470.4	161.8
5–10	0.04–0.21	0.88	94.7	25.7
10–15	0.21–0.92	0.89	38.4	20.7
15–20	0.92–2.09	0.89	18.2	7.9
20–25	2.09–3.99	0.88	9.5	5.0
25–30	3.99–6.59	0.90	5.0	4.9

Panel D: Differences in differences, 2001–4

	(1)	(2)	(3)
	Give amount ($ thousand)	Give 1/0	Cond. amount ($ thousand)
Year = 2004	8.082	−0.115	11.233
	[2.08]**	[−1.09]	[1.74]*
Stockholder	7.059	0.154	6.202
	[3.08]***	[1.93]*	[2.26]**
Stockholder x 2004	−10.623	0.108	−14.254
	[−2.43]**	[0.99]	[−2.08]**
Demi-decile effects	Y	Y	Y
Σ weight	18,355	18,355	15,156
N	2,687	2,687	2,461
R-squared	0.104	0.075	0.106

Panel E: Differences in differences, 2004–7

	(1)	(2)	(3)
	Give amount ($ thousand)	Give	Cond. amount ($ thousand)
Year = 2007	−7.933	0.032	−11.044
	[−1.88]*	[0.32]	[−1.57]
Stockholder	−2.840	0.260	−6.917
	[−0.78]	[3.45]***	[−1.11]
Stockholder x 2007	11.239	0.015	14.284
	[2.52]**	[0.15]	[1.98]**
Demi-decile effects	Y	Y	Y
Σ weight	17,347	17,347	14,554
N	2,680	2,680	2,476
R-squared	0.105	0.103	0.106

Panels A, B, and C report summary statistics. Panels D and E report results from a weighted differences-in-differences estimation where we indicate the left-hand-side variables are the amount given, an indicator for whether or not the household gave, and the amount given (only including households who gave). In Panels D and E, the right-hand-side variables are an indicator for 2004 (2007), an indicator for stock ownership, the interaction between these two, as well as demi-decile effects (not reported for brevity). Dollar amounts are reported in real 2014 dollars adjusted using the Consumer Price Index All Items series. For Panels A–C, we compute totals and averages using all five implicates for each household, dividing the weight for each implicate by five. For Panels D and E, we first average values across all implicates for a household before applying the average weight. Standard errors are white heteroscedasticity-robust. */**/*** indicates significance at the 10 percent, 5 percent, and 1 percent levels, respectively.

and the amount given if a household participated. While there was little change in participation rates, we find that the richest stockholders cut their giving by an average of $10,000 compared to the non-stockholders after the 2003 Bush Tax Cuts. Panel E shows that this cut is reversed subsequently between 2003 and 2006. There was no significant change in the giving patterns between stock- versus non-stockholders from 2000 to 2006. In short, it appears that substitution effects of tax cuts offset any of the positive effects insinuated in Gates' supposition.

CONCLUSION

This essay has explored two factors identified by Bill Gates as influencing philanthropy by the very wealthy: esteem competition and taxes. Gates has, with Warren Buffett, attempted to change the economy of esteem among the rich by challenging them to give away most of their wealth to philanthropic causes. He has also suggested that tax cuts could play a positive role in encouraging philanthropy by households at the top of the income distribution, and thereby help ameliorate income inequality.

Our research suggests that tax cuts are unlikely to stimulate greater giving by the very wealthy. Examining the response of the rich to the unanticipated 2003 Bush Tax Cuts, we find that the substitution effects of these cuts, which increased the relative price of giving by reducing the value of the charitable tax deduction, dominated income, altruism, and status effects. Our initial results suggest that tax policies are a first-order determinant of philanthropy for the richest households, but not in the direction expected by tax cut advocates.

Our study does not directly measure the effect of status competition on philanthropy by the rich. Nor does our SCF data, from 2001, 2004, and 2007, tell us anything about the potential for increasing philanthropy by altering the economy of esteem. Gates and Buffett issued their Giving Pledge challenge—an explicit attempt to change the economy of esteem for philanthropy—in 2010. While they have publicized a list of those who have joined the pledge, no data on how much they have pledged are available. Nevertheless, our anthropological evidence on esteem competition by conspicuous giving suggests considerable potential for influencing philanthropy by this route.

We conclude with some reflections on the welfare implications of three different methods of redistributing the wealth of the rich: philanthropy, state taxation for public works or transfer programs, and corporate largesse. Gates' view, quoted at the beginning of this essay, reflects an opinion widely shared among the very wealthy: that private philanthropy is a better way to redistribute wealth than the state tax-and-transfer system. Wealthy donors tend to resist taxation. They also draw a sharp distinction between charity (direct transfers to needy individuals, which they consider a state responsibility) and philanthropy (private support for organizations that provide public goods, such as schools) (Ostrower 1995: Kindle loc. 48–63). This view reflects the ideology of Andrew Carnegie (1889), who launched the modern American philanthropic movement among the wealthy. The welfare case for favoring philanthropy over state redistribution thus depends on several assumptions: that the rich care more about, and know better than the state or the less advantaged, how best to promote the welfare of the latter, and that others' welfare is better promoted by private non-profit organizations than by state-run organizations or direct transfers to the less advantaged.

One difficulty with mobilizing esteem competition to promote welfare via philanthropy is that the donations that win admiration need not track the welfare of the less advantaged. Ostrower did not find that her subjects considered relative welfare impacts in deciding where to donate. Rather, they gave to organizations to which they were personally connected, such as their alma mater; to the causes of their family members and associates, to whom they owed reciprocal obligations of giving; and to the most prestigious organizations, where they sought board seats. Hence, donations to elite schools and cultural institutions far outstripped those to social services, youth, and human rights organizations (Ostrower 1995: 418–60, 603).

Since Ostrower's study, organizations such as the Center for Effective Philanthropy, GuideStar, and GiveWell have arisen, with the aims of directing donors to causes that have a measurable impact, and incentivizing charities to spend more efficiently. However, even if such effective giving organizations make charities more responsive to donors' interests, it doesn't follow that they are responsive to the needs of recipients. This is of particular concern where needs are greatest, in the least developed countries. Private non-profits, in substituting for state provision of public goods in least developed countries, may impair the development of state capacity needed for development, and may reinforce despotic governments by reducing their accountability to the people (Deaton 2013: chapter 7). Finally, to the extent that the rich have acquired their fortunes through reneging on norms of reciprocity toward other stakeholders in the firms they control, and exploitation of monopoly advantages and other market failures, the appropriation and redistribution of rents is liable to be less welfare-promoting than if they were never appropriated in the first place.

State tax-and-transfer programs will promote welfare more effectively than philanthropy if the less advantaged know more about how to promote their welfare than the rich do. State provision of public goods in democratic countries will be superior to philanthropic provision to the extent that democratic accountability enables greater responsiveness to public interests than private philanthropy. Yet there are downsides to reliance on state redistribution. States may be unable to overcome resistance to the taxation needed to fund effective programs. Their foreign aid programs are more likely to reinforce despotic regimes than private foreign relief. States may also be excessively risk-averse. Private foundations may be able to test novel approaches through experiments that states would not risk (Reich 2013).

Corporate largesse offers a third method of redistribution. By this we do not mean corporate philanthropy, which we have shown is marginal relative to individual efforts, and which is subject to at least as many drawbacks as private philanthropy. Rather, we refer to redistribution of rents among the firm's stakeholders, away from top executives and shareholders, toward workers, subcontractors, customers, and the communities in which the firms operate. The vast majority of UHNW philanthropists are executives of major firms (Wealth-X and Arton Capital 2014: 8). They enjoy considerable power not only over the size of their own compensation packages, but over the distribution of rents among stakeholders. An extreme example of corporate largesse is the decision of Dan Price, CEO of Gravity Payments, to take a huge pay cut and redistribute the firm's profits to pay his employees a minimum wage of $70,000 per year (Cohen 2015a).

Such a firm-centered model of redistribution offers some potential advantages. It can be implemented voluntarily. It takes advantage of the superior knowledge executives have of the interests of those with whom they regularly interact, relative to their knowledge of the interests of distant recipients. It takes advantage of the longevity of firms, which are able to undertake long-term projects promoting social progress that extend beyond the lifetimes of individual donors. Finally, it may fulfill, to a greater extent than the other models, the norms of reciprocity that lie at the origins of esteem competition (Anderson 2015).

A disadvantage of corporate largesse is that it would require a substantially greater alteration in the economy of esteem among the very wealthy than the effective philanthropy movement is attempting. Dan Price, far from receiving praise from his wealthy peers for raising his workers' salaries, faced a backlash (Cohen 2015b). Yet this reflects a relatively recent alteration in the economy of esteem. In 1955, *Fortune* reported on the lives of major corporate executives in America who earned $50,000 or more annually (about $435,000 in today's purchasing power). The typical executive, they reported, owned two cars, lived in a seven-room house with 2.5 bathrooms, and spent his leisure time golfing and fishing (*Fortune* 2012). Such a lifestyle would be considered modest even by the standards of the merely upper middle class today. *Fortune* attributed its modesty to highly progressive taxation. Nevertheless, leading executives of the era enjoyed superior prestige. They did so in virtue of presiding over firms with many employees who themselves enjoyed good salaries, and in virtue of the central contributions their firms were seen to be making to an economy that extended growing prosperity to the vast majority. Because esteem is based on nothing more than the opinions of others, it is subject to dramatic alteration by changing people's standards of what is estimable.

These reflections are not intended to offer a definitive answer to the question of how redistribution is best effected, but only to raise considerations relevant to such an assessment. We have suggested that the prospects for the wealthy to derive utility from spending their wealth on purely private, personal consumption are limited by time constraints. The remaining options are spending for altruism, and spending on esteem competition, either through conspicuous consumption or conspicuous giving. Besides being inherently inefficient (Frank 2000), conspicuous consumption may yield less utility to the spender than conspicuous giving, while conspicuous giving, along with altruism, may yield considerable utility to others as well. It may be possible to alter the economy of esteem to align the status interests of the wealthy more closely with the welfare of everyone else. This might be done through effective philanthropy movements, corporate largesse, or traditional tax-and-transfer policies, which prod the wealthy to base their claims to esteem on the contributions their firms make to the public good.

This essay leaves for future research the crucial question of how effectively norm entrepreneurs such as Gates and Buffett can change the economy of esteem among their peers, and how others might be able to steer it toward other practices that spread benefits beyond the 1 percent. As with all norm change, the wealthy face a collective action problem in altering their shared standards of esteem. Yet they also face a collective action problem with the status quo. Piketty (2014) argues on historical and theoretical grounds that the rich countries of the world are headed for ever-widening inequality. This trend may not be sustainable. Hanauer (2014) argues that the 99 percent will not indefinitely tolerate it. Nor does the prosperity of the wealthy depend on it. To the contrary: although businesspeople "love our customers rich and our employees poor," when they consider only their own interests in isolation, this forgets that the customers of every business are nearly all the employees of other businesses. Businesspeople therefore have a collective interest in the prosperity of employees as well as customers. Alterations in the economy of esteem among the rich may offer one way they can spur each other to realize this collective interest.

· ·

COMMENTS AND DISCUSSION

Anderson, Cheng, and Hong consider the motives that drive philanthropy among the wealthiest individuals, and assess the merits of private philanthropy compared to public investment as a means of advancing the social good. They offer a nuanced picture of interaction among esteem, income, and tax incentives as driving motivations. Human history suggests that "esteem hierarchies" could be harnessed more effectively to motivate private giving, though they express concern that private philanthropy is often unresponsive to important public needs.

Is private philanthropy undemocratic, and in what respects exactly is that problematic?

A number of participants at the Society for Progress' second assembly observed the way in which big philanthropy tends to be driven by the narrow or idiosyncratic preferences of donors, rather than a regard for the social concerns requiring most investment. Frank and Risse, for example, both observed the enormous need for infrastructure improvements in the United States. A number of comments also made reference to Angus Deaton's observation (Deaton 2013) that private philanthropy tends to crowd out the public sector. A further problem here is that, as Pettit noted, big philanthropists wield enormous social power through their giving. In the case of corporations, Davis observed that giving is by necessity limited to goods (arts funding, for example) that do not entail controversial value commitments. What is the right balance here between public and private investment? What institutional mechanisms can most effectively achieve that balance?

What are the social and institutional conditions under which private philanthropy most effectively serves social causes?

"It is hard to do good," Anderson observed, noting the difficulties that so many aid organizations have in achieving their mission. Mendiola suggested that there is a "sweet spot" for companies when they are able to make social investments that are specifically responsive to their impact on the community. Sen likewise observed that the most effective private philanthropists tend to have some kind of personal background that connects them to a given cause and inspires the necessary level of commitment. As Hammami observed, the growing approach to for-profit models of social investment suggests yet another way of driving the needed commitment and competence. Citing the example of the Twin Cities (Minneapolis and St. Paul), Davis observed that giving among the wealthy tends to be largest in close-knit communities of high-status individuals where there are strong norms connecting status to philanthropy. At the same time, this kind of communal structure can tend to favor splashy, prestige giving (museums, operas, etc.) at the expense of more mundane public goods. Here, again, concerns about democracy become relevant. At the same time, as Schmidtz observed, private philanthropists have the opportunity to be "experimental" with investment in ways that governments simply cannot.

References

Anderson, E. 2015. "The Business Enterprise as an Ethical Agent." In S. Rangan (ed.), *Performance and Progress: Essays on Capitalism, Business, and Society*. New York and Oxford: Oxford University Press.

Andreoni, J. 1990. "Impure Altruism and Donations to Public Goods: A Theory of Warm-glow Giving." *The Economic Journal* 100(401): 464–77.

Auerbach, A. J. and Hassett, K. A. 2005. "The 2003 Dividend Tax Cuts and the Value of the Firm: An Event Study." No. w11449. National Bureau of Economic Research.

Boehm, C. 1999. *Hierarchy in the Forest: The Evolution of Egalitarian Behavior*. Cambridge, MA: Harvard University Press.

Buffett, W. 2015. "My Philanthropic Pledge." <http://givingpledge.org/Content/media/My%20Philanthropic%20Pledge.pdf>. Accessed October 20, 2015.

Carnegie, A. 1889. "Wealth." *North American Review* 148(391): 653–65.

Cheng, I.-H., Hong, H., and Shue, K. 2013. "Do Managers Do Good with Other People's Money?" No. w19432. National Bureau of Economic Research.

Chetty, R. and Saez, E. 2004. "Dividend Taxes and Corporate Behavior: Evidence from the 2003 Dividend Tax Cut." No. w10841. National Bureau of Economic Research.

CNN Money 2015. "10 More Billionaires Join Buffett-Gates Giving Pledge." <http://money.cnn.com/2015/06/02/news/companies/giving-pledge-billionaires-buffett-gates/index.html?section=money_topstories>. Accessed February 23, 2018.

Cohen, P. 2015a. "One Company's New Minimum Wage: $70,000 a Year." *New York Times*, 13 April.

Cohen, P. 2015b. "A Company Copes with Backlash Against the Raise That Roared." *New York Times*, 31 July.

Deaton, A. 2013. *The Great Escape: Health, Wealth, and the Origins of Inequality*. Princeton: Princeton University Press.

Flannery, K. and Marcus, J. 2012. *The Creation of Inequality: How Our Prehistoric Ancestors Set the Stage for Monarchy, Slavery, and Empire*. Cambridge, MA: Harvard University Press.

Fortune 2012. "How Top Executives Live (Fortune 1955)." *Fortune*, 6 May. <http://fortune.com/2012/05/06/how-top-executives-live-fortune-1955/>. Accessed February 23, 2018.

Frank, R. 2000. *Luxury Fever: Why Money Fails to Satisfy in an Era of Excess*. Princeton: Princeton University Press.

Fried, M. H. 1967. *The Evolution of Political Society: An Essay in Political Anthropology*. New York: Random House.

Gates, B. 2014. "Why Inequality Matters." The Blog of Bill Gates <http://www.gatesnotes.com>. Accessed February 23, 2018.

Giving Pledge. 2015. <http://givingpledge.org/index.html>. Accessed February 23, 2018.

Giving USA Foundation. 2015. "Annual Report on Philanthropy for the Year 2014 Data Tables." Indiana University.

Hanauer, N. 2014. "The Pitchforks Are Coming . . . For Us Plutocrats." *Politico*, July/August. <http://www.politico.com/magazine/story/2014/06/the-pitchforks-are-coming-for-us-plutocrats-108014_full.html#.U7SO_7EmXKc>. Accessed February 23, 2018.

Harrison, E. K. 2007. "Estate Planning Under the Bush Tax Cuts." *National Tax Journal* 60(3): 371–84.

Heffetz, O. and Frank, R. H. 2008. "Preferences for Status: Evidence and Economic Implications." In J. Benhabib, A. Bisin, and M. Jackson (eds.), *Handbook of Social Economics*, volume 1. San Diego: Elsevier, 69–91.

Indiana University. nd. Lilly Family School of Philanthropy, Million Dollar List. <http://www.milliondollarlist.org/>. Accessed February 23, 2018.

Lancet 2009. "What Has the Gates Foundation Done for Global Health?" *The Lancet* 373(9675): 1577.

Linder, S. B. 1970. *The Harried Leisure Class*. New York: Columbia University Press.

List, J. A. 2011. "The Market for Charitable Giving." *The Journal of Economic Perspectives* 25(2): 157–80.

Ostrower, F. 1995. *Why the Wealthy Give: The Culture of Elite Philanthropy*. Princeton: Princeton University Press.

Piketty, T. 2014. *Capital in the Twenty-First Century*. Trans. Arthur Goldhammer. Cambridge, MA: Harvard University Press.

Poterba, J. 2004. "Taxation and Corporate Payout Policy." No. w10321. National Bureau of Economic Research.

Reich, R. 2013. "What Are Foundations For?" *Boston Review*, 1 March. <https://www.bostonreview.net/forum/foundations-philanthropy-democracy>. Accessed February 23, 2018.

Smith, A. 1759 [1976]. *The Theory of Moral Sentiments*. Edited by D. D. Raphael and A. L. Macfie. *Glasgow Edition of the Works and Correspondence of Adam Smith*. Oxford: Oxford University Press.

Smith, A. 1776 [1981]. *An Inquiry Into the Nature and Causes of the Wealth of Nations*, volume 1. *Glasgow Edition of the Works and Correspondence*. Indianapolis: Liberty Fund.

U.S. Trust and Lilly Family School of Philanthropy at Indiana University. 2014. *The 2014 U.S. Trust Study of High Net Worth Philanthropy*. <http://www.ustrust.com/publish/content/application/pdf/GWMOL/USTp_ARV3FMVF_2015-11.pdf>. Accessed February 23, 2018.

Wealth-X and Arton Capital. 2014. *Wealth-X and Arton Capital Philanthropy Report 2014*. <http://global-citizen.org/wp-content/uploads/2014/10/WX_AC-Philanthropy-Report-2014-Web.pdf>. Accessed February 23, 2018.

Zucman, G. 2013. "The Missing Wealth of Nations: Are Europe and the US net Debtors or net Creditors?" *The Quarterly Journal of Economics* 128(3): 1321–64.

CHAPTER 15

···

RECOGNIZING AND EMBRACING OUR SHARED HUMANITY

···

VALERIE TIBERIUS AND JAMES P. WALSH

Recognizing our shared humanity and our biological nature as beings whose happiness is dependent on others, we learn to open our hearts, and in so doing we gain a sense of purpose and a sense of connection with those around us.

Dalai Lama, Facebook post, October 2, 2012

Abstract

Real progress occurs when individual lives change for the better. Colleges and universities formerly aspired to develop the character of their students. The trend of late has been to treat students as "customers." Can we once again help students to recognize what matters to them and help them develop a philosophy of life? This chapter describes one approach and tool. Drawing on social psychologists' findings of patterned regularity in the world, it aims to reveal commonalities especially in individual values. While we don't want to "tell" students, simply asking them to recall and report is inadequate. Rather we want them to discover. Knowing where your values come from, and in particular knowing what personal and cultural experiences shape what matters, is crucial to understanding what is important in life. The chapter outlines a pedagogical tool to elicit this sharing and recognition.

Interdisciplinary work is all the rage these days. Partnerships and collaborations between the likes of musicians and historians, visual artists and neuroscientists, and engineers and physicians, for example, are sought and encouraged by university administrators and granting agencies. Why is this? What is interdisciplinarity's promise? The answer is rooted in the assumption that two heads are better than one. Or, more to the point, that two perspectives are better than one. Diverse approaches to imagination, creativity, and analysis may reveal new ways to address the complex problems attendant to what has been called the Anthropocene Era. We live in a period when, for the first time in history, the human species is shaping life on the planet (Sanderson et al. 2002). In fact, we humans dominate the earth's ecosystems (Hoffman and Jennings 2015). Some worry that we are not taking our stewardship responsibilities seriously, that we are actually flirting with human extinction if we do not amend our ways (Bostrom 2013; Matheny 2007). We must recognize and embrace our common humanity if we are to dodge the bullet of extinction and beyond that, create a world of prosperity for all.

A noteworthy partnership is beginning to emerge between philosophy and business in the world of higher education (Colby et al. 2011). With business as perhaps the most powerful transnational institution on the world's stage today, the idea is that those who teach the next generation of business leaders would do well to marry their analytic skills with those who for centuries have considered what it means to live a good life. At times like this, businesspeople would do well to think more broadly about the ends of commerce (Donaldson and Walsh 2015). This kind of partnership is just one of many that embody the hopes of those who suggest that natural and social scientists alike must join forces with those in the humanities if we are to forestall extinction, if not create a more prosperous world (Palsson et al. 2013; Wilson 2014).[1] A product of the imagination of a philosopher and business professor, our work here represents an attempt to bridge difference in an attempt to inspire and enable a better world.

To begin, we needed to find points of connection. Successful interdisciplinary work grows out of relationships between people who have something in common and who trust each other. Complete strangers, we knew nothing of each other when we began. Subramanian Rangan and his dream for the Society for Progress brought us together. We voiced our different perspectives and discovered shared values and interests in our early conversations. In time, we developed a friendship. The good news is that we learned quickly that we share three key points of connection. First, we share a deep commitment to social progress, broadly defined to include (among other things) an end to racism, a cure for AIDS, and the elimination of war, famine, and poverty. Second, we know that whatever we might do to create social progress, we must attend to individual lives. Institutional change matters but lives are lived one at a time. Real progress occurs when individual lives change for the better. And third, as professors, we believe in the power of education to inspire and enable individuals to make the world a better place. Our faith in education encompasses not only formal education, but also the kind of learning that happens when individuals from different perspectives connect in a meaningful way. At its best, education helps reveal and stir our common humanity.

We found too that we were united by a wary concern for the contemporary state of higher education. Colleges and universities formerly aspired to develop the character of

---

[1] Palsson et al. (2013: 10) succinctly capture such an aspiration: "To remedy the lack of understanding of the Anthropocene, it is essential to enhance and intensify the social sciences and humanities' work on how directionality could be articulated, democratically anchored, and implemented in the search for new technologies, medical knowledge, economic paradigms, and forms of social organization."

their students (James 1907). The trend of late, however, has been to treat students as customers. We often take students as we find them and simply work to satisfy their desire for marketable skills. We teach but we may do little to inspire them to lives of purpose, meaning, and contribution (March 2003). Many fall into a trap of teaching instrumental reasoning, not judgment or wisdom. James (1907) warned us off such an orientation years ago. Such students, he warned, "are made into an efficient instrument for doing a definite thing" but he remarked that "they may remain a crude and smoky kind of petroleum, incapable of spreading light." Lamenting the current situation, Harvard's President Drew Gilpin Faust (2009) summed up our challenge: "Human beings need meaning, understanding and perspective as well as jobs."

These common starting points led us to a mutual interest in developing a pedagogical tool that would help students grasp what matters to them and, we dare say, identify a philosophy of life that may stem from their desires. Upon reflection and even reconsideration, this may even serve as a foundation for a life of purpose, meaning, and contribution. Note that we are not imagining solitary reflection. This is to be a social intervention. Engaging with others, students will gain not just a better perspective on who they are, but in reflection and dialogue they will quickly discover that they share more in common with others than they might imagine. Apparent differences can blind one to fundamental commonalities. In a way, the project we propose is an expression of the optimism that brought the two of us together. We found that we had much in common, supposed divides notwithstanding. We hope to foster that same kind of connection among our students, and maybe eventually even among the world's citizens.

In this essay, we will describe our idea and how it could be used in various university settings (and even beyond). As we consider its benefits, we will pay particular attention to how it could spur social progress. Neither of us has much technological acumen, and so we will not address the details of the technology that will help bring our ideas to life. Rather, we will discuss the idea and how it might be deployed for the common good.

RECOGNIZING OUR COMMON HUMANITY

We live in a world of difference. We are inclined to sift and sort others, and even ourselves, into identity groups based on age, race, color, religion, sex, gender identity, national origin, height, weight, disability, and so many others—athletic ability, taste in music, hobbies, hair color, and so on. We draw inferences about each other and often discriminate—positively and negatively—based on what we observe about others. That said, for all our supposed differences, we are all human. We are profoundly alike, as well.

Dahlsgaard et al. (2005), for example, examined the world's major religious traditions and found six virtues common to all: courage, justice, humanity, temperance, wisdom, and transcendence. Relatedly, social psychologists often find patterned regularity when they examine morality in the world. Rokeach (1973), an eminent social psychologist, developed a value survey comprising thirty-six values (eighteen terminal and eighteen instrumental values) and found commonality the world over. The former includes such values as a world at peace, family security, and freedom; the latter includes values such as being honest, ambitious, and responsible. Years later, Braithwaite and Scott (1991) found broad support for his work. Schwartz (2006) too has since found some universality in the list. Haidt and Kesebir (2010) also find evidence of moral cohesion the world over. Still, we know that social life is marked by variance. Not everyone holds the same value with the same intensity. Ask people to rank what is important to them and even if the lists are similar, the rankings may vary dramatically. Nevertheless, despite these differences of priority, we believe (in keeping with the above value research) that there are commonalities to be discovered. Our pedagogical tool and intervention ideas aim to reveal these commonalities.

To begin, we believe that we need to develop a new way to uncover one's values. Rooted in cognitive appraisal, survey analyses have their limitations, particularly if you think of values as having a cognitive and an affective dimension (Tiberius 2008). As illuminating as an abstract appraisal of our values may be, untethered to lived experience they may be a poor indication of the emotional or affective aspect of valuing, and therefore a poor stimulus for conversation, mutual understanding, and action. If we think of values as mutually reinforcing patterns of attitudes (both cognitive and emotional) that people take to govern their deliberation and choices, then survey research may not be the best tool for revealing values.

Simply asking people to report their values is inadequate for our purposes, then, but other techniques (such as interviews and reflective prompts) run the risk of imposing values on a person artificially. Further, we want to avoid a temptation to "teach" values as one might teach the periodic table. For one thing, we don't exactly have a consensus about what the "right" values are. Perhaps if we lived in a more homogenous culture, or if our concerns were confined to a small community of like-minded people, we could posit specific shared values and propose that institutions of higher education teach these values to their students. But we do not live in such a world. Our concerns encompass the global community, a diverse community marked by a pluralistic set of values. Moreover, in many cultures, teaching a specific set of values goes against the culturally supported values of autonomy and value-neutrality on the part of the state. Is there a better way? We believe so. In short, we think the right path begins with helping people to recognize the origins of their values and to see these values as emerging from a set of experiences in a way that is open to consideration.[2]

Knowing where your values come from, and in particular knowing just what personal and cultural experiences shape what matters to you, is a part of the process of developing an understanding of what matters in life. We may find commonality in

---

[2] "[C]ompassion, altruism and empathy. [T]hese prosocial traits are innate to us and lie at the very centerpiece of our common humanity. Our capacity to feel compassion has ensured the survival and thriving of our species over millennia." These words ground the work of Stanford University's Center for Compassion and Altruism Research and Education, and indeed, our own. See <http://ccare.stanford.edu/about/mission-vision/#sthash.ifm20SEa.dpuf>.

the fact that similar life events shape us, even if we draw different conclusions from those same events. For example, some people reacted to the 9/11 terrorist attacks by becoming wary of others and preoccupied with security; others reacted by reaching out to others and working for peace. Today, some people applaud Donald Trump's call to bar people of the Muslim faith from entering America, while others plant signs in their yards proclaiming solidarity with their Muslim neighbors.[3] And so, people with very different core values (a commitment to self and security or a commitment to others and harmony) may find that they have much more in common than they imagine. Their values, however different, are rooted in the same experience. When we talk about that experience—and our different reactions to it—we may find ourselves on common ground. In this way, we might be able to bridge seemingly insuperable differences. We believe that we can best appreciate our shared humanity when we recognize our shared experiences.

Life's Defining Moments

To begin, people need to identify the defining moments in their lives. The first step in our pedagogy is to ask people to do just that. Imagining for the moment that we are working with college students between the ages of eighteen and twenty-six in the US, Table 15.1 captures our early thinking about what some of those moments might be. Some are publicly shared and some will be intensely private. The columns to the right capture a first approximation of some public moments between 1990 and 2015 that may have affected people's lives and worldview. We first tried to generate a list of possible life-shaping events on both the world and the US stage (of course, this list will be refined with experience). We then looked deeper into the realms of economics, business, technology, and culture for other possible moments. We ask students to look over the list, add other moments that mean something to them, and then identify those that matter most. The next step is to ask them to reflect on these significant moments and generate a list of moments and events in their private lives that mattered deeply to them. They may have been experienced alone (or alone yet among strangers), with friends, or with family members. These events may include births, deaths, loves, loves lost, moments of triumph, moments of humiliation, moments of indescribable joy, and moments of unspeakable sadness. In the end, each person will be looking at a broad array of life-defining moments.

The next broad step is to ask people to make sense of them. We imagine a four-step process of discovery. First, looking at the broad array of meaningful life moments, we expect that people will see variations on themes. That is, we expect that many of these moments can be clustered in some fashion. We ask them to do that clustering. Looking for similarities and differences across the many moments, we ask the participants to sort them into categories that "go together" in their minds. Once clustered, the second task is to name them. For example, one might categorize events into those that have to

---

[3] <http://www.1humanfamily.org/>.

Table 15.1. Defining moments, 1990–2015

	Personal moments	Family moments	Friendship moments	World events	United States events	Economics	Business	Technology	Culture
1990				Iraq invades Kuwait; Nelson Mandela released from prison; East and West Germany unite				First web page; Hubble Telescope launched	
1991				Soviet Union is dissolved; Gulf War begins					
1992				Bosnian War begins; European Union is created	Bill Clinton elected		Mall of America opens	Search browsers introduced	
1993				European Union established	First World Trade Center attack			More emails sent than letters mailed	Beanie Baby craze
1994				Rwanda genocide; Nelson Mandela elected South African president; England–France tunnel opens		NAFTA established	Criticism of Nike's supply chain practices in *New York Times*, ABC-TV and *The Economist*	Sale of genetically modified food is okayed	*The Lion King* released
1995					Oklahoma City bombing		eBay is founded		*Toy Story* released; OJ Simpson acquitted
1996				Kathie Lee Gifford sweatshop scandal	Bill Clinton re-elected			Dolly the sheep is cloned; DVDs introduced	
1997				Hong Kong handed over to China; Princess Diana dies				IBM computer beats Garry Kasparov in chess	First Harry Potter book released
1998				US embassies bombed in Kenya and Tanzania	Bill Clinton–Monica Lewinsky scandal		Google is founded	Broadband appears in homes; iMac introduced	Titanic wins eleven Oscars

(continued)

Table 15.1. Continued

	Personal moments	Family moments	Friendship moments	World events	United States events	Economics	Business	Technology	Culture
1999					Bill Clinton impeachment trial	Euro is introduced			
2000				USS Cole attacked; Antarctic ozone hole seen as largest ever	George Bush elected	Dot-com bubble bursts	Napster is launched		
2001				US invades Afghanistan; No Y2K crisis	9/11 attack		First iPod; Wikipedia launch; ENRON bankrupt		
2002				Chechen hostage killing in Russia; Bali bombing	Columbine shootings; DC sniper; Axis of Evil speech		WorldCom bankruptcy		
2003				US invades Iraq	Department of Homeland Security created			Human genome mapped; space shuttle disintegrates	Michael Jackson arrested on child molestation charges
2004				East Asia tsunami; Abu Ghraib prison scandal; Al Qaeda Madrid bombing	George Bush re-elected		Facebook founded		Red Sox win first World Series since 1918
2005				Al Qaeda London bombing	Hurricane Katrina		YouTube is founded; Dennis Kozlowski convicted		Lance Armstrong wins seventh Tour de France
2006				Hezbollah declares war on Israel; Saddam Hussein is hanged		Muhammad Yunus and Grameen Bank win Nobel Peace Prize			
2007					Virginia Tech shootings	Great Recession begins	First iPhone released		*An Inconvenient Truth* wins Academy Award

Table 15.1. Continued

	Personal moments	Family moments	Friendship moments	World events	United States events	Economics	Business	Technology	Culture
2008					Obama elected; Rod Blagojevich arrested for corruption	Oil hits $100/gallon	Lehman Bros files for bankruptcy; melamine poisoning scandal		Michael Phelps wins eight Olympic gold medals
2009				Sri Lankan civil war ends			Bernie Madoff gets 150-year sentence		Michael Jackson dies; Tiger Woods admits "transgressions"
2010				Haitian earthquake	WikiLeaks; "Obamacare" is law; Citizens United decision		BP Gulf oil spill		World Cup held in South Africa
2011				Tunisia's president resigns, launching Arab Spring; Fukushima nuclear plant damaged in tsunami	Joplin, MO tornado; Occupy Wall Street protests			Steve Jobs dies	Penn State sex abuse scandal
2012					Barack Obama re-elected; Sandy Hook shooting; Hurricane Sandy				
2013				Bangladesh garment factory collapses; Sichuan earthquake; Turkey street protests	Detroit files for bankruptcy; gay marriage legalized		Data stolen from an estimated forty million Target customers		Boston Marathon bombing; Lance Armstrong confesses to doping
2014				Ebola epidemic; ISIS beheadings	Ferguson explodes with racial tension; Snowden leaks				Malala wins Nobel Peace Prize; Robin Williams commits suicide
2015				Europe's migrant crisis; *Charlie Hebdo* Paris attack	Full US–Cuba diplomatic ties established		Volkswagen emissions scandal		FIFA corruption scandal

do with love, fear, and loss. Someone else might categorize events in terms of family, friendship, and career. Third, we ask every person to look at those named clusters of significant life moments and write an essay that articulates their philosophy of life. Finally, we ask them to step back, look both at their life-defining moments and their philosophy of life, and articulate the short list of principles or values that guide them in their day-to-day lives.

We imagine that this can all be done on an IT platform of some sort (details to be addressed later). The important point to note is that we aim to provide each person with a summary document that identifies the named clusters of his or her life-defining moments, his or her philosophy of life, and his or her life-guiding principles and values. We suspect that having that document in hand will itself be a significant life moment for many.

EMBRACING OUR COMMON HUMANITY

Looking to bridge differences and ultimately to recognize and embrace our shared humanity, our work cannot stop with personal documents, however useful they might be to the individual. We are looking to use these insights to establish connections with others. Four things can happen when we engage others about what matters most. First, we find that many aspects of life that we imagine to be idiosyncratic are, in fact, shared. Tell a story of a family member with a life-threatening illness, and we find many who confront or have confronted the exact same situation. Many couples suffer infertility and miscarriage in silence. Share their experience with others and they soon discover a host of people in the same boat. We do not live alone. Second, we may find that our differences are rooted in similarity. While we may interpret life's defining moments in entirely different ways, we share many of the same moments. Take the time to look behind value differences and we often discover similarity, and if not similarity, certainly empathy and sympathy. Third, we may find that our life principles are rooted in shallow soil. Some inferences we draw from life experience may stand re-examination. For instance, realizing that you care about preserving historic opera houses because your parents rewarded you with candy when they took you to the opera as a child might prompt you to rethink your personal commitment to historic preservation. Reflection on other sorts of experiences, however, may have the opposite effect. A recognition that your concern for the welfare of oppressed people was influenced by your father's participation in World War II, for example, may reaffirm your values. And finally, we find community. The simple fact of sharing one's life with others inevitably draws people together. We may not be able to solve each other's problems but sharing life's burdens and joys with each other helps to make life worth living. As the Dalai Lama said, our happiness is dependent on others. Unfortunately, too many of us needlessly live "alone together."

There are two broad ways to share our defining moments and the inferences we draw from them. We can do this in person and/or we can do it virtually. But the most important question to ask about this work is not "How?" but "Why?" We need context. The context itself may determine the best way for people to encounter each other. We began talking about doing this kind of work on campus. While we can imagine a range of professors picking up this pedagogy for their own uses, we think the obvious place to begin this work is in a university's Office of Student Life. The name of the office varies by campus but just about every university in America has an initiative to bring people together across difference. These offices provide a natural home for our ideas. Consider our own universities.

The University of Minnesota has an Office for Equity and Diversity.[4] The office offers an incredible range of services, education and training initiatives, awards, scholarships, and events. Diversity is a core value at the University of Minnesota. The office's work is grounded in this laudatory aspiration statement:

> An academy of the highest stature, as measured against ideals of both academic excellence and social justice, is one in which diversity is never an add-on or afterthought, never just "another thing to think about," not a problem to be fixed. In a University culture of excellence, diversity is intrinsic; excellence and diversity are inextricably intertwined—not *either-or*, but *both-and*.

Long committed to diversity, equity, and inclusion,[5] the University of Michigan has a special Program on Intergroup Relations.[6] This too would provide fertile ground for the kind of work we envision. Note too Michigan's high aspirations:

> The Program on Intergroup Relations (IGR) is a social justice education program. IGR blends theory and experiential learning to facilitate students' learning about social group identity, social inequality, and intergroup relations. The program prepares students to live and work in a diverse world and educates them in making choices that advance equity, justice, and peace. IGR was founded in 1988 and was the first program of its kind. IGR is a partnership between Student Life and the College of Literature, Science, and the Arts.

We can imagine these offices drawing students together with our exercise to foster dialogue and understanding among and between various identity groups. These connections would happen in person. That said, we can also imagine a university scaling the Defining Moments exercise as a stimulus to campus-wide awareness, dialogue, and understanding. Admittedly, this may be most attractive to universities roiled by identity conflict (Heller 2016). For example, both the University of Missouri and Yale University were recently engulfed in controversy and protest about race relations. Both the president and chancellor of the University of Missouri stepped down after their poor handling of manifestly racist incidents on campus in the fall of 2015 (Calamur 2015). In that same fall, Yale exploded in controversy after a faculty member wrote to students with Halloween costume advice (Friedersdorf 2015). Had everyone

---

[4] <https://diversity.umn.edu/>.
[5] <https://diversity.umich.edu/our-commitment/>.
[6] <https://igr.umich.edu/about>.

on campus completed the Defining Moments exercise (online and anonymously but with identity markers), the university would then have had a searchable database in hand that students, faculty, and staff alike could draw upon to establish and reestablish bonds in times of seemingly intractable difference. For instance, one can imagine a university-sponsored teach-in (to revive a practice from the 1960s) where reflecting upon these experience-based philosophies of life, people of different races could engage with each other to find common ground. Perhaps that would help address the kind of incivility or worse that we saw at Missouri when on October 5, the "Legion of Black Collegians were called the N-word while rehearsing for homecoming festivities" and then again on October 24, when "a swastika was drawn with human feces at a university residence hall" (Calamur 2015). Incivility was present at Yale too. In the midst of their controversy, a student told a faculty member at the center of their storm, "You should not sleep at night! You are disgusting!" (Friedersdorf 2015).

The in-person and online pedagogies would differ, of course. In person, one might imagine that students would complete their Defining Moments reflections beforehand and then come together in a workshop to read their philosophies of life aloud to each other in small groups. When done, they could share their core values and invite a conversation about their philosophy of life, core values, and the origins of both. This could be done in a round-robin fashion. In the end, the group as a whole would step back and make sense of what they heard each other say. Do this in a group comprising members of different identity groups, and mutual understanding and respect can only emerge.

The online experience is different. Here, one would collect the Defining Moments information to build a searchable database, one that with imagination could be used in a variety of helpful ways. In essence, each participant (ideally, all entering freshmen) would create a profile that could be amended over time as they wish. This profile would be searchable and visible to the university community (though students could opt to hide some entries if they preferred). While no personal information would be revealed (names, addresses, personal photographs, and the like), people would self-identify by the kinds of categories and identity groups that people commonly employ. We imagined a host of them at the beginning of this paper—age, race, color, religion, sex, gender identity, national origin, height, weight, disability, and the like. Searchable and open to sorting, it would be an easy matter to generate a compendium of Defining Moments and what they mean to people of different races, gender identities, and religious groups (to name three groups that matter so much these days).

Open for personal edification and inspiration at any time of the day or night, this database could also be used more formally by faculty and staff at the university. Freshman writing instructors might use it as a stimulus for variety of writing assignments. Social science faculty members could ask their students to analyze the database. Courses focusing on particular periods in history could target one relevant Defining Moment for discussion. Intergroup workshop leaders could use selected entries as a stimulus for all kinds of debate and conversation. And yes, in a crisis of the kind Missouri and Yale experienced, everyone could read entries from their colleagues across whatever divide is problematic at the moment. Finding commonality in moments of acute difference can only help to ease tension.[7]

Faculty and staff could also complete the Defining Moments exercise. Having the life stories and philosophies of everyone in the university online and a just mouse click away from everyone, would do much to bring the shared humanity of that university to life. Knowing that everyone on campus completed such an exercise would open the door to meaningful conversations with strangers. Find yourself with a small group of others and you can always ask people about their life philosophies. As such, we would stimulate "big talk" rather than "small talk" (Boomer 2016). With a common knowledge that everyone has a philosophy of life in hand and ready for sharing, meaningful conversations are likely to happen in the most unexpected times and places. Such openness would go a long way toward turning a university into a university community.

At the risk of getting ahead of ourselves and dreaming too big, we can't resist pointing out the benefits of this kind of database if it were to go viral. The day one university embraces such an initiative is the day others follow suit. To be sure, the admissions office of the university that embraces this kind of practice would celebrate their open and engaging community with prospective students. Other universities would eagerly move to emulate the practice. In short order, we imagine that almost every college and university would embrace the practice. The same is true of corporations. At a time when so many organizations are trying their best to create open and compassionate work environments (Cameron and Spreitzer 2013), a Defining Moments database—with all of the attendant workshop and engagement possibilities at the ready—would certainly prove attractive to innovative companies.[8] With its worth proven, the practice would likely diffuse quickly in this arena too.

Finally, given the right technological platform, one can imagine this scaling up to encompass larger and larger segments of the world. Translation capabilities being what they are today, people could create their Defining Moment profile and share it with the world. Add some new identifiers and we can all learn about the lives and interior lives of people all over the world. To be sure, such a tool might go a long way to resolving conflict and enabling a better world. Imagine, for example, if the Palestinians and Israelis knew each other's defining life moments and what they meant to each other. That fact alone might help to bring peace to the region. Expand the searchable identifiers and people from

---

[7] There is reason to think it would also increase compassion, though this would require further investigation. Our preliminary look at compassion interventions reveals two kinds of strategies that tend to be effective: one that produces self-affirmation and the other that creates shared experiences. Since our pedagogical tool combines these two elements, it seems reasonable to hope that it would have a positive effect on compassion. See Lim et al. (2015), Condon et al. (2013), Sherman and Cohen (2002), and Crocker et al. (2008) for links to the psychology literature on these kinds of interventions.

[8] Of course, if this exercise is expanded to include people of different ages and nationalities, then the list of possible defining moments in Table 15.1 will need to change accordingly. Just as obviously, with so many students born and raised outside of the United States on US campuses today, the initial list of publicly shared moments in Table 15.1 will likely need to be expanded before it is used. In time, we can imagine building a drop-down menu of events for every country in the world.

both sides of a conflict, not to mention the world at large, could appreciate what it is really like to suffer the loss of a parent, child, aunt, uncle, cousin, brother, or sister in a war.[9] Pinker (2011) suggested that the invention of the printing press marked the point in human history when violence started to subside. With life stories accessible to the general public in written form, people began to appreciate the fact that others had an inner life. As such, violence started to subside. Here, we imagine using the Internet to bring the lives and stories of everyday people to even more people (in vivid and memorable ways). Such a process can only help to foster progress, peace, and prosperity.

CONCLUSION

Joseph Stalin is reported to have said, "The death of one man is a tragedy, the death of millions is a statistic." He and his followers deliberately killed six million civilians (Snyder 2011). We know that six million murders are an unspeakable horror, but at some level Stalin was correct—not being able to wrap our minds around events of that magnitude, the world was in some measure unmoved by those deaths. With 7.4 billion people in the world today, we know that we are likely to continue to suffer at each other's hands. We may even know that the human race faces a real probability of extinction. But such events, happening as they do on a massive scale, overwhelm us. Statistics simply cannot convey the true meaning of a dispute, an atrocity, or even the real possibility of human extinction. Slovic (2007) calls this phenomenon "psychic numbing." Cognitively overwhelmed, we become immune to great problems.

Thankfully, Mother Teresa offers an antidote to Stalin's reasoning. She said, "If I look at the mass I will never act. If I look at the one, I will." Somehow we need to recognize and deeply appreciate others' lives if our collective well-being is to flourish. The good news is that if everyone acts in their own small way, these acts can scale to effect great change (Weick 1984). Slovic and Slovic (2015: 220) summarized their book on the topic with these words:

> one of the essential lessons of our book is that how information is communicated (whether in large quantities or small)—such as the intertwining of numerical and narrative descriptions or sometimes the extension of abstract numerical data into narrative or visual analogues—may be particularly essential to our apprehending (and perhaps counteracting) the dangers and injustices human beings impose upon ourselves and the planet.

Simply put, we need to see and appreciate each other as human beings. We hope that the narrative descriptions revealed in our Defining Moments reflection exercise, and in the interventions it allows in universities, corporations, and maybe even around the

---

[9] Such an intervention may also serve as an antidote to any explicit attempt to dehumanize others (Haslam 2006; Kelman 1973).

world, will reveal to us our shared humanity. In the end, we hope it will enable us all to realize the possibility of a collective life well-lived.[10]

. . . .

COMMENTS AND DISCUSSION

Since markets are designed above all to give people the things they value, the question of what people value, and what in fact is worth valuing, is central to any diagnosis of the present economic system. Drawing on research in psychology, Tiberius and Walsh imaginatively explore the prospect for a tool that might enable people to better develop

---

[10] We read Parker Palmer's 2009 book, *A Hidden Wholeness*, just after finishing this essay. In a moment of what some would call synchronicity, we learned that he too carries our intuition about the importance of sharing with each other our lives' defining moments and how we make sense of them. We would like to end our essay by quoting him at length (Palmer 2009: 123–4):

> Because our stories make us vulnerable to being fixed, exploited, dismissed, or ignored, we have learned to tell them guardedly or not at all. Neighbors, coworkers, and even family members can live side by side for years without learning much about each other's lives. As a result, we lose something of great value, for the more we know about another's story, the harder it is to hate or harm that person.
>
> Instead of telling our vulnerable stories, we seek safety in abstractions, speaking to each other about our opinions, ideas, and beliefs rather than about our lives. Academic culture blesses this practice by insisting that the more abstract our speech, the more likely we are to touch the universal truths that unite us. But what happens is exactly the reverse: as our discourse becomes more abstract, the less connected we feel. There is less sense of community among intellectuals than in the most "primitive" society of storytellers.
>
> I learned something about the connection between storytelling and community while sitting in a Quaker meeting for worship, a communal silence out of which people occasionally speak. I listened as one man grieved the recent death of his best friend, telling a moving story about an experience the two of them had shared. I did not know this man or his friend, but the story he told took me deep into my own life: it brought my own friends to mind and reminded me of how precious they are and of how important it is that I let them know that fact.
>
> After 10 or 15 minutes of silence, another person spoke, describing with uncanny accuracy what had happened within me as I listened to the first person speak: "We believe that we will find shared truth by going up into big ideas," she said. "But it is only when we go down, drawing deep from the well of personal experience, that we tap into the living water that supplies all of our lives."
>
> I know of dialogue groups where this principle is given an acid test. People who are at each other's throats over thorny issues like abortion or the death penalty are brought together for a facilitated weekend retreat. During their time together, they are forbidden from announcing, explaining, or defending their position on the issue at hand. Instead, they are invited to tell personal stories about the experiences that brought them to whatever position they hold, while others listen openly.
>
> This process often creates more mutual understanding than other modes of conflict resolution—especially as people are reminded that similar experiences can lead different individuals to very different conclusions. We find common bonds in the shared details of the human journey, not in the divergent conclusions we draw from those details.

a sense of their own values, and how those values overlap with the perspective of others. The key idea here is that, in general, people share more in their sense of value, meaning, and purpose than is evident in the normal means available for interacting with others. Thus they envision a method by which we might progressively elicit information and reflection from individuals on what matters to them, what their defining experiences have been, and how these various responses might fit together into a scheme of values, or perhaps even a "philosophy of life." Those responses could then be aggregated—using an IT platform of some kind—to identify commonalities that could facilitate valuable mutual engagement among diverse individuals.

> *In what ways and to what extent exactly are individual values defined and constrained by a social context?*

Tiberius and Walsh's approach centers on eliciting the perspective of individuals on their own values. At the Society for Progress' second assembly several people commented, however, on the important respects in which individual values are shaped by the individual's relation to a broader social context. Drawing on examples of slave abolitionists, Anderson observed that social change depends not only on getting people to care about certain values, but also on coordinating social norms and practices so that it is possible to act on them effectively. Following up on this point, Autor noted data showing that the tendency of individuals to come out as gay was closely tied to specific features of their friend network. In this respect, it looks as if our individual identity is shaped and constituted in important ways by our social networks. Looking to trends in the education world, Meyer observed that the increasing emphasis on empathy and individual connection has tended to personalize our understanding of world events and, at the same time, to reduce the significance of a longer historical perspective as our perception shrinks to present human relationships.

> *What constitutes the right kind of reflection on values, and what should we expect to get out of such reflection, exactly?*

Kitcher suggested that the attempt to elicit "principles" from people as a consequence of this kind of reflection might be overly constraining. Couldn't people just aspire to some pattern of behavior? And Fuerstein observed the important differences between therapeutic forms of intervention—in which people principally try to get clear about what they believe—as opposed to a more normative kind of reflection, in which people aim in some sense to improve their values. Both Fuerstein's and Kitcher's observations raise questions about what we should really expect from people in articulating their values. As Kitcher observed, there is some resemblance between Tiberius and Walsh's proposal and group therapy. In that context, however, much of the value derives from the role of a skilled moderator; perhaps this is crucial. Drawing on Jonathan Haidt's recent work in moral psychology, Risse observed that many of our important value commitments are layered somewhere in our subconscious. Beyond asking people to reflect on what they believe, perhaps it is crucial that we find ways of accessing their beliefs and commitments of which they are unaware. Rangan noted that recent technological developments—such as the Fitbit or smartwatch—might hold some promise as ways of accessing and maintaining value judgments on a more ongoing, spontaneous basis.

REFERENCES

Boomer, T. 2016. "The End of Small Talk." *New York Times*, January 14. <http://www. nytimes.com/2016/01/17/fashion/dating-the-end-of-small-talk.html?_r=o>.

Bostrom, M. 2013. "Existential Risk Prevention As Global Priority." *Global Policy* 4(1): 15–31.

Braithwaite, V. A. and Scott, W. A. 1991. "Values." In J. P. Robinson, P. R. Shaver, and L. S. Wrightsman (eds.), *Measures of Personality and Social Psychology Attitudes*. San Diego, CA: Academic Press, 661–753.

Calamur, K. 2015. "What's Happening at the University of Missouri?" *The Atlantic*, November 9. <http://www.theatlantic.com/national/archive/2015/11/whats-happening-at-the-university-of-missouri/414870/>.

Cameron, K. S. and Spreitzer, G. M. 2013. *The Handbook of Positive Organizational Scholarship*. Oxford: Oxford University Press.

Colby, A., Ehrlich, T., Sullivan, W. M., and Dolle, J. R. 2011. *Rethinking Undergraduate Education: Liberal Learning for the Profession*. San Francisco: Jossey-Bass.

Condon, P., Desbordes, G., Miller, W. B., and DeSteno, D. 2013. "Meditation Increases Compassionate Responses to Suffering." *Psychological Science* 24(10): 2125–7.

Crocker, J., Niiya, Y., and Mischkowski, D. 2008. "Why Does Writing About Important Values Reduce Defensiveness? Self-Affirmation and the Role of Positive Other-directed Feelings." *Psychological Science* 19(7): 740–7.

Dahlsgaard, K., Peterson, C., and Seligman, M. E. P. 2005. "Shared Virtue: The Convergence of Valued Human Strengths Across Culture and History." *Review of General Psychology* 9(3): 203–13.

Donaldson, T. and Walsh, J. P. 2015. "Toward a Theory of Business." *Research in Organizational Behavior* 35: 181–207.

Faust, D. G. 2009. "The University's Crisis of Purpose." *New York Times*, September 6. <http://www.nytimes.com/2009/09/06/books/review/Faust-t.html?_r=1>.

Friedersdorf, K. 2015. "The New Intolerance of Student Activism." *The Atlantic*, November 9. <http://www.theatlantic.com/politics/archive/2015/11/the-new-intolerance-of-student-activism-at-yale/414810/>.

Haslam, N. 2006. "Dehumanization: An Integrative Review." *Personality and Social Psychology Review* 10(3): 252–64.

Haidt, J. and Kesebir, S. 2010. "Morality." In S. Fiske, D. Gilbert, and G. Lindzey (eds.), *Handbook of Social Psychology*, 5th edition, volume 5. Hoboken, NJ: Wiley, 797–832.

Heller, N. 2016. "The Big Uneasy: What's Roiling the Liberal Arts Campus?" *The New Yorker*, May 30: 48–57.

Hoffman, A. J. and Jennings, P. D. 2015. "Institutional Theory and the Natural Environment: Research in (and on) the Anthropocene." *Organization & Environment*, 28: 8–31.

James, W. 1907. "The Social Value of the College-Bred." Address Delivered at a Meeting of the Association of American Alumnae at Radcliff College, November 7. <http://www.uky.edu/~eushe2/Pajares/jaCollegeBred.html>.

Kelman, H. G. 1973. "Violence Without Moral Restraint: Reflections on the Dehumanization of Victims and Victimizers." *Journal of Social Issues* 29: 25–61.

Lim, D., Condon, P., and DeSteno, D. 2015. "Mindfulness and Compassion: An Examination of Mechanism and Scalability." *PloS One* 10(2): e0118221.

March, J. G. 2003. "A Scholar's Quest." *Journal of Management Inquiry* 12(3): 205–7.

Matheny, J. G. 2007. "Reducing the Risk of Human Extinction." *Risk Analysis* 27(5): 1335–44.

Palmer, P. J. 2009. *A Hidden Wholeness: The Journey Toward an Undivided Life*. New York: John Wiley and Sons.

Palsson, G., Szerszynski, B., Sorlin, S., Marks, J., Avril, B., Crumley, C., Hackmann, H., Holm, P., Ingram, J., Kirman, A., Buendıa, M. P., and Weehuizen, R. 2013. "Reconceptualizing the 'Anthropos' in the Anthropocene: Integrating the Social Sciences and Humanities in Global Environmental Change Research." *Environmental Science & Policy* 28: 3–13.

Pinker, S. 2011. *The Better Angels of our Nature: Why Violence Has Declined*. New York: Penguin Books.

Rokeach, M. 1973. *The Nature of Human Values*. New York: Free Press.

Sanderson, E. W., Jaiteh, M., Levy, M. A., Redford, K. H., Wannebo, A. V., and Woolmer, G. 2002. "The Human Footprint and the Last of the Wild." *BioScience* 52(10): 891–904.

Schwartz, S. H. 2006. "Basic Human Values: Theory, Measurement, and Applications." *Revue Française de Sociologie* 47(4): 249–88.

Sherman, D. K. and Cohen, G. L. 2002. "Accepting Threatening Information: Self–Affirmation and the Reduction of Defensive Biases." *Current Directions in Psychological Science* 11(4): 119–23.

Slovic, P. 2007. "'If I Look at the Mass I Will Never Act': Psychic Numbing and Genocide." *Judgment and Decision Making* 2(2): 79–95.

Slovic, S. and Slovic, P. 2015. "Postscript." In S. Slovic and P. Slovic (eds.), *Numbers and Nerves: Information, Emotion, and Meaning and in a World of Data*. Corvallis, OR: Oregon State University Press, 217–20.

Snyder, T. 2011. "Hitler vs. Stalin: Who Killed More?" *New York Review of Books*, March 10. <http://www.nybooks.com/articles/2011/03/10/hitler-vs-stalin-who-killed-more/>.

Tiberius, V. 2008. *The Reflective Life: Living Wisely with Our Limits*. Oxford: Oxford University Press.

Weick, K. 1984. "Small Wins: Redefining the Scale of Social Problems." *American Psychologist* 39(1): 40–9.

Wilson, E. O. 2014. *The Meaning of Human Existence*. New York: Liveright Publishing Corporation.

CHAPTER 16

THE GOVERNMENT'S CATALYTIC ROLE IN DRIVING SOCIETAL PROGRESS

RABIH ABOUCHAKRA, MONA HAMMAMI, AND JIM HAGEMANN SNABE

Abstract

Governments can contribute more effectively and efficiently to societal progress. The traditional government machinery is however inadequate, underfunded, and wrongly funded, and still overly focused on economic output rather than societal outcomes. New approaches need to deal better with multidimensional problems, some massive (such as migration), and better integrate behavioral insights and big data. This chapter highlights: (1) outcome-conditional taxes and transfers (such as a sugar tax aimed at obesity, and cash for school attendance family transfers); (2) corrective rather than just preventive regulation (as exemplified by Germany's paternal leave policy which aims to correct demographic decline); (3) nudge policies (such as opt-out rather than opt-in voluntary pension savings); (4) innovative financing (such as government matching of foreign remittance by expats to finance infrastructure in Mexico); and (5) greater use of big data to compare interventions and outcomes (as attempted by the US Department of Education).

INTRODUCTION

CONSIDER the many challenges governments around the world continue to face in the second decade of the twenty-first century. Growing global inequality, booming urbanization and rising slums, high unemployment, low life expectancy, obesity, reduced trust in governments, a major shortage of global talent—all are among the increasingly complex issues governments must now grapple with. These challenges are all occurring in the context of larger global economic, political, and environmental issues that only add to the difficulties governments everywhere must come to terms with. Already, their failure to meet some of the basic needs of their citizens has resulted in protests and major regime change in many parts of the world.

Overcoming these challenges won't be easy. While many governments have been able to exert some control over their countries' economies, through various fiscal and monetary policy structures, they do not have a strong track record of solving a wide variety of social and economic problems. Too many continue to depend on archaic and unresponsive policy mechanisms, while financial restrictions only add to the difficulties of executing the policies they do devise.

With the digital revolution changing the way we do business, the way we interact, and the way we live, the speed of change has accelerated to unprecedented levels. In order for governments to help shape the future at the speed needed and benefit from the new digital opportunities, a new approach is needed.

In short, governments around the world need a new way to create the policies that go beyond traditional development goals to solve the many problems they face at the speed needed—a new policy mantra designed to shape how leaders envision the way to societal progress. And they need a new set of innovative tools for carrying out those policies if they are to become truly sustainable in the long run. How that can be achieved is the subject of this essay.

THE LARGER CONTEXT

We have reached a point where many of the challenges we face are growing and evolving faster than ever, and solving them has come to seem virtually impossible. Such issues have been termed "wicked problems"—problems that are difficult to define, caused by a multiplicity of factors, and have many interdependencies. The unstable nature of these wicked problems makes them hugely complex to resolve, with dramatic social implications. Overcoming them hinges on coordination from numerous stake-holders, and requires behavioral change and the reversal of years of policy failures.

Consider the increasingly high levels of CO_2 emissions, a major driver of global warming, that have now reached an unprecedented 400 parts per million (ppm) in our atmosphere. That's more than 100 ppm higher than at any time in the last million years, and possibly higher than any time in the last 25 million years (see Figure 16.1). At the current rate of increase in CO_2 emissions, the world will not meet its target of limiting global warming to just 2°C over the pre-industrial average, since the 1990s. Global warming, like other such challenges, requires a response right now because the time required to solve them is running out. "The problem will, at some point, be too acute, have had too much impact, or be too late to stop or reverse."[1]

The global economy is also evolving quickly, with the world undergoing a third wave of industrial upheaval. The first two industrial revolutions, brought about by the

---

[1] Chris Riedy, Associate Professor at the Institute for Sustainable Futures, University of Technology Sydney. <http://chrisriedy.me/2013/05/29/climate-change-is-a-super-wicked-problem/>.

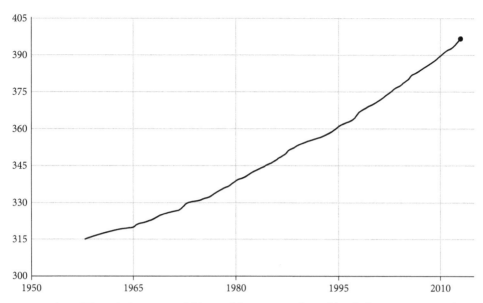

FIGURE **16.1.** CO_2 emissions are quickly reaching unprecedented levels (1963–2013, ppm)

invention of the steam engine and then electricity, the horseless carriage, and countless other inventions, transformed the world and made people's lives immeasurably better—even though it led, at first, to the loss of millions of jobs.

Now comes the digital revolution, which if not a true "wicked problem," is already creating a new wave of invention, and of economic disruption. Driven by powerful new technologies capable of delivering innovations like mass-customization and robotics, this revolution has already enabled the automation of activities in virtually every industry. The question it poses for governments now is whether digitization will lead to massive job destruction, without creating the many opportunities the previous two industrial revolutions led to. Is it also likely to exacerbate inequality as it makes labor with the wrong skills obsolete?

On the other hand, the digital revolution has enabled a flood of information on an unprecedented scale. The spread of information into every corner of our lives has given people the ability to look much more closely into the activities of their governments, to hold them more accountable, to voice their opinions through any number of new channels, and to challenge existing policies and norms. The sheer amount of data now available to governments, and the rise of new techniques for analyzing it, will enable them to better understand critical economic and social trends, and dramatically affect how they design and carry out policies. Indeed, simply finding the talent needed to manage such large volumes of data will be a challenge going forward.

These are just two of the major challenges governments face in our rapidly evolving world; others include rapid urbanization and the risk of growing slums, rising obesity in some areas and persistent malnutrition in others, growing and aging populations, resource scarcity, and loss of biodiversity. All will demand that governments respond by creating and carrying out new policies, and doing so more quickly and more effectively.

GOVERNMENT MACHINERY

Despite the promise of the digital revolution, and the relative success governments have had in boosting economic growth, many countries continue to struggle to address critical issues of social progress. Global inequality remains high, illiteracy remains prevalent in many parts of the world, and poverty, while decreasing, remains a major issue in parts of South Asia and Africa. Even the United Nations' Millennium Development Goals, which came to an end in 2015, have not been met. Corruption, weak institutions, the fickle rule of law, and uninviting environments for doing business—all are still common features in much of the emerging and developing world. Governments, of course, are not the only culprits. But they need to play a vital role in addressing these issues, and so far they have failed. Where have they gone wrong? In many ways, the machinery of government itself has faced several challenges, including the following.

Unresponsive operations. Governments have suffered from poor productivity improvements for many years. The frequent absence of market pressures—the primary driver of private sector behavior and productivity gains—reduces the pressure for cost savings and innovation. Instead, governments have remained stuck in traditional ways, bureaucratic, slow to change, and lacking in innovation in many of their policies and tools. And they have long operated within economic structures defined by the industrial revolution model, and come late to the realization that the information age requires a new mindset and a new way of approaching how to make and carry out policy. This also means that governments have been slow to adapt to change, and as such have not been able to anticipate and prepare for the new and rapidly evolving challenges now confronting them. This lack of agility has been a significant deterrent to progress.

Financially burdened—the "unaffordable" government. The recent financial crisis forced most governments into a long period of fiscal consolidation, leading them to cut spending on long-term initiatives and focus on short-term reactive spending, and in many cases it continues to this day. As a result, they have struggled to spend adequately on complex challenges of health, education, the environment, and other critical issues. Moreover, by taking a traditional approach to its long-standing role as the primary financier of social initiatives, governments have not kept up with the complexities of "wicked problems," either as funders of solutions or actors in carrying them out. Tapping into new innovative financing techniques will be essential, especially given the evolving nature of financing itself and the rise of "social impact" funds.

Lack of adequate measures of progress. Most of the traditional ways of measuring how governments perform have relied on measures of input and output rather than looking at outcomes. Of equal concern is the fact that governments overall typically use measures of progress that are heavily reliant on economic performance as an objective gauge of social progress, the most common being GDP. Such metrics are relatively easy to capture and to use in making comparisons between countries and over time. As a result, discussions of the problems facing governments have typically been dominated by economists and businesspeople with a vested interest in concentrating on indicators that mostly indicate bottom-line results.

Metrics such as GDP, however, do not adequately capture issues of quality of life or the distribution of wealth across a population. For example, spending on things like cigarettes, gun sales, and oil spills are included in GDP calculations, but the results do not capture just how socially or environmentally destructive they are. Nor are economic concerns such as income inequality considered. In short, GDP has long been criticized as unreflective of "societal progress"—countries can grow richer even as they perform poorly on social and environmental indicators. Rapidly developing countries like China release massive amounts of greenhouse gases into the atmosphere, while diabetes and other major health concerns are rampant in highly developed countries like the US.

GDP metrics can even miss substantial sources of economic progress. Some economists have tried to capture the impact of technological evolution on GDP, yet free digital services from companies like Google, Wikipedia, Skype, Twitter, Facebook, and YouTube, among others, are left out, despite their clear positive impact on productivity, and can even appear to indicate a drop in performance as measured by GDP.

Only recently have more accurate measures of social outcomes started to become more common. A variety of new metrics are now being proposed as alternatives to such purely economic measures (see Box 16.1). No clear consensus has emerged as to the best approach for measuring well-being as well as development. In fact, the report by

Box 16.1. Measuring well-being

New approaches to policy require new ways to measure progress in meeting policy goals. The development of measures of social progress and well-being that go beyond GDP has been thriving recently, both in academic and policy circles:

- In the academic sphere, the Sen–Nussbaum approach, otherwise known as the capability approach,[2] has received considerable attention, thanks in part to the flourishing Human Development and Capability Association. In this approach to well-being, economist Amartya Sen initially considered five components in the assessment of capabilities: the importance of real freedoms; individual differences in the ability to transform resources into valuable activities; the multitude of activities giving rise to happiness; the balance of materialistic and non-materialistic factors in evaluating human welfare; and concern for the distribution of opportunities within society. Economist Martha Nussbaum argued further that the core capabilities that should be supported by all democracies are life; bodily health; bodily integrity; senses, imagination, and thought; emotions; practical reason; affiliation; coexistence and interest for other species; playing; and control over one's environment. Recently,

(continued)

[2] D. Clark, 2006. "The Capability Approach: Its Development, Critiques and Recent Advances," ESRC Research Group.

Box 16.1 Continued

however, this approach has been challenged in the face of growing interest in measuring various subjective indicators of satisfaction with life, such as happiness.

- In policy circles, the best-known example of a measure that extends beyond GDP is the Human Development Index (HDI), which measures the performance of different countries in terms of their income, health, and education. Proposed by the United Nations Development Programme, it is heavily inspired by the capability approach.
- Other measures, such as the "Better Life Index" launched by the Organisation for Economic Co-operation and Development, look at satisfaction with life, combining such factors as access to education, housing, healthcare, and the like. Some measures now include a Happiness Index. The Social Progress Initiative's index offers a holistic overview of societal progress by using fifty-two social and environmental indicators to measure 160 countries, and is noteworthy in its exclusion of economic variables.

the French government's Commission on the Measurement of Economic Performance and Social Progress, known as the Stiglitz–Sen–Fitoussi report, highlights the conflicts and contradictions between the different approaches.[3] Clearly, any truly effective measure must be multidimensional, and not just a measure of economic progress, and it should look beyond the well-being of the current generation to the sustainability of well-being for generations to come.

Lack of focus on the customer. All too often, governments have seen their role as governing *over* their constituents rather than *with* them, an attitude that has led to poor engagement with constituents. With more information at their disposal, however, people are increasingly holding their governments accountable for more engagement in interventions and faster, more citizen-centric policy results.[4]

The New Policy Mantra Requires an Innovative Toolbox

Given the new realities and new challenges governments now face, it is time for a new policy mantra—one that will serve as a guide for leaders as they shape their vision of our evolving world. It would be difficult, if not impossible, to draw up a clear set of policies that will meet the needs of every government and society. It will also be impossible to assume that all governments act the same or have the same philosophical and political orientation. It is clear that taking into account the political economy of countries will

---

[3] <http://archives.cerium.ca/IMG/pdf/1-Measurement.pdf>; <http://www.oecd.org/site/worldforumindia/OECD-World-Forum-2012-India-proceedings.pdf>.

[4] PwC, 2013. "Future of Government." <https://www.pwc.com/gx/en/psrc/publications/assets/pwc_future_of_government_pdf.pdf>

have different implications on the choice of mantra as well as the different toolboxes governments are likely to use. Keeping in mind this caveat, this essay seeks to focus on the government in general as a conduit/agent of progress in the absolute sense. Future work might add a political economy lens and explore its implications.

However, the evolving nature of the world around us and the need to integrate progress into the design of our policies necessitates a new philosophy of thinking—a new policy mantra. This philosophy will require the design of a set of policies that are more inclusive, participatory, and sustainable.

But if the desired outcomes are to be inclusive, sustainable, and participatory, how can governments help catalyze such outcomes? To devise and implement this new policy mantra, governments must reinvent their policy toolbox, either by relying on traditional tools or developing new and innovative ways to achieve the intended outcomes of their new policies. What is important in this new way of thinking is that governments have to utilize tools much more innovatively. The difference between past government tools and new ones is that such tools now need to:

1. *Deal with multidimensional problems.* They need to address much more complex issues that governments have not paid attention to in the past. This will mean designing tools with issues that have not typically been on the government agenda, such as climate change.
2. *Respond to massive scale issues.* Tools have to deal with problems that have reached an unbearable size, be it large rural–urban migration, massive cross-border migration, or fast aging and a large elderly population.
3. *Capture policy trade-offs.* Many of the devised government policy tools might promote one outcome while compromising another. For instance, a welfare benefit to help the unemployed might promote longer periods out of the labor force. Tools have to make sure that such trade-offs are balanced and that no outcome is compromised.
4. *Promote outcomes affordably.* Government resources must be maximized in the most efficient way while meeting social outcomes of progress. With highly indebted public treasuries, governments need to meet social outcomes through resources beyond their means through engaging with private partners.
5. *Integrate behavioral insights.* Governments must question the typical premise that all households and economic agents are always rational. They have to try and better understand human behavior by integrating it into the design of their policies to achieve the intended outcomes.
6. *Be smart.* Governments have to leverage an amount and type of data that has never been available before in the form of structured and unstructured information (e.g. social media and people sentiment).

The policy tools available are new and traditional forms of regulations, economic incentives, information, nudges, and new ways to raise and channel funding. These tools could be used together or individually to meet government priorities.

Economic incentives are a powerful tool as they affect people's behavior, directing it toward societal outcomes that the government wants to promote. As such, by providing money or taking money from people or economic/social agents you are driving them with a different set of priorities. In addition, economic incentives have the ability to price market externalities and as such internalize them to the decision maker. Incentives are among the most powerful tools available to governments, especially if well designed.

Regulation is one of the standard tools to reward or prohibit a behavior that might affect socio-economic outcomes. The power of regulations lies in the ability to apply them across so many domains. For them to be effective governments have to be capable of enforcing them and ensuring that they do not stifle or inhibit innovation.

Nudges are relatively new tools that factor in behavioral insights on people's preferences and decision-making process and then use such insights to provide people with a positive re-enforcement or a "nudge" toward making decisions that fit within government-promoted policies. By assuming that not all agents are rational, such tools allow governments to experiment with policy tools that might be closer to reality. Nudges are still relatively new tools mostly seen as complementary to other government policies. They still need to be tested and tried on a wider spectrum.

With government machinery suffering from lack of funding and resources, governments have to look into creative means of raising money. However, the intention is not just to raise money, but to ensure that by doing so it is involving other social participants in meeting societal outcomes. By developing *creative financing mechanisms* governments can share the risk with private players and deliver public goods and services that would not have been possible otherwise.

Lastly, through *information* governments can better listen, and as such understand the needs and concerns of people and better disseminate messages and new policies they want to drive. A government can also analyze large pieces of information and feed this directly into its policy design. Information can also be used in designing policies to affect people's intentions and behavior toward social outcomes. Information as a tool could either be used passively, as in displaying more information about the benefits and drawbacks of something and hope people will react in the intended direction; or it could be used actively, where information is used to persuade people to promote social outcomes. Information could also be used to feed into policy.

Tool 1: Economic Incentives

Governments have access to a variety of economic incentives, including taxes, fines, subsidies, and grants, to carry out their policy goals. These are perhaps the most important tools that governments can utilize. Negative incentives such as taxes and fines are typically designed to deter undesirable behavior, even if they are not perceived to be punitive enough to do so. Subsidies and grants, on the other hand, are used as positive influencers, but if not properly designed and clearly targeted, they may distort behavior and promote abuse of the benefits.

Innovative ways of employing incentives include the use of fiscal policy to change people's behavior. Rather than using untargeted subsidies to help the poor, governments can use cash transfers uncoupled from price. An even better solution is the use of conditional cash transfers, whereby the intended benefit is not provided unless the people targeted change their behavior—sending their children to school, for example. Incentives can also be used to deter people from harming themselves, for example by eating unhealthy food. However, the effectiveness of such policies will depend on other, interrelated laws and regulations (ability to smuggle) and on elasticities such as the availability of substitutes for the goods taxed, among other issues.

When Mexico's economic crisis of 1994–5 threatened to increase its level of poverty sharply, for example, the country's new administration considered a variety of approaches to providing greater social protection, driven by new evidence on the role of health, nutrition, and education in reducing poverty and trends in maximizing efficiency toward these goals. In 1997, as a result, a series of programs were rolled out, including a plan called PROGRESA[5] that tied transfers to investments in human capital.

PROGRESA used geographical targeting to select localities especially in need of assistance. The health benefits offered included a grant for food for children under age 16, pregnant and lactating women, and nutritional supplements for children aged 4–24 months, pregnant and lactating women, and children aged 2–5 years with signs of malnutrition. The program also provided transfers for attendance at primary and secondary schools, and included conditions for compliance, including required health center visits for children, prenatal and postnatal check-ups for mothers, attendance at nutrition and health education lectures, and a minimum of 85 percent attendance at schools.

A follow-up study assessing the impact of the program showed that it significantly reduced poverty in the targeted communities. The number of people living in poverty decreased by 17 percent and the severity of poverty by 46 percent.

Denmark, too, has tried economic incentives as a way to encourage healthy eating habits, though with less success. In October 2011, the country introduced a tax on food with excess amounts of saturated fat, as well as a tax on beverages sweetened with sugar. Statistics from FDB, Denmark's largest consumer goods retailer, showed that Danish shoppers increased their purchase of leaner and low-fat meat between November 2011 and August 2012, while decreasing purchases of butter and mixed-butter products as well.[6] However, the tax was abolished thirteen months after it was rolled out, due to fierce opposition from the food industry and limited involvement of stakeholders, authorities, and experts, according to critics, as well as administrative challenges.

Economic incentives devised to price a market externality, and thus internalize it, through the utilization of a tax can be deterring because the cost is high enough. In

---

[5] International Food Policy Research Institute, 2010. "Conditional Cash Transfers in Latin America."

[6] Center for Public Health Liverpool John Moores University, 2013. "Exploring the Acceptability of a Tax on Sugar-Sweetened Beverages"; Ecorys, 2014. "Food Taxes and their Impact on Competitiveness in the Agri-Food Sector."

countries with strong taxing agencies and a well-functioning tax system, such regulations can, however, be highly effective.

In its efforts to reduce the overall atmospheric levels of sulfur dioxide and the nitrous oxides that cause acid rain, for example, the US' Environmental Protection Agency targeted coal-burning power plants, limiting their SO_2 emissions.[7] Eventually, the plants were allowed to buy and sell emission permits through the Clean Air Act as amended in 1990. The goal was to decrease emissions by 10 million tons from 1980 levels, when emissions totaled 25.9 million tons. The amendment set a decreasing cap on emissions in the following years.

The program led to a decrease of SO_2 emissions by 40 percent, reaching the target prior to the 2010 statutory deadline, with costs at a fraction of what was originally estimated. While the intended benefits of the program were aimed at reducing the acidification of aquatic ecosystems, assessments revealed that the greatest benefit came in the form of better health due to reduced levels of airborne particles.

Examples of similar policies include carbon taxes that have been rolled out in several countries and several states within the United States. Revenues generated by carbon taxes are used for a variety of purposes, such as being given to households, especially the poorest, through tax credits or direct payments to offset the higher prices they would have to pay for gasoline, electricity, and other goods and services because of the tax, or used to invest in renewable energy and public transportation, or to lower other taxes.

Lately we have seen a move toward a global carbon tax. For example, Tirole and Gollier argue that the rationale behind such a tax is simple: if you put the same price on carbon in all sectors and all countries, the environmental cost of economic activities can become apparent to investors and consumers, and markets can efficiently work to reduce emissions, wherever they are the cheapest.[8] However, many still debate the effectiveness of such a policy, especially given the difference in economic, social, and political setting across countries. Others argue that setting a price on carbon as a policy on its own is not enough. Nevertheless, this is an example of changing the global economic and political discourse to try and solve a cross-national issue.

The discussion of taxes on carbon and pollution fits within the movement created by some economists (namely Walter R. Stahel and Geneviève Reday-Mulvey), which argues that in the transition to a "circular economy" taxation should become sustainable, i.e. shift from being imposed on renewable resources to be only imposed on non-renewable ones.[9] Given that logic, governments should shift their taxation policies away from labor and wages to consumption of materials, waste, and emissions. Currently, the wrong set of economic incentives is applied where the non-renewable source of "unemployment" is being subsidized through welfare systems while the

---

[7] Harvard Environmental Economics Program, 2012. "The SO2 Allowance Trading System and the Clean Air Act Amendments of 1990: Reflecting on Twenty Years of Policy Innovation," literature review.

[8] C. Gollier and J. Tirole, 2015. "Thinking Beyond a Global Carbon Price," *The Economist*, June.

[9] <http://www.product-life.org/en/sustainable-taxation-creates-regional-jobs-in-a-circular-economy>; <http://www.makingitmagazine.net/?p=6793>.

renewable part of employment is being taxed. Circular economy advocates increasingly push for a change to this type of thought, arguing that taxes should shift from labor to natural resource use and consumption.[10]

Tool 2: Regulations and Restrictions

Regulations, whether economic, social, or administrative in nature, can either stimulate innovation or slow it down. Governments often use regulations to implement and manage their strategies and policies. They devise restrictions, bans, compliance rules, and similar forms of regulation to impose behavioral limitations designed to achieve policy goals, and expect people and businesses to comply with them. Regulations have proved to be useful if the consequences of not following them are real enough that they act as a true deterrent. In addition, regulations set clear protocols and expectations of what is required and serve as reference points or benchmarks for behavior.

A major drawback to this policy tool, however, has been the difficulty of enforcement, due to the lack of adequate enforcement mechanisms. Moreover, the imposition of regulations has often been too rigid and taken too long to devise, amend, and implement. Innovative new regulatory processes, however, can successfully overcome these shortcomings.

An example of a regulation that has been set up to mitigate the threat of a declining European population (coupled with a rapidly aging society) is the German paternal leave regulation. Such a regulation has played an important role in promoting larger families. The German Parental Allowance and Parental Leave Act allows employees to get paid parental leave in addition to mandatory maternity leave after childbirth. Following a 2015 reform of the law, it is now possible, in addition to the previous parental allowance of a maximum of twelve months paid parental leave (or fourteen months if the other parent decides to go on parental leave too), to have a Parental Allowance Plus (available for parents of children born on and after July 1, 2015) that allows employees to have up to twenty-four months of paid parental leave, or twenty-eight months if both parents go on parental leave.

Further, the allowance is paid by the state rather than the private sector, which provides an incentive for businesses to support their employees' decisions as they do not bear the costs. This contrasts with US regulations, which do not provide paid leave and often put the burden on private companies. Despite its highly protective welfare policies, Germany has been one of the most successful models in Europe for lowering unemployment and raising employment participation, while meeting a demographic challenge.

In some areas, regulations have not kept pace with the evolving nature of the global economy. The spread of the sharing economy, for instance, is one example where

---

[10] The Ex'tax Project in cooperation with Deloitte, EY, KPMG, and PwC, 2014. "New Era. New Plan. Fiscal Reforms for An Inclusive Circular Economy."

government regulation has lagged. In many cases regulations have been set to stifle the growth of such platforms, thus diminishing their potentially evolutionary impact. In the past government intervention in regulating peer-to-peer activities was required to adjust for market failure. But the spread of the digital revolution has led to a new set of digitally enabled exchanges. This form of exchange has expanded dramatically in recent years, mediated by digital platforms like Uber, Airbnb, and Funding Circle among others. The difference in these new forms of exchange is that the distinction between personal and professional in the provision of commercial services is not necessarily as clear as it used to be. Moreover, it often involves a somehow "anonymous" set of transactions.[11] This means that regulation in its traditional sense could be challenging, and imposing it could hinder innovation and slow down the growth in employment that happens through such platforms.

Tool 3: Nudges

In addition to regulations, governments can adopt programs that leverage behavioral economics and other behavioral insights to "nudge" people toward better decisions and actions. Instead of placing regulatory restrictions on behavior or offering economic incentives, nudges influence behavior by changing how behavioral choices are presented. While a relatively new tool, nudges are becoming a key element of the policymaker's toolkit as they have been shown to have real impacts on behavior. And in some cases, nudges are easier to implement than regulation or economic incentives.

Many examples of the use of nudges are still in the experimental phase, but the UK has already experienced considerable success with the technique in boosting contributions to private, company-sponsored pension plans. Current UK rules on the management of private pensions have led to underfunded individual pension plans that don't adequately replace pre-retirement income. Not only are contributions to private pensions failing to rise as expected, but increasing life expectancy will create additional pressures that cannot be alleviated by raising the pension age alone. There are currently around seven million people in the UK who are not saving enough to generate the income they are likely to need in retirement. Initiatives to stimulate savings in personal pension plans have not worked; nor have policies using more information to persuade people to make better choices.[12]

There are many reasons for the low level of pension saving. Joining a scheme requires an active decision, but all too often sheer inertia keeps people from acting. The problem is especially acute for pensions because the decision involves thinking about a far-off future scenario. Most people find it difficult to imagine old age, so the

---

[11] M. Cohen and A. Sundararajan, 2015. "Self-Regulation and Innovation in the Peer-to-Peer Sharing Economy." University of Chicago Law Review Dialogue 116.

[12] K. Ly and D. Soman, 2013. "Nudging Around The World." Rotman School of Management. University of Toronto.

decision to act to create the conditions for retirement does not seem to be a high priority—after all, it can always be deferred.

While many people claim they want to "have to save," many actually respond adversely to the idea of compulsory savings. Currently, the onus is almost always on employees to make the effort to join their company's pension plan or buy a personal pension—the "default" option when employees first join a company is for them *not* to join. The concept adopted by the Pensions Commission was to change the default, such that employees automatically join a pension plan, while having the option to opt out if they wish.

Changing the default meant that inertia was now working in favor of retirement savings, while preserving the opt-out option meant that the system wasn't compulsory. The reform also introduced a compulsory "matching" contribution from employers, obliging them to contribute to employees' pensions. Evidence in the US shows that such defaults have increased participation in private pensions dramatically.

Tool 4: Innovative Financing

Governments have long suffered from a lack of the financial resources needed to carry out social policies, a situation that has become especially acute since the financial crisis of 2008–9. In the hope of increasing the funds available for new social programs, *public–private partnerships* (PPPs) have grown in popularity as a way for governments to share investment risk (with each entity managing that aspect of the risk involved that it can best manage). Initially used to fund physical infrastructure projects, PPPs are increasingly employed in social services to build and manage prisons, hospitals, and schools.

The effectiveness of PPPs depends, however, on how they are set up, financed, and managed. Typically, they are funded through social impact bonds, which are financed by the government with repayment contingent on the successful completion of the project. This form of financing allows the government to partner with innovative and effective service providers while ensuring that taxpayers will not pay for the programs unless they demonstrate success in achieving the desired outcomes.

Among the most innovative, if still infrequently employed, forms of non-public financing to achieve public benefits is the use of *social impact bonds*. The UK's Centre for Social Impact Bonds, part of the government's Cabinet Office, has been issuing social impact bonds for several years.[13] As of April 2013, the center had issued fourteen social impact bonds, with more in the pipeline. One bond was designed to improve the plight of the homeless in London, as measured by the number of resettlements of homeless people to permanent accommodations, reconnections abroad, increase in employment, and fewer hospital visits.

[13] Centre for Social Impact Bonds at the UK Cabinet Office website. <https://www.gov.uk/guidance/social-impact-bonds>.

The service is funded by a combination of investment from social investors and from two service providers. In this model, the service providers share the risk and can make a financial return if the project is successful. Payments against the outcomes of this project are delivered quarterly and can be reinvested so that only a portion of the service costs need to be funded by investment in the bonds themselves.

A typical example of the use of social impact bonds has been with the Finnish government, which announced that part of dealing with the European Union's refugee crisis could be through the use of such bonds. The aim of the program (rolled out in spring 2016) is to employ immigrants in the economy quickly and as such integrate them into society and release the pressure on the government for supporting them. The Finnish Ministry of Employment and the Economy, in cooperation with Sitra, are the main sponsors. If immigrants get into work fast enough and therefore reach the government's intended goal (saving public money that would have been otherwise spent on refugee support), the state will reimburse some of the money saved to the projects.[14]

Another form of creative financing involves the deployment of philanthropic and private money to deliver specific goods and services. This technique relies heavily on the concept of impact investing, in which investors contribute to a specific fund in the hope of receiving real financial returns as well as social benefits.

An example of impact investing involves the creative use of *structured financing*. For example, in 2008 Australia's largest private provider of childcare, ABC Learning, went bankrupt, and its childcare centers were put up for sale. This prompted four organizations—Social Ventures Australia, the Benevolent Society, the Brotherhood of St. Laurence, and Mission Australia—to come together to form the Goodstart Consortium, which registered as a non-profit with the goal of transforming early learning in Australia.[15]

The consortium determined that the best way to attract funding was through a variety of layered funding structures, each of which could accommodate the different risk appetites of investors. The National Australia Bank agreed to provide senior debt to the syndicate, while the Australian government made a loan to the consortium that could be repaid at a much later stage. A final layer of finance came from forty-one social investors—a mix of individuals and foundations. To attract these investors, the consortium created a new financial instrument called a social capital note, which paid a 12 percent rate of return.

Through these multiple investors, the consortium managed to secure AUS$95 million in cash to purchase ABC Learning's 678 childcare centers, and another AUS$70 million to fund its ongoing operations. Goodstart is now one of the country's most successful social enterprises, showing what can be achieved through clever collaboration across sectors.

---

[14] <http://www.nordiclabourjournal.org/nyheter/news-2015/article.2015-12-07.3565624712>.

[15] P. Lomax and R. Wharton, 2014. "10 Innovations in Global Philanthropy." <http://www.thinknpc.org/publications/10-innovations/>.

The *remittances* sent home from migrant workers in other countries have also been used creatively to finance socially beneficial projects. A particularly successful example is Mexico's so-called 3-for-1 Program.[16] Tens of millions of Mexicans have left their country in search of a better life and economic opportunities in the United States. Many of these migrants leave their families and communities behind, so it is not surprising that they send a large amount of remittances back home every year. In 2010, remittances from Mexicans living in the US to their home country amounted to more than $20 billion.

In an effort to channel this large revenue stream into projects that would yield a wider societal benefit, Mexico's government launched what it called the 3-for-1 Program. The program offered a simple proposition: for every dollar raised by a given immigrant association in the US for a specific project, each of the three levels of government (municipal, state, and federal) would match it dollar for dollar, using money received from tax receipts and oil revenue from Mexico's state oil company.

As a result, the amount of money available for social development and public infrastructure projects, already a large sum of money, tripled, boosting significantly Mexico's efforts to improve the country's societal well-being.

Tool 5: Information, Education, and Persuasion

Information and education programs are commonly used to enhance learning and individual knowledge, and ultimately to increase awareness and influence behavior. The assumption is that when consumers have more information they are likely to make better, more informed decisions. For instance, financial literacy programs aim at equipping individuals with enough knowledge to make informed decisions regarding savings and retirement. With this knowledge, it is assumed that individuals will be motivated to create and follow through with a savings and retirement plan.

In addition, governments have tried active persuasion to influence behavior. This is often developed through targeted advertisement campaigns designed to promote a specific behavior. Communications programs that appeal to people's moral or civic responsibilities have often been used to persuade individuals to make better choices for themselves and for the betterment of society.

In the hope of boosting dissemination of information to the US government, in 2009 President Barack Obama and the White House introduced an online portal in the form of a crowdsourcing competition; federal employees would be able to submit their ideas on how the US government could save money to help it become more effective and efficient. The ideas that captured most votes and that were considered noteworthy by the government were chosen as winners and would later be reflected in the government's plans.

---

[16] Future Challenges, 2011. "Mexico's 3x1 Program Aims to Channel Remittance."

Tens of thousands of cost-minimization ideas have been submitted by federal employees over the past five years with dozens of the most promising ideas included in the president's budget, specifically in the Cuts, Consolidations, and Savings section. The President's SAVE Award[17] is a prime example of how governments are using information and online media to engage people and facilitate the creation of ideas, actions, policies, and laws that impact society as a whole. This type of approach allows for greater consideration and inclusion of society's demands to be reflected in governmental agendas and action plans.

But data are not only used as a source of information for persuasion. They are also utilized by governments to deliver better impact. One example of the need to integrate the large sets of information into government policy has been through the US Department of Education incorporation of big data into the National Education Technology Plan. In the education sector, developers use data mining to apply lessons for learning specific competencies. The plan designed by the US Department of Education aims at eventually using similar big data tools to analyze courses, schools, and even entire districts. These plans are in the early stages but represent an exciting new field within education.

With the growing volume and velocity in data it has become imperative to think of how best to analyze and integrate the findings into policymaking. Governments are major collectors of data but they often do not invest in analyzing them and deriving trends and policies from them.

ENABLERS

If governments are to overcome their traditional shortcomings and succeed in delivering on the new policy mantra, they must become more entrepreneurial, more innovative, and more agile, capable of channeling expertise and attracting the talent and funding needed to bring about true societal well-being. And they must be able to do so in partnership with a variety of new social players engaged in the same mission. In order to ensure that their policies and tools become more effective in responding to social challenges, governments need to put in place several key enablers.

Trustworthiness. Perhaps the most important enabler is trust, which can only be developed through a willingness to be transparent, to communicate, and to deliver consistently and effectively on policy promises.

Linked closely to social trust is a sense of shared purpose and direction, both among the broader population and among important stakeholder groups such as business or unions. Trust and a sense of shared purpose, in turn, makes the task of strategic

---

[17] The White House, 2015. "The President's SAVE Award"; Information Week, 2012. "Top 14 Government Social Media Initiatives."

communication with all stakeholders easier to undertake. Research indicates that countries with higher levels of trust and a strong sense of common ground are better able to make good policy decisions and to generate stronger economic outcomes.

Tough choices about policy matters are easier to make in countries with high levels of trust and shared purpose. Iceland, Ireland, and Estonia are good recent examples in Europe, where more rapid fiscal consolidation has taken place. Incidentally in many of these countries trust has been high and as such the passage of harsh policies has been much easier. Indeed, countries blessed with both have been able to perform strongly over the past few decades, because it is easier to sustain a medium-term policy direction and to respond quickly to new challenges and changing circumstances when necessary.

Transparency. Transparency is critical to build trust and ensure progress. Just as business leaders are expected to report the performance of companies on a regular basis, governments should report the progress of society. The progress of society should be measured in multiple dimensions: income, health, and education—as suggested by the HDI. For each measure of progress a government should define targets and measure progress against them. Through online access to measures of progress for all citizens, governments can inspire society to focus on specific areas and create a foundation for long-term policymaking. Finding the measures that government needs to focus on will be quite challenging but essential going forward.

Attracting and retaining talent. In order for the government machinery to be capable of driving progress globally it should be able to attract and retain the type of talent that is capable of driving such an agenda. The new tier of public servants has to understand the challenges at hand, be well paid and well trained, and have the vision and leadership required to take on the progress agenda. An example of a government that has already invested heavily in attracting public sector talent is Singapore. Some of the policies include: talent attracted through scholarships; rigorous selection, with a public service division setting policies on recruitment; civil servants paid the highest salaries in the world in order to attract talent and avoid corruption; salaries pegged to the private sector; bonuses tied to the performance of the economy; and promotion based on an appraisal system (reporting system and performance ranking system).

Communication. In the digital age, governments are increasingly using social media platforms to communicate with their citizens. In the UK, for instance, the government teamed up with Facebook to create a dedicated space for users to come up with ideas on how to create savings in public spending. According to the Prime Minister's Office, the first phase was open to public sector workers in the hope of gathering their professional insights and views on everything from how to cut back on wasteful spending to how to radically change the way services are provided. The second phase will not only source people's ideas but also allow the government to hear what people thought about the ideas already put forward. The UK government is already transforming how it interacts with its citizens, boosting both transparency and accountability. This sense of communication also helps build the trust further, but more importantly allows for transparency and accountability.

Agility. Governments must ensure that their policy machinery is agile and flexible enough to meet the many challenges they face. That demands, first, that they fully understand those challenges; here, an integrated risk management or horizon-scanning office can help alert policymakers to issues that will likely affect their countries in the long term. Second, governments need to build adaptable institutions that, by using innovative technology and other tools, can function in our highly uncertain environment, anticipating short-term problems and reacting quickly and effectively, without compromising or sabotaging their long-term options.

Continuously reinventing itself. Governments' ability to sense change, detect it, and respond to it is core. It goes beyond just the agility and flexibility of government to suggest that they need to reinvent themselves, and they need to do so continuously. The pace of change happening globally is tremendous and right now governments are running behind. The danger lies in the fact that instead of catalyzing progress and enabling successful change, governments are inhibiting progress by simply being too late to the game.

For instance, the digital revolution is likely to bring along a large wave of job destruction. However, parallel to the typical model of employment a new model is emerging. This new model of creating jobs is allowing for self-employment and alternative ways of starting businesses. Take the example of Uber. Uber doesn't employ people directly but it creates a platform which enables people to be employed by providing their services within this shared economy perspective. Governments, however, have not enabled such models to flourish. In fact they have over-regulated such models, defending traditional models and hampering growth. This has been an inhibitor and it is time to rethink the role of government, turning it from an obstructer to an enabler.

Leading by example. Governments can promote their social goals and improve policy outcomes by taking the lead on actions that would benefit society as a whole and adopting programs internally before rolling them out to society. For instance, if the goal is increased energy efficiency, governments could start by ensuring that all government bodies increase their own efficiency, through the use of LED bulbs and other efficient devices, and then promoting their own success to the public at large.

Connected within and across. No government can function optimally and deliver services efficiently unless they can break down the many barriers that currently exist between their many siloed departments and functions, while learning to work with non-governmental and private partners. This will require a strong central organization that can establish connections between all internal and external players, and orchestrate how they operate together. Doing so will also require that governments make major cultural changes, boosting collaboration across sectors, borders, and organizations and building new capabilities in partnering, co-ventures, co-creation, and co-design.

PUTTING IT ALL TOGETHER

Executing the new policy mantra will require that governments prioritize the actions they must take, better understand the challenges they face, transform how they devise new policies to respond to those challenges, put those new policies into practice, and measure the outcomes on an ongoing basis. To that end, we suggest the following prioritization roadmap:

1. Widen the discussion among leadership and policymakers beyond the narrow discussion of economic development to include the broad concept of societal progress, happiness, well-being, etc. This will also mean ensuring that leadership adopts such concepts as a driving force behind their vision.
2. Internalize the new philosophy mantra into government and leadership thinking. This will create a better understanding of the ways to measure outcome and progress, as well as a new process to think of policies that are of societal relevance and at the same time inclusive, participatory, and sustainable.
3. Work on modernizing government machinery to make it agile, citizen-centric, service-oriented, networked, and most importantly trustworthy. At the heart of such an effort is the need to make the public sector an attractive hub for talent and innovation. This center can then deliver new innovative tools of policymaking.
4. Leverage the tools available to governments for addressing new and evolving challenges, while making sure that such tools are multidimensional, smart, and affordable, reflect behavioral insights, and are capable of balancing policy trade-offs.
5. Finally, the information gathered through the constant assessment of progress and outcomes must be fed back into the overarching policymaking body, with the goal of generating a virtuous circle of continuous improvement.

AREAS OF FURTHER ASSESSMENT/INVESTIGATION

Perhaps no government is able to solve perfectly all the challenges and problems it faces. But all governments can do a better job than they are doing now, by simply rethinking their policy toolbox in light of the dramatic changes happening globally. The key is to develop policies that are truly inclusive, participatory, smart, innovative, and sustainable, to remain alert to continuously changing circumstances, and to adapt at the speed needed in the digital world. If done well, governments have a unique opportunity to become the catalyst for progress in society and shape a more sustainable future.

This essay has attempted to set the stage for understanding the basic role of government in driving progress, but by doing so it has left a few questions that are worth exploring further. What are some measures that governments can use to measure progress? How easy is it for governments to share such metrics with the people and really show change? The essay also highlights some of the tools governments can use. These include economic incentives, and although we present initial evidence of some other, innovative incentives, it is worth further exploring a framework of how economic incentives could best operate. Another angle worth exploring is the effect of different political orientations/models on the choice of government tools and how we can reconcile progress within such a political economy model. These are just a few questions to start the discussion and are certainly worth exploring further.

· ·

COMMENTS AND DISCUSSION

Abouchakra, Hammami, and Snabe's essay considers the distinctive role of government in contributing to the better alignment of business objectives with the social good, as well as the distinctive challenges that governments confront in the contemporary era. They propose a "toolbox" of approaches that might enable governments to make more effective contributions. They envision a nimble government that makes targeted "nudges," leverages incentives, and works in partnership with the business and non-profit world.

What structural challenges confront governments in trying to make effective interventions for social good?

Pointing to India's struggles in implementing large-scale improvements in education, at the Society for Progress' second assembly Sen observed that governments must continually confront the corruption of politics by large financial interests in the business sector. Even if businesses would benefit from wholesale improvements in education, their immediate financial interests typically cut against these kinds of large public investments. Proposals for government approaches to social problems are in some sense premised on addressing this more fundamental problem. Likewise, Mendiola and Barney both noted the disincentives for the most skilled and qualified to work in politics. Anderson noted that public–private partnerships seem like a promising approach to some important problems. Yet, here again, there are problems with incentives, as the gains of private partners can too easily come at the expense of public goods (consider, Anderson noted, the case of such partnerships in American schools). What domains are best suited to such partnerships, and what governance structures can ensure that gains are fairly distributed?

How can traditionally big and slow government bureaucracies work effectively for the social good in a fast-changing marketplace?

As Barney noted, governments tend to be behind market trends, almost by definition, since it is notoriously difficult to see where trends are going until they emerge from the marketplace itself. Frank suggested that governments have a particular role to play in rectifying clearly identifiable market failures through smart social science. Consider the case of congestion pricing: people tend to recoil at penalties more than they leap at incentives. We might thus mitigate public recoil by redistributing the proceeds of taxing peak driving. Autor observed that governments should not be afraid to make big interventions but that, at the same time, they ought to make commensurate investments in collecting data that would allow for an evaluation of success. Snabe noted that, culturally, it can be difficult to balance the traditional negative role of governments in regulating with a more positive approach focused on investing. As Pettit noted, the appropriateness of a given approach can vary significantly across different types of governments, which are susceptible to varying measures of legislative coherence, corruption, and technocratic delegation, for example.

Index of Names

Note: Boxes and figures are indicated by an italic *b* or *f* following the page number.

INDEX OF SUBJECTS

Note: Tables, figures, and boxes are indicated by an italic *t*, *f*, or *b* following the page number.